GREENB[...]
GUIDE [...]
DEPARTMENT 56®
VILLAGES

NINTH EDITION
1999

Including:

THE ORIGINAL SNOW VILLAGE®
THE ORIGINAL SNOW VILLAGE® ACCESSORIES

THE HERITAGE VILLAGE COLLECTION®
Dickens' Village Series®
New England Village®
Alpine Village Series™
Christmas In The City®
Little Town Of Bethlehem™
North Pole Series™
Disney Parks Village™

THE HERITAGE VILLAGE COLLECTION® ACCESSORIES

SEASONS BAY™
SEASONS BAY™ ACCESSORIES
SEASONS BAY™ GENERAL ACCESSORIES

MEADOWLAND
BACHMAN'S®
PROFILES™
HISTORICAL LANDMARK SERIES™

ADDITIONAL VILLAGE ACCESSORIES

ORNAMENTS

**The Most Respected Guides To Popular Collectibles
& Their After Market Values**

P.O. Box 645
Pacific Grove, CA 93950
831.656.9000
FAX 831.656.9004
www.greenbooks.com

Printed in Canada

ISBN 0-923628-76-2

Table Of Contents

Louise Patterson Langenfeld is unique in collectible annals, for she grew up immersed in collectibles. Her father developed the BRADEX, the first comprehensive listing of collector plates and their secondary market values, for the world renowned BRADFORD EXCHANGE. A graduate of Michigan State University, during summers and school breaks, Louise helped her Dad with his successful limited edition plate publishing business. Louise attended many South Bend Conventions, greeting and getting to know collectors in the exhibit.

After graduation, Louise gained a thorough education in retailing, working for New York Department Stores Abraham & Strauss. In the early eighties, she joined her father full time.

In 1985, they realized that there was no comprehensive, complete guide to one of the most popular new products, Enesco's Precious Moments Collection. Encouraged by her Dad, Louise proudly published the first GREENBOOK Guide to the Enesco Precious Moments Collection in 1986.

Louise can muddle through the most confusing complexity of information, reducing it to comprehensible components. Collectors appreciate her clear thinking and ability to discern the important facets of a collection. GREENBOOK Guides, deceptively simple in appearance, are chock-full of every fact any collector seeks. Every new Guide enjoys ever growing audiences, and imitators. Like the words Kleenex or Xerox have come to represent facial tissues and photocopies, GREENBOOK has come to mean secondary market price guide to many. GREENBOOK Guides are vastly different, collectors learn, for no detail is overlooked, and pricing is based on research, not fiction.

GREENBOOK is Louise. Her vision and concern for the collector is legend. As collectors' tastes and interests change, Louise is at the forefront, documenting and reflecting current enthusiasms. Her innovation and understanding of the collectible marketplace led GREENBOOK to be the first to document the Enesco Cherished Teddies Collection, and, more recently, Ty Beanie Babies. When a new product becomes hot, collectors, retailers, secondary market dealers and even makers turn to GREENBOOK, urging publication of the definitive GREENBOOK Guide.

1997 saw the launch of the very first GREENBOOK Guide on CD-Rom. Computer-savy collectors are delighted, for this innovative product makes everything much easier, from insurance documentation to shopping wishlists.

Louise's husband, Nick, joined GREENBOOK in 1998 to bear the administrative load leaving Louise free to develop even more Guides. And to enjoy some leisure time watching their 10-year-old daughter, Ally, compete on her horse, Bubble Bath.

Editor & Publisher Louise Langenfeld

GREENBOOK–WHAT WE DO & HOW WE DO IT

LISTINGS

The GREENBOOK Listings developed for the Department 56® Villages feature color photographs, factual information and GREENBOOK TRUMARKET VALUES for each piece.

Factual information consists of:
- Name
- Item Number
- Year Of Introduction
- Market Status
- Description
- Variations
- Particulars

GREENBOOK TRUMARKET VALUE Listings include:
- Original Suggested Retail Price (OSRP)
- GREENBOOK TRUMARKET Secondary Market Value (GBTru$)
- The percentage up or down as compared to last year's 8th Ed. Guide (or "No Change" if the value is unchanged)
- The GBTru$ History Line–tracking the GREENBOOK Secondary Market Value for each piece over the years. If a piece is Current, the GBTru$ History Line tracks the Suggested Retail Price.

GREENBOOK TRUMARKET VALUES

Secondary Market values are from actual sales that have taken place in every region of the country. The data is compiled, checked for accuracy, and a value established as a benchmark as a result of this research. There are many factors which determine the price a collector will pay for a piece; most acquisitions are a matter of personal judgement. The price will fluctuate with the time of year, section of the country and type of sale. GREENBOOK takes all of these factors into consideration when determining TRUMARKET Values, and so **GREENBOOK TRUMARKET Values are never an absolute number**. Use them as a basis for comparison, as a point of information when considering an acquisition, and as a guide when insuring for replacement value.

The GREENBOOK does not trade on the Secondary Market. The GREENBOOK monitors and reports prices, in the same way as the Wall Street Journal reports trades on the stock markets in the United States and abroad.

HOW TO USE THIS GUIDE

The Guide is divided into the following main sections: The Original Snow Village®, The Heritage Village Collection®, Seasons Bay™, Special Releases, Additional Village Accessories and Ornaments. Special Releases include Meadowland, Bachman's®, Profiles™ and the Historical Landmark Series™.

Within each section, GREENBOOK Listings are in year of introduction order, with the May Releases appearing before the December Releases. Within each group of May or December introductions, the pieces appear in Department 56® Item Number order.

It's important to remember "the year of introduction indicates the year in which the piece was designed, sculpted and copyrighted" and the piece is generally available to collectors the following calendar year.

The GREENBOOK History List serves as an outline of each section, use it as your map through each Village.

Percent
Change
From 1998
GBTru$

Original   1999
Suggested   GREENBOOK
Item   Year Of   Retail   True Market
Name   Number   Issue   Status   Price   Value

| DICKENS' VILLAGE MILL | ITEM #
6519-6 | INTRO
1985 | RETIRED
LTD ED 2,500 | OSRP
$35 | GBTRU
$4755 | ↓
5% |

Roughhewn stone makes up 3-section mill with large wooden mill wheel. Two sets double doors—one large set to allow carriage to be brought directly into building, smaller doors open into silo area.
Notable: Early release to Gift Creations Concepts (GCC). Some sleeves read "Dickens' Village Cottage."

| DATE: ___ $ ___
○ WISH   ○ HAVE | **'91**
$5550 | **'92**
5550 | **'93**
5550 | **'94**
5150 | **'95**
5000 | **'96**
4850 | **'97**
4995 | **'98**
5025 |

GBTru$ History Line

Peter George, GREENBOOK's Department 56® Historian, is the publisher of the Village Chronicle magazine which he founded in 1991. Along with his publishing responsibilities, he also writes some of the articles and features for the magazine. Considered a Department 56® authority, he is a frequent guest speaker at gatherings and other Department 56, Inc. related events throughout the United States. As you might expect, one of his favorite pastimes is collecting Department 56® Villages. The following is Peter's schedule of appearances for 1999 and those already booked for 2000. If you're nearby we hope you'll take the opportunity to stop in and say hi.

MAY 1999
  2 Nuance's 4th Annual Collectors' Cruise, **Barrington, RI**
 16 Garden State Villagers Meeting **(NJ)**

JUNE 1999
  4-6 Tropical Gathering in Florida, Wyndham Resort & Spa,
       Ft. Lauderdale, FL
 26-27 International Collectible Expo,
        Rosemont Convention Center, **Rosemont, IL**

JULY 1999
 23-25 Texas Round-Up, Austin Marriott, **Austin, TX**

AUGUST 1999
  6-8 Southern Regional Gathering, Embassy Suites Hotel,
       Greenville, SC
 28-29 Bachman's® Village Gathering,
        Minneapolis Convention Center, **Minneapolis, MN**

SEPTEMBER 1999
 19 Delaware Valley 56ers Meeting, **Philadelphia, PA** Area
 24-26 Occasion Gifts & Collectibles Annual Department 56® Gathering
        Rockaway, NJ

OCTOBER 1999
 1-3 Display Expo 1999, Fort William Henry Resort, **Lake George, NY**

NOVEMBER 1999
 5-7 Nancy's Hallmark Retirement Party, **Sharonville, OH**

MARCH 2000
 24-26 California Gold Gathering, Marriott Hotel, **Irvine, CA**

MAY 2000
 5-7 PA5-6000, Lancaster Host & Convention Center, **Lancaster, PA**

Throughout this edition of the Guide are a variety of articles by Peter George, GREENBOOK's Department 56® Historian, that were previously printed in *the Village Chronicle* magazine. These articles cover topics including particular buildings and accessories and collecting Department 56® in general. We think you will enjoy reading these articles for their historical, informational and entertainment value.

the **Village Chronicle.**

If you enjoy the articles from *the Village Chronicle* subscribe to it today and continue the fun. Each issue entertains and informs you with page after page of:

- accurate, timely information
- articles about each of the Villages
- varied points of view from nationally recognized authorities
- display advice & tips
- product highlights
- secondary market updates
- a calendar of Department 56® events
- collector's corner
- and always much more

$27 for one year - 6 issues   (International: $32 US funds)
$48 for two years - 12 issues   (International: $53 US funds)
                                     R.I. residents add 7% sales tax.
Visa, MasterCard, Discover, American Express, Checks accepted

Subscribe by phone, fax, mail, internet.
           Phone: 401-467-9343
              Fax: 401-467-9359
    Internet: http://www.villagechronicle.com
          Mail: the Village Chronicle
                   757 Park Ave.
                   Cranston, RI 02910

Department 56® Time Line

1976 ♦ First lighted houses, *Snow Village*, are introduced.

1977 ♦ First six *Snow Village* pieces are available at stores.
♦ Three more *Snow Village* houses are introduced, creating an on-going collection.

1978 ♦ First stickers with "Manufactured in Taiwan for Department 56" begin to appear.

1979 ♦ The first pieces, ten buildings, are retired.
♦ An American flag is featured on a building for the first time.
♦ First accessory, *Carolers*, is introduced.
♦ The Meadowland Series, though not part of *Snow Village*, is introduced.
♦ Name of building and copyright information begin to appear on bottom of buildings.

1980 ♦ The first vehicle, *Ceramic Car*, makes its debut.
♦ Dated stickers appear on bottom of buildings.

1982 ♦ *Gabled House* and *New Stone Church* are the first "Early Release" pieces offered to GCC.
♦ *Snowman With Broom* is introduced, becoming the first accessory manufactured with another material other than ceramic.

1983 ♦ The word "*Original*" is added to the *Snow Village* title.

1984 ♦ The first porcelain village, Dickens' Village Series®, is announced.

1985 ♦ Pieces are sold in styrofoam boxes and sleeves for the first time.
♦ The first limited edition, the *Dickens' Village Mill*—limited to 2,500 pieces, is introduced.

1986 ♦ *Snow Village Traditions*, a small book illustrated by Kristi Jensen (now Kristi Jensen Pierro), is published to commemorate the 10th Anniversary of The Original Snow Village®.
♦ New England Village® becomes the second porcelain village.
♦ Alpine Village Series™ becomes the third porcelain village.
♦ *Christmas Carol Collection*, the first of a number of series based on the works of Charles Dickens, is introduced.
♦ The first Snowbabies™, 16 in all, are introduced.

1987
- The Original Snow Village® accessories are scaled down.
- Porcelain villages are placed under the "umbrella" of The Heritage Village Collection®.
- Christmas In The City®, the fourth porcelain village, is added.
- Little Town Of Bethlehem™ becomes the fifth porcelain village.
- Bachman's® Hometown Series, a short-lived village, is introduced; though porcelain, it is not part of The Heritage Village Collection®.
- Cold Cast Porcelain (CCP) replicas of Dickens' Village Series® and New England Village® pieces are introduced.
- Lite-Ups, miniature versions of Dickens' Village Series® and New England Village® pieces, are introduced.
- First Snowbabies™ retire.

1988
- The first of its five newsletters, predecessors to the *Quarterly*, are published by Department 56, Inc.
- The first Dickens' Village Series® pieces are retired.
- The first Snowbabies™ limited edition, *Frosty Frolic*—limited to 4,800 pieces, is introduced.

1989
- First Christmas In The City® limited edition, *Dorothy's Dress Shop*—limited to 12,500, is introduced.
- Department 56, Inc. exhibits at the International Collectible Exposition in South Bend, Indiana for the first time.
- The consumer service phone line, 800-LIT-TOWN, is made available to collectors.
- Miniature pewter Snowbabies™ are introduced.

1990
- The first interracial accessory, *Here We Come A Caroling* (The Original Snow Village®), is issued.
- The first Bachman's® Village Gathering is held in Minneapolis, MN.
- The Original Snow Village® American Architecture Series is introduced.
- The sixth in the Heritage Village Collection®, North Pole Series™, is introduced.

1991
- Department 56, Inc. moves to new headquarters, One Village Place, in Eden Prairie, MN.
- The first issue of the *Quarterly* is published.
- Dated stickers appear on bottom of The Original Snow Village® buildings for the last time.

1992 ♦ *Crown & Cricket Inn*, first in a series of buildings included in the Charles Dickens' Signature Series, is issued.
♦ *The Gate House*, the first Event Piece, is sold at dealers' open house events.
♦ Six Department 56, Inc. sponsored Gatherings are scheduled.
♦ Bachman's®, the parent company, sells Department 56, Inc. to Forstmann, Little for a reported $270 million.

1993 ♦ Department 56, Inc. exhibits at the Long Beach, CA International Collectible Exposition for the first time.
♦ Forstmann, Little and Company files with the Securities and Exchange Commission to sell 4.6 million public shares of Department 56, Inc. stock.
♦ Ed Bazinet becomes the company's first CEO.
♦ *Nantucket Renovation*, the first Original Snow Village® limited piece, is issued and limited to one year of production.
♦ Production of the limited edition *Cathedral Church Of St. Mark* ceases due to production problems—only 3,024 of the planned 17,500 are produced.
♦ *Boarding & Lodging School #18* is issued to commemorate the 150th Anniversary of the publishing of Dickens' *A Christmas Carol*.
♦ First Heritage Village Collection® interracial accessory, *Playing In The Snow* (Christmas In The City®), is issued.
♦ Special "Road Show" gold van is manufactured to be given to prospective investors.
♦ The second Event Piece, the Snowbabies™ *Can I Open It Now?*, is available at selected dealers' open houses.
♦ The first Snowbabies™ piece to have an annual mark, *Somewhere In Dreamland*, is issued.

1994 ♦ Department 56, Inc. exhibits at the Secaucus, New Jersey International Collectible Exposition for the first time.
♦ Susan Engel is appointed as President after Todd Bachman announces his departure.
♦ Disney Parks Village™, the seventh village in The Heritage Village Collection®, is announced.
♦ 13 Department 56, Inc. sponsored Gatherings are held.
♦ The Original Snow Village® *Starter Kit* contains the first pieces to be sold in kit form.
♦ The 10th Anniversary of Dickens' Village Series® is commemorated with the *Postern*.
♦ *Jack Frost...A Touch of Winter's Magic*, the first Snowbabies™ piece featuring a person other than a Snowbaby, is introduced.

1995
- First "Homes For The Holidays" Event is held, featuring a Dickens' Village Series® *Start A Tradition* Set.
- Production of *Mickey's New Friend*, a Snowbabies™ piece produced exclusively for Disney, ceases.
- Dickens' Village Series® *Christmas Carol Set* retires.
- Snowbunnies first appear on dealers' shelves.

1996
- Approximately fifty dealers are eliminated for not adhering to Department 56 Inc.'s marketing strategies.
- *Ramsford Palace*—limited to 27,500—is issued for Dickens' Village Series®—its first limited in eight years.
- The entire Disney Parks Village™ is retired at midyear, the first village to be retired completely.
- First buildings with smoking chimneys are introduced—one for The Original Snow Village®, one for Dickens' Village Series®.
- Numbering system is changed to include a different number for each piece in a set, and individual buildings within sets are retired. Dealers are allowed to purchase (and sell) individual pieces from sets.
- Limited Edition Snowbabies™ piece, *Climb Every Mountain*—limited to 22,500 pieces—is issued.
- Snowbabies™ glass ornaments are introduced.
- Snowbabies™ Starter Kit, *Star Gazing*, is introduced.
- Ed Bazinet resigns as Chief Executive Officer and is replaced by Susan Engel.
- Retirement Day moves from December to November.
- Department 56, Inc. and QVC sell village sets as a "test" on the cable television shopping network.
- The first Limited Edition accessory, *A Christmas Carol Reading by Charles Dickens*, is announced.
- The first Profiles™ building, *Heinz House*, is made available through the H. J. Heinz Company.
- The first Storybook Village designs are issued.

1997
- The last Charles Dickens' Signature Series building, *Gad's Hill Place*, is introduced.
- Department 56, Inc. contracts with Enesco and Goebel to sell its products in Europe.
- The first Mother's Day promotion is held featuring a Limited Edition print with a purchase of the Snowbabies™ piece *Once Upon a Time*.
- *Tower Of London*, the first Historical Landmark Series™ piece, is introduced for Dickens' Village Series®.
- The Classic Ornament Series debuts.
- The Snowbabies™ Friendship Club, Department 56, Inc.'s first collectors' club, is announced.
- *Ronald McDonald House® (The House That ❤ Built™)*, the first building produced as a fund raiser and not intended for retail sales, is issued.
- GCC's Twentieth Anniversary is marked by The Original Snow Village® building, *Mainstreet Gift Shop*, produced for sale exclusively by GCC member retailers.
- Ed Bazinet resigns as Chairman and is replaced by Susan Engel.
- The second Profiles™ building, *Main Street Memories*, is sold to State Farm Insurance employees, agents, and retirees.
- Department 56, Inc. donates $1 million to Ronald McDonald House® Charities.

1998
- Department 56, Inc. introduces the *Kensington Palace* at the International Collectible Exposition in Rosemont.
- The first Halloween-related building, *Haunted Mansion*, is introduced.
- Two of The Orignal Snow Village® buildings, *Haunted Mansion* and *Rock Creek Mill*, are produced with no glaze.
- The first animated buildings, *Haunted Mansion* and *Carousel*, debut.
- *Collectors Club House*, a building produced by Department 56, Inc. for members of collectors' clubs affiliated with the National Council of 56 Clubs, is announced.
- The second *Ronald McDonald House®* is issued & limited to 5,600 pcs.
- Limited to 5,000 pieces, the *Lionel® Electric Train Shop* is sold through Allied Model Trains in California.
- Forstmann, Little divests itself of Department 56, Inc. holdings.
- Village brochures for current and retired pieces make their debut.
- The first Snowbabies™ Guest Series piece, *I Have the Feeling We're Not in Kansas Anymore*, is announced.

Department 56® Time Line

1998 (cont.)

- The first set in the Literary Series—*Great Expectations Satis Manor*—is introduced.
- *Independence Hall*, the first Historical Landmark Series™ design not intended for Dickens' Village Series®, is announced. It is classified as a Heritage Village Collection® piece.
- Seasons Bay™, a village with pewter accessories for all four seasons and no snow, makes its debut.
- The first Storybook Village designs are retired.
- *Let's Be Friends*, a customized Snowbabies™ piece—limited to 1,200 pieces—is issued at the Disneyana Convention.
- Winter Silhouette's name is changed to Silhouette Treasures and Silhouette Santa.
- Elf Land, a subdivision of the North Pole Series™, debuts with three buildings.
- The first July event is announced and slated for 1999.

the **Village Chronicle.**

The Original Snow Village®

The Original Snow Village® Accessories

Dickens' Village Series®

NEW ENGLAND VILLAGE®

ALPINE VILLAGE SERIES™

CHRISTMAS IN THE CITY®

Little Town Of Bethlehem™

NORTH POLE SERIES™

Disney Parks Village™

The Heritage Village Collection® Accessories

Seasons Bay™

Seasons Bay™ Accessories

Special Releases

Additional Village Accessories

Ornaments

Item#	Name	Intro	Retired	OSRP$	GBTru$	Wish	Have	Date	Qty	Paid Each	Total
5001-3	Mountain Lodge	1976	1979	20	390	○	○				
5002-1	Gabled Cottage	1976	1979	20	365	○	○				
5003-9	Inn, The	1976	1979	20	450	○	○				
5004-7	Country Church	1976	1979	18	375	○	○				
5005-4	Steepled Church	1976	1979	25	620	○	○				
5006-2	Small Chalet	1976	1979	15	460	○	○				
5007-0	Victorian House	1977	1979	30	445	○	○				
5008-8	Mansion	1977	1979	30	450	○	○				
5009-6	Stone Church–"Original, Version 1"	1977	1979	35	615	○	○				
5009-6	Stone Church–"Original, Version 2"	1977	1979	35	595	○	○				
5011-2	Homestead	1978	1984	30	225	○	○				
5012-0	General Store–"White"	1978	1980	25	465	○	○				
5012-0	General Store–"Tan"	1978	1980	25	545	○	○				
5012-0	General Store–"Gold"	1978	1980	25	495	○	○				
5013-8	Cape Cod	1978	1980	20	365	○	○				
5014-6	Nantucket	1978	1986	25	265	○	○				
5015-3	Skating Rink/Duck Pond Set	1978	1979	16	1110	○	○				
5016-1	Small Double Trees–"Blue Birds"	1978	1989	13.50	165	○	○				
5016-1	Small Double Trees–"Red Birds"	1978	1989	13.50	50	○	○				
5054-2	Victorian	1979	1982	30	360	○	○				
5055-9	Knob Hill–"Gray"	1979	1981	30	335	○	○				
5055-9	Knob Hill–"Yellow"	1979	1981	30	365	○	○				
5056-7	Brownstone	1979	1981	36	575	○	○				
5057-5	Log Cabin	1979	1981	22	445	○	○				
5058-3	Countryside Church	1979	1984	27.50	250	○	○				
5059-1	Stone Church	1979	1980	32	945	○	○				
5060-9	School House	1979	1982	30	375	○	○				
5061-7	Tudor House	1979	1981	25	305	○	○				
5062-5	Mission Church	1979	1980	30	1765	○	○				
5063-3	Mobile Home	1979	1980	18	1690	○	○				
5065-8	Giant Trees	1979	1982	20	270	○	○				
5066-6	Adobe House	1979	1980	18	2735	○	○				

OSV Page 1 Totals: 789.50 18,865.00

Item#	Name	Intro	Retired	OSRP$	GBTru$	Wish	Have	Date	Qty	Paid Each	Total
5067-4	Cathedral Church	1980	1981	36	2900	○	○				
5068-2	Stone Mill House	1980	1982	30	440	○	○				
5070-9	Colonial Farm House	1980	1982	30	285	○	○				
5071-7	Town Church	1980	1982	33	320	○	○				
5086-5	Train Station With 3 Train Cars	1980	1985	100	400	○	○				
5087-3	"	1980									
5072-5	Wooden Clapboard	1981	1984	32	240	○	○				
5073-3	English Cottage	1981	1982	25	295	○	○				
5074-1	Barn	1981	1984	32	395	○	○				
5076-8	Corner Store	1981	1983	30	225	○	○				
5077-6	Bakery	1981	1983	30	260	○	○				
5078-4	English Church	1981	1982	30	325	○	○				
5080-6	Large Single Tree	1981	1989	17	45	○	○				
5085-6	Train Station With 3 Train Cars	1981	1985	100	385	○	○				
5017-2	Skating Pond	1982	1984	25	350	○	○				
5019-9	Street Car	1982	1984	16	335	○	○				
5020-2	Centennial House	1982	1984	32	315	○	○				
5021-0	Carriage House	1982	1984	28	295	○	○				
5022-9	Pioneer Church	1982	1984	30	295	○	○				
5023-7	Swiss Chalet	1982	1984	28	425	○	○				
5024-5	Bank	1982	1983	32	600	○	○				
5081-4	Gabled House	1982	1983	30	370	○	○				
5082-2	Flower Shop	1982	1983	25	465	○	○				
5083-0	New Stone Church	1982	1984	32	330	○	○				
5000-8	Town Hall	1983	1984	32	335	○	○				
5001-6	Grocery	1983	1985	35	315	○	○				
5002-4	Victorian Cottage	1983	1984	35	375	○	○				
5003-2	Governor's Mansion	1983	1985	32	320	○	○				
5004-0	Turn Of The Century	1983	1986	36	200	○	○				
5025-3	Gingerbread House	1983	1984	24	325	○	○				
5026-1	Village Church	1983	1984	30	430	○	○				
5028-8	Gothic Church	1983	1986	36	250	○	○				
5029-6	Parsonage	1983	1985	35	325	○	○				
5031-8	Wooden Church	1983	1985	30	325	○	○				

OSV Page 2 Totals: 1,128.00 13,495.00

The Original Snow Village® GB History List

Item#	Name	Intro	Retired	OSRP$	GBTru$	Wish Have	Date	Qty	Paid Each	Total
5032-6	Fire Station	1983	1984	32	475	○ ○ ○	—	—	—	—
5033-4	English Tudor	1983	1985	30	245	○ ○ ○	—	—	—	—
5084-9	Chateau	1983	1984	35	425	○ ○ ○	—	—	—	—
5005-9	Main Street House	1984	1986	27	250	○ ○ ○	—	—	—	—
5007-5	Stratford House	1984	1986	28	145	○ ○ ○	—	—	—	—
5008-3	Haversham House	1984	1987	37	225	○ ○ ○	—	—	—	—
5009-1	Galena House	1984	1985	32	365	○ ○ ○	—	—	—	—
5010-5	River Road House	1984	1987	36	170	○ ○ ○	—	—	—	—
5012-1	Delta House	1984	1986	32	275	○ ○ ○	—	—	—	—
5015-6	Bayport	1984	1986	30	215	○ ○ ○	—	—	—	—
5034-2	Congregational Church	1984	1985	28	625	○ ○ ○	—	—	—	—
5035-0	Trinity Church	1984	1986	32	280	○ ○ ○	—	—	—	—
5036-9	Summit House	1984	1985	28	365	○ ○ ○	—	—	—	—
5037-7	New School House	1984	1986	35	225	○ ○ ○	—	—	—	—
5039-3	Parish Church	1984	1986	32	320	○ ○ ○	—	—	—	—
5045-8	Stucco Bungalow	1985	1986	30	345	○ ○ ○	—	—	—	—
5046-6	Williamsburg House	1985	1988	37	130	○ ○ ○	—	—	—	—
5047-4	Plantation House	1985	1987	37	95	○ ○ ○	—	—	—	—
5048-2	Church Of The Open Door	1985	1988	34	140	○ ○ ○	—	—	—	—
5049-0	Spruce Place	1985	1987	33	235	○ ○ ○	—	—	—	—
5050-4	Duplex	1985	1987	35	135	○ ○ ○	—	—	—	—
5051-2	Depot And Train With 2 Train Cars	1985	1988	65	135	○ ○ ○	—	—	—	—
5052-0	Ridgewood	1985	1987	35	140	○ ○ ○	—	—	—	—
5041-5	Waverly Place	1986	1986	35	305	○ ○ ○	—	—	—	—
5042-3	Twin Peaks	1986	1986	32	370	○ ○ ○	—	—	—	—
5043-1	2101 Maple	1986	1986	32	295	○ ○ ○	—	—	—	—
5060-1	Lincoln Park Duplex	1986	1988	33	140	○ ○ ○	—	—	—	—
5062-8	Sonoma House	1986	1988	33	145	○ ○ ○	—	—	—	—
5063-6	Highland Park House	1986	1988	35	135	○ ○ ○	—	—	—	—
5065-2	Beacon Hill House	1986	1988	31	170	○ ○ ○	—	—	—	—
5066-0	Pacific Heights House	1986	1988	33	90	○ ○ ○	—	—	—	—
5067-9	Ramsey Hill House	1986	1989	36	90	○ ○ ○	—	—	—	—
5068-7	Saint James Church	1986	1988	37	155	○ ○ ○	—	—	—	—

OSV PAGE 3 TOTALS: 1,117.00   7,855.00

The Original Snow Village® GB History List

Item#	Name	Intro	Retired	OSRP$	GBTru$	Wish	Have	Date	Qty	Paid Each	Total
5070-9	All Saints Church	1986	1997	38	65	○	○				
5071-7	Carriage House	1986	1988	29	105	○	○				
5073-3	Toy Shop	1986	1990	36	100	○	○				
5076-8	Apothecary	1986	1990	34	95	○	○				
5077-6	Bakery	1986	1991	35	85	○	○				
5078-4	Diner	1986	1987	22	595	○	○				
5006-7	St. Anthony Hotel & Post Office	1987	1989	40	95	○	○				
5013-0	Snow Village Factory	1987	1989	45	120	○	○				
5019-9	Cathedral Church	1987	1990	50	100	○	○				
5024-5	Cumberland House	1987	1995	42	70	○	○				
5027-0	Springfield House	1987	1990	40	70	○	○				
5030-0	Lighthouse	1987	1988	36	550	○	○				
5081-4	Red Barn	1987	1992	38	90	○	○				
5082-2	Jefferson School	1987	1991	36	170	○	○				
5089-0	Farm House	1987	1992	40	75	○	○				
5091-1	Fire Station No. 2	1987	1989	40	195	○	○				
5092-0	Snow Village Resort Lodge	1987	1989	55	130	○	○				
5044-0	Village Market	1988	1991	39	80	○	○				
5054-7	Kenwood House	1988	1990	50	145	○	○				
5121-7	Maple Ridge Inn	1988	1990	55	65	○	○				
5122-5	Village Station And Train	1988	1992	65	110	○	○				
5123-3	Cobblestone Antique Shop	1988	1992	36	65	○	○				
5124-1	Corner Cafe	1988	1991	37	90	○	○				
5125-0	Single Car Garage	1988	1990	22	50	○	○				
5126-8	Home Sweet Home/House & Windmill	1988	1991	60	110	○	○				
5127-6	Redeemer Church	1988	1992	42	65	○	○				
5128-4	Service Station	1988	1991	37.50	260	○	○				
5140-3	Stonehurst House	1988	1994	37.50	55	○	○				
5141-1	Palos Verdes	1988	1990	37.50	70	○	○				
5114-4	Jingle Belle Houseboat	1989	1991	42	180	○	○				
5119-5	Colonial Church	1989	1992	60	85	○	○				
5120-9	North Creek Cottage	1989	1992	45	60	○	○				
5142-0	Paramount Theater	1989	1993	42	185	○	○				
5143-8	Doctor's House	1989	1992	56	100	○	○				

OSV Page 4 Totals: 1,419.50   4,485.00

Item#	Name	Intro	Retired	OSRP$	GBTru$	Wish	Have	Date	Qty	Paid Each	Total
5144-6	Courthouse	1989	1993	65	185	O	O				
5145-4	Village Warming House	1989	1992	42	65	O	O				
5149-7	J. Young's Granary	1989	1992	45	85	O	O				
5150-0	Pinewood Log Cabin	1989	1995	37.50	60	O	O				
5151-9	56 Flavors Ice Cream Parlor	1990	1992	42	175	O	O				
5152-7	Morningside House	1990	1992	45	65	O	O				
5153-5	Mainstreet Hardware Store	1990	1993	42	80	O	O				
5154-3	Village Realty	1990	1993	42	60	O	O				
5155-1	Spanish Mission Church	1990	1992	42	70	O	O				
5156-0	Prairie House	1990	1993	42	70	O	O				
5157-8	Queen Anne Victorian	1990	1996	48	75	O	O				
5097-0	Christmas Shop, The	1991	1996	37.50	65	O	O				
5400-3	Oak Grove Tudor	1991	1994	42	50	O	O				
5401-1	Honeymooner Motel, The	1991	1993	42	85	O	O				
5402-0	Village Greenhouse	1991	1995	35	55	O	O				
5403-8	Southern Colonial	1991	1994	48	80	O	O				
5404-6	Gothic Farmhouse	1991	1997	48	70	O	O				
5405-4	Finklea's Finery Costume Shop	1991	1993	45	70	O	O				
5406-2	Jack's Corner Barber Shop	1991	1994	42	75	O	O				
5407-0	Double Bungalow	1991	1994	45	65	O	O				
5420-8	Grandma's Cottage	1992	1996	42	80	O	O				
5421-6	St. Luke's Church	1992	1994	45	65	O	O				
5422-4	Village Post Office	1992	1995	35	65	O	O				
5423-2	Al's TV Shop	1992	1995	40	60	O	O				
5424-0	Good Shepherd Chapel & Church School	1992	1996	72	85	O	O				
5425-9	Print Shop & Village News	1992	1994	37.50	65	O	O				
5426-7	Hartford House	1992	1995	55	75	O	O				
5427-5	Village Vet And Pet Shop	1992	1995	32	70	O	O				
5437-2	Craftsman Cottage	1992	1995	55	75	O	O				
5438-0	Village Station	1992	1997	65	70	O	O				
5439-9	Airport	1992	1996	60	85	O	O				

OSV Page 5 Totals: 1,415.50   2,400.00

Item#	Name	Intro	Retired	OSRP$	GBTru$	Wish Have	Date	Qty	Paid Each	Total
5441-0	Nantucket Renovation	1993	1993 Annual	55	65	○				
5442-9	Mount Olivet Church	1993	1996	65	75	○				
5443-7	Village Public Library	1993	1997	55	75	○				
5444-5	Woodbury House	1993	1996	45	65	○				
5445-3	Hunting Lodge	1993	1996	50	145	○				
5446-1	Dairy Barn	1993	1997	55	80	○				
5447-0	Dinah's Drive-In	1993	1996	45	95	○				
5448-8	Snowy Hills Hospital	1993	1996	48	90	○				
5460-7	Fisherman's Nook Resort	1994	Current	75	75	○				
5461-5	Fisherman's Nook Cabins, Set/2	1994	Current	50	50	○				
	Fisherman's Nook Bass Cabin	1994								
	Fisherman's Nook Trout Cabin	1994								
5462-3	Snow Village Starter Set	1994	1996	49.99	65	○				
	Shady Oak Church									
5464-0	Wedding Chapel	1994	Current	55	55	○				
5465-8	Federal House	1994	1997	50	75	○				
5466-6	Carmel Cottage	1994	1997	48	55	○				
5467-4	Skate & Ski Shop	1994	1998	50	55	○				
5468-2	Glenhaven House	1994	1997	45	65	○				
5469-0	Coca-Cola® brand Bottling Plant	1994	1997	65	90	○				
5470-4	Marvel's Beauty Salon	1994	1997	37.50	55	○				
5483-6	Christmas Cove Lighthouse	1995	Current	60	60	○				
5484-4	Coca-Cola® brand Corner Drugstore	1995	1998	55	90	○				
54850	Snow Carnival Ice Palace	1995	1998	95	115	○				
54851	Pisa Pizza	1995	1998	35	50	○				
5485-2	Peppermint Porch Day Care	1995	1997	45	70	○				
54853	Village Police Station	1995	1998	48	60	○				
54854	Holly Brothers Garage	1995	1998	48	60	○				
54855	Ryman Auditorium®	1995	1997	75	95	○				
54856	Dutch Colonial	1995	1996	45	70	○				
54857	Beacon Hill Victorian	1995	1998	60	90	○				
54858	Bowling Alley	1995	1998	42	60	○				
54859	Starbucks® Coffee	1995	Current	48	48	○				

OSV Page 6 Totals: 1,599.49   2,198.00

ITEM#	NAME	INTRO	RETIRED	OSRP$	GBTRU$	WISH	HAVE	DATE	QTY	PAID EACH	TOTAL
54871	NICK'S TREE FARM	1996	CURRENT	40	40	O	O	——	——	——	——
54872	SMOKEY MOUNTAIN RETREAT	1996	CURRENT	65	65	O	O	——	——	——	——
54873	BOULDER SPRINGS HOUSE	1996	1997	60	75	O	O	——	——	——	——
54874	REINDEER BUS DEPOT	1996	1997	42	60	O	O	——	——	——	——
54880	ROCKABILLY RECORDS	1996	1998	45	55	O	O	——	——	——	——
54881	CHRISTMAS LAKE HIGH SCHOOL	1996	CURRENT	52	52	O	O	——	——	——	——
54882	BIRCH RUN SKI CHALET	1996	CURRENT	60	60	O	O	——	——	——	——
54883	ROSITA'S CANTINA	1996	CURRENT	50	50	O	O	——	——	——	——
54884	SHINGLE VICTORIAN	1996	CURRENT	55	55	O	O	——	——	——	——
54885	SECRET GARDEN FLORIST, THE	1996	CURRENT	50	50	O	O	——	——	——	——
54886	HARLEY-DAVIDSON® MOTORCYCLE SHOP	1996	CURRENT	65	65	O	O	——	——	——	——
8802	BACHMAN'S® FLOWER SHOP	1997	PROMO	50	110	O	O	——	——	——	——
8960	RONALD MCDONALD HOUSE® (THE HOUSE THAT ♥ BUILT™)	1997	EVENT PIECE	*	395	O	O	——	——	——	——
54887	MAINSTREET GIFT SHOP	1997	1997	50	75	O	O	——	——	——	——
54902	ORIGINAL SNOW VILLAGE START A TRADITION SET, THE KRINGLES TOY SHOP A HOT CHOCOLATE STAND	1997	1998	100	100	O	O	——	——	——	——
54903	OLD CHELSEA MANSION	1997	1998	85	95	O	O	——	——	——	——
54904	NEW HOPE CHURCH	1997	1998	60	80	O	O	——	——	——	——
54910	CHRISTMAS BARN DANCE	1997	CURRENT	65	65	O	O	——	——	——	——
54911	ITALIANATE VILLA	1997	CURRENT	55	55	O	O	——	——	——	——
54912	FARM HOUSE	1997	CURRENT	50	50	O	O	——	——	——	——
54913	HERSHEY'S™ CHOCOLATE SHOP	1997	CURRENT	55	55	O	O	——	——	——	——
54914	MCDONALD'S®	1997	CURRENT	65	65	O	O	——	——	——	——
54915	GRACIE'S DRY GOODS & GENERAL STORE	1997	CURRENT	70	70	O	O	——	——	——	——
54916	ROLLERAMA ROLLER RINK	1997	CURRENT	56	56	O	O	——	——	——	——
54917	LINDEN HILLS COUNTRY CLUB	1997	CURRENT	60	60	O	O	——	——	——	——
54918	BRANDON BUNGALOW, THE	1997	CURRENT	55	55	O	O	——	——	——	——
2202	LIONEL® ELECTRIC TRAIN SHOP	1998	LTD ED 5,000	55	110	O	O	——	——	——	——
2203	BACHMAN'S® GREENHOUSE	1998	PROMO	60	95	O	O	——	——	——	——
2210	RONALD MCDONALD HOUSE® (THE HOUSE THAT ♥ BUILT™)	1998	LTD ED 5,600	*	400	O	O	——	——	——	——

OSV PAGE 7 TOTALS: 1,575.00   2,618.00

Item#	Name	Intro	Retired	OSRP$	GBTru$	Wish	Have	Date	Qty	Paid Each	Total
54932	Rock Creek Mill House	1998	1998	64	95	O	O				
54933	Carnival Carousel	1998	Current	150	150	O	O				
54934	Snowy Pines Inn Exclusive Gift Set	1998	Event Gift Set	65	90	O	O				
54935	Haunted Mansion	1998	Current	110	110	O	O				
54940	Center For The Arts	1998	Current	64	64	O	O				
54941	Uptown Motors Ford®	1998	Current	95	95	O	O				
54942	Fire Station #3	1998	Current	70	70	O	O				
54943	Stick Style House	1998	Current	60	60	O	O				
54944	Hidden Ponds House	1998	Current	50	50	O	O				
54945	...Another Man's Treasure Garage	1998	Current	60	60	O	O				
54946	Farmer's Co-Op Granary, The	1998	Current	64	64	O	O				
54947	Lionel® Electric Train Shop	1998	Current	55	55	O	O				
54948	Harley-Davidson® Manufacturing	1998	Current	80	80	O	O				
54949	Secret Garden Greenhouse, The	1998	Current	60	60	O	O				
	OSV Page 8 Totals:			1,047.00	1,103.00						

	OSRP$	GBTru$
OSV Page 1 Totals:	789.50	18,865.00
OSV Page 2 Totals:	1,128.00	13,495.00
OSV Page 3 Totals:	1,117.00	7,855.00
OSV Page 4 Totals:	1,419.50	4,485.00
OSV Page 5 Totals:	1,415.50	2,400.00
OSV Page 6 Totals:	1,599.49	2,198.00
OSV Page 7 Totals:	1,575.00	2,618.00
OSV Page 8 Totals:	1,047.00	1,103.00
OSV Grand Totals:	**10,090.99**	**53,019.00**

MOUNTAIN LODGE

Item #	Intro	Retired	OSRP	GBTru	NO
5001-3	1976	1979	$20	**$390**	CHANGE

One of the "Original 6." Color on roof is different from piece to piece. Bright colored skis lean against two-story lodge, upper windows painted to appear as lead panes, sunburst on end of building, snow-laden tree at side.

DATE: ____ $ ____	'91	'92	'93	'94	'95	'96	'97	'98
O Wish O Have	$525	550	405	370	375	325	375	390

GABLED COTTAGE

Item #	Intro	Retired	OSRP	GBTru	↓
5002-1	1976	1979	$20	**$365**	4%

One of the "Original 6." Four-peaked roof with two chimneys, curtained windows, welcome mat. Ivy climbs walls to roof and door, several windows have wreath design. Attached snow-laden tree with bluebird.

DATE: ____ $ ____	'91	'92	'93	'94	'95	'96	'97	'98
O Wish O Have	$450	475	395	385	350	350	365	380

INN, THE

Item #	Intro	Retired	OSRP	GBTru	NO
5003-9	1976	1979	$20	**$450**	CHANGE

One of the "Original 6." Colors on roof are not consistent. Two large brick chimneys, full length covered porch, welcome mat at timbered front doors, attached snow-laden tree on side, bright yellow door on opposite side.

DATE: ____ $ ____	'91	'92	'93	'94	'95	'96	'97	'98
O Wish O Have	$525	500	475	490	450	365	425	450

COUNTRY CHURCH

Item #	Intro	Retired	OSRP	GBTru	↑
5004-7	1976	1979	$18	**$375**	6%

One of the "Original 6." Also known as "Wayside Chapel." Vines and painted welcome on walls, short-spired, door ajar, circular upper window, painted side windows, snow-laden tree shades one wall.
Notable: Authentic Department 56® pieces have hand-lettered signs. If they appear "rubber-stamped," they are not Department 56®.

DATE: ____ $ ____	'91	'92	'93	'94	'95	'96	'97	'98
O Wish O Have	$325	435	375	375	385	345	360	355

The Original Snow Village®

Steepled Church

Item #	Intro	Retired	OSRP	GBTru	↑
5005-4	1976	1979	$25	**$620**	7%

One of the "Original 6." Colors on roof are not consistent. One spire, large circular window over double wood front doors flanked by leaded lattice design windows, side chapel, snow-covered tree, bluebird on steeple.

Date: ____ $ ____	'91	'92	'93	'94	'95	'96	'97	'98
○ Wish ○ Have	$775	675	675	640	625	515	550	580

Small Chalet

Item #	Intro	Retired	OSRP	GBTru	↑
5006-2	1976	1979	$15	**$460**	8%

One of the "Original 6." Also known as "Gingerbread Chalet." Variation in number of flowers in box (4, 5 or 7) and in color–tan to dark brown. Two-story small gingerbread look home, flower box with snow-covered plants, attached tree.

Date: ____ $ ____	'91	'92	'93	'94	'95	'96	'97	'98
○ Wish ○ Have	$360	415	415	365	400	375	445	425

Victorian House

Item #	Intro	Retired	OSRP	GBTru	↓
5007-0	1977	1979	$30	**$445**	4%

Variations in color–rust/white, salmon/white, pink/white & orange/yellow. Variations in birds–some to none. Orange/yellow color combination has no attached tree. Textured to portray shingles and clapboard. Steps lead up to front door. Stained glass inserts above windows.

Date: ____ $ ____	'91	'92	'93	'94	'95	'96	'97	'98
○ Wish ○ Have	$400	485	375	435	455	395	430	465

Mansion

Item #	Intro	Retired	OSRP	GBTru	↓
5008-8	1977	1979	$30	**$450**	24%

Building is white brick with porch supported by pillars, windows are shuttered, two chimneys plus cupola on roof. Attached snow-laden evergreen tree.
Notable: Variation in roof color–either forest green or turquoise. Forest green is considered to be the first shipped and is much harder to find. Amount and placement of snow varies with the roof colors.

Date: ____ $ ____	'91	'92	'93	'94	'95	'96	'97	'98
○ Wish ○ Have	$600	600	500	550	495	495	515	590

STONE CHURCH– "ORIGINAL, VERSION 1"

ITEM #	INTRO	RETIRED	OSRP	GBTru	↓
5009-6	1977	1979	$35	**$615**	5%

Notable: There are two Stone Churches: 1977, #5009-6 and 1979, #5059-1. There are Two Versions of #5009-6. Both versions of the original 1977 Church have 10 1/2" steeples. The color on Version 1 is usually a pale mint green; the finish is very glossy. Version 1's top step on the tree side is flush with the edge of the bottom step. Both versions have a separate bell attached by wire.

DATE: ____ $ ____	'91	'92	'93	'94	'95	'96	'97	'98
○ WISH ○ HAVE	$825	715	650	725	625	555	555	645

STONE CHURCH– "ORIGINAL, VERSION 2"

	GBTru	↓
	$595	7%

The color on Version 2 of the original Church is usually a deeper greenish yellow. Version 2's top step is indented from the bottom step on the right-hand side.

DATE: ____ $ ____	'91	'92	'93	'94	'95	'96	'97	'98
○ WISH ○ HAVE	$825	715	650	725	625	555	555	640

HOMESTEAD

ITEM #	INTRO	RETIRED	OSRP	GBTru	↑
5011-2	1978	1984	$30	**$225**	5%

Old-fashioned farmhouse, front porch full length of house. Second-floor bay windows. Triple window in front gable. Attached tree.

DATE: ____ $ ____	'91	'92	'93	'94	'95	'96	'97	'98
○ WISH ○ HAVE	$250	310	285	240	250	195	245	215

NOTES: _____
_____
_____
_____
_____
_____

GENERAL STORE–"WHITE"

ITEM #	INTRO	RETIRED	OSRP	GBTRU	↓
5012-0	1978	1980	$25	**$465**	5%

General Stores supply food, postal service and gas.
Notable: Variations in color–White, Tan & Gold–affect GBTru$ Value. This "White" General Store w/gray roof is considered to be the first shipped, however the "Tan" and "Gold" are much harder to find. The sign on the "White" General Store most often is, "General Store, Y & L Brothers." All three colors have Christmas trees on the porch roof.

DATE: ___ $ ___	'91	'92	'93	'94	'95	'96	'97	'98
○ WISH ○ HAVE	$440	500	450	450	450	435	455	490

GENERAL STORE–"TAN"

GBTRU	↓
$545	4%

This is the "Tan" General Store. The sign above the porch most often reads, "General Store, S & L Brothers."

DATE: ___ $ ___	'91	'92	'93	'94	'95	'96	'97	'98
○ WISH ○ HAVE	$440	500	605	605	585	535	600	565

GENERAL STORE–"GOLD"

GBTRU	↓
$495	2%

This is the "Gold" General Store. The sign above the porch most often reads simply, "General Store."

DATE: ___ $ ___	'91	'92	'93	'94	'95	'96	'97	'98
○ WISH ○ HAVE	$440	500	560	560	550	545	525	505

CAPE COD

ITEM #	INTRO	RETIRED	OSRP	GBTRU	↑
5013-8	1978	1980	$20	**$365**	1%

Steep gabled roof with chimney, small dormer and painted landscaping. Attached snow-laden tree.

DATE: ___ $ ___	'91	'92	'93	'94	'95	'96	'97	'98
○ WISH ○ HAVE	$385	385	375	360	375	385	375	360

NANTUCKET

ITEM #	INTRO	RETIRED	OSRP	GBTRU	↑
5014-6	1978	1986	$25	**$265**	2%

Yellow cottage with green roof. Small front porch, attached greenhouse. Attached tree. Some have garland above two front windows, some don't.
Notable: Also see the *Nantucket Renovation,* 1993, #5441-0.

DATE: ____ $ ____	'91	'92	'93	'94	'95	'96	'97	'98
○ WISH ○ HAVE	$235	250	250	315	275	235	255	260

SKATING RINK/ DUCK POND SET

ITEM #	INTRO	RETIRED	OSRP	GBTRU	↑
5015-3	1978	1979	$16	**$1110**	4%

Lighted. Set of 2. (The *Skating Rink* is the piece with the snowman, the *Duck Pond* is the piece with the bench and blue birds.)
Notable: One of the first non-house pieces. In this set the trees were attached directly to the pond bases where their size and weight caused frequent breakage, therefore they were retired in 1979. The revised *Skating Pond,* 1982, #5017-2, was also a set of 2 with one piece being the pond and the other piece double lighted trees. Because the *Skating Rink* and *Duck Pond* are frequently sold separately on the secondary market there is confusion between the *Skating Rink* and *Skating Pond.* The Rink has one single lighted tree attached to the base, the Pond has separate double trees.

DATE: ____ $ ____	'91	'92	'93	'94	'95	'96	'97	'98
○ WISH ○ HAVE	$1100	1200	950	1000	1000	970	1045	1070

NOTES: _____
_____
_____
_____
_____
_____

SMALL DOUBLE TREES– "BLUE BIRDS"

ITEM #	INTRO	RETIRED	OSRP	GBTRU	NO
5016-1	1978	1989	$13.50	**$165**	CHANGE

Lighted. Approximately 8 to 8 1/2" tall.
Notable: One of the first non-house accessory pieces. Variations in color of birds–blue or red–affect GBTru$ Value. Blue are considered to be the first ones shipped; the change to red was made in late 1979. There were mold changes and a variation in the amount of snow over the years as well.

DATE: ____ $ ____	'91	'92	'93	'94	'95	'96	'97	'98
○ WISH ○ HAVE	$150	150	225	175	175	175	180	165

SMALL DOUBLE TREES– "RED BIRDS"

	GBTRU	NO
	$50	CHANGE

This is the Small Double Trees–"Red Birds" and a photo illustrating changes in the mold and the variation in the amount of snow.

DATE: ____ $ ____	'91	'92	'93	'94	'95	'96	'97	'98
○ WISH ○ HAVE	$40	48	48	52	50	40	45	50

VICTORIAN

ITEM #	INTRO	RETIRED	OSRP	GBTRU	↓
5054-2	1979	1982	$30	**$360**	6%

Notable: There are variations in color and in exterior finish. They are peach with smooth walls (1979), gold with smooth walls (1980) and gold clapboard (1981 on). The peach is the most difficult to find but the gold and the gold clapboard look nicer and are preferred by collectors.

DATE: ____ $ ____	'91	'92	'93	'94	'95	'96	'97	'98
○ WISH ○ HAVE	$345	440	435	380	350	315	350	385

NOTES: _____

_____

_____

_____

_____

_____

KNOB HILL–"GRAY"

	ITEM #	INTRO	RETIRED	OSRP	GBTru	↑
	5055-9	1979	1981	$30	**$335**	2%

Notable: Variations in color in this three-story San Francisco-style Victorian row house–"Gray" or "Yellow"–affect GBTru$ Value. This is the "Gray" Knob Hill with a red roof and black trim. The "Gray" Knob Hill is considered to be the first shipped.

DATE: ____ $ ____	'91	'92	'93	'94	'95	'96	'97	'98
○ WISH ○ HAVE	$350	350	350	350	295	265	350	330

KNOB HILL–"YELLOW"

	GBTru	↓
	$365	4%

This is the "Yellow" Knob Hill with a red roof and gray trim.

DATE: ____ $ ____	'91	'92	'93	'94	'95	'96	'97	'98
○ WISH ○ HAVE	$350	350	350	350	375	345	365	380

BROWNSTONE

	ITEM #	INTRO	RETIRED	OSRP	GBTru	↓
	5056-7	1979	1981	$36	**$575**	4%

Building is three stories with wreath trimmed bay windows on all floors, overall flat roof.
Notable: There are two roof colors–originally introduced with a gray roof, the following year the roof was red. Red is the most desired.

DATE: ____ $ ____	'91	'92	'93	'94	'95	'96	'97	'98
○ WISH ○ HAVE	$475	495	540	560	575	545	565	600

LOG CABIN

	ITEM #	INTRO	RETIRED	OSRP	GBTru	↓
	5057-5	1979	1981	$22	**$445**	4%

Rustic log house with stone chimney, roof extends to cover porch, log pile at side, skis by door.

DATE: ____ $ ____	'91	'92	'93	'94	'95	'96	'97	'98
○ WISH ○ HAVE	$450	475	475	475	475	400	440	465

COUNTRYSIDE CHURCH

ITEM #	INTRO	RETIRED	OSRP	GBTRU	↓
5058-3	1979	1984	$27.50	**$250**	4%

White clapboard church with central bell steeple, attached tree has all lower branches pruned.
Notable: For a "no snow" version, see 1979 Meadowland *Countryside Church,* Item #5051-8.

DATE: ____ $ ____		'91	'92	'93	'94	'95	'96	'97	'98
○ WISH ○ HAVE		$275	295	295	295	295	260	275	260

STONE CHURCH

ITEM #	INTRO	RETIRED	OSRP	GBTRU	↓
5059-1	1979	1980	$32	**$945**	3%

8 1/2" steeple. The color is yellow. It has a Department 56® sticker dated 1980 on the bottom.
Notable: See also the original *Stone Church,* 1977, Item #5009-6.

DATE: ____ $ ____		'91	'92	'93	'94	'95	'96	'97	'98
○ WISH ○ HAVE		$750	850	910	1000	1000	915	955	975

SCHOOL HOUSE

ITEM #	INTRO	RETIRED	OSRP	GBTRU	↓
5060-9	1979	1982	$30	**$375**	6%

Flag flies from a roof peak above the brick one-room school. The flag pole is metal and removable.
Notable: Color varies from rust to dark brown. The first design to feature the American flag.

DATE: ____ $ ____		'91	'92	'93	'94	'95	'96	'97	'98
○ WISH ○ HAVE		$400	360	405	340	345	365	360	400

TUDOR HOUSE

ITEM #	INTRO	RETIRED	OSRP	GBTRU	↓
5061-7	1979	1981	$25	**$305**	5%

Brick chimney and fireplace on simple L-shaped, timber-trimmed home with split-shingle roof.

DATE: ____ $ ____		'91	'92	'93	'94	'95	'96	'97	'98
○ WISH ○ HAVE		$415	385	330	330	325	285	295	320

MISSION CHURCH

ITEM #	INTRO	RETIRED	OSRP	GBTRU	↑
5062-5	1979	1980	$30	**$1765**	35%

Sun-dried clay with structural timbers visible at roof line. Small arched bell tower above entry. Ceramic bell is attached by wire.

DATE: ____ $ ____

	'91	'92	'93	'94	'95	'96	'97	'98
○ WISH ○ HAVE	$785	950	950	1260	1250	1100	1275	1310

MOBILE HOME

ITEM #	INTRO	RETIRED	OSRP	GBTRU	↑
5063-3	1979	1980	$18	**$1690**	2%

Similar to aluminum-skinned Airstream mobile home. To be towed by car or truck for travel.

DATE: ____ $ ____

	'91	'92	'93	'94	'95	'96	'97	'98
○ WISH ○ HAVE	$1350	1625	1700	1700	1750	1865	1725	1650

GIANT TREES

ITEM #	INTRO	RETIRED	OSRP	GBTRU	↓
5065-8	1979	1982	$20	**$270**	4%

Lighted snow-covered large evergreen trees. Approximately 11" tall. Birds perch on branches.

DATE: ____ $ ____

	'91	'92	'93	'94	'95	'96	'97	'98
○ WISH ○ HAVE	$310	295	295	360	360	335	295	280

ADOBE HOUSE

ITEM #	INTRO	RETIRED	OSRP	GBTRU	↑
5066-6	1979	1980	$18	**$2735**	9%

Small sun-dried clay home. Outside oven on side, chili peppers hang from roof beams.

DATE: ____ $ ____

	'91	'92	'93	'94	'95	'96	'97	'98
○ WISH ○ HAVE	$1000	2000	2400	2495	2500	2150	2400	2500

CATHEDRAL CHURCH

ITEM #	INTRO	RETIRED	OSRP	GBTRU	↑
5067-4	1980	1981	$36	**$2900**	7%

First of two Original Snow Village® Cathedral Churches. (See also 1987, Item #5019-9.) This church has a central dome with two shorter bell towers. The stained glass windows are acrylic. Production problems (fragile domes) forced retirement after one year.
Notable: Inspired by St. Paul's Cathedral in St. Paul, MN.

DATE: ____ $ ____	'91	'92	'93	'94	'95	'96	'97	'98
○ WISH ○ HAVE	$725	825	2300	1895	2000	2100	2500	2700

STONE MILL HOUSE

ITEM #	INTRO	RETIRED	OSRP	GBTRU	↓
5068-2	1980	1982	$30	**$440**	22%

Water wheel on dark weathered stone block mill, separate bag of oats hung with wire from block and tackle, another bag propped by door. Many pieces available on the secondary market are missing the separate bag of oats.
Notable: The GBTru$ for a piece without the bag of oats is $350.

DATE: ____ $ ____	'91	'92	'93	'94	'95	'96	'97	'98
○ WISH ○ HAVE	$635	635	575	545	495	425	535	565

COLONIAL FARM HOUSE

ITEM #	INTRO	RETIRED	OSRP	GBTRU	NO CHANGE
5070-9	1980	1982	$30	**$285**	

House with wide front porch, two front dormers in attic, symmetrical layout of windows.
Notable: The same Item # was used for the 1986 *All Saints Church*.

DATE: ____ $ ____	'91	'92	'93	'94	'95	'96	'97	'98
○ WISH ○ HAVE	$425	425	400	365	375	315	325	285

TOWN CHURCH

ITEM #	INTRO	RETIRED	OSRP	GBTRU	↓
5071-7	1980	1982	$33	**$320**	9%

A short bell tower rises from central nave area, an attached tree tucks in close to the side chapel.
Notable: The same Item # was used for the 1986 *Carriage House*.

DATE: ____ $ ____	'91	'92	'93	'94	'95	'96	'97	'98
○ WISH ○ HAVE	$410	385	385	355	375	355	350	350

The Original Snow Village®

TRAIN STATION WITH 3 TRAIN CARS

ITEM #	INTRO	RETIRED	OSRP	GBTRU	NO
5086-5	1980	1985	$100	**$400**	CHANGE
5087-3					

Set of 4. First Original Snow Village® train & station design.

Notable: *Train Station With 3 Train Cars* was sold until 1981 under the Item #'s 5087-3 and 5086-5, respectively. Although boxed separately, they were sold together. This Station has 6 window panes, a round window in the door, and brick on the front only. The three lighted train cars–an engine, passenger car and baggage/mail caboose have "G & N RR" on the cars. All four pieces are lit and were made in Japan. After introduction it was thought the train was too large for the station. In 1981 a larger station, now packaged with the train, Item #5085-6, was released.

DATE: ___ $ ___	'91	'92	'93	'94	'95	'96	'97	'98
○ WISH ○ HAVE	$350	375	375	375	395	425	400	400

WOODEN CLAPBOARD

ITEM #	INTRO	RETIRED	OSRP	GBTRU	↓
5072-5	1981	1984	$32	**$240**	6%

White house with green roof and trim and wraparound porch. Red brick chimney.

DATE: ___ $ ___	'91	'92	'93	'94	'95	'96	'97	'98
○ WISH ○ HAVE	$300	320	300	260	260	210	230	255

ENGLISH COTTAGE

ITEM #	INTRO	RETIRED	OSRP	GBTRU	↑
5073-3	1981	1982	$25	**$295**	2%

Cottage with thatched roof and timbered frame, two chimneys, 1 1/2 stories. The roof comes down to meet the top of the first story.

Notable: The same Item # was used for the 1986 *Toy Shop*.

DATE: ___ $ ___	'91	'92	'93	'94	'95	'96	'97	'98
○ WISH ○ HAVE	$300	350	325	285	295	275	295	290

BARN

ITEM # 5074-1	INTRO 1981	RETIRED 1984	OSRP $32	GBTRU **$395**	↓ 7%

Red barn and silo. Gray roof, two vents on roof ridge, root cellar on side, hay loft over animals and equipment.
Notable: Also known as the "Original Barn."

DATE: ___ $ ___	'91 $450	'92 425	'93 425	'94 460	'95 460	'96 410	'97 430	'98 425
○ WISH ○ HAVE								

CORNER STORE

ITEM # 5076-8	INTRO 1981	RETIRED 1983	OSRP $30	GBTRU **$225**	↓ 10%

Red brick building with one large display window, entry door on corner, bay window in family living area, shutters on windows, shingled roof.
Notable: The same Item # was used for the 1986 *Apothecary.*

DATE: ___ $ ___	'91 $260	'92 260	'93 260	'94 260	'95 245	'96 205	'97 245	'98 250
○ WISH ○ HAVE								

BAKERY

ITEM # 5077-6	INTRO 1981	RETIRED 1983	OSRP $30	GBTRU **$260**	↓ 5%

A white building with a green roof, bakery store beneath the family living area and a half turret form giving a unique angle to the front and second-story bay window
Notable: The same Item # was used for the 1986 *Bakery*–a brown building in a new and different design. There is a wide difference in secondary market value between the two bakery designs. Check all your factual information prior to a purchase. The original *Bakery* is modeled after the Scofield Building in Northfield, MN.

DATE: ___ $ ___	'91 $275	'92 275	'93 275	'94 275	'95 250	'96 255	'97 265	'98 275
○ WISH ○ HAVE								

ENGLISH CHURCH

ITEM # 5078-4	INTRO 1981	RETIRED 1982	OSRP $30	GBTRU **$325**	↓ 12%

Church with steep pitched roof, side chapel, a steeple topped by a gold cross, arched windows, and triangular window in gable above the entry double doors. The cross is separate and inserts into the steeple.
Notable: The same Item # was used for the 1986 *Diner.*

DATE: ___ $ ___	'91 $250	'92 375	'93 375	'94 390	'95 395	'96 365	'97 375	'98 370
○ WISH ○ HAVE								

LARGE SINGLE TREE

ITEM #	INTRO	RETIRED	OSRP	GBTRU	↓
5080-6	1981	1989	$17	**$45**	18%

One lighted snow-covered evergreen tree approximately 9" tall with birds perched on the branches.
Notable: There were mold changes and variations in the amount of snow over the years.

DATE: ____ $ ____		'91	'92	'93	'94	'95	'96	'97	'98
○ WISH ○ HAVE		$50	50	50	55	45	35	45	55

TRAIN STATION WITH 3 TRAIN CARS

ITEM #	INTRO	RETIRED	OSRP	GBTRU	NO
5085-6	1981	1985	$100	**$385**	CHANGE

Revised Original Snow Village® train and station design. Set of 4. (Original was 1980, #5086-5 and #5087-3.) All 4 pieces are lit. This larger station, w/8 window panes, 2 windows in the door,  brick on the front & side wings, and Tudor style cross beams, is in better proportion to the train cars.

DATE: ____ $ ____		'91	'92	'93	'94	'95	'96	'97	'98
○ WISH ○ HAVE		$350	375	325	325	325	330	360	385

SKATING POND

ITEM #	INTRO	RETIRED	OSRP	GBTRU	NO
5017-2	1982	1984	$25	**$350**	CHANGE

Set of 2. A small snow-covered skating pond with a snowman on the edge and tree trunks piled together to provide seating is one piece. The second piece is two lighted evergreen trees.
Notable: This set replaced, and is sometimes confused with, the *Skating Rink/Duck Pond Set,* 1978, #5015-3. In this piece, the trees are separate from the pond.

DATE: ____ $ ____		'91	'92	'93	'94	'95	'96	'97	'98
○ WISH ○ HAVE		$350	350	350	390	380	360	355	350

STREET CAR

ITEM #	INTRO	RETIRED	OSRP	GBTRU	↓
5019-9	1982	1984	$16	**$335**	12%

Lighted bright yellow with green "Main Street" sign on side. #2 car, hookup on top for pole to connect to electric power.
Notable: Same Item # was used for the 1987 *Cathedral Church.*

DATE: ____ $ ____		'91	'92	'93	'94	'95	'96	'97	'98
○ WISH ○ HAVE		$375	350	325	368	395	325	375	380

CENTENNIAL HOUSE

ITEM #	INTRO	RETIRED	OSRP	GBTRU	NO
5020-2	1982	1984	$32	**$315**	CHANGE

Two-story clapboard house, square tower, carved and curved window frames, wooden balcony and porch.

DATE: ___ $ ___	'91	'92	'93	'94	'95	'96	'97	'98
○ WISH ○ HAVE	$365	365	370	350	350	305	325	315

CARRIAGE HOUSE

ITEM #	INTRO	RETIRED	OSRP	GBTRU	NO
5021-0	1982	1984	$28	**$295**	CHANGE

In this carriage house, bright lamps flank the entry to the storage area for the carriages. The driver has a small apartment above.

DATE: ___ $ ___	'91	'92	'93	'94	'95	'96	'97	'98
○ WISH ○ HAVE	$300	315	300	305	325	290	315	295

PIONEER CHURCH

ITEM #	INTRO	RETIRED	OSRP	GBTRU	↓
5022-9	1982	1984	$30	**$295**	8%

Simple cedar shake shingle church with front notice board sending joy to all who pass. Building has a short steeple on the front of the roof ridge.

DATE: ___ $ ___	'91	'92	'93	'94	'95	'96	'97	'98
○ WISH ○ HAVE	$285	355	305	310	300	310	320	320

SWISS CHALET

ITEM #	INTRO	RETIRED	OSRP	GBTRU	↓
5023-7	1982	1984	$28	**$425**	3%

Stone base walls support the timber upper stories of the chalet. The upper floor has a front balcony with a railing and is enclosed by a roof overhang. This building has a very unusual roof.

DATE: ___ $ ___	'91	'92	'93	'94	'95	'96	'97	'98
○ WISH ○ HAVE	$335	450	435	415	450	410	430	440

BANK

Item #	Intro	Retired	OSRP	GBTru	↓
5024-5	1982	1983	$32	**$600**	3%

Building is a corner bank with entry by revolving door. Outside there's a covered stairway leading to a second story. The "BANK" sign is part of the corner design.
Notable: The same Item # was used for the 1987 *Cumberland House*.

		'91	'92	'93	'94	'95	'96	'97	'98
Date: ___ $ ___									
○ Wish ○ Have		$415	635	715	600	600	585	600	620

GABLED HOUSE

Item #	Intro	Retired	OSRP	GBTru	NO
5081-4	1982	1983	$30	**$370**	CHANGE

Production pieces of this design are quite different from the house pictured on the Original Snow Village® poster. The house is white shingled with a very dark blue-green variegated four gabled roof. In addition, the building has two small covered porches.
Notable: The same Item # was used for the 1987 *Red Barn*. Early Release to Gift Creations Concepts (GCC).

		'91	'92	'93	'94	'95	'96	'97	'98
Date: ___ $ ___									
○ Wish ○ Have		$350	400	425	360	390	320	355	370

FLOWER SHOP

Item #	Intro	Retired	OSRP	GBTru	NO
5082-2	1982	1983	$25	**$465**	CHANGE

Flower boxes rest outside by the large display window. Shop has rolled-up awnings above the front windows.
Notable: There is a variation in the color of the window frames–they are either green or brown. The same Item # was used for the 1987 *Jefferson School*.

		'91	'92	'93	'94	'95	'96	'97	'98
Date: ___ $ ___									
○ Wish ○ Have		$420	450	475	425	450	450	480	465

NEW STONE CHURCH

Item #	Intro	Retired	OSRP	GBTru	↓
5083-0	1982	1984	$32	**$330**	12%

Church of stone block construction with long nave with side chapel, steeple rises on side opposite chapel. Front has arched windows and two lamps.
Notable: Early release to Gift Creations Concepts (GCC).

		'91	'92	'93	'94	'95	'96	'97	'98
Date: ___ $ ___									
○ Wish ○ Have		$245	325	325	370	395	330	370	375

TOWN HALL

ITEM #	INTRO	RETIRED	OSRP	GBTru	↑
5000-8	1983	1984	$32	**$335**	3%

Brick & stone Town Hall with 2 corner covered side entries. Building has symmetrical design (window over window) and a steeple above the front main wall. There's a ceramic bell in the tower.

Notable: A separate, stamped metal weathervane came in an envelope inside the box. It's rare to find a piece that still has it. No doubt many were unknowingly discarded.

DATE: ___ $ ___	'91	'92	'93	'94	'95	'96	'97	'98
○ WISH ○ HAVE	$225	300	330	330	345	315	335	325

GROCERY

ITEM #	INTRO	RETIRED	OSRP	GBTru	↓
5001-6	1983	1985	$35	**$315**	10%

Red brick grocery with full painted display windows and decorative cornice trim above and below front windows. The outside staircase leads to family quarters.

DATE: ___ $ ___	'91	'92	'93	'94	'95	'96	'97	'98
○ WISH ○ HAVE	$250	325	325	300	325	325	360	350

VICTORIAN COTTAGE

ITEM #	INTRO	RETIRED	OSRP	GBTru	NO
5002-4	1983	1984	$35	**$375**	CHANGE

Cottage has ornate carved woodwork on front and an ornamental arched entry. First-floor French windows are separated by pillars.

DATE: ___ $ ___	'91	'92	'93	'94	'95	'96	'97	'98
○ WISH ○ HAVE	$340	375	350	360	365	305	360	375

GOVERNOR'S MANSION

ITEM #	INTRO	RETIRED	OSRP	GBTru	↑
5003-2	1983	1985	$32	**$320**	2%

Brick mansion with metal ironwork featured on the roof cupola (missing from photo). Building has wide entry steps, a repetitive design above the door, a second story and central attic windows.

DATE: ___ $ ___	'91	'92	'93	'94	'95	'96	'97	'98
○ WISH ○ HAVE	$285	285	290	300	275	280	305	315

Turn Of The Century

Item #	Intro	Retired	OSRP	GBTru	↓
5004-0	1983	1986	$36	**$200**	22%

Steps lead to the covered entry and a front triangular ornate design crown the front gable of this building. A squared turret rises from the left front corner and ends in the highest roof peak. The pictured piece is missing a chimney–the center peak should have a chimney. **Notable:** The bottom of the piece reads, "Turn The Time Of Century."

		'91	'92	'93	'94	'95	'96	'97	'98
Date: ____ $ ____									
○ Wish ○ Have		$250	265	265	235	235	245	250	255

Gingerbread House

Item #	Intro	Retired	OSRP	GBTru	↓
5025-3	1983	1984	$24	**$325**	6%

Two Versions: Lighted house and coin bank–not lighted. The coin bank version is extremely difficult to find. Designed like a Christmas edible treat. Cookies trim sides while candy canes and sugar hearts decorate the roof.

		'91	'92	'93	'94	'95	'96	'97	'98
Date: ____ $ ____									
○ Wish ○ Have		$310	370	395	270	270	280	335	345

Village Church

Item #	Intro	Retired	OSRP	GBTru	↑
5026-1	1983	1984	$30	**$430**	2%

Stone steps of the church lead to double carved doors. The design over the door repeats on the roof trim. The steeple has long narrow openings and pointed arch windows. **Notable:** Collectors often confuse this piece with the 1984 *Parish Church,* Item #5039-3. Early release to Gift Creations Concepts (GCC).

		'91	'92	'93	'94	'95	'96	'97	'98
Date: ____ $ ____									
○ Wish ○ Have		$290	330	335	375	375	385	395	420

Gothic Church

Item #	Intro	Retired	OSRP	GBTru	↑
5028-8	1983	1986	$36	**$250**	2%

Stone block church with the steeple rising straight from large double doors ending in a cross. The bell chamber has ornate grillwork. Smaller entry doors flank the central area repeating the design.

		'91	'92	'93	'94	'95	'96	'97	'98
Date: ____ $ ____									
○ Wish ○ Have		$225	250	245	275	275	235	255	245

PARSONAGE

ITEM #	INTRO	RETIRED	OSRP	GBTRU	↓
5029-6	1983	1985	$35	**$325**	16%

A tower rises above the entry of the parsonage. The front gable has ornate coping topped by a cross. The coping details are repeated around the windows, doors and small balcony. There are community rooms on first floor and the family lives upstairs.

DATE: ____ $ ____	'91	'92	'93	'94	'95	'96	'97	'98
○ WISH ○ HAVE	$225	375	380	380	350	300	375	385

WOODEN CHURCH

ITEM #	INTRO	RETIRED	OSRP	GBTRU	↓
5031-8	1983	1985	$30	**$325**	8%

White clapboard church with crossed timber design that repeats over the door, roof peak and steeple. The side chapel has a separate entry door.

DATE: ____ $ ____	'91	'92	'93	'94	'95	'96	'97	'98
○ WISH ○ HAVE	$400	400	375	375	350	285	350	355

FIRE STATION

ITEM #	INTRO	RETIRED	OSRP	GBTRU	↓
5032-6	1983	1984	$32	**$475**	17%

The central door of the fire station opens to reveal a red fire truck. Brick columns from the base to the roof add to the sturdy look. A Dalmatian sits by the entry, ready when necessary.
Notable: Some pieces are without the dog.

DATE: ____ $ ____	'91	'92	'93	'94	'95	'96	'97	'98
○ WISH ○ HAVE	$675	675	650	650	625	550	575	575

ENGLISH TUDOR

ITEM #	INTRO	RETIRED	OSRP	GBTRU	↓
5033-4	1983	1985	$30	**$245**	13%

Stucco finish building with brick chimneys. The three front roof peaks create the front gable design.

DATE: ____ $ ____	'91	'92	'93	'94	'95	'96	'97	'98
○ WISH ○ HAVE	$275	300	300	260	295	225	275	280

CHATEAU

ITEM #	INTRO	RETIRED	OSRP	GBTRU	↓
5084-9	1983	1984	$35	**$425**	14%

First-story large windows which include front and side bow windows are a feature of this building. There's a diamond design on the roof shingles, stone for walls and a cylindrical chimney with a domed flue cap. The front dormers and side peaks exhibit an ornate carved design. **Notable:** Early release to Gift Creations Concepts (GCC).

		'91	'92	'93	'94	'95	'96	'97	'98
DATE: ____ $ ____									
○ WISH ○ HAVE		$290	375	420	470	475	445	475	495

MAIN STREET HOUSE

ITEM #	INTRO	RETIRED	OSRP	GBTRU	NO
5005-9	1984	1986	$27	**$250**	CHANGE

White and green 1 1/2-story house with clapboard lower story and timbered upper story. There are two lamps on either side of the front door.
Notable: Early release to Gift Creations Concepts (GCC).

		'91	'92	'93	'94	'95	'96	'97	'98
DATE: ____ $ ____									
○ WISH ○ HAVE		$165	250	250	250	275	225	240	250

STRATFORD HOUSE

ITEM #	INTRO	RETIRED	OSRP	GBTRU	↓
5007-5	1984	1986	$28	**$145**	24%

English Tudor style house featuring vertical ornamental timbers. All gables rise to the same height.

		'91	'92	'93	'94	'95	'96	'97	'98
DATE: ____ $ ____									
○ WISH ○ HAVE		$110	225	225	215	195	165	175	190

HAVERSHAM HOUSE

ITEM #	INTRO	RETIRED	OSRP	GBTRU	↓
5008-3	1984	1987	$37	**$225**	20%

All gables, balconies and porch are decorated with ornately carved woodwork.
Notable: Early release to Gift Creations Concepts (GCC). Early release pieces were larger than subsequent ones.

		'91	'92	'93	'94	'95	'96	'97	'98
DATE: ____ $ ____									
○ WISH ○ HAVE		$200	240	295	310	300	240	280	280

GALENA HOUSE

ITEM #	INTRO	RETIRED	OSRP	GBTRU	↑
5009-1	1984	1985	$32	$365	3%

Steps lead to double entry doors of this brick home. A bay window fills one side. The second floor is incorporated into the roof construction.

DATE: ___ $ ___	'91	'92	'93	'94	'95	'96	'97	'98
○ WISH ○ HAVE	$285	330	330	330	345	285	320	355

RIVER ROAD HOUSE

ITEM #	INTRO	RETIRED	OSRP	GBTRU	↓
5010-5	1984	1987	$36	$170	17%

A large and grand white house with many windows. **Notable:** There are 3 Versions: Version 1 has cut out transoms above the two front windows and above the middle arch over front door; Version 2 repeats the cut out transoms with a solid middle arch; Version 3 has a cut out middle arch and solid transoms. Early release to Gift Creations Concepts (GCC).

DATE: ___ $ ___	'91	'92	'93	'94	'95	'96	'97	'98
○ WISH ○ HAVE	$150	150	220	220	215	185	200	205

DELTA HOUSE

ITEM #	INTRO	RETIRED	OSRP	GBTRU	↓
5012-1	1984	1986	$32	$275	13%

A large brick house with a balcony above the wraparound porch which is separate from the entry. The decorative porch trim design is repeated where the roof and brick meet and on turret. **Notable:** The pictured piece is without the ornamental "iron works" atop the tower. Many collectors are unaware of the trim, in fact it's rare to find a piece that still has it. It came in an envelope inside the box.

DATE: ___ $ ___	'91	'92	'93	'94	'95	'96	'97	'98
○ WISH ○ HAVE	$350	325	335	345	310	260	300	315

BAYPORT

ITEM #	INTRO	RETIRED	OSRP	GBTRU	↓
5015-6	1984	1986	$30	$215	4%

Gray clapboard corner entry home with a turret addition positioned between the two main wings of the two-story house.

DATE: ___ $ ___	'91	'92	'93	'94	'95	'96	'97	'98
○ WISH ○ HAVE	$215	230	230	230	235	210	235	225

CONGREGATIONAL CHURCH

ITEM #	INTRO	RETIRED	OSRP	GBTRU	↑
5034-2	1984	1985	$28	**$625**	5%

Brick church with fieldstone front. The stone is repeated on the steeple. There are louver vents on the belfry.

DATE: ____ $ ____	'91	'92	'93	'94	'95	'96	'97	'98
○ WISH ○ HAVE	$250	360	415	540	595	615	645	595

TRINITY CHURCH

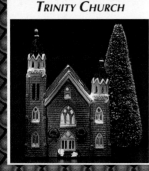

ITEM #	INTRO	RETIRED	OSRP	GBTRU	↑
5035-0	1984	1986	$32	**$280**	2%

Church has steeples of different heights, clerestory windows to bring additional light to the nave and two large wreaths by the front doors.

DATE: ____ $ ____	'91	'92	'93	'94	'95	'96	'97	'98
○ WISH ○ HAVE	$220	265	305	305	305	245	285	275

SUMMIT HOUSE

ITEM #	INTRO	RETIRED	OSRP	GBTRU	↑
5036-9	1984	1985	$28	**$365**	6%

Pink corner house features a rounded turret and large entry door with side lights. Cornices appear to support the roof edge. Each second-story window is capped by a molded projection.

DATE: ____ $ ____	'91	'92	'93	'94	'95	'96	'97	'98
○ WISH ○ HAVE	$375	375	395	385	385	310	340	345

NEW SCHOOL HOUSE

ITEM #	INTRO	RETIRED	OSRP	GBTRU	↓
5037-7	1984	1986	$35	**$225**	12%

Two-story schoolhouse with bell tower and clock.
Notable: There is a separate cloth flag on a wooden pole that can be inserted into a hole in the base.

DATE: ____ $ ____	'91	'92	'93	'94	'95	'96	'97	'98
○ WISH ○ HAVE	$240	270	275	275	275	215	235	255

The Original Snow Village ®

PARISH CHURCH

ITEM #	INTRO	RETIRED	OSRP	GBTRU	↓
5039-3	1984	1986	$32	**$320**	4%

White country church with unique three level steeple has arched windows, a red door and a circular window over the entry.
Notable: Collectors often confuse this piece with the 1993 *Village Church,* Item #5026-1.

DATE: ____ $ ____	'91	'92	'93	'94	'95	'96	'97	'98
○ WISH ○ HAVE	$310	345	370	370	370	285	315	335

STUCCO BUNGALOW

ITEM #	INTRO	RETIRED	OSRP	GBTRU	↓
5045-8	1985	1986	$30	**$345**	7%

Two-story small house with one roof dormer as a mini tower has a second dormer featuring a timbered design. The entry door is built into the archway under a low roof peak. A wreath and garland decorate the door.

DATE: ____ $ ____	'91	'92	'93	'94	'95	'96	'97	'98
○ WISH ○ HAVE	$105	375	360	385	395	340	365	370

WILLIAMSBURG HOUSE

ITEM #	INTRO	RETIRED	OSRP	GBTRU	↓
5046-6	1985	1988	$37	**$130**	21%

A traditional two-story colonial with all windows shuttered, three dormers, two chimneys and a covered entry topped by a second-floor balcony.

DATE: ____ $ ____	'91	'92	'93	'94	'95	'96	'97	'98
○ WISH ○ HAVE	$95	110	135	145	135	165	165	165

PLANTATION HOUSE

ITEM #	INTRO	RETIRED	OSRP	GBTRU	↓
5047-4	1985	1987	$37	**$95**	14%

The house features an entry with two-story wood columns, three dormers, two chimneys and four first-floor windows with canopies.

DATE: ____ $ ____	'91	'92	'93	'94	'95	'96	'97	'98
○ WISH ○ HAVE	$80	95	118	118	115	120	115	110

CHURCH OF THE OPEN DOOR

ITEM #	INTRO	RETIRED	OSRP	GBTru	↑
5048-2	1985	1988	$34	**$140**	4%

Church with a steeple on the side chapel has design over front entry above circular window that is repeated in motif on eaves.

Date: ____ $ ____		'91	'92	'93	'94	'95	'96	'97	'98
○ Wish ○ Have		$110	105	135	135	125	130	145	135

SPRUCE PLACE

ITEM #	INTRO	RETIRED	OSRP	GBTru	↓
5049-0	1985	1987	$33	**$235**	13%

Victorian house has a windowed turret rising above a covered porch. There's decorative molding above the porch, windows and dormer. A circular window over the porch is decorated with a wreath.

Date: ____ $ ____		'91	'92	'93	'94	'95	'96	'97	'98
○ Wish ○ Have		$275	315	320	270	275	255	270	270

DUPLEX

ITEM #	INTRO	RETIRED	OSRP	GBTru	↓
5050-4	1985	1987	$35	**$135**	10%

The duplex is a two-family house with a shared entry. Each family has up and down rooms and a bay window. The building has a small second-story balcony and roof dormers.

Date: ____ $ ____		'91	'92	'93	'94	'95	'96	'97	'98
○ Wish ○ Have		$100	105	110	165	165	155	165	150

DEPOT AND TRAIN WITH 2 TRAIN CARS

ITEM #	INTRO	RETIRED	OSRP	GBTru	↓
5051-2	1985	1988	$65	**$135**	18%

Second Original Snow Village® train & station design. Set of 4. Train is non-lighting. Depot has 2 wings, each w/chimney, connected by a central area. **Notable:** There are 3 Versions: 1st Version of the depot (pictured) was brown w/gray cornerstones & yellow passenger car windows; 2nd Version was a variegated brick w/no cornerstones & yellow passenger car windows; 3rd Version was the brick w/white passenger car windows.

Date: ____ $ ____		'91	'92	'93	'94	'95	'96	'97	'98
○ Wish ○ Have		$110	125	135	135	145	150	160	165

RIDGEWOOD

ITEM #	INTRO	RETIRED	OSRP	GBTRU	↓
5052-0	1985	1987	$35	**$140**	18%

Porches run the length of both the first and second story on this house. The first-floor front windows are arched as is the window over the front door and the window in the attic.

DATE: ___ $ ___	'91	'92	'93	'94	'95	'96	'97	'98
○ WISH ○ HAVE	$125	130	150	165	170	180	180	170

WAVERLY PLACE

ITEM #	INTRO	RETIRED	OSRP	GBTRU	↓
5041-5	1986	1986	$35	**$305**	3%

This ornate Victorian home has two different turret-like window designs. The second story features half-moon window highlights and carved moldings.
Notable: Designed after the Gingerbread Mansion in Ferndale, CA. Early release to Gift Creations Concepts (GCC), Fall 1985.

DATE: ___ $ ___	'91	'92	'93	'94	'95	'96	'97	'98
○ WISH ○ HAVE	$265	300	300	300	325	290	300	315

TWIN PEAKS

ITEM #	INTRO	RETIRED	OSRP	GBTRU	↓
5042-3	1986	1986	$32	**$370**	13%

Building has two matching three-story stone turrets with a multitude of windows on each story to soften the fortress look. Wide steps lead to the red entry doors.
Notable: Early release to Gift Creations Concepts (GCC), Fall 1985.

DATE: ___ $ ___	'91	'92	'93	'94	'95	'96	'97	'98
○ WISH ○ HAVE	$275	285	325	510	525	445	440	425

2101 MAPLE

ITEM #	INTRO	RETIRED	OSRP	GBTRU	↓
5043-1	1986	1986	$32	**$295**	14%

Brick two-story home with the side of the front porch built out from a stone turret. The second-story windows are capped by a half-circle window.
Notable: Early release to Gift Creations Concepts (GCC), Fall 1985.

DATE: ___ $ ___	'91	'92	'93	'94	'95	'96	'97	'98
○ WISH ○ HAVE	$195	330	330	360	375	325	345	345

LINCOLN PARK DUPLEX

ITEM #	INTRO	RETIRED	OSRP	GBTru	NO
5060-1	1986	1988	$33	**$140**	CHANGE

Two-family attached home reminiscent of Chicago's Lincoln Park. Occupants share a front door. The floor plan's unique feature is the placement of chimneys–as if the floor plans are reversed–one is at the front, the other is at the rear.

DATE: ___ $ ___	'91	'92	'93	'94	'95	'96	'97	'98
○ WISH ○ HAVE	$90	115	100	125	125	135	135	140

SONOMA HOUSE

ITEM #	INTRO	RETIRED	OSRP	GBTru	NO
5062-8	1986	1988	$33	**$145**	CHANGE

Building exhibits the flavor of the Southwest with stucco walls and red roof. The decorative curved front rises 2 1/2 stories. A square turret adjacent to the front door is capped by the same decorative design which also repeats on the chimney.
Notable: Early release to Gift Creations Concepts (GCC), Fall 1985.

DATE: ___ $ ___	'91	'92	'93	'94	'95	'96	'97	'98
○ WISH ○ HAVE	$85	110	115	118	120	140	145	145

HIGHLAND PARK HOUSE

ITEM #	INTRO	RETIRED	OSRP	GBTru	↓
5063-6	1986	1988	$35	**$135**	21%

Brick, timbered and gabled house brings English Tudor design to cozy home. Rounded arch front door repeats theme in two windows in mid-roof gable. Brick chimney on side.
Notable: Early release to Gift Creations Concepts (GCC), Fall 1986.

DATE: ___ $ ___	'91	'92	'93	'94	'95	'96	'97	'98
○ WISH ○ HAVE	$100	105	120	150	150	160	160	170

BEACON HILL HOUSE

ITEM #	INTRO	RETIRED	OSRP	GBTru	↓
5065-2	1986	1988	$31	**$170**	6%

A green with black roof row house, typical of urban Boston neighborhoods. Home features bay windows on first and second story highlighted by paneled framing.

DATE: ___ $ ___	'91	'92	'93	'94	'95	'96	'97	'98
○ WISH ○ HAVE	$95	120	150	165	150	165	175	180

Pacific Heights House

Item #	Intro	Retired	OSRP	GBTru	↓
5066-0	1986	1988	$33	**$90**	14%

A beige with tan roof West Coast row house that appears tall and narrow due to the vertical theme of the front porch balcony support columns.

Date: _____ $ _____

		'91	'92	'93	'94	'95	'96	'97	'98
○ Wish	○ Have	$115	90	95	100	100	105	100	105

Ramsey Hill House

Item #	Intro	Retired	OSRP	GBTru	↓
5067-9	1986	1989	$36	**$90**	10%

Victorian home with double chimneys. There are steps to the front door and a porch adjacent to the entry. The side door also features a small porch. A low balustrade fronts the second-story windows. Hand painting adds detailing to the design.

Notable: Early release to Gift Creations Concepts (GCC), Fall 1986. The early release piece colors are more vibrant.

Date: _____ $ _____

		'91	'92	'93	'94	'95	'96	'97	'98
○ Wish	○ Have	$90	96	96	98	95	95	100	100

Saint James Church

Item #	Intro	Retired	OSRP	GBTru	↓
5068-7	1986	1988	$37	**$155**	11%

Church with long central nave flanked by lower roofed side sections fronted by two towers. The main center cross is reinforced by smaller crosses on each section of the tower roof. Smaller round side windows repeat the central window shape.

Date: _____ $ _____

		'91	'92	'93	'94	'95	'96	'97	'98
○ Wish	○ Have	$105	140	170	160	175	155	160	175

All Saints Church

Item #	Intro	Retired	OSRP	GBTru	NO
5070-9	1986	1997	$38	**$65**	CHANGE

A small country church with simple design of long nave and entry door in the base of the bell tower.

Notable: The same Item # was used for the 1980 *Colonial Farm House.*

Date: _____ $ _____

		'91	'92	'93	'94	'95	'96	'97	'98
○ Wish	○ Have	$45	45	45	45	45	45	45	65

CARRIAGE HOUSE

ITEM #	INTRO	RETIRED	OSRP	GBTᴿᵁ	↓
5071-7	1986	1988	$29	**$105**	19%

A small home converted from a building originally used to house carriages. A second story is achieved with many dormer windows. The fieldstone foundation allowed great weight when it was used for carriages.
Notable: The same Item # was used for the 1980 *Town Church.*

DATE: ____ $ ____	'91	'92	'93	'94	'95	'96	'97	'98
○ WISH ○ HAVE	$95	110	110	110	110	115	125	130

TOY SHOP

ITEM #	INTRO	RETIRED	OSRP	GBTᴿᵁ	NO
5073-3	1986	1990	$36	**$100**	CHANGE

The shop's front windows display toys while the roof molding draws attention to the teddy bear under the pediment.
Notable: This Main Street design is based on the Finch Building in Hastings, MN. The same Item # was used for the 1981 *English Cottage.*

DATE: ____ $ ____	'91	'92	'93	'94	'95	'96	'97	'98
○ WISH ○ HAVE	$75	100	95	90	90	90	95	100

APOTHECARY

ITEM #	INTRO	RETIRED	OSRP	GBTᴿᵁ	↓
5076-8	1986	1990	$34	**$95**	14%

Two doors flank a central display bow window. A mortar and pestle, symbolizing the profession of the proprietor, is on the front panel above the second floor family quarters windows.
Notable: Some sleeves read "Antique Shop." The same Item # was used for the 1981 *Corner Store.* This Main Street design is based on the former City Hall in Hastings, MN.

DATE: ____ $ ____	'91	'92	'93	'94	'95	'96	'97	'98
○ WISH ○ HAVE	$70	92	92	85	90	100	105	110

BAKERY

ITEM #	INTRO	RETIRED	OSRP	GBTᴿᵁ	NO
5077-6	1986	1991	$35	**$85**	CHANGE

The corner bakery has two large multi-paned display windows protected by a ribbed canopy. Greek key designs around the roof edging highlight the bas-relief cupcake topped by a cherry that is centrally placed over the entry.
Notable: The same Item # was used for the first Original Snow Village® *Bakery* in 1981. This Main Street design is based on the Scofield Building in Northfield, MN.

DATE: ____ $ ____	'91	'92	'93	'94	'95	'96	'97	'98
○ WISH ○ HAVE	$37.50	80	70	80	85	85	90	85

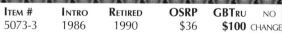

DINER

ITEM #	INTRO	RETIRED	OSRP	GBTRU	↓
5078-4	1986	1987	$22	**$595**	8%

Diners are an eating place based on the railroads' famous dining cars with a reputation for good, wholesome food. The glass block entry protects diners from the weather. **Notable:** The same Item # was used for the 1981 *English Church*. Also known as "Mickey's." Designed after Mickey's Diner in St. Paul, MN.

DATE: ___ $ ___		'91	'92	'93	'94	'95	'96	'97	'98
○ WISH	○ HAVE	$270	420	425	530	550	650	655	650

ST. ANTHONY HOTEL & POST OFFICE

ITEM #	INTRO	RETIRED	OSRP	GBTRU	↓
5006-7	1987	1989	$40	**$95**	17%

This Main Street design three-story red brick building with green trim is dated "1886" and has an address of "56 Main Street." An American flag flies outside the ground floor of the Post Office.
Notable: Metal flag is separate.

DATE: ___ $ ___		'91	'92	'93	'94	'95	'96	'97	'98
○ WISH	○ HAVE	$85	100	110	115	110	115	105	115

SNOW VILLAGE FACTORY

ITEM #	INTRO	RETIRED	OSRP	GBTRU	↓
5013-0	1987	1989	$45	**$120**	20%

Set of 2. Smokestack is separate. The wood building rises on a stone block base with a tall smokestack at the rear. Factory products are sold in the small shop in the front.

DATE: ___ $ ___		'91	'92	'93	'94	'95	'96	'97	'98
○ WISH	○ HAVE	$90	105	110	110	120	130	135	150

CATHEDRAL CHURCH

ITEM #	INTRO	RETIRED	OSRP	GBTRU	↓
5019-9	1987	1990	$50	**$100**	13%

Second of two Original Snow Village® Cathedral Churches. (See also 1980, Item #5067-4.) Cathedral has mosaic stained glass decorating the Gothic windows on all sides as well as the large turret.
Notable: Same Item # was used for the 1982 *Street Car*.

DATE: ___ $ ___		'91	'92	'93	'94	'95	'96	'97	'98
○ WISH	○ HAVE	$85	110	110	110	100	105	110	115

CUMBERLAND HOUSE

ITEM #	INTRO	RETIRED	OSRP	GBTʀᴜ	
5024-5	1987	1995	$42	**$70**	NO CHANGE

Large garland-decorated house has multicolored roof supported by four columns, two chimneys and shuttered windows.
Notable: The same Item # was used for the 1982 *Bank*.

DATE: ____ $ ____	'91	'92	'93	'94	'95	'96	'97	'98
○ WISH ○ HAVE	$44	44	45	45	45	65	75	70

SPRINGFIELD HOUSE

ITEM #	INTRO	RETIRED	OSRP	GBTʀᴜ	↓
5027-0	1987	1990	$40	**$70**	22%

Williamsburg blue clapboard home's lower level has two multi-paned bay windows–one is bowed. The upper level windows are shuttered. Roof dormers are half-circle sunbursts. A stone chimney completes this house.

DATE: ____ $ ____	'91	'92	'93	'94	'95	'96	'97	'98
○ WISH ○ HAVE	$90	100	85	100	75	80	80	90

LIGHTHOUSE

ITEM #	INTRO	RETIRED	OSRP	GBTʀᴜ	
5030-0	1987	1988	$36	**$550**	NO CHANGE

A favorite with collectors. Five-story lighthouse beacon rises from sturdy stone slab base and is connected to a caretaker's cottage.
Notable: There are 2 Versions: one has a white unglazed tower, the other has an off-white glazed tower.

DATE: ____ $ ____	'91	'92	'93	'94	'95	'96	'97	'98
○ WISH ○ HAVE	$255	340	340	650	595	605	595	550

RED BARN

ITEM #	INTRO	RETIRED	OSRP	GBTʀᴜ	↓
5081-4	1987	1992	$38	**$90**	14%

Wooden barn has stone base, double cross-buck doors on the long side, and hayloft above the main doors. There are three ventilator cupolas on the roof ridge. A cat sleeps in the hayloft.
Notable: The same Item # was used for the 1982 *Gabled House.* Early release to Gift Creations Concepts (GCC).

DATE: ____ $ ____	'91	'92	'93	'94	'95	'96	'97	'98
○ WISH ○ HAVE	$42	42	75	75	75	85	85	105

JEFFERSON SCHOOL

Item #	Intro	Retired	OSRP	GBTru	↑
5082-2	1987	1991	$36	**$170**	6%

A two-room schoolhouse with large multi-paned windows with top transoms. There's a short bell tower incorporated into the roof.
Notable: The same Item # was used for the 1982 *Flower Shop.* Early release to Gift Creations Concepts (GCC).

Date: ___ $ ___	'91	'92	'93	'94	'95	'96	'97	'98
○ Wish ○ Have	$40	90	108	115	145	155	170	160

FARM HOUSE

Item #	Intro	Retired	OSRP	GBTru	NO
5089-0	1987	1992	$40	**$75**	CHANGE

A 2 1/2-story wood frame home with front full-length porch. The roof interest is two low peaks and one high peak with attic window in highest peak.

Date: ___ $ ___	'91	'92	'93	'94	'95	'96	'97	'98
○ Wish ○ Have	$44	45	70	75	65	75	75	75

FIRE STATION NO. 2

Item #	Intro	Retired	OSRP	GBTru	NO
5091-1	1987	1989	$40	**$195**	CHANGE

Fire Station has two large double doors housing two engines, the side stair leads to living quarters. It's a brick building with a stone arch design at engine doors and front windows.
Notable: Early release to Gift Creations Concepts (GCC).

Date: ___ $ ___	'91	'92	'93	'94	'95	'96	'97	'98
○ Wish ○ Have	$70	120	140	140	185	220	200	195

SNOW VILLAGE RESORT LODGE

Item #	Intro	Retired	OSRP	GBTru	↓
5092-0	1987	1989	$55	**$130**	13%

Bright yellow and green lodge with scalloped roof, covered porch and side entry. There are bay windows on the front house section. The back section rises to dormered 3 1/2 stories. Ventilator areas are directly under the roof cap.

Date: ___ $ ___	'91	'92	'93	'94	'95	'96	'97	'98
○ Wish ○ Have	$100	120	120	120	140	145	145	150

VILLAGE MARKET

ITEM #	INTRO	RETIRED	OSRP	GBTRU	↓
5044-0	1988	1991	$39	**$80**	16%

Silk-screened glass windows detail the merchandise available at the market. A red and white canopy protects shoppers using the in/out doors. There's a sign over the second-story windows.
Notable: The color varies from mint green to cream. Sisal tree on top is separate. Early release to Gift Creations Concepts (GCC).

DATE: ____ $ ____	'91	'92	'93	'94	'95	'96	'97	'98
○ Wish ○ Have	$40	85	74	75	65	75	75	95

KENWOOD HOUSE

ITEM #	INTRO	RETIRED	OSRP	GBTRU	NO CHANGE
5054-7	1988	1990	$50	**$145**	

Three-story home has an old-fashioned wraparound verandah with arched openings. The front facade features scalloped shingles on third story.
Notable: Early release to Gift Creations Concepts (GCC).

DATE: ____ $ ____	'91	'92	'93	'94	'95	'96	'97	'98
○ Wish ○ Have	$100	105	105	100	125	130	130	145

MAPLE RIDGE INN

ITEM #	INTRO	RETIRED	OSRP	GBTRU	↓
5121-7	1988	1990	$55	**$65**	13%

Inn is a replica of a Victorian mansion. The ornamental roof piece concealed lightning rods.
Notable: This piece is an interpretation of an American landmark in Cambridge, NY. 1991 Gift Creations Concepts (GCC) Catalog Exclusive at $75.00.

DATE: ____ $ ____	'91	'92	'93	'94	'95	'96	'97	'98
○ Wish ○ Have	$100	98	92	75	65	75	75	75

VILLAGE STATION AND TRAIN

ITEM #	INTRO	RETIRED	OSRP	GBTRU	↓
5122-5	1988	1992	$65	**$110**	8%

Set of 4. The third Original Snow Village® train and station design. Station features an outside ticket window, soft drink vending machine and outside benches.
Notable: The three train cars do not light.

DATE: ____ $ ____	'91	'92	'93	'94	'95	'96	'97	'98
○ Wish ○ Have	$70	70	105	105	100	115	110	120

COBBLESTONE ANTIQUE SHOP

ITEM #	INTRO	RETIRED	OSRP	GBTru	NO
5123-3	1988	1992	$36	**$65**	CHANGE

The silk-screened front windows display antiques for sale and a bay window fills the second-story width. A building date of "1881" is on the arched cornice.

DATE: ____ $ ____		'91	'92	'93	'94	'95	'96	'97	'98
○ WISH	○ HAVE	$37.50	37.50	65	70	65	70	75	65

CORNER CAFE

ITEM #	INTRO	RETIRED	OSRP	GBTru	↓
5124-1	1988	1991	$37	**$90**	10%

There's "Pie" and "Coffee" silk-screened on the windows of this corner restaurant with red, white, and blue striped awnings. A building date of "1875" is inscribed on the turret.

DATE: ____ $ ____		'91	'92	'93	'94	'95	'96	'97	'98
○ WISH	○ HAVE	$37.50	75	75	80	90	90	100	100

SINGLE CAR GARAGE

ITEM #	INTRO	RETIRED	OSRP	GBTru	↓
5125-0	1988	1990	$22	**$50**	17%

Double doors open to house the car, there are two outside lights for safety and convenience. Designed to look like a house, the windows have shutters and the roof has dormers. The roof projects over a wood pile, keeping it dry.

DATE: ____ $ ____		'91	'92	'93	'94	'95	'96	'97	'98
○ WISH	○ HAVE	$50	50	50	65	50	55	55	60

HOME SWEET HOME/ HOUSE & WINDMILL

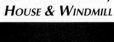

ITEM #	INTRO	RETIRED	OSRP	GBTru	↓
5126-8	1988	1991	$60	**$110**	8%

Set of 2. The saltbox home has an asymmetrical arrangement of windows. Doors for root cellar are at the front corner and there's one central brick chimney. The four-bladed metal windmill is separate.

Notable: Inspired by the East Hampton, NY historic landmark home of John Howard Payne, composer of "Home Sweet Home."

DATE: ____ $ ____		'91	'92	'93	'94	'95	'96	'97	'98
○ WISH	○ HAVE	$60	105	105	110	115	120	120	120

REDEEMER CHURCH

ITEM #	INTRO	RETIRED	OSRP	GBTRU	↓
5127-6	1988	1992	$42	**$65**	13%

The stone corners add strength and support to this church and bell tower. Arched windows and heavy wooden double doors complete the design.

Date: ____ $ ____		'91	'92	'93	'94	'95	'96	'97	'98
○ Wish ○ Have		$45	45	74	75	60	70	70	75

SERVICE STATION

ITEM #	INTRO	RETIRED	OSRP	GBTRU	NO
5128-4	1988	1991	$37.50	**$260**	CHANGE

Set of 2. Includes building and gas pumps. Pumps do not light. There's a big difference in the secondary market value if the pumps are missing. Bill's has a candy machine, restroom, work area and office.
Notable: More commonly known as "Bill's Service Station."

Date: ____ $ ____		'91	'92	'93	'94	'95	'96	'97	'98
○ Wish ○ Have		$37.50	90	112	165	295	295	265	260

STONEHURST HOUSE

ITEM #	INTRO	RETIRED	OSRP	GBTRU	↓
5140-3	1988	1994	$37.50	**$55**	21%

Home of red brick punctuated with black and white painted bricks. The half-circle sunburst design second-story dormers restate the arch shape of the first-floor windows.

Date: ____ $ ____		'91	'92	'93	'94	'95	'96	'97	'98
○ Wish ○ Have		$37.50	37.50	37.50	37.50	60	65	65	70

PALOS VERDES

ITEM #	INTRO	RETIRED	OSRP	GBTRU	↓
5141-1	1988	1990	$37.50	**$70**	22%

Spanish style stucco home with green tiled roof, covered entry porch, and second-floor shuttered windows. Coming forward from the main wing is a two-story round turret and ground-floor window alcove. There's a separate potted miniature sisal tree on the porch.

Date: ____ $ ____		'91	'92	'93	'94	'95	'96	'97	'98
○ Wish ○ Have		$60	85	75	75	80	85	85	90

Jingle Belle Houseboat

Item #	Intro	Retired	OSRP	GBTru	↑
5114-4	1989	1991	$42	**$180**	9%

This floating house sports a Christmas tree on the wheelhouse roof and rear deck. The boat's name is stenciled on the bow and life preservers.
Notable: The stamped metal bell that hangs on the side is separate and often lost.

Date: ____ $ ____	'91	'92	'93	'94	'95	'96	'97	'98
○ Wish ○ Have	$42	90	80	80	100	115	150	165

Colonial Church

Item #	Intro	Retired	OSRP	GBTru	↑
5119-5	1989	1992	$60	**$85**	13%

Church has front entry with four floor-to-roof columns supporting the roof over the porch. The front facade repeats the design with four half columns set into the wall. A metal cross tops the three-tier steeple bell tower.
Notable: Early release to Gift Creations Concepts (GCC).

Date: ____ $ ____	'91	'92	'93	'94	'95	'96	'97	'98
○ Wish ○ Have	$60	60	85	75	75	80	70	75

North Creek Cottage

Item #	Intro	Retired	OSRP	GBTru	↓
5120-9	1989	1992	$45	**$60**	20%

Cape Cod style home with a colonial columned front porch. In addition, there's an attached garage with a deck on top, a front dormer and stone chimney.
Notable: Early release to Gift Creations Concepts (GCC).

Date: ____ $ ____	'91	'92	'93	'94	'95	'96	'97	'98
○ Wish ○ Have	$45	45	70	65	55	70	65	75

Paramount Theater

Item #	Intro	Retired	OSRP	GBTru	↓
5142-0	1989	1993	$42	**$185**	5%

The theater is a Spanish theme art deco building with double marques. A ticket booth in the center is flanked by two double doors. Corner billboards advertise "White Christmas" is *Now Showing* and "It's A Wonderful Life" is *Coming Soon*.

Date: ____ $ ____	'91	'92	'93	'94	'95	'96	'97	'98
○ Wish ○ Have	$42	42	42	78	85	125	160	195

DOCTOR'S HOUSE

ITEM #	INTRO	RETIRED	OSRP	GBTRU	↓
5143-8	1989	1992	$56	**$100**	5%

The Doctor's home and office are within this house. A rounded turret completes the front. The three-story building has arched, porthole, and bay windows to add to its Victorian charm.

DATE: ____ $ ____	'91	'92	'93	'94	'95	'96	'97	'98
○ WISH ○ HAVE	$56	56	85	85	95	100	105	105

COURTHOUSE

ITEM #	INTRO	RETIRED	OSRP	GBTRU	↓
5144-6	1989	1993	$65	**$185**	5%

Courthouse has four corner roof turrets with a central clock tower, windows with half-circle sunbursts, decorative molding on the second story with two front windows being clear half-circles.
Notable: The design is based on the Gibson County Courthouse in Princetown, IN.

DATE: ____ $ ____	'91	'92	'93	'94	'95	'96	'97	'98
○ WISH ○ HAVE	$65	65	65	110	125	150	180	195

VILLAGE WARMING HOUSE

ITEM #	INTRO	RETIRED	OSRP	GBTRU	↓
5145-4	1989	1992	$42	**$65**	13%

Used by skaters to warm up from the chill, this small red house has a steep front roof. The bench at the side is available for a brief rest. Sisal trees detach.

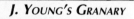

DATE: ____ $ ____	'91	'92	'93	'94	'95	'96	'97	'98
○ WISH ○ HAVE	$42	42	70	60	60	70	65	75

J. YOUNG'S GRANARY

ITEM #	INTRO	RETIRED	OSRP	GBTRU	NO
5149-7	1989	1992	$45	**$85**	CHANGE

Granary has a central water wheel for grinding grain, a stone silo on one side and a small store and storage area on other side.
Notable: Named for Julia Young, a Department 56, Inc. retailer in New Jersey.

DATE: ____ $ ____	'91	'92	'93	'94	'95	'96	'97	'98
○ WISH ○ HAVE	$45	45	65	75	65	75	80	85

PINEWOOD LOG CABIN

ITEM #	INTRO	RETIRED	OSRP	GBTRU	↓
5150-0	1989	1995	$37.50	**$60**	14%

Cabin of log construction with two fireplaces for heating and cooking, tree trunk porch pillars, firewood stack and attached tree. The house name appears on the sign above the porch.
Notable: Early release to Gift Creations Concepts (GCC), Fall 1990.

		'91	'92	'93	'94	'95	'96	'97	'98
DATE: ___ $ ___									
○ WISH ○ HAVE		$37.50	37.50	37.50	37.50	37.50	60	60	70

56 FLAVORS ICE CREAM PARLOR

ITEM #	INTRO	RETIRED	OSRP	GBTRU	NO
5151-9	1990	1992	$42	**$175**	CHANGE

Ice cream parlor is decorated like a sundae. Peppermint pillars flank the door, there's a sugar cone roof with a cherry on its peak and window boxes hold ice cream cones. Cherry and stem on top are extremely fragile.
Notable: Early release to Gift Creations Concepts (GCC).

		'91	'92	'93	'94	'95	'96	'97	'98
DATE: ___ $ ___									
○ WISH ○ HAVE		$42	45	78	80	80	105	145	175

MORNINGSIDE HOUSE

ITEM #	INTRO	RETIRED	OSRP	GBTRU	NO
5152-7	1990	1992	$45	**$65**	CHANGE

Home is a pink split-level house with one-car garage. It has a fieldstone chimney, curved front steps and terraced landscaping with removable sisal trees.

		'91	'92	'93	'94	'95	'96	'97	'98
DATE: ___ $ ___									
○ WISH ○ HAVE		$45	45	55	50	50	65	60	65

MAINSTREET HARDWARE STORE

ITEM #	INTRO	RETIRED	OSRP	GBTRU	↓
5153-5	1990	1993	$42	**$80**	11%

A three-story building with the store on the ground level. Access to the rental rooms on the second and third story is by the outside staircase. The store was originally photo-graphed with blue awnings and window trim, however production pieces had green awnings and trim.

		'91	'92	'93	'94	'95	'96	'97	'98
DATE: ___ $ ___									
○ WISH ○ HAVE		$42	42	42	55	65	75	80	90

VILLAGE REALTY

ITEM #	INTRO	RETIRED	OSRP	GBTRU	↓
5154-3	1990	1993	$42	**$60**	20%

The two-story main building houses a real estate office. A front bay display window showcases available properties. The small adjacent building is an intimate Italian restaurant with colorful striped awning.
Notable: "J. Saraceno" over the door is a tribute to Department 56, Inc.'s late National Sales Manager.

DATE: ____ $ ____	'91	'92	'93	'94	'95	'96	'97	'98
○ WISH ○ HAVE	$42	42	42	60	70	75	70	75

SPANISH MISSION CHURCH

ITEM #	INTRO	RETIRED	OSRP	GBTRU	↓
5155-1	1990	1992	$42	**$70**	18%

Sun-dried clay creates this adobe Spanish style church. The arcade along one side gives protected access.
Notable: Designed after the Enga Memorial Chapel in Minneapolis, MN.

DATE: ____ $ ____	'91	'92	'93	'94	'95	'96	'97	'98
○ WISH ○ HAVE	$42	42	72	72	60	75	80	85

PRAIRIE HOUSE

ITEM #	INTRO	RETIRED	OSRP	GBTRU	NO
5156-0	1990	1993	$42	**$70**	CHANGE

American Architecture Series. Two-story home with upper floor set in and back atop the first story. A large chimney rises up through the first story. Two large pillars support the covered entry with separate, removable sisal trees on either side.

DATE: ____ $ ____	'91	'92	'93	'94	'95	'96	'97	'98
○ WISH ○ HAVE	$42	42	44	50	60	70	70	70

QUEEN ANNE VICTORIAN

ITEM #	INTRO	RETIRED	OSRP	GBTRU	NO
5157-8	1990	1996	$48	**$75**	CHANGE

American Architecture Series. Broad steps lead up to a pillared porch with a unique corner gazebo style sitting area. An ornate turret on the corner of the second story is decorated with scalloped shingles.

DATE: ____ $ ____	'91	'92	'93	'94	'95	'96	'97	'98
○ WISH ○ HAVE	$48	48	50	50	50	50	65	75

CHRISTMAS SHOP, THE

Item #	Intro	Retired	OSRP	GBTru	
5097-0	1991	1996	$37.50	**$65**	NO CHANGE

Pediment on the brick building advertises the holiday, the French "NOEL." There's a large teddy bear by the front window.
Notable: Early release to Gift Creations Concepts (GCC) and Showcase Dealers.

Date: ____ $ ____	'91	'92	'93	'94	'95	'96	'97	'98
○ Wish ○ Have	$37.50	37.50	37.50	37.50	37.50	37.50	60	65

OAK GROVE TUDOR

Item #	Intro	Retired	OSRP	GBTru	↓
5400-3	1991	1994	$42	**$50**	29%

Red brick base with stucco, and timbered second-story home. There's a fireplace of brick and stone by the entry door. Rough stone frames the door and foundation.
Notable: Early release to Showcase Dealers.

Date: ____ $ ____	'91	'92	'93	'94	'95	'96	'97	'98
○ Wish ○ Have	$42	42	42	42	60	65	65	70

HONEYMOONER MOTEL, THE

Item #	Intro	Retired	OSRP	GBTru	
5401-1	1991	1993	$42	**$85**	NO CHANGE

A moon and stars sign above the office door is an advertisement for the motel. Motel is a white building with blue awnings and doors. There's a soda and ice machine by the office door. Middle class auto travelers were attracted to stay-over facilities that provided the privacy and luxury offered by Mom & Pop enterprises. By the 1940's there were motels coast to coast.
Notable: Early release to Showcase Dealers.

Date: ____ $ ____	'91	'92	'93	'94	'95	'96	'97	'98
○ Wish ○ Have	$42	42	44	75	70	70	80	85

VILLAGE GREENHOUSE

Item #	Intro	Retired	OSRP	GBTru	↓
5402-0	1991	1995	$35	**$55**	21%

Plant growing area has bricked bottom and glass roof to allow sunlight in. Attached small store sells accessories. It has brick chimney, shingled roof and covered entry.

Date: ____ $ ____	'91	'92	'93	'94	'95	'96	'97	'98
○ Wish ○ Have	$35	35	36	36	36	75	65	70

SOUTHERN COLONIAL

ITEM #	INTRO	RETIRED	OSRP	GBTRU	NO
5403-8	1991	1994	$48	**$80**	CHANGE

American Architecture Series. Four columns rise from the ground to the roof with a second-story verandah across the front. Double chimneys are surrounded by a balustrade. Shutters by each window both decorate and shut out the heat of the sun. Two urns flank steps of entryway.

DATE: ____ $ ____	'91	'92	'93	'94	'95	'96	'97	'98
O WISH O HAVE	$48	48	50	50	65	75	75	80

GOTHIC FARMHOUSE

ITEM #	INTRO	RETIRED	OSRP	GBTRU	NO
5404-6	1991	1997	$48	**$70**	CHANGE

American Architecture Series. Clapboard home with diamond patterned roof shingles has columned front porch and entry. The first floor has a large bay window. The second story rises to a gable with carved molding which is repeated on the two dormer windows over the porch.

DATE: ____ $ ____	'91	'92	'93	'94	'95	'96	'97	'98
O WISH O HAVE	$48	48	48	48	48	48	48	70

FINKLEA'S FINERY COSTUME SHOP

ITEM #	INTRO	RETIRED	OSRP	GBTRU	NO
5405-4	1991	1993	$45	**$70**	CHANGE

Dressed stone trims the facade of the three-story brick building. There are red awnings over the first-floor display windows and a hood projects over the third-floor piano teacher's windows. The attached side setback is two stories with a decorated rental return door and an awning on upper window.

DATE: ____ $ ____	'91	'92	'93	'94	'95	'96	'97	'98
O WISH O HAVE	$45	45	45	70	55	60	60	70

JACK'S CORNER BARBER SHOP

ITEM #	INTRO	RETIRED	OSRP	GBTRU	NO
5406-2	1991	1994	$42	**$75**	CHANGE

The barber shop also houses M. Schmitt Photography Studio and a second-floor tailor shop. A two-story turret separates two identical wings of the brick building. The fantail window design is repeated on the doors and on roof peaks.
Notable: M. Schmitt is in honor of Department 56, Inc.'s photographer, Matthew Schmitt.

DATE: ____ $ ____	'91	'92	'93	'94	'95	'96	'97	'98
O WISH O HAVE	$42	42	42	42	55	65	70	75

The Original Snow Village ®

DOUBLE BUNGALOW

ITEM #	INTRO	RETIRED	OSRP	GBTru	↓
5407-0	1991	1994	$45	**$65**	7%

An early two-family home–double entry doors, each side has bow window downstairs, a roof dormer, and its own chimney. A brick facade dresses up the clapboard house.

DATE: ____ $ ____	'91	'92	'93	'94	'95	'96	'97	'98
○ Wish ○ Have	$45	45	45	45	55	65	65	70

GRANDMA'S COTTAGE

ITEM #	INTRO	RETIRED	OSRP	GBTru	↑
5420-8	1992	1996	$42	**$80**	14%

A small porch is nestled between two identical house sections. Each section has a hooded double window, flanked by evergreens. Chimneys rise off the main roof.
Notable: Early release to Gift Creations Concepts (GCC).

DATE: ____ $ ____	'92	'93	'94	'95	'96	'97	'98
○ Wish ○ Have	$42	45	45	45	45	65	70

ST. LUKE'S CHURCH

ITEM #	INTRO	RETIRED	OSRP	GBTru	↓
5421-6	1992	1994	$45	**$65**	13%

Brick church features three square based steeples. The central steeple rises off the nave roof. The side steeples have doors at their base and are at the front corners of church. Trefoil designs on either side are repeated on the center main entry doors.
Notable: Early release to Gift Creations Concepts (GCC).

DATE: ____ $ ____	'92	'93	'94	'95	'96	'97	'98
○ Wish ○ Have	$45	45	45	60	70	65	75

VILLAGE POST OFFICE

ITEM #	INTRO	RETIRED	OSRP	GBTru	↓
5422-4	1992	1995	$35	**$65**	19%

Doric columns support porch to the double entry doors. Building is a two-story brick with a two-story turret rising above the sign. A Greek key incised design separates the stories.
Notable: Early release to Showcase Dealers.

DATE: ____ $ ____	'92	'93	'94	'95	'96	'97	'98
○ Wish ○ Have	$35	37.50	37.50	37.50	70	70	80

AL'S TV SHOP

ITEM #	INTRO	RETIRED	OSRP	GBTRU	↓
5423-2	1992	1995	$40	**$60**	8%

TV Shop has antenna on the roof. There are red awnings on the upper windows and a red canopy over the lower display window. The store entry is on the corner of the building.

DATE: ____ $ ____
○ WISH ○ HAVE

	'92	'93	'94	'95	'96	'97	'98
	$40	40	40	40	65	65	65

GOOD SHEPHERD CHAPEL & CHURCH SCHOOL

ITEM #	INTRO	RETIRED	OSRP	GBTRU	↓
5424-0	1992	1996	$72	**$85**	11%

Set of 2. The white chapel with a red roof rises on a stone base and has a steeple at the front entry. The church school has double doors, tall windows, a small bell tower, and a stone chimney on the side. The church side door meets the school side door.

DATE: ____ $ ____
○ WISH ○ HAVE

	'92	'93	'94	'95	'96	'97	'98
	$72	72	72	72	72	95	95

PRINT SHOP & VILLAGE NEWS

ITEM #	INTRO	RETIRED	OSRP	GBTRU	↓
5425-9	1992	1994	$37.50	**$65**	13%

The stone in the front pediment notes a "1893" construction date. A symmetrical building design is emphasized by double chimneys, matching windows and columns. The brick building also houses a Muffin Shop.

DATE: ____ $ ____
○ WISH ○ HAVE

	'92	'93	'94	'95	'96	'97	'98
	$37.50	37.50	37.50	55	60	70	75

HARTFORD HOUSE

ITEM #	INTRO	RETIRED	OSRP	GBTRU	↓
5426-7	1992	1995	$55	**$75**	6%

Home has a steeply pitched roof with an ornate front covered entry pediment design which is repeated in the steep front gable. Molding surrounds windows and is on the side porch columns.

DATE: ____ $ ____
○ WISH ○ HAVE

	'92	'93	'94	'95	'96	'97	'98
	$55	55	55	55	80	80	80

VILLAGE VET AND PET SHOP

Item #	Intro	Retired	OSRP	GBTru	NO
5427-5	1992	1995	$32	$70	CHANGE

Building has arched crescents over picture windows that are screened designs depicting dogs, kittens, fish and birds. An ornamental molding outlines the roof edge. A dog sits on the entry steps to the Vet's Office.
Notable: In the first shipments the hand lettered sign was misspelled "Vetrinary."

Date: ____ $ ____
○ Wish ○ Have

'92	'93	'94	'95	'96	'97	'98
$32	32	32	32	65	65	70

CRAFTSMAN COTTAGE

Item #	Intro	Retired	OSRP	GBTru	NO
5437-2	1992	1995	$55	$75	CHANGE

American Architecture Series. A stone based porch extends across the front of the house ending in a stone chimney. Large squared pillars are part of the support for the second-story room above the entryway. There's a small dormer by chimney.

Date: ____ $ ____
○ Wish ○ Have

'92	'93	'94	'95	'96	'97	'98
$55	55	55	55	75	75	75

VILLAGE STATION

Item #	Intro	Retired	OSRP	GBTru	↓
5438-0	1992	1997	$65	$70	13%

A clock tower rises on one side of the two-story red brick station. The platform sign behind a stack of luggage announces arrivals and departures. The many-windowed waiting room for travelers extends the length of the station.

Date: ____ $ ____
○ Wish ○ Have

'92	'93	'94	'95	'96	'97	'98
$65	65	65	65	65	65	80

AIRPORT

Item #	Intro	Retired	OSRP	GBTru	NO
5439-9	1992	1996	$60	$85	CHANGE

The airport's semicircular vaulted roof extends the length of the plane hangar with the control tower rising off the central rear of the building. A one-engine prop plane sits in the hangar entrance. There's a fuel tank pump at the corner, plus thermometer, and a crop-dusting schedule. The door at the opposite front corner is for passengers and freight business.

Date: ____ $ ____
○ Wish ○ Have

'92	'93	'94	'95	'96	'97	'98
$60	60	60	60	60	75	85

NANTUCKET RENOVATION

ITEM #	INTRO	RETIRED	OSRP	GBTRU	↓
5441-0	1993	1993 ANNUAL	$55	**$65**	7%

Notable: Available for one year only through retailers who carried The Original Snow Village® in 1986, Showcase Dealers and select buying groups. For the original *Nantucket,* see 1978, Item #5014-6. Special box and hang tag. Blueprints of the renovation included.

DATE: _____ $ _____
○ WISH ○ HAVE

'93	'94	'95	'96	'97	'98
$55	105	70	75	75	70

MOUNT OLIVET CHURCH

ITEM #	INTRO	RETIRED	OSRP	GBTRU	↓
5442-9	1993	1996	$65	**$75**	6%

Handsome brick church with large circular stained-glass window above double door entry. Square bell tower with steeple roof. Smaller stained-glass window design repeated on side chapel entry.

DATE: _____ $ _____
○ WISH ○ HAVE

'93	'94	'95	'96	'97	'98
$65	65	65	65	80	80

VILLAGE PUBLIC LIBRARY

ITEM #	INTRO	RETIRED	OSRP	GBTRU	↑
5443-7	1993	1997	$55	**$75**	15%

Sturdy brick and stone building with four Greek columns supporting the front portico. Entry is from the side steps through the double doors. A brick cupola rises from the center of the roof.

DATE: _____ $ _____
○ WISH ○ HAVE

'93	'94	'95	'96	'97	'98
$55	55	55	55	55	65

WOODBURY HOUSE

ITEM #	INTRO	RETIRED	OSRP	GBTRU	↓
5444-5	1993	1996	$45	**$65**	7%

Turned spindle posts support the front porch of this clapboard home. It has a double gable design with the lower gable featuring two-story bow windows. A brick chimney extends through the roof.

DATE: _____ $ _____
○ WISH ○ HAVE

'93	'94	'95	'96	'97	'98
$45	45	45	45	65	70

HUNTING LODGE

ITEM #	INTRO	RETIRED	OSRP	GBTRU	↑
5445-3	1993	1996	$50	**$145**	4%

Lodge is a rustic log structure on a stone foundation with stone fireplace. Antlers decorate the front gable above the porch entry. Wreaths and garland add the final touch.

DATE: _____ $ _____
O WISH   O HAVE

'93	'94	'95	'96	'97	'98
$50	50	50	50	80	140

DAIRY BARN

ITEM #	INTRO	RETIRED	OSRP	GBTRU	↑
5446-1	1993	1997	$55	**$80**	7%

Cow barn with attached silo, tin mansard roof and cow weathervane. Silo holds grain for winter feed. Wind-run ventilator fan keeps hay bales from collecting moisture.

DATE: _____ $ _____
O WISH   O HAVE

'93	'94	'95	'96	'97	'98
$55	55	55	55	55	75

DINAH'S DRIVE-IN

ITEM #	INTRO	RETIRED	OSRP	GBTRU	NO
5447-0	1993	1996	$45	**$95**	CHANGE

A burger in a bun and a bubbly soda top the circular fast-food drive-in. As car travel increased, so did a need for informal eating places. A favorite stop for teenagers, children, and parents on a limited budget.

DATE: _____ $ _____
O WISH   O HAVE

'93	'94	'95	'96	'97	'98
$45	45	45	45	75	95

SNOWY HILLS HOSPITAL

ITEM #	INTRO	RETIRED	OSRP	GBTRU	NO
5448-8	1993	1996	$48	**$90**	CHANGE

A brick hospital with steps leading to double main entry doors. The roof of the Emergency entrance drive-up on the side is topped by a Christmas tree. Wreaths decorate the second-story windows.

DATE: _____ $ _____
O WISH   O HAVE

'93	'94	'95	'96	'97	'98
$48	48	48	48	75	90

FISHERMAN'S NOOK RESORT

Item #	Intro	Retired	OSRP	GBTru	
5460-7	1994	Current	$75	$75	NO CHANGE

Building is office for cabin rental, store for bait and gas for boats, plus places for boats to tie up.

Date: ____ $ ____
O Wish   O Have

'94	'95	'96	'97	'98
$75	75	75	75	75

FISHERMAN'S NOOK CABINS

Item #	Intro	Retired	OSRP	GBTru	
5461-5	1994	Current	$50	$50	NO CHANGE

Set of 2. Midyear release. Includes *Fisherman's Nook Bass Cabin* and *Fisherman's Nook Trout Cabin*. Sold only as a set.

see below

Date: ____ $ ____
O Wish   O Have

'94	'95	'96	'97	'98
$50	50	50	50	50

FISHERMAN'S NOOK BASS CABIN

Item #	Intro	Retired	OSRP	GBTru
5461-5	1994	Current	*	*

1 of a 2-piece set. *Sold only as a set. See FISHERMAN'S NOOK CABINS. Midyear release. Each cabin named for fish–rustic wood cabin with wood pile and fireplace for heat.

Date: ____ $ ____
O Wish   O Have

FISHERMAN'S NOOK TROUT CABIN

Item #	Intro	Retired	OSRP	GBTru
5461-5	1994	Current	*	*

1 of a 2-piece set. *Sold only as a set. See FISHERMAN'S NOOK CABINS. Midyear release. Each cabin named for fish–rustic wood cabin with wood pile and fireplace for heat.

Date: ____ $ ____
O Wish   O Have

SNOW VILLAGE STARTER SET

ITEM #	INTRO	RETIRED	OSRP	GBTRU	↓
5462-3	1994	1996	$49.99	**$65**	13%

Set of 6. Set includes *Shady Oak Church* building, *Sunday School Serenade* accessory, 3 assorted "bottle-brush" sisal trees, and a bag of Real Plastic Snow.
Notable: Featured at Department 56, Inc.'s National Open Houses hosted by participating Gift Creation Concepts (GCC) retailers the first weekend in November, 1994.

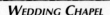

DATE: _____ $ _____
○ WISH ○ HAVE

'94	'95	'96	'97	'98
$49.99	50	50	70	75

WEDDING CHAPEL

ITEM #	INTRO	RETIRED	OSRP	GBTRU	NO
5464-0	1994	CURRENT	$55	**$55**	CHANGE

A white clapboard church with a brick tower supporting a wooden steeple. A bell hangs in the tower above the door. The arched windows have green shutters. Attached snow-covered tree.

DATE: _____ $ _____
○ WISH ○ HAVE

'94	'95	'96	'97	'98
$55	55	55	55	55

FEDERAL HOUSE

ITEM #	INTRO	RETIRED	OSRP	GBTRU	↑
5465-8	1994	1997	$50	**$75**	7%

American Architecture Series. Stately symmetrical brick structure has a white portico and columns at the front door. Roof dormers and four chimneys complete the mirrored effect. The lower windows are decorated with wreaths. Attached snow-covered tree.

DATE: _____ $ _____
○ WISH ○ HAVE

'94	'95	'96	'97	'98
$50	50	50	50	70

CARMEL COTTAGE

ITEM #	INTRO	RETIRED	OSRP	GBTRU	↓
5466-6	1994	1997	$48	**$55**	15%

Cottage with stucco walls, a steep pitched roof, dormer on side and chimney at rear. Stone trims the door, side passage and windows.

DATE: _____ $ _____
○ WISH ○ HAVE

'94	'95	'96	'97	'98
$48	48	48	48	65

SKATE & SKI SHOP

ITEM #	INTRO	RETIRED	OSRP	GBTRU	↑
5467-4	1994	1998	$50	**$55**	10%

Chalet style shop has stone chimney and slate roof. Timber trims the windows and base.

DATE: _____ $ _____
○ WISH ○ HAVE

	'94	'95	'96	'97	'98
	$50	50	50	50	50

GLENHAVEN HOUSE

ITEM #	INTRO	RETIRED	OSRP	GBTRU	↑
5468-2	1994	1997	$45	**$65**	8%

2 1/2-story home with bay windows on first floor. Small porch at entrance. House has formal look with an ornate pediment highlighting the attic windows on the front gable. Two trees attached at the right front corner.

DATE: _____ $ _____
○ WISH ○ HAVE

	'94	'95	'96	'97	'98
	$45	45	45	45	60

COCA–COLA® BRAND BOTTLING PLANT

ITEM #	INTRO	RETIRED	OSRP	GBTRU	↑
5469-0	1994	1997	$65	**$90**	6%

Large, red Coca-Cola logo sign set on roof above entry doors. Vending machine sits at back of loading dock, two cases sit at front. Two smoke stacks rise from roof near skylights. Early samples did not have cases of soda on loading dock.

DATE: _____ $ _____
○ WISH ○ HAVE

	'94	'95	'96	'97	'98
	$65	65	65	65	85

MARVEL'S BEAUTY SALON

ITEM #	INTRO	RETIRED	OSRP	GBTRU	↑
5470-4	1994	1997	$37.50	**$55**	10%

Brick first story houses the Beauty Salon where a picture window displays styles. The stucco second story houses a Wig Shop.
Notable: Named for Marvel Foster who worked for Department 56, Inc.

DATE: _____ $ _____
○ WISH ○ HAVE

	'94	'95	'96	'97	'98
	$37.50	37.50	37.50	37.50	50

CHRISTMAS COVE LIGHTHOUSE

ITEM #	INTRO	RETIRED	OSRP	GBTRU	NO
5483-6	1995	CURRENT	$60	$60	CHANGE

Midyear release. Ship beacon atop white block tower. Steps lead to brick home of keeper. Attached trees. 2-light socket cord. Lift-off top allows access to bulb in tower.

DATE: ____ $ ____
○ WISH ○ HAVE

'95	'96	'97	'98
$60	60	60	60

COCA–COLA® BRAND CORNER DRUGSTORE

ITEM #	INTRO	RETIRED	OSRP	GBTRU	↑
5484-4	1995	1998	$55	$90	64%

Midyear release. Oversize Coke bottle and logo sign is advertisement for soda shop in drugstore. Stone trims the corner shop with bow windows and roof cornices.

DATE: ____ $ ____
○ WISH ○ HAVE

'95	'96	'97	'98
$55	55	55	55

SNOW CARNIVAL ICE PALACE

ITEM #	INTRO	RETIRED	OSRP	GBTRU	↑
54850	1995	1998	$95	$115	21%

Set of 2. Turrets trim a fantasy, frosty ice palace for festival King and Queen. Entry welcome gate with snowy trees leads to the magical creation built of blocks of ice. Northern American and Canadian cities often have Winter Holiday Festivals with grand ice buildings and sculptures.

DATE: ____ $ ____
○ WISH ○ HAVE

'95	'96	'97	'98
$95	95	95	95

PISA PIZZA

ITEM #	INTRO	RETIRED	OSRP	GBTRU	↑
54851	1995	1998	$35	$50	43%

A replica of the Leaning Tower of Pisa, a landmark building in Italy, is the central design on restaurant. Flanking doors and window have striped canopies.

DATE: ____ $ ____
○ WISH ○ HAVE

'95	'96	'97	'98
$36	35	35	35

PEPPERMINT PORCH DAY CARE

ITEM #	INTRO	RETIRED	OSRP	GBTRU	NO
5485-2	1995	1997	$45	$70	CHANGE

Midyear release. Day-care center in white clapboard house. Mint candy theme on pillars and balcony. Boots, teddy bear on porch.
Notable: Original sample had "Peppermint Place" as the name on the building.

DATE: _____ $ _____
○ WISH   ○ HAVE

'95	'96	'97	'98
$45	45	45	70

VILLAGE POLICE STATION

ITEM #	INTRO	RETIRED	OSRP	GBTRU	↑
54853	1995	1998	$48	$60	25%

The 56th Precinct is housed in a two-story brick building with stone coping capping off the roof edge. Arched windows accent the double entry design. There are awnings on the three upper windows with Department name above. Doughnut shop next door for a quick pick-me-up break.

DATE: _____ $ _____
○ WISH   ○ HAVE

'95	'96	'97	'98
$48	48	48	48

HOLLY BROTHERS GARAGE

ITEM #	INTRO	RETIRED	OSRP	GBTRU	↑
54854	1995	1998	$48	$60	25%

Gas station with two pumps. Coke machine, wall phone, repair stalls, tires, free air, office and rest rooms are housed in a white building. Owner's name above gas pumps.

DATE: _____ $ _____
○ WISH   ○ HAVE

'95	'96	'97	'98
$48	48	48	48

RYMAN AUDITORIUM®

ITEM #	INTRO	RETIRED	OSRP	GBTRU	↑
54855	1995	1997	$75	$95	6%

Nashville's country music auditorium. Featured acts are country western artists.

DATE: _____ $ _____
○ WISH   ○ HAVE

'95	'96	'97	'98
$75	75	75	90

DUTCH COLONIAL

ITEM #	INTRO	RETIRED	OSRP	GBTRU	NO
54856	1995	1996	$45	**$70**	CHANGE

American Architecture Series. Second story of colonial home is constructed as part of mansard roof that extends down to first floor level. Shuttered double windows frame front door two steps up from walk. One bedroom accesses an upper balustraded outdoor sitting area.

DATE: ____ $ ____
○ WISH ○ HAVE

'95	'96	'97	'98
$45	45	70	70

BEACON HILL VICTORIAN

ITEM #	INTRO	RETIRED	OSRP	GBTRU	↑
54857	1995	1998	$60	**$90**	50%

Covered porch encloses turret structure that rises up entire height of house and features shuttered windows. Brick home with transverse roof has ornate wood molding trim on gables. Snowy fir trees on front corner.

DATE: ____ $ ____
○ WISH ○ HAVE

'95	'96	'97	'98
$60	60	60	60

BOWLING ALLEY

ITEM #	INTRO	RETIRED	OSRP	GBTRU	↑
54858	1995	1998	$42	**$60**	43%

Bowling pins and ball atop brick building advertise sports activity within. Pins flank Village Lanes sign above archway of double entry doors. Snowy trees next to entrance.

DATE: ____ $ ____
○ WISH ○ HAVE

'95	'96	'97	'98
$42	42	42	42

STARBUCKS® COFFEE

ITEM #	INTRO	RETIRED	OSRP	GBTRU	NO
54859	1995	CURRENT	$48	**$48**	CHANGE

Corner building features many varieties of coffee and baked treats. Stone structure with starred canopies over upper windows and larger awnings atop windows on street level. Store logo displayed on roof pediment.

DATE: ____ $ ____
○ WISH ○ HAVE

'95	'96	'97	'98
$48	48	48	48

NICK'S TREE FARM

ITEM #	INTRO	RETIRED	OSRP	GBTRU	NO
54871	1996	CURRENT	$40	**$40**	CHANGE

Set of 10. Midyear release. Small wood hut provides office and warming area for Nick on a farm where he or you can select a live or cut tree. Nick pulls a cut tree on a sled.

DATE: _____ $ _____
O WISH   O HAVE

'96	'97	'98
$40	40	40

SMOKEY MOUNTAIN RETREAT

ITEM #	INTRO	RETIRED	OSRP	GBTRU	NO
54872	1996	CURRENT	$65	**$65**	CHANGE

Midyear release. Log structure with two stone fireplaces has exposed log beams, covered entry and porch areas to hold sleds and outdoor gear. This building debuts a smoking chimney feature. A built-in Magic Smoking Element, powered by a separate transformer, heats a supplied nontoxic liquid causing it to smoke. See Trims, Item #52620, for refill *Village Magic Smoke*.

DATE: _____ $ _____
O WISH   O HAVE

'96	'97	'98
$65	65	65

BOULDER SPRINGS HOUSE

ITEM #	INTRO	RETIRED	OSRP	GBTRU	↑
54873	1996	1997	$60	**$75**	7%

Midyear release. Clapboard house with 2 1/2 stories has covered entry and front porch. Shutters frame front gable windows, attached tree behind side bow window.

DATE: _____ $ _____
O WISH   O HAVE

'96	'97	'98
$60	60	70

REINDEER BUS DEPOT

ITEM #	INTRO	RETIRED	OSRP	GBTRU	NO
54874	1996	1997	$42	**$60**	CHANGE

Midyear release. Depot is two stories with restaurant and waiting room flanking central entry topped by depot name and vertical bus sign.

DATE: _____ $ _____
O WISH   O HAVE

'96	'97	'98
$42	42	60

ROCKABILLY RECORDS

ITEM #	INTRO	RETIRED	OSRP	GBTRU	↑
54880	1996	1998	$45	**$55**	22%

Art deco styled Rockabilly recording studio and business office. Roof sign created to look like vinyl record. Jukebox design on front building corners highlight coin operated record players found in soda fountains and entertainment areas. Light brick with barrel roll molding between the first and second floor.

DATE: ____ $ ____
○ WISH ○ HAVE

'97	'98
$45	45

CHRISTMAS LAKE HIGH SCHOOL

ITEM #	INTRO	RETIRED	OSRP	GBTRU	NO
54881	1996	CURRENT	$52	**$52**	CHANGE

Variegated brick two-story school building has name above double entry doors with dedication date plaque in central roof gable. There are two chimneys where the side wings meet with the central portion of the building. Bell cupola above center gable. Basketball hoop by side entrance.

DATE: ____ $ ____
○ WISH ○ HAVE

'97	'98
$52	52

BIRCH RUN SKI CHALET

ITEM #	INTRO	RETIRED	OSRP	GBTRU	NO
54882	1996	CURRENT	$60	**$60**	CHANGE

Peeled rough-hewn logs used for ski lodge. Large fieldstone fireplace provides cozy lounge area after all day skiing. Chalet offers rooms, refreshments and even a first aid station for minor mishaps.

DATE: ____ $ ____
○ WISH ○ HAVE

'97	'98
$60	60

ROSITA'S CANTINA

ITEM #	INTRO	RETIRED	OSRP	GBTRU	NO
54883	1996	CURRENT	$50	**$50**	CHANGE

Mexican restaurant in Southwest design to resemble smooth adobe with tile roof. Diners are invited to taste the spicy food guaranteed to warm from the inside-out. El Loco Bar is tucked in at the side for those who want a beverage and a snack instead of dinner.

DATE: ____ $ ____
○ WISH ○ HAVE

'97	'98
$50	50

SHINGLE VICTORIAN

ITEM #	INTRO	RETIRED	OSRP	GBTRU	NO
54884	1996	CURRENT	$55	**$55**	CHANGE

American Architecture Series. Bright blue and white three-story home with wraparound porch. Top story features dormer windows. Formal living room has triple front window and a bow side window. Double entry doors with diamond shaped glass design. Saw-toothed roof ridge plus two chimneys.

DATE: ____ $ ____
O WISH   O HAVE

'97	'98
$55	55

SECRET GARDEN FLORIST, THE

ITEM #	INTRO	RETIRED	OSRP	GBTRU	NO
54885	1996	CURRENT	$50	**$50**	CHANGE

Canvas awning with silk-screened lettering protects front of shop that features display boxes of flower arrangements and plants. Bridal planning is also available upstairs over the shop.

DATE: ____ $ ____
O WISH   O HAVE

'97	'98
$50	50

HARLEY-DAVIDSON® MOTORCYCLE SHOP

ITEM #	INTRO	RETIRED	OSRP	GBTRU	NO
54886	1996	CURRENT	$65	**$65**	CHANGE

Showroom and maintenance shop devoted to 'Hog' devotees. Cycle display on front entry reinforced canopy. Soda can and bottle ice chest and gas pump allow cyclist and cycle to fill-er-up. Repair area with roll-up garage door and large disposal drums.

DATE: ____ $ ____
O WISH   O HAVE

'97	'98
$65	65

BACHMAN'S® FLOWER SHOP

ITEM #	INTRO	RETIRED	OSRP	GBTRU	↑
8802	1997	PROMO	$50	**$110**	47%

Personalized for Bachman's® Village Gathering with a purple canvas awning with silk screened lettering. Company logo and year of establishment on front of shop. Display boxes with flower arrangements and plants. Bridal planning is also available upstairs.

DATE: ____ $ ____
O WISH   O HAVE

'97	'98
$50	75

RONALD MCDONALD HOUSE® (THE HOUSE THAT ♥ BUILT™)

ITEM #	INTRO	RETIRED	OSRP	GBTRU	↓
8960	1997	EVENT PIECE	*	$395	15%

Midyear announcement. Two-story home with heart-trimmed tree and picket fence decorated with holly. These homes-away-from-home were created for the care and well-being of families of children undergoing treatment at nearby hospitals for very serious illnesses. This was a very limited piece available only to 1997 Homes For The Holidays participants. *The piece was not for retail sale. They were raffled at the Department 56, Inc.'s Homes For The Holiday Event, with proceeds going to the Ronald McDonald Houses.

DATE: _____ $ _____		'97	'98
○ WISH ○ HAVE		$NE	465

MAINSTREET GIFT SHOP

ITEM #	INTRO	RETIRED	OSRP	GBTRU	↓
54887	1997	1997	$50	$75	17%

An actual Original Snow Village® house display is used as a focal point in the acrylic front window of the shop.
Notable: Available only to Gift Creation Concepts (GCC) dealers to celebrate the 20th Anniversary of GCC. Two medallions came with the piece allowing display of the GCC Dealer logo or it could be personalized with the store name. A special GCC decal bottomstamp was added to the usual Department 56, Inc. embossed stamp.

DATE: _____ $ _____		'97	'98
○ WISH ○ HAVE		$50	90

ORIGINAL SNOW VILLAGE START A TRADITION SET, THE

ITEM #	INTRO	RETIRED	OSRP	GBTRU	NO
54902	1997	1998	$100*	$100	CHANGE

Set of 8. Midyear release. Two lighted buildings– *Kringles Toy Shop* w/revolving front door & acrylic windows, *A Hot Chocolate Stand* in the shape of a mug. Accessories are: *Saturday Morning Downtown* (little girl sips a mug of chocolate & boy pulls sled of presents); 2 trimmed trees in drum bases; bag of Snow & Cobblestone Road.
Notable: It was first available at the Department 56, Inc.'s Homes For The Holidays Event held November 1–9, 1997. * Reduced to $75 during Event. Also: The hangtag for Nikki's reads "Kringle's Cocoa Shop."

DATE: _____ $ _____		'97	'98
○ WISH ○ HAVE		$100	100

OLD CHELSEA MANSION

ITEM #	INTRO	RETIRED	OSRP	GBTRU	↑
54903	1997	1998	$85	$95	12%

Midyear release. The brick three-story house has steps at the front entry and a door flanked by columns. Classical proportions produce a stately house.
Notable: Represents the New York home of Clement Clarke Moore, the author of *A Visit From St. Nicholas*. Commemorates the 175th Anniversary of the poem. A 32-page hardcover, illustrated, full color book is included. The history of Moore, his home and the poem make this collector's book a Village "first."

DATE: _____ $ _____		'97	'98
○ WISH ○ HAVE		$85	85

New Hope Church

Item #	Intro	Retired	OSRP	GBTru	↑
54904	1997	1998	$60	**$80**	33%

Midyear release. Brick church with turret-like tower features acrylic stained glass windows. Community Bingo enthusiasts attend and enjoy an evening out in the company of friends.

Date: ____ $ ____
○ Wish ○ Have

	'97	'98
	$60	60

Christmas Barn Dance

Item #	Intro	Retired	OSRP	GBTru	NO
54910	1997	Current	$65	**$65**	CHANGE

Red barn with double silo and mansard roof is site of holiday dance. Doors open to decorated area. Features many complex attachments, including metal ladder, lightning posts, weathervane, hanging lantern and pigeons.

Date: ____ $ ____
○ Wish ○ Have

'98
$65

Italianate Villa

Item #	Intro	Retired	OSRP	GBTru	NO
54911	1997	Current	$55	**$55**	CHANGE

American Architecture Series. Double entry door design is base for turret that rises up through roof in center of front facade. Windows feature molding and pediments. Ornate coping design highlights roof. Hanging porch swing. Sisal trees and metal lightning rod.

Date: ____ $ ____
○ Wish ○ Have

'98
$55

Farm House

Item #	Intro	Retired	OSRP	GBTru	NO
54912	1997	Current	$50	**$50**	CHANGE

Porch protects front entry of 1 1/2-story brick home. Roof line accented by two gables over shuttered windows. Large bay window on first floor with special glass wax stencils. Attached tree.

Date: ____ $ ____
○ Wish ○ Have

'98
$50

HERSHEY'S™ CHOCOLATE SHOP

ITEM #	INTRO	RETIRED	OSRP	GBTRU	NO
54913	1997	CURRENT	$55	$55	CHANGE

Chocolate kisses decorate front store windows while lighted billboard on roof advertises candy bars. Red canopy over entry doors to sweet shop.

DATE: ____ $ ____
○ WISH   ○ HAVE

'98
$55

McDONALD'S®

ITEM #	INTRO	RETIRED	OSRP	GBTRU	NO
54914	1997	CURRENT	$65	$65	CHANGE

Golden Arches fast food restaurant, circa the 1950's where burgers, fries and shakes are tops on the menu. Illuminated arches. Acrylic windows. Children sitting on bench are first time figurines have been used as an attachment.

DATE: ____ $ ____
○ WISH   ○ HAVE

'98
$65

GRACIE'S DRY GOODS & GENERAL STORE

ITEM #	INTRO	RETIRED	OSRP	GBTRU	NO
54915	1997	CURRENT	$70	$70	CHANGE

Set of 2. Columns flank front door and display windows. Upper story created as a flat wall to feature store name sign. Forerunner of supermarket and department store, this store had something for everyone. Separate gas pump allowed for a quick refill.

DATE: ____ $ ____
○ WISH   ○ HAVE

'98
$70

ROLLERAMA ROLLER RINK

ITEM #	INTRO	RETIRED	OSRP	GBTRU	NO
54916	1997	CURRENT	$56	$56	CHANGE

Oval 1950's design skating rink is housed in building with domed roof similar to Quonset hut design. Boy and girl shadow design art work by front entry. Lights around marquee, acrylic signs and rooftop skylight illuminate.

DATE: ____ $ ____
○ WISH   ○ HAVE

'98
$56

LINDEN HILLS COUNTRY CLUB

ITEM #	INTRO	RETIRED	OSRP	GBTru	
54917	1997	Current	$60	**$60**	NO CHANGE

Set of 2. Brick and stone building with 2 1/2 story gable over front entry doors houses restaurant and recreation facilities for member families. Pro Golf Shop on the side. Metal lanterns that light from within.
Notable: Linden Hills is an area near downtown Minneapolis, close to Lake Harriet.

DATE: _____ $ _____
○ WISH ○ HAVE

'98
$60

BRANDON BUNGALOW, THE

ITEM #	INTRO	RETIRED	OSRP	GBTru	
54918	1997	Current	$55	**$55**	NO CHANGE

Stone and clapboard home. Stone fireplace chimney rises through roof. Family car sits in open garage. Evergreen shrubs set off front porch and railings.
Notable: Named for a small resort town in northern Minnesota.

DATE: _____ $ _____
○ WISH ○ HAVE

'98
$55

LIONEL® ELECTRIC TRAIN SHOP

ITEM #	INTRO	RETIRED	OSRP	GBTru	
2202	1998	Ltd Ed 5,000	$55	**$110**	↑ 100%

Notable: This building was produced exclusively for Allied Model Trains of California. The date at the top of the building, 1946, was the year that Allied opened its doors. The address on the awning, 4411, is Allied's actual street address. The building was re-issued later with slight alterations for sale by all Original Snow Village® dealers, 1998 Item #54947.

DATE: _____ $ _____
○ WISH ○ HAVE

'98
$55

BACHMAN'S® GREENHOUSE

ITEM #	INTRO	RETIRED	OSRP	GBTru	
2203	1998	Promo	$60	**$95**	↑ 58%

"The design was inspired by a small greenhouse that once stood adjacent to Bachman's® flagship store, and it is lit like no other piece. The unusual interior lights hang over the plant tables and they actually work. The piece also has see-through panes that duplicate the curved glass of the original greenhouse." - from *The Bachman's® Village News*
Notable: An exclusive created for the 1998 Bachman's® Village Gathering. Companion piece to 1997 exclusive *Bachman's® Flower Shop*. It was re-issued as *The Secret Garden Greenhouse*, 1998 Item #54949.

DATE: _____ $ _____
○ WISH ○ HAVE

'98
$60

RONALD McDONALD HOUSE® (THE HOUSE THAT ♥ BUILT™)

ITEM #	INTRO	RETIRED	OSRP	GBTRU
2210	1998	LTD ED 5,600	*	**$400**

Notable: This was a very limited piece available to Department 56, Inc.'s 1998 Homes For The Holidays participating dealers. Two-story bright and cheery yellow house carries out the heart motif. *The piece was not for retail sale. It was raffled at the Event with proceeds going to the Ronald McDonald Houses. These homes-away-from-home were created for the care and well-being of families of children undergoing treatment at nearby hospitals for very serious illnesses.

DATE: ____ $ ____   '98
○ WISH   ○ HAVE $NE

ROCK CREEK MILL HOUSE

ITEM #	INTRO	RETIRED	OSRP	GBTRU	↑
54932	1998	1998	$64	**$95**	48%

Midyear release. Large water wheel is two stories tall and actually turns to generate power to have a functioning mill. Stone foundation and chimney. Several attached trees.
Notable: Released in matte finish. Sample versions (limited number) were produced with a glossy finish.
GBTru$ for shiny version is $275.

DATE: ____ $ ____   '98
○ WISH   ○ HAVE $64

CARNIVAL CAROUSEL

ITEM #	INTRO	RETIRED	OSRP	GBTRU	NO
54933	1998	CURRENT	$150	**$150**	CHANGE

Midyear release. Colorfully painted and decorated building houses ornately carved carousel to delight children of all ages. Musical lighted piece plays 30 songs, has off/on switch and volume control. Motorized screen casts shadows. Has own adapter.

DATE: ____ $ ____   '98
○ WISH   ○ HAVE $150

SNOWY PINES INN EXCLUSIVE GIFT SET

ITEM #	INTRO	RETIRED	OSRP	GBTRU	↑
54934	1998	EVENT GIFT SET	$65	**$90**	38%

Set of 9. Midyear release. One lighted building–a resort inn with facilities to rent rooms, dine, and enjoy winter recreation in the area. Accessory Set of 2, entitled *Decorate the Tree,* has children trimming tree. 4 sisal trees, Brick Road, 1.5 oz. bag of Village Fresh Fallen Snow. Tinsel garland adds sparkle.
Notable: One of three Gift Sets featured at Department 56, Inc.'s National Homes For The Holidays Open House Event, November 5–9, 1998.

DATE: ____ $ ____   '98
○ WISH   ○ HAVE $65

HAUNTED MANSION

ITEM #	INTRO	RETIRED	OSRP	GBTRU	NO
54935	1998	CURRENT	$110	$110	CHANGE

Midyear release. Gothic looking house has front entry doors that hang open adding to haunted look. Building does not have snow trim. Motorized screen projects ghosts, bats and witches on the windows. Comes with its own adapter.

DATE: _____ $ _____
O WISH   O HAVE

'98
$110

CENTER FOR THE ARTS

ITEM #	INTRO	RETIRED	OSRP	GBTRU
54940	1998	CURRENT	$64	$64

This building includes three art-related enterprises—Mackenzie's Studio Of Dance, Andrew's Art Supplies, and Alexandria Gallery.

DATE: _____ $ _____
O WISH   O HAVE

UPTOWN MOTORS FORD®

ITEM #	INTRO	RETIRED	OSRP	GBTRU
54941	1998	CURRENT	$95	$95

Set of 3. A particular feature of this building is its animated, revolving 1964 Mustang in the showroom.

DATE: _____ $ _____
O WISH   O HAVE

FIRE STATION #3

ITEM #	INTRO	RETIRED	OSRP	GBTRU
54942	1998	CURRENT	$70	$70

A noted feature of this station is the finished interior beyond the opened bay doors. Around back are kennels for the station's Dalmatians.

DATE: _____ $ _____
O WISH   O HAVE

The Circle Of Life

In this column in the September/October '98 issue, I wrote about how things have changed during the seven years that we have been publishing *the Village Chronicle*. I covered changes in the publication, changes in collecting, and changes in the quality of Department 56, Inc.'s designs. What I didn't mention is that this constant state of change is turning full circle.

In that article, I wrote about the displays that many collectors now create, how they differed from the "all-in-a-row" scenes that were so often the first display attempts for many of us. Yet it's "full-blown" displays that I'd like to cover here—not those created by collectors, but those created by dealers and, in essence, by Department 56, Inc.

In 1994, Department 56, Inc. developed a new tier of dealer, the Key Dealer. Once appointed as a Key Dealer, a store receives particular perks from Department 56, Inc. in exchange for its extra efforts in promoting its products. One of the criteria is the ability to prominently present and market the product. This is the reason we now see such wonderful displays in many of the stores we visit. This wasn't the only reason dealers switched from their own version of "all-in-a-row" displays. Many dealers, getting feedback and ideas from collectors, had every intention of creating their own impressive displays. In many cases, creative collectors were asked to design and build scenes for stores.

Because of this, collectors have enjoyed viewing displays ranging from interesting to drop-dead unbelievable. Running water, trains, carousels, drawbridges, fireworks, moving sidewalks, rising and setting suns, sound effects, twinkling stars, and more features than can be listed here have been incorporated into these creations. It's not unusual to find rooms dedicated to Department 56®, specifically designed to show the buildings, accessories, and the maker's creativity in a way no other collectible is presented. Several stores have built additions to showcase Department 56® collectibles, their number one line. Not only is it enjoyable to see such rooms, it's actually fascinating when you think about the time, effort, and money put into such ventures.

But (there's *always* a but, isn't there?) as a man once sang, "The times, they are a-changin'." No, the rooms are not going to go away. Yet there is a need for a new style of retail display. Or is it an old style…with a twist?

Yes, everyone likes to look at the large displays. Collectors, both novice and experienced, derive ideas from them, and collectors and non-collectors alike just enjoy these cold-weather scenes. However, this style of display often does little to attract new collectors, something every store needs. Put in a rather simple way, potential collectors look at a scene, admire it, and think about the effort involved in such an endeavor, the space it would require, and its cost. Boy, better think about another hobby!

It's not difficult to understand the psychology behind this. When I was young, I always wanted a train set. When I got older and could afford a quality set, I visited a hobby shop. This shop had a display that featured multiple trains running simultaneously, flowing water, varying levels, blinking lights, crevasses, trestles, and more. It all seemed too complicated, and I never thought about buying a set again.

continued page 84

The Circle Of Life *(cont. from page 83)*

But then Allied Model Trains began selling its limited edition Department 56® train cars, one per year. I bought the first, and guess what! It was easy, no pain at all. More than that, I couldn't wait for the next one. Now I'm getting my first train set, something I never would have had if all I had ever seen was large, complicated—though beautiful and mechanically amazing—displays.

Should stores go back to just placing the buildings on a shelf? Well, no, not really. But perhaps they should begin to put more emphasis on vignettes. It seems to make sense that a quality collectible/giftware such as a Department 56® village building would be very appealing to many more consumers when set in such a scene.

This is not only my opinion, but it appears to be Department 56, Inc.'s as well. Think about the push the company has been putting on vignettes over the past few years. They appear in their ads, in their *Quarterly*, in their display-making seminars, everywhere, it seems.

Case in point…a Gold Key dealer recently remodeled their store and dismantled its free-standing The Heritage Village Collection® display and placed the pieces in vignettes on den-styled bookshelves in a "home" setting. It was interesting to notice during the store's grand re-opening that collectors and non-collectors alike were standing in front of the shelves commenting on the vignettes while few were admiring the still free-standing The Original Snow Village® display.

And the times…they are a changin'!

the **Village Chronicle.**

STICK STYLE HOUSE	**ITEM #** 54943	**INTRO** 1998	**RETIRED** CURRENT	**OSRP** $60	**GBTRU** $60

American Architecture Series. This 2 1/2-story clapboard home features a porch that runs the width of the house.

DATE: ____ $ ____
○ WISH ○ HAVE

HIDDEN PONDS HOUSE	**ITEM #** 54944	**INTRO** 1998	**RETIRED** CURRENT	**OSRP** $50	**GBTRU** $50

Cat lovers rejoice! This wonderful little house includes a tiny kitten at the two bottles of milk on the side of the house. This marks the first cat attachment in the Village.

DATE: ____ $ ____
○ WISH ○ HAVE

...ANOTHER MAN'S TREASURE GARAGE

ITEM #	INTRO	RETIRED	OSRP	GBTRU
54945	1998	CURRENT	$60	**$60**

Set of 22. Apparently it's time to sell some keepsakes to make room for more little houses. Lantern in wreath is metal. Lamp hangs from actual chain.

DATE: _____ $ _____
O WISH O HAVE

FARMER'S CO-OP GRANARY, THE

ITEM #	INTRO	RETIRED	OSRP	GBTRU
54946	1998	CURRENT	$64	**$64**

A large sign advertises that this building produces Rock Creek Enriched Flour. One of its large front doors is partially opened.

DATE: _____ $ _____
O WISH O HAVE

LIONEL® ELECTRIC TRAIN SHOP

ITEM #	INTRO	RETIRED	OSRP	GBTRU
54947	1998	CURRENT	$55	**$55**

Similar to the limited edition *Lionel® Electric Train Shop*, 1998 Item #2202.
Notable: Differences include: name and new address have been added to awning, and graphics have been changed.

DATE: _____ $ _____
O WISH O HAVE

HARLEY-DAVIDSON® MANUFACTURING

ITEM #	INTRO	RETIRED	OSRP	GBTRU
54948	1998	CURRENT	$80	**$80**

Set of 3. The name of these famous motorcycles appears in various places on this large manufacturing plant, including on the front, on the smoke stacks, and on the roof-level sign.
Notable: Its address is the actual address of the Harley-Davidson® offices in Milwaukee, WI.

DATE: _____ $ _____
O WISH O HAVE

SECRET GARDEN GREENHOUSE, THE

ITEM #	INTRO	RETIRED	OSRP	GBTRU
54949	1998	CURRENT	$60	**$60**

"The design was inspired by a small greenhouse that once stood adjacent to Bachman's flagship store, and it is lit like no other piece. The unusual interior lights hang over the plant tables and they actually work. The piece also has see-through panes that duplicate the curved glass of the original greenhouse." - from *The Bachman's® Village News*
Notable: This is a re-issue of the *Bachman's® Greenhouse*, 1998 Item #2203.

DATE: _____ $ _____
○ WISH   ○ HAVE

Artists' Appearances

Artists' appearances—at a major collectible event or a store's open house—are nothing new in the collectible industry. Manufacturers have been scheduling artists at consumer-based events for years. Doing so has served at least three purposes, including offering the opportunity for collectors to meet the artist of their favorite collectible; allowing the artist to interact with the collector and therefore determine what is popular, what is not; and drawing collectors into retail stores.

Department 56, Inc. has participated in this practice in the past…to a point. Their artists have appeared at the International Collectible Expositions, but appearances in stores have been another matter entirely. By limiting the appearances to the Expos, only two of the three afore-mentioned purposes were met. The artists and the collectors interacted and benefited from the experiences in their own ways. *But*, what about the third purpose? What about getting collectors into the stores. This is certainly not to be overlooked.

In the past collectors were sure to go to stores, mill around for a while, examine the new pieces, re-examine the older ones, perhaps even purchase a building or accessory from a village that wasn't necessarily one they collected. Now, however, things have changed. It's not unusual for collectors to call the retailer and instruct the stores to put all the new pieces aside to be picked up all at once. The collector is in and out in a matter of a few minutes. In many cases, the pieces are already charged to a credit card.

So what's the difference? The retailer is still making sales, right? Yes, and possibly no. Remember how I said collectors might even buy a piece to another village? Popular retailing theory suggests that once consumers are in a store they might buy something in addition to their intended purchase. In short, Department 56® products were selling well, but, to a lesser degree than in prior years. Were they providing the retailer with the opportunity for add-on sales—a retailing requisite?

Furthermore, many collectors were opting not to attend open houses…at least not in the exorbitant hordes as in earlier years. This did not suggest that there was less excitement for the product, just less urgency. "Why rush?" many thought. "I'll just get the event piece a day or two after the event."

By scheduling artist appearances in stores, Department 56, Inc. is now providing the urgency. Collectors will make a point of going to retailers on a specific day. They'll take part in the other scheduled events of the day, and yes, they'll most likely purchase some additional items. There's nothing quite like a win-win-win situation! *the* **Village Chronicle.**

Item#	Name	Intro	Retired	OSRP$	GBTru$	Wish	Have	Date	Qty	Paid Each	Total
5064-1	CAROLERS	1979	1986	12	135	O	O				
5069-0	CERAMIC CAR	1980	1986	5	45	O	O				
5079-2	CERAMIC SLEIGH	1981	1986	5	45	O	O				
5018-0	SNOWMAN WITH BROOM	1982	1990	3	12	O	O				
6460-2	MONKS-A-CAROLING	1982	N/A	6	195	O	O				
6459-9	MONKS-A-CAROLING	1983	1984	6	75	O	O				
5038-5	SCOTTIE WITH TREE	1984	1985	3	160	O	O				
5040-7	MONKS-A-CAROLING	1984	1988	6	50	O	O				
5053-9	SINGING NUNS	1985	1987	6	120	O	O				
5055-5	AUTO WITH TREE—"SQUASHED"	1985	VARIATION	5	90	O	O				
5055-5	AUTO WITH TREE	1985	CURRENT	5	6.50	O	O				
5056-3	SNOW KIDS SLED, SKIS	1985	1987	11	38	O	O				
5057-1	FAMILY MOM/KIDS, GOOSE/GIRL—"LARGE"	1985	1988	11	28	O	O				
5057-1	FAMILY MOM/KIDS, GOOSE/GIRL—"SMALL"	1985	1988	11	26	O	O				
5059-8	SANTA/MAILBOX—"LARGE"	1985	1988	11	40	O	O				
5059-8	SANTA/MAILBOX—"SMALL"	1985	1988	11	40	O	O				
5094-6	KIDS AROUND THE TREE—"LARGE"	1986	1990	15	45	O	O				
5094-6	KIDS AROUND THE TREE—"SMALL"	1986	1990	15	35	O	O				
5095-4	GIRL/SNOWMAN, BOY	1986	1987	11	50	O	O				
5096-2	SHOPPING GIRLS WITH PACKAGES—"LARGE"	1986	1988	11	45	O	O				
5096-2	SHOPPING GIRLS WITH PACKAGES—"SMALL"	1986	1988	11	35	O	O				
NONE	SNOW VILLAGE HOUSE FOR SALE SIGN	1987	N/A	GIFT	25	O	O				
5102-0	3 NUNS WITH SONGBOOKS	1987	1988	6	125	O	O				
5103-9	PRAYING MONKS	1987	1988	6	40	O	O				
5104-7	CHILDREN IN BAND	1987	1989	15	27	O	O				
5105-5	CAROLING FAMILY	1987	1990	20	24	O	O				
5106-3	TAXI CAB	1987	CURRENT	6	6.50	O	O				
5107-1	CHRISTMAS CHILDREN	1987	1990	20	22	O	O				
5108-0	HOUSE FOR SALE SIGN	1987	1989	3.50	10	O	O				
581-9	HOUSE FOR SALE SIGN—"GCC BLANK"	1987	PROMO	*	10	O	O				
5113-6	SNOW KIDS	1987	1990	20	32	O	O				

OSVA PAGE 1 TOTALS: 276.50   1,637.00

The Original Snow Village® Accessories GB History List   87

Item#	Name	Intro	Retired	OSRP$	GBTru$	Wish	Have	Date	Qty	Paid Each	Total
5116-0	Man On Ladder Hanging Garland	1988	1992	7.50	14	O	O				
5117-9	Hayride	1988	1990	30	55	O	O				
5118-7	School Children	1988	1990	15	30	O	O				
5129-2	Apple Girl/Newspaper Boy	1988	1990	11	15	O	O				
5130-6	Woodsman And Boy	1988	1991	13	24	O	O				
5131-4	Doghouse/Cat In Garbage Can	1988	1992	15	25	O	O				
5132-2	Fire Hydrant & Mailbox	1988	1998	6	8	O	O				
5133-0	Water Tower	1988	1991	20	75	O	O				
2510-4	Water Tower–"John Deere"	1988	Promo	24	675	O	O				
5135-7	Nativity	1988	Current	7.50	7.50	O	O				
5136-5	Woody Station Wagon	1988	1990	6.50	28	O	O				
5137-3	School Bus, Snow Plow	1988	1991	16	50	O	O				
5138-1	Tree Lot	1988	Current	33.50	37.50	O	O				
8183-3	Sisal Tree Lot	1988	1991	45	78	O	O				
5146-2	Village Gazebo	1989	1995	27	35	O	O				
5147-0	Choir Kids	1989	1992	15	20	O	O				
5148-9	Special Delivery	1989	1990	16	45	O	O				
5166-7	For Sale Sign	1989	1998	4.50	4.50	O	O				
539-8	For Sale Sign–"Bachman's®"	1989	Promo	4.50	26	O	O				
5167-5	Street Sign	1989	1992	7.50	12	O	O				
5168-3	Kids Tree House	1989	1991	25	50	O	O				
5169-1	Bringing Home The Tree	1989	1992	15	20	O	O				
5170-5	Skate Faster Mom	1989	1991	13	25	O	O				
5171-3	Crack The Whip	1989	1996	25	27	O	O				
5172-1	Through The Woods	1989	1991	18	22	O	O				
5173-0	Statue Of Mark Twain	1989	1991	15	28	O	O				
5174-8	Calling All Cars	1989	1991	15	75	O	O				
5177-2	Flag Pole	1989	Current	8.50	8.50	O	O				
5179-9	Mailbox	1989	1990	3.50	15	O	O				
9948-1	Snow Village Promotional Sign	1989	1990	Promo	25	O	O				
5134-9	Kids Decorating The Village Sign	1990	1993	12.50	25	O	O				
5158-6	Down The Chimney He Goes	1990	1993	6.50	9	O	O				
5159-4	Sno-Jet Snowmobile	1990	1993	15	24	O	O				
5160-8	Sleighride	1990	1992	30	50	O	O				

OSVA Page 2 Totals: 526.50   1,668.00

Item#	Name	Intro	Retired	OSRP$	GBTru$	Wish	Have	Date	Qty	Paid Each	Total
5161-6	Here We Come A Caroling	1990	1992	18	30	O	O				
5162-4	Home Delivery	1990	1992	16	25	O	O				
5163-2	Fresh Frozen Fish	1990	1993	20	40	O	O				
5164-0	A Tree For Me	1990	1995	7.50	12	O	O				
5165-9	A Home For The Holidays	1990	1996	6.50	15	O	O				
5197-7	Special Delivery	1990	1992	16	27	O	O				
5198-5	Village Mail Box	1990	1998	3.50	3.50	O	O				
5408-9	Wreaths For Sale	1991	1994	27.50	28	O	O				
5409-7	Winter Fountain	1991	1993	25	50	O	O				
5410-0	Cold Weather Sports	1991	1994	27.50	32	O	O				
5411-9	Come Join The Parade	1991	1992	12.50	20	O	O				
5412-7	Village Marching Band	1991	1992	30	54	O	O				
5413-5	Christmas Cadillac	1991	1994	9	12	O	O				
5414-3	Snowball Fort	1991	1993	27.50	36	O	O				
5415-1	Country Harvest	1991	1993	13	22	O	O				
5428-3	Village Used Car Lot	1992	1997	45	60	O	O				
5429-1	Village Phone Booth	1992	Current	7.50	7.50	O	O				
5430-5	Nanny And The Preschoolers	1992	1994	27.50	30	O	O				
5431-3	Early Morning Delivery	1992	1995	27.50	32	O	O				
5432-1	Christmas Puppies	1992	1996	27.50	30	O	O				
5433-0	Round & Round We Go!	1992	1995	18	22	O	O				
5434-8	A Heavy Snow Fall	1992	Current	16	16	O	O				
5435-6	We're Going To A Christmas Pageant	1992	1994	15	21	O	O				
5436-4	Winter Playground	1992	1995	20	30	O	O				
5440-2	Spirit Of Snow Village Airplane	1992	1996	32.50	42	O	O				
5449-6	Safety Patrol	1993	1997	27.50	30	O	O				
5450-0	Christmas At The Farm	1993	1996	16	30	O	O				
5451-8	Check It Out Bookmobile	1993	1995	25	28	O	O				
5452-6	Tour The Village	1993	1997	12.50	18	O	O				
5453-4	Pint-Size Pony Rides	1993	1996	37.50	40	O	O				
5454-2	Pick-up And Delivery	1993	Current	10	10	O	O				
5455-0	A Herd Of Holiday Heifers	1993	1997	18	25	O	O				
5457-7	Classic Cars	1993	1998	22.50	30	O	O				

OSVA Page 3 Totals: 665.00 908.00

Item#	Name	Intro	Retired	OSRP$	GBTru$	Wish	Have	Date	Qty	Paid Each	Total
5458-5	Spirit Of Snow Village Airplane	1993	1996	12.50	25	○	○				
5459-3	Village News Delivery	1993	1996	15	18	○	○				
5462-3*	Sunday School Serenade	1994	1996	*	*	○	○				
5463-1	Caroling At The Farm	1994	Current	35	35	○	○				
5471-2	Stuck In The Snow	1994	1998	30	38	○	○				
5472-0	Pets On Parade	1994	1998	16.50	20	○	○				
5473-9	Feeding The Birds	1994	1997	25	35	○	○				
5474-7	Mush!	1994	1997	20	25	○	○				
5475-5	Skaters & Skiers	1994	Current	27.50	27.50	○	○				
5476-3	Going To The Chapel	1994	Current	20	20	○	○				
5477-1	Santa Comes To Town, 1995	1994	1995 Annual	30	40	○	○				
5478-0	Marshmallow Roast	1994	Current	32.50	32.50	○	○				
5479-8	Coca-Cola® brand Delivery Truck	1994	1998	15	25	○	○				
5480-1	Coca-Cola® brand Delivery Men	1994	1998	25	32	○	○				
5481-0	Coca-Cola® brand Billboard	1994	1997	18	27	○	○				
Various	A Visit With Santa	1995	Promo	25	45	○	○				
54860	Frosty Playtime	1995	1997	30	45	○	○				
54861	Poinsettias For Sale	1995	1998	30	40	○	○				
54862	Santa Comes To Town, 1996	1995	1996 Annual	32.50	40	○	○				
54863	Chopping Firewood	1995	Current	16.50	16.50	○	○				
54864	Firewood Delivery Truck	1995	Current	15	15	○	○				
54865	Service With A Smile	1995	1998	25	32	○	○				
54866	Pizza Delivery	1995	1998	20	30	○	○				
54867	Grand Old Opry Carolers	1995	1997	25	36	○	○				
54868	Snow Carnival Ice Sculptures	1995	1998	27.50	36	○	○				
54869	Snow Carnival King & Queen	1995	1998	35	45	○	○				
54870	Starbucks® Coffee Cart	1995	Current	27.50	27.50	○	○				
54879	Just Married	1995	Current	25	25	○	○				
Various	Here Comes Santa	1996	Promo	25	35	○	○				
54875	A Ride On The Reindeer Lines	1996	1997	35	40	○	○				
54890	Treetop Tree House	1996	Current	35	35	○	○				
54891	On The Road Again	1996	Current	20	20	○	○				
54892	Moving Day	1996	1998	32.50	40	○	○				
54893	Holiday Hoops	1996	Current	20	20	○	○				

OSVA Page 4 Totals: 823.50 1,023.00

Item#	Name	Intro	Retired	OSRP$	GBTru$	Wish	Have	Date	Qty	Paid Each	Total
54894	Men At Work	1996	1998	27.50	36	○	○				
54895	Terry's Towing	1996	Current	20	20	○	○				
54896	Caroling Through The Snow	1996	Current	15	15	○	○				
54897	Heading For The Hills	1996	Current	8.50	8.50	○	○				
54898	A Harley-Davidson® Holiday	1996	Current	22.50	22.50	○	○				
54899	Santa Comes To Town, 1997	1996	1997 Annual	35	40	○	○				
54900	Harley-Davidson® Fat Boy & Softail	1996	Current	16.50	16.50	○	○				
54901	Harley-Davidson® Sign	1996	Current	18	18	○	○				
54902*	Saturday Morning Downtown	1997	1998	*	*	○	○				
54905	Whole Family Goes Shopping, The	1997	Current	25	25	○	○				
54921	A Holiday Sleigh Ride Together	1997	Current	32.50	32.50	○	○				
54922	Christmas Kids	1997	Current	27.50	27.50	○	○				
54923	Let It Snow, Let It Snow	1997	Current	20	20	○	○				
54924	Kids Love Hershey's™!	1997	Current	30	30	○	○				
54925	McDonald's®... Lights Up The Night	1997	Current	30	30	○	○				
54926	Kids, Candy Canes... & Ronald McDonald®	1997	Current	30	30	○	○				
54927	He Led Them Down The Streets Of Town	1997	Current	30	30	○	○				
54928	Everybody Goes Skating At Rollerama	1997	Current	25	25	○	○				
54929	At The Barn Dance, It's Allemande Left	1997	Current	30	30	○	○				
54930	Hitch-Up The Buckboard	1997	Current	40	40	○	○				
54931	Farm Accessory Set	1997	Current	75	75	○	○				
2204	Say It With Flowers	1998	Promo	30	40	○	○				
54920	Santa Comes To Town, 1998	1998	1998 Annual	30	40	○	○				
54934*	Decorate The Tree	1998	Event G/S Acc.	*	*	○	○				
54936	First Round Of The Year	1998	Current	30	30	○	○				
54937	Trick Or Treat Kids	1998	Current	33	33	○	○				
54938	Carnival Tickets & Cotton Candy	1998	Current	30	30	○	○				
54939	Two For The Road, 3 Assorted	1998	Current	20/ea	20/ea	○	○				
52780	Uptown Motors Ford® Billboard	1998	Current	20	20	○	○				
54950	1955 Ford® Automobiles, 6 Assorted	1998	Current	10/ea	10/ea	○	○				
54951	1964-1/2 Ford® Mustang, 3 Assorted	1998	Current	10/ea	10/ea	○	○				
54952	Village Fire Truck	1998	Current	22.50	22.50	○	○				
54953	Fireman To The Rescue	1998	Current	30	30	○	○				

OSVA Page 5 Totals: 823.50 | 857.00

The Original Snow Village® Accessories GB History List

Item#	Name	Intro	Retired	OSRP$	GBTru$	Wish	Have	Date	Qty	Paid Each	Total
54954	Fun At The Firehouse	1998	Current	27.50	27.50	○					
54955	Farmer's Flatbed	1998	Current	17.50	17.50	○					
54956	Catch Of The Day, The	1998	Current	30	30	○					
54957	Christmas Visit To The Florist	1998	Current	30	30	○					
54958	Santa Comes To Town, 1999	1998	1999 Annual	30	30	○					
54959	Village Service Vehicles	1998	Current	45	45	○					
54970	Quality Service At Ford®	1998	Current	27.50	27.50	○					
54971	Patrolling The Road	1998	Current	20	20	○					
54972	Couldn't Wait Until Christmas	1998	Current	17	17	○					
54973	Costumes For Sale	1998	Current	60	60	○					
54974	Uncle Sam's Fireworks Stand	1998	Event Piece 1999	45	45	○					
54975	Harley-Davidson® Water Tower	1998	Current	37.50	37.50	○					
54976	...Another Man's Treasure Accessories	1998	Current	27.50	27.50	○					
	OSVA Page 6 Totals:			414.50	414.50						
	OSVA Page 1 Totals:			276.50	1,637.00						
	OSVA Page 2 Totals:			526.50	1,668.00						
	OSVA Page 3 Totals:			665.00	908.00						
	OSVA Page 4 Totals:			823.50	1,023.00						
	OSVA Page 5 Totals:			823.50	857.00						
	OSVA Page 6 Totals:			414.50	414.50						
	OSVA Grand Totals:			3,529.50	6,507.50						

CAROLERS

ITEM #	INTRO	RETIRED	OSRP	GBTʀᴜ	↑
5064-1	1979	1986	$12	**$135**	8%

Set of 4. Couple, girl, garlanded lamppost, snowman.
Notable: First people in the Village and first accessory.

DATE: ____ $ ____		'91	'92	'93	'94	'95	'96	'97	'98
○ Wɪsʜ	○ Hᴀᴠᴇ	$95	105	110	125	125	125	125	125

CERAMIC CAR

ITEM #	INTRO	RETIRED	OSRP	GBTʀᴜ	↓
5069-0	1980	1986	$5	**$45**	25%

First vehicle, no other cars were available until 1985.
Open roadster holds lap rugs, Christmas tree and wrapped presents.
Notable: Did not come in a box.

DATE: ____ $ ____		'91	'92	'93	'94	'95	'96	'97	'98
○ Wɪsʜ	○ Hᴀᴠᴇ	$20	42	48	52	50	55	60	60

CERAMIC SLEIGH

ITEM #	INTRO	RETIRED	OSRP	GBTʀᴜ	↓
5079-2	1981	1986	$5	**$45**	25%

Patterned after old-fashioned wood sleigh, holds Christmas tree and wrapped presents.
Notable: Did not come in a box.

DATE: ____ $ ____		'91	'92	'93	'94	'95	'96	'97	'98
○ Wɪsʜ	○ Hᴀᴠᴇ	$20	52	55	55	55	55	65	60

SNOWMAN WITH BROOM

ITEM #	INTRO	RETIRED	OSRP	GBTʀᴜ	↓
5018-0	1982	1990	$3	**$12**	20%

Snowman with top hat and red nose holds straw broom.

DATE: ____ $ ____		'91	'92	'93	'94	'95	'96	'97	'98
○ Wɪsʜ	○ Hᴀᴠᴇ	$10	15	15	15	10	12	12	15

MONKS-A-CAROLING

ITEM #	INTRO	RETIRED	OSRP	GBTRU	↓
6460-2	1982	N/A	$6	**$195**	5%

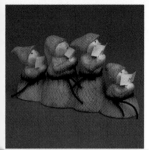

Notable: These original four friars singing carols were giftware adopted as an Original Snow Village® piece by collectors. The piece is unglazed, the Monks carry paper song books and have real cord for sashes.

DATE: ___ $ ___		'97	'98
○ Wish ○ Have		$200	205

MONKS-A-CAROLING

ITEM #	INTRO	RETIRED	OSRP	GBTRU	↑
6459-9	1983	1984	$6	**$75**	15%

Notable: This is the 2nd *Monks-A-Caroling.* It was retired after one year due to the maker's inability to supply. This version is slightly smaller than the giftware piece, glazed, and the Monks carry ceramic songbooks and have painted-on rope sashes. The diffused rosy blush in the Monks' cheeks differentiate this piece from the 3rd Version Monks (1984, Item #5040-7 from another supplier).

DATE: ___ $ ___	'91	'92	'93	'94	'95	'96	'97	'98
○ Wish ○ Have	$70	70	75	75	70	65	65	65

SCOTTIE WITH TREE

ITEM #	INTRO	RETIRED	OSRP	GBTRU	↓
5038-5	1984	1985	$3	**$160**	9%

A black dog waits by a snow-covered tree.
Notable: Some pieces have a white star on top of the tree.

DATE: ___ $ ___	'91	'92	'93	'94	'95	'96	'97	'98
○ Wish ○ Have	$95	115	132	140	150	165	165	175

MONKS-A-CAROLING

ITEM #	INTRO	RETIRED	OSRP	GBTRU	↓
5040-7	1984	1988	$6	**$50**	23%

Notable: Replaced the 1983 *Monks-A-Caroling,* Item #6459-9. On this piece the Monks have a distinct pink circle to give the cheeks blush.

DATE: ___ $ ___	'91	'92	'93	'94	'95	'96	'97	'98
○ Wish ○ Have	$25	25	30	38	40	38	50	65

SINGING NUNS

ITEM # 5053-9	INTRO 1985	RETIRED 1987	OSRP $6	GBTRU **$120**	↓ 8%

Four nuns in habits, sing carols.

DATE: ____ $ ____		'91	'92	'93	'94	'95	'96	'97	'98
○ WISH ○ HAVE		$65	75	85	105	125	130	135	130

AUTO WITH TREE– "SQUASHED"

ITEM # 5055-5	INTRO 1985	RETIRED VARIATION	OSRP $5	GBTRU **$90**	NO CHANGE

Notable: First Version of red VW Beetle with sisal tree strapped to roof looks as if the tree's weight crushed the car. Did not come in a box.

DATE: ____ $ ____	'97	'98
○ WISH ○ HAVE	$75	90

AUTO WITH TREE

	RETIRED CURRENT	OSRP $5	GBTRU **$6.50**	NO CHANGE

Notable: Second Version of red VW Beetle with sisal tree strapped to roof. Did not come in a box.

DATE: ____ $ ____	'91	'92	'93	'94	'95	'96	'97	'98
○ WISH ○ HAVE	$6.50	6.50	6.50	6.50	6.50	6.50	6.50	6.50

SNOW KIDS SLED, SKIS

ITEM # 5056-3	INTRO 1985	RETIRED 1987	OSRP $11	GBTRU **$38**	↓ 24%

Set of 2. Three children on a toboggan and one child on skis.
Notable: See *Snow Kids,* 1987, Item #5113-6, for these kids as part of a set of 4 in a scaled down size.

DATE: ____ $ ____	'91	'92	'93	'94	'95	'96	'97	'98
○ WISH ○ HAVE	$20	48	48	50	50	50	55	50

FAMILY MOM/KIDS, GOOSE/GIRL–"LARGE"

ITEM #	INTRO	RETIRED	OSRP	GBTRU	↓
5057-1	1985	1988	$11	$28	44%

Set of 2. Mother holds hands of two children, one girl feeds corn to geese.
Notable: First Version. This is the original larger size. By 1987 the piece was downscaled.

DATE: ____ $ ____	'91	'92	'93	'94	'95	'96	'97	'98
○ WISH ○ HAVE	$30	35	35	45	45	48	42	50

FAMILY MOM/KIDS, GOOSE/GIRL–"SMALL"

	GBTRU	↓
	$26	42%

Set of 2.
Notable: Second Version. This is the downscaled version. In addition to being smaller, there is more detail in the pieces.

DATE: ____ $ ____	'91	'92	'93	'94	'95	'96	'97	'98
○ WISH ○ HAVE	$30	35	35	45	45	48	42	45

SANTA/MAILBOX–"LARGE"

ITEM #	INTRO	RETIRED	OSRP	GBTRU	↓
5059-8	1985	1988	$11	$40	27%

Set of 2. Santa with toy bag and girl mails letter to Santa as dog watches.
Notable: First Version. This is the original larger size. Girl has brown hair. By 1987 the piece was downscaled. 1997 was the first year we tracked secondary market performance separately.

DATE: ____ $ ____	'91	'92	'93	'94	'95	'96	'97	'98
○ WISH ○ HAVE	$25	40	46	48	50	53	60	55

SANTA/MAILBOX–"SMALL"

	GBTRU	↓
	$40	20%

Set of 2.
Notable: Second Version. This is the downscaled version. In addition to being shorter, Santa and the girl are also trimmer. In this version the girl has blonde hair. 1997 was the first year we tracked secondary market performance separately.

DATE: ____ $ ____	'91	'92	'93	'94	'95	'96	'97	'98
○ WISH ○ HAVE	$25	40	46	48	50	53	57	50

KIDS AROUND THE TREE— "LARGE"

ITEM #	INTRO	RETIRED	OSRP	GBTRU	↓
5094-6	1986	1990	$15	**$45**	25%

Children join hands to make a ring around the snow-covered tree with a gold star.
Notable: First Version of *Kids Around The Tree*. This is the original larger size, 5 3/4" in height. By 1987 the piece was dramatically downscaled.

DATE: ___ $ ___	'91	'92	'93	'94	'95	'96	'97	'98
○ WISH ○ HAVE	$60	60	60	70	60	60	55	60

KIDS AROUND THE TREE— "SMALL"

	GBTRU	↓
	$35	24%

Notable: Second Version of *Kids Around The Tree*. This is the downscaled version, 4 1/2" in height.

DATE: ___ $ ___	'91	'92	'93	'94	'95	'96	'97	'98
○ WISH ○ HAVE	$30	32	32	40	35	38	40	46

GIRL/SNOWMAN, BOY

ITEM #	INTRO	RETIRED	OSRP	GBTRU	↓
5095-4	1986	1987	$11	**$50**	31%

Set of 2. Girl puts finishing touches on snowman as boy reaches to place decorated hat atop head.
Notable: See *Snow Kids,* 1987, Item #5113-6, for these kids as part of a set of 4 in a scaled down size.

DATE: ___ $ ___	'91	'92	'93	'94	'95	'96	'97	'98
○ WISH ○ HAVE	$35	50	55	70	70	62	65	72

NOTES: _____

_____

_____

_____

_____

_____

SHOPPING GIRLS WITH PACKAGES—"LARGE"

ITEM #	INTRO	RETIRED	OSRP	GBTRU	↓
5096-2	1986	1988	$11	**$45**	10%

Set of 2. Girls dressed toasty for shopping with hats, mittens, coats, boots, stand by some of their wrapped packages.
Notable: First Version. This is the original larger size–3" in height. By 1987 the piece was downscaled. 1997 was the first year we tracked secondary market performance separately.

DATE: ____ $ ____	'91	'92	'93	'94	'95	'96	'97	'98
○ WISH ○ HAVE	$25	35	38	44	45	48	50	50

SHOPPING GIRLS WITH PACKAGES—"SMALL"

	GBTRU	↓
	$35	22%

Set of 2.
Notable: Second Version. This is the downscaled version– 2 3/4" in height. 1997 was the first year we tracked secondary market performance separately.

DATE: ____ $ ____	'91	'92	'93	'94	'95	'96	'97	'98
○ WISH ○ HAVE	$25	35	38	44	45	48	47	45

SNOW VILLAGE HOUSE FOR SALE SIGN

ITEM #	INTRO	RETIRED	OSRP	GBTRU
NONE	1987	N/A	GIFT	$25

Notable: This sign was given to dealers who attended trade shows and showrooms around the country. It was never intended for resale and is one of the rarest Original Snow Village® accessories. It came packed in a blister pack.

DATE: ____ $ ____	'91	'92	'93	'94	'95	'96	'97	'98
○ WISH ○ HAVE	NE	NE	NE	NE	NE	NE	NE	NE

3 NUNS WITH SONGBOOKS

ITEM #	INTRO	RETIRED	OSRP	GBTRU	↓
5102-0	1987	1988	$6	**$125**	11%

Three nuns in habits standing side-by-side carry songbooks to sing carols.

DATE: ____ $ ____	'91	'92	'93	'94	'95	'96	'97	'98
○ WISH ○ HAVE	$50	75	95	115	125	128	135	140

PRAYING MONKS

Item #	Intro	Retired	OSRP	GBTru	↓
5103-9	1987	1988	$6	**$40**	17%

Three monks, standing side-by-side, praying.

Date: ___ $ ___		'91	'92	'93	'94	'95	'96	'97	'98
○ Wish ○ Have		$30	32	42	42	40	44	50	48

CHILDREN IN BAND

Item #	Intro	Retired	OSRP	GBTru	↓
5104-7	1987	1989	$15	**$27**	23%

One child conducts three band players: horn, drum and tuba.

Date: ___ $ ___		'91	'92	'93	'94	'95	'96	'97	'98
○ Wish ○ Have		$25	35	28	24	25	32	30	35

CAROLING FAMILY

Item #	Intro	Retired	OSRP	GBTru	↓
5105-5	1987	1990	$20	**$24**	31%

Set of 3. Father holds baby, mother and son, and girl with pup.

Date: ___ $ ___		'91	'92	'93	'94	'95	'96	'97	'98
○ Wish ○ Have		$25	35	30	32	30	28	35	35

TAXI CAB

Item #	Intro	Retired	OSRP	GBTru	NO
5106-3	1987	Current	$6	**$6.50**	CHANGE

Yellow Checker cab.

Date: ___ $ ___		'91	'92	'93	'94	'95	'96	'97	'98
○ Wish ○ Have		$6.50	6.50	6.50	6.50	6.50	6.50	6.50	6.50

CHRISTMAS CHILDREN

ITEM #	INTRO	RETIRED	OSRP	GBTRU	↓
5107-1	1987	1990	$20	**$22**	37%

Set of 4. Children at outdoor activities: girl and pup on sled, boy, girl holding wreath and girl feeding carrot to bunny.

DATE: ___ $ ___		'91	'92	'93	'94	'95	'96	'97	'98
○ WISH ○ HAVE		$25	35	35	30	30	35	35	35

HOUSE FOR SALE SIGN

ITEM #	INTRO	RETIRED	OSRP	GBTRU	NO
5108-0	1987	1989	$3.50	**$10**	CHANGE

First "For Sale Sign." This ceramic sign is trimmed with holly.
Notable: See also *For Sale Sign,* 1989 Item #5166-7.

DATE: ___ $ ___		'91	'92	'93	'94	'95	'96	'97	'98
○ WISH ○ HAVE		$8	12	12	10	10	10	10	10

HOUSE FOR SALE SIGN— "GCC BLANK"

ITEM #	INTRO	RETIRED	OSRP	GBTRU	↓
581-9	1987	PROMO	*	**$10**	55%

Notable: Gift Creations Concepts (GCC) 1989 Christmas Catalog Exclusive, *free with any $100 Department 56® purchase. Holly trims blank sign for personalization.

DATE: ___ $ ___	'97	'98
○ WISH ○ HAVE	$25	22

SNOW KIDS

ITEM #	INTRO	RETIRED	OSRP	GBTRU	↓
5113-6	1987	1990	$20	**$32**	43%

Set of 4. Three kids on toboggan, child on skis, boy and girl putting finishing touches on snowman.
Notable: Incorporates *Snow Kids Sled, Skis,* 1985, Item #5056-3, and *Girl/Snowman, Boy,* 1986, Item #5095-4, re-scaled to the smaller size.

DATE: ___ $ ___		'91	'92	'93	'94	'95	'96	'97	'98
○ WISH ○ HAVE		$30	52	52	48	45	50	55	56

MAN ON LADDER HANGING GARLAND

ITEM #	INTRO	RETIRED	OSRP	GBTRU	↓
5116-0	1988	1992	$7.50	**$14**	26%

Man carries garland up ladder to decorate eaves of house. Man is ceramic, ladder is wooden, garland is sisal.

DATE: ____ $ ____	'91	'92	'93	'94	'95	'96	'97	'98
○ WISH ○ HAVE	$8	8	18	16	18	16	16	19

HAYRIDE

ITEM #	INTRO	RETIRED	OSRP	GBTRU	↓
5117-9	1988	1990	$30	**$55**	19%

Farmer guides horse-drawn hay-filled sleigh with children as riders.

DATE: ____ $ ____	'91	'92	'93	'94	'95	'96	'97	'98
○ WISH ○ HAVE	$45	65	70	65	60	60	60	68

SCHOOL CHILDREN

ITEM #	INTRO	RETIRED	OSRP	GBTRU	↓
5118-7	1988	1990	$15	**$30**	6%

Set of 3. Three children carrying school books.

DATE: ____ $ ____	'91	'92	'93	'94	'95	'96	'97	'98
○ WISH ○ HAVE	$20	30	25	28	25	25	30	32

APPLE GIRL/NEWSPAPER BOY

ITEM #	INTRO	RETIRED	OSRP	GBTRU	↓
5129-2	1988	1990	$11	**$15**	40%

Set of 2. Girl holds wood tray carrier selling apples for 5¢, newsboy sells the Village News.

DATE: ____ $ ____	'91	'92	'93	'94	'95	'96	'97	'98
○ WISH ○ HAVE	$20	25	20	22	20	22	22	25

WOODSMAN AND BOY

ITEM #	INTRO	RETIRED	OSRP	GBTRU	↓
5130-6	1988	1991	$13	**$24**	33%

Set of 2. Man chops and splits logs and boy prepares to carry supply to fireplace.

DATE: ____ $ ____		'91	'92	'93	'94	'95	'96	'97	'98
○ WISH ○ HAVE		$13	26	22	25	30	30	30	36

DOGHOUSE/ CAT IN GARBAGE CAN

ITEM #	INTRO	RETIRED	OSRP	GBTRU	↓
5131-4	1988	1992	$15	**$25**	17%

Set of 2. Dog sits outside doghouse decorated with wreath; cat looks at empty boxes and wrappings in garbage can.

DATE: ____ $ ____		'91	'92	'93	'94	'95	'96	'97	'98
○ WISH ○ HAVE		$15	15	30	30	25	27	27	30

FIRE HYDRANT & MAILBOX

ITEM #	INTRO	RETIRED	OSRP	GBTRU	↑
5132-2	1988	1998	$6	**$8**	33%

Set of 2. Red fire hydrant and rural curbside mailbox on post.

DATE: ____ $ ____		'91	'92	'93	'94	'95	'96	'97	'98
○ WISH ○ HAVE		$6	6	6	6	6	6	6	6

WATER TOWER

ITEM #	INTRO	RETIRED	OSRP	GBTRU	↓
5133-0	1988	1991	$20	**$75**	17%

2 pieces. Metal scaffold base holds red ceramic Original Snow Village® water container with green top, ladder leads to top.

DATE: ____ $ ____		'91	'92	'93	'94	'95	'96	'97	'98
○ WISH ○ HAVE		$22	48	48	52	65	70	75	90

WATER TOWER– "JOHN DEERE"

ITEM #	INTRO	RETIRED	OSRP	GBTru	↑
2510-4	1988	PROMO	$24	**$675**	8%

Notable: Special piece, *John Deere Water Tower* is exactly the same as the *Original Snow Village® Water Tower* with the exception that it reads, "Moline Home of John Deere." It was offered for sale through the John Deere catalog.

DATE: ___ $ ___	'91	'92	'93	'94	'95	'96	'97	'98
○ WISH ○ HAVE	$125	125	150	395	650	675	695	625

NATIVITY

ITEM #	INTRO	RETIRED	OSRP	GBTru	NO
5135-7	1988	CURRENT	$7.50	**$7.50**	CHANGE

Holy Family, lamb, in crèche scene.

DATE: ___ $ ___	'91	'92	'93	'94	'95	'96	'97	'98
○ WISH ○ HAVE	$7.50	7.50	7.50	7.50	7.50	7.50	7.50	7.50

WOODY STATION WAGON

ITEM #	INTRO	RETIRED	OSRP	GBTru	↓
5136-5	1988	1990	$6.50	**$28**	20%

"Wood" paneled sides on station wagon.

DATE: ___ $ ___	'91	'92	'93	'94	'95	'96	'97	'98
○ WISH ○ HAVE	$12	20	22	30	25	25	30	35

SCHOOL BUS, SNOW PLOW

ITEM #	INTRO	RETIRED	OSRP	GBTru	↓
5137-3	1988	1991	$16	**$50**	25%

Set of 2. Yellow school bus and red sand gravel truck with snow plow.

DATE: ___ $ ___	'91	'92	'93	'94	'95	'96	'97	'98
○ WISH ○ HAVE	$16	25	25	55	50	57	55	67

TREE LOT

ITEM #	INTRO	RETIRED	OSRP	GBTRU	NO
5138-1	1988	CURRENT	$33.50	**$37.50**	CHANGE

Christmas lights on tree lot's fence plus decorated shack and trees for sale. The shack is ceramic, the fence is wood and the trees are sisal.

DATE: ____ $ ____	'91	'92	'93	'94	'95	'96	'97	'98
○ WISH ○ HAVE	$37.50	37.50	37.50	37.50	37.50	37.50	37.50	37.50

SISAL TREE LOT

ITEM #	INTRO	RETIRED	OSRP	GBTRU	↓
8183-3	1988	1991	$45	**$78**	13%

A variety of cut trees for sale at a street lot. Signs identify the trees in each row.

DATE: ____ $ ____	'91	'92	'93	'94	'95	'96	'97	'98
○ WISH ○ HAVE	$45	80	85	85	75	85	95	90

VILLAGE GAZEBO

ITEM #	INTRO	RETIRED	OSRP	GBTRU	↓
5146-2	1989	1995	$27	**$35**	17%

Small, open, red roofed garden structure that will protect folks from rain and snow, or be a private place to sit.

DATE: ____ $ ____	'91	'92	'93	'94	'95	'96	'97	'98
○ WISH ○ HAVE	$27.50	28	30	30	30	42	40	42

CHOIR KIDS

ITEM #	INTRO	RETIRED	OSRP	GBTRU	↓
5147-0	1989	1992	$15	**$20**	33%

Four kids in white and red robes with green songbooks, caroling.

DATE: ____ $ ____	'91	'92	'93	'94	'95	'96	'97	'98
○ WISH ○ HAVE	$15	15	20	28	25	25	28	30

SPECIAL DELIVERY

ITEM #	INTRO	RETIRED	OSRP	GBTRU	↓
5148-9	1989	1990	$16	**$45**	21%

Set of 2. Mailman and mailbag with his mail truck in USPO colors of red, white and blue with the eagle logo.
Notable: Discontinued due to licensing problems with the U.S. Postal Service. Replaced with 1990, *Special Delivery*, Item #5197-7.

DATE: ___ $ ___	'91	'92	'93	'94	'95	'96	'97	'98
○ WISH ○ HAVE	$45	42	42	42	45	40	50	57

FOR SALE SIGN

ITEM #	INTRO	RETIRED	OSRP	GBTRU	NO
5166-7	1989	1998	$4.50	**$4.50**	CHANGE

Enameled metal sign can advertise "For Sale" or "SOLD" depending which side is displayed. Birds decorate and add color.

DATE: ___ $ ___	'91	'92	'93	'94	'95	'96	'97	'98
○ WISH ○ HAVE	$4.50	4.50	4.50	4.50	4.50	4.50	4.50	4.50

FOR SALE SIGN— "BACHMAN'S®"

ITEM #	INTRO	RETIRED	OSRP	GBTRU	↑
539-8	1989	PROMO	$4.50	**$26**	4%

Enameled metal sign reads "Bachman's Village Gathering 1990". Birds decorate and add color.
Notable: Bachman's® Exclusive for their Village Gathering in 1990.

DATE: ___ $ ___	'96	'97	'98
○ WISH ○ HAVE	$25	25	25

STREET SIGN

ITEM #	INTRO	RETIRED	OSRP	GBTRU	NO
5167-5	1989	1992	$7.50	**$12**	CHANGE

6 pieces per package. Green metal street signs. Use the street names provided (Lake St., Maple Dr., Park Ave., River Rd., Elm St., Ivy Lane...) or personalize to give each village street a unique name.

DATE: ___ $ ___	'91	'92	'93	'94	'95	'96	'97	'98
○ WISH ○ HAVE	$7.50	7.50	NE	8	8	12	10	12

KIDS TREE HOUSE

ITEM #	INTRO	RETIRED	OSRP	GBTRU	↓
5168-3	1989	1991	$25	**$50**	23%

Decorated club house built on an old dead tree. Steps lead up to the hideaway. Material is resin.

DATE: ___ $ ___	'91	'92	'93	'94	'95	'96	'97	'98
○ WISH ○ HAVE	$25	48	45	45	50	55	60	65

BRINGING HOME THE TREE

ITEM #	INTRO	RETIRED	OSRP	GBTRU	↓
5169-1	1989	1992	$15	**$20**	29%

A man pulls a sled holding the tree as the girl watches to make sure it doesn't fall off. Tree is sisal.

DATE: ___ $ ___	'91	'92	'93	'94	'95	'96	'97	'98
○ WISH ○ HAVE	$15	15	20	22	25	27	25	28

SKATE FASTER MOM

ITEM #	INTRO	RETIRED	OSRP	GBTRU	↓
5170-5	1989	1991	$13	**$25**	11%

Two children sit in the sleigh as their skating Mom pushes them across the ice.

DATE: ___ $ ___	'91	'92	'93	'94	'95	'96	'97	'98
○ WISH ○ HAVE	$13	30	28	24	20	28	30	28

CRACK THE WHIP

ITEM #	INTRO	RETIRED	OSRP	GBTRU	↓
5171-3	1989	1996	$25	**$27**	10%

Set of 3. A fast moving line of skaters hold tightly to the person in front of them. The first person does slow patterns but as the line snakes out, the last people are racing to keep up and they whip out.

DATE: ___ $ ___	'91	'92	'93	'94	'95	'96	'97	'98
○ WISH ○ HAVE	$25	25	25	25	25	25	32	30

THROUGH THE WOODS

ITEM #	INTRO	RETIRED	OSRP	GBTRU	↓
5172-1	1989	1991	$18	$22	27%

Set of 2. Children bring a tree and a basket of goodies to Grandma.

DATE: _____ $ _____
○ WISH   ○ HAVE

'91	'92	'93	'94	'95	'96	'97	'98
$18	30	30	22	25	23	28	30

STATUE OF MARK TWAIN

ITEM #	INTRO	RETIRED	OSRP	GBTRU	↓
5173-0	1989	1991	$15	$28	38%

A tribute to the author who wrote about lives of American folk.

DATE: _____ $ _____
○ WISH   ○ HAVE

'91	'92	'93	'94	'95	'96	'97	'98
$15	28	28	30	30	35	40	45

CALLING ALL CARS

ITEM #	INTRO	RETIRED	OSRP	GBTRU	↑
5174-8	1989	1991	$15	$75	7%

Set of 2. Police car and patrolman directing traffic.

DATE: _____ $ _____
○ WISH   ○ HAVE

'91	'92	'93	'94	'95	'96	'97	'98
$15	32	30	30	35	35	65	70

FLAG POLE

ITEM #	INTRO	RETIRED	OSRP	GBTRU	
5177-2	1989	CURRENT	$8.50	$8.50	NO CHANGE

Resin base, metal pole, cloth flag and thread rope.

DATE: _____ $ _____
○ WISH   ○ HAVE

'91	'92	'93	'94	'95	'96	'97	'98
$8.50	8.50	8.50	8.50	8.50	8.50	8.50	8.50

MAILBOX

ITEM #	INTRO	RETIRED	OSRP	GBTRU	↓
5179-9	1989	1990	$3.50	**$15**	25%

Freestanding public mailbox in USPO colors, red, white and blue with logo.
Notable: Discontinued due to licensing problems with the U.S. Postal Service. Replaced with 1990 *Mailbox,* Item #5198-5.

DATE: ____ $ ____	'91	'92	'93	'94	'95	'96	'97	'98
○ WISH ○ HAVE	$20	20	15	20	20	20	20	20

SNOW VILLAGE PROMOTIONAL SIGN

ITEM #	INTRO	RETIRED	OSRP	GBTRU	NO
9948-1	1989	1990	PROMO	**$25**	CHANGE

Sign displays the Original Snow Village® logo. Brickwork at the base supports the sign. Earthenware.
Notable: Intended to be used by Department 56, Inc. retailers as a promotional item.

DATE: ____ $ ____	'95	'96	'97	'98
○ WISH ○ HAVE	$15	20	22	25

KIDS DECORATING THE VILLAGE SIGN

ITEM #	INTRO	RETIRED	OSRP	GBTRU	↓
5134-9	1990	1993	$12.50	**$25**	4%

Two children place garland on a Original Snow Village® sign.

DATE: ____ $ ____	'91	'92	'93	'94	'95	'96	'97	'98
○ WISH ○ HAVE	$12.50	12.50	12.50	21	20	22	22	26

DOWN THE CHIMNEY HE GOES

ITEM #	INTRO	RETIRED	OSRP	GBTRU	↓
5158-6	1990	1993	$6.50	**$9**	40%

Santa with a big bag of toys enters chimney to make delivery on Christmas Eve. Chimney can be attached to a house rooftop.

DATE: ____ $ ____	'91	'92	'93	'94	'95	'96	'97	'98
○ WISH ○ HAVE	$6.50	6.50	6.50	14	14	15	15	15

SNO-JET SNOWMOBILE

ITEM #	INTRO	RETIRED	OSRP	GBTRU	↓
5159-4	1990	1993	$15	$24	14%

Red and silver trimmed snowmobile with front ski runners and rear caterpillar treads.

DATE: ____ $ ____		'91	'92	'93	'94	'95	'96	'97	'98
○ WISH	○ HAVE	$15	15	15	24	24	25	25	28

SLEIGHRIDE

ITEM #	INTRO	RETIRED	OSRP	GBTRU	↓
5160-8	1990	1992	$30	$50	17%

Family rides in open old-fashioned green sleigh pulled by one horse.

DATE: ____ $ ____		'91	'92	'93	'94	'95	'96	'97	'98
○ WISH	○ HAVE	$30	30	52	54	55	50	60	60

HERE WE COME A CAROLING

ITEM #	INTRO	RETIRED	OSRP	GBTRU	NO
5161-6	1990	1992	$18	$30	CHANGE

Set of 3. Children and pet dog sing carols.

DATE: ____ $ ____		'91	'92	'93	'94	'95	'96	'97	'98
○ WISH	○ HAVE	$18	18	25	25	25	24	28	30

HOME DELIVERY

ITEM #	INTRO	RETIRED	OSRP	GBTRU	↓
5162-4	1990	1992	$16	$25	34%

Set of 2. Milkman and milk truck.

DATE: ____ $ ____		'91	'92	'93	'94	'95	'96	'97	'98
○ WISH	○ HAVE	$16	16	30	30	30	33	35	38

FRESH FROZEN FISH

Item #	Intro	Retired	OSRP	GBTru	↓
5163-2	1990	1993	$20	**$40**	9%

Set of 2. Ice fisherman and ice house.

Date: ___ $ ___	'91	'92	'93	'94	'95	'96	'97	'98
○ Wish ○ Have	$20	20	20	35	35	36	42	44

A TREE FOR ME

Item #	Intro	Retired	OSRP	GBTru	↓
5164-0	1990	1995	$7.50	**$12**	20%

2 pieces per package. Ceramic snowman with top hat, corn cob pipe and red muffler carries his own small snow-covered sisal tree.

Date: ___ $ ___	'91	'92	'93	'94	'95	'96	'97	'98
○ Wish ○ Have	$7.50	7.50	8	8	8	14	12	15

A HOME FOR THE HOLIDAYS

Item #	Intro	Retired	OSRP	GBTru	↑
5165-9	1990	1996	$6.50	**$15**	25%

Birdhouse with blue bird sitting on roof. Pole is decorated with garland and there's a small snow-covered evergreen.

Date: ___ $ ___	'91	'92	'93	'94	'95	'96	'97	'98
○ Wish ○ Have	$6.50	6.50	7	7	7	7	10	12

SPECIAL DELIVERY

Item #	Intro	Retired	OSRP	GBTru	↓
5197-7	1990	1992	$16	**$27**	36%

Set of 2. The Original Snow Village® postman and truck in red and green Snow Village Mail Service colors.
Notable: "S.V. Mail Service" replaced the discontinued 1985 *Special Delivery,* Item #5148-9. (Postman remained the same, only the truck changed.)

Date: ___ $ ___	'91	'92	'93	'94	'95	'96	'97	'98
○ Wish ○ Have	$16	16	22	38	35	36	36	42

VILLAGE MAIL BOX

ITEM #	INTRO	RETIRED	OSRP	GBTRU	NO
5198-5	1990	1998	$3.50	**$3.50**	CHANGE

The Original Snow Village® mail receptacle in red and green Snow Village Mail Service colors.
Notable: "S.V. Mail" replaced the discontinued 1985 *Mailbox*, Item #5179-9.

DATE: ___	$ ___	'91	'92	'93	'94	'95	'96	'97	'98
○ WISH	○ HAVE	$3.50	3.50	3.50	3.50	3.50	3.50	3.50	3.50

WREATHS FOR SALE

ITEM #	INTRO	RETIRED	OSRP	GBTRU	↓
5408-9	1991	1994	$27.50	**$28**	38%

Set of 4. Girl holds for sale sign, boy holds up wreaths, child pulls sled. Fence holds wreaths. Materials are ceramic, wood and sisal.

DATE: ___	$ ___	'91	'92	'93	'94	'95	'96	'97	'98
○ WISH	○ HAVE	$27.50	27.50	27.50	27.50	45	40	40	45

WINTER FOUNTAIN

ITEM #	INTRO	RETIRED	OSRP	GBTRU	↓
5409-7	1991	1993	$25	**$50**	19%

Angel holds sea shell with water frozen as it flowed. Materials are ceramic and acrylic.

DATE: ___	$ ___	'91	'92	'93	'94	'95	'96	'97	'98
○ WISH	○ HAVE	$25	25	25	45	50	50	55	62

COLD WEATHER SPORTS

ITEM #	INTRO	RETIRED	OSRP	GBTRU	↓
5410-0	1991	1994	$27.50	**$32**	24%

Set of 4. Three children play ice hockey.

DATE: ___	$ ___	'91	'92	'93	'94	'95	'96	'97	'98
○ WISH	○ HAVE	$27.50	27.50	27.50	27.50	45	45	45	42

Come Join The Parade

Item #	Intro	Retired	OSRP	GBTru	NO
5411-9	1991	1992	$12.50	**$20**	CHANGE

Two children carry parade banner.

Date: ____ $ ____	'91	'92	'93	'94	'95	'96	'97	'98
○ Wish ○ Have	$12.50	12.50	22	18	20	20	22	20

Village Marching Band

Item #	Intro	Retired	OSRP	GBTru	↓
5412-7	1991	1992	$30	**$54**	19%

Set of 3. Drum major, two horn players and two drummers.

Date: ____ $ ____	'91	'92	'93	'94	'95	'96	'97	'98
○ Wish ○ Have	$30	30	68	45	50	55	60	67

Christmas Cadillac

Item #	Intro	Retired	OSRP	GBTru	↓
5413-5	1991	1994	$9	**$12**	33%

Pink car holds sisal tree and presents.

Date: ____ $ ____	'91	'92	'93	'94	'95	'96	'97	'98
○ Wish ○ Have	$9	9	9	9	10	15	15	18

Snowball Fort

Item #	Intro	Retired	OSRP	GBTru	↓
5414-3	1991	1993	$27.50	**$36**	18%

Set of 3. One boy behind wall, one hides behind tree, one in open clearing, all with snowballs to throw.

Date: ____ $ ____	'91	'92	'93	'94	'95	'96	'97	'98
○ Wish ○ Have	$27.50	27.50	27.50	40	40	40	40	44

COUNTRY HARVEST

Item #	Intro	Retired	OSRP	GBTru	↓
5415-1	1991	1993	$13	**$22**	12%

Farm folk with market basket and pitchfork.
Notable: Reminiscent of Grant Wood's *American Gothic* painting.

DATE: ___ $ ___	'91	'92	'93	'94	'95	'96	'97	'98
○ Wish ○ Have	$13	13	13	25	25	18	27	25

VILLAGE USED CAR LOT

Item #	Intro	Retired	OSRP	GBTru	↑
5428-3	1992	1997	$45	**$60**	11%

Set of 5. Small office on a stone base with stone chimney. Attached tree. Free-standing sign plus office sign advertises used cars and good terms. Three cars in the lot.

DATE: ___ $ ___	'92	'93	'94	'95	'96	'97	'98
○ Wish ○ Have	$45	45	45	45	45	45	54

VILLAGE PHONE BOOTH

Item #	Intro	Retired	OSRP	GBTru	NO
5429-1	1992	CURRENT	$7.50	**$7.50**	CHANGE

Silver and red outdoor phone booth with accordion open/close doors.

DATE: ___ $ ___	'92	'93	'94	'95	'96	'97	'98
○ Wish ○ Have	$7.50	7.50	7.50	7.50	7.50	7.50	7.50

NANNY AND THE PRESCHOOLERS

Item #	Intro	Retired	OSRP	GBTru	↓
5430-5	1992	1994	$27.50	**$30**	21%

Set of 2. Two girls and a boy hold onto Nanny's shopping basket as she pushes carriage with baby.

DATE: ___ $ ___	'92	'93	'94	'95	'96	'97	'98
○ Wish ○ Have	$27.50	27.50	27.50	30	38	40	38

EARLY MORNING DELIVERY

ITEM #	INTRO	RETIRED	OSRP	GBTRU	↓
5431-3	1992	1995	$27.50	**$32**	24%

Set of 3. Village kids deliver morning newspaper. One tosses to house, one pushes sled, and Dalmatian holds next paper in mouth.

DATE: _____ $ _____
○ WISH ○ HAVE

	'92	'93	'94	'95	'96	'97	'98
	$27.50	27.50	27.50	27.50	34	40	42

CHRISTMAS PUPPIES

ITEM #	INTRO	RETIRED	OSRP	GBTRU	↓
5432-1	1992	1996	$27.50	**$30**	29%

Set of 2. One girl hugs a pup as two kids take box of pups for a ride in red wagon.

DATE: _____ $ _____
○ WISH ○ HAVE

	'92	'93	'94	'95	'96	'97	'98
	$27.50	27.50	27.50	27.50	27.50	40	42

ROUND & ROUND WE GO!

ITEM #	INTRO	RETIRED	OSRP	GBTRU	↓
5433-0	1992	1995	$18	**$22**	21%

Set of 2. Two kids go sledding on round saucer sleds.

DATE: _____ $ _____
○ WISH ○ HAVE

	'92	'93	'94	'95	'96	'97	'98
	$18	18	18	18	22	30	28

A HEAVY SNOW FALL

ITEM #	INTRO	RETIRED	OSRP	GBTRU	
5434-8	1992	CURRENT	$16	**$16**	NO CHANGE

Set of 2. Girl stops to look at bird perched on handle of her shovel as boy shovels snow off the walkway.

DATE: _____ $ _____
○ WISH ○ HAVE

	'92	'93	'94	'95	'96	'97	'98
	$16	16	16	16	16	16	16

WE'RE GOING TO A CHRISTMAS PAGEANT

ITEM #	INTRO	RETIRED	OSRP	GBTRU	↓
5435-6	1992	1994	$15	$21	16%

Children wear costumes of Santa, a decorated tree, and a golden star.

DATE: _____ $ _____
○ WISH   ○ HAVE

'92	'93	'94	'95	'96	'97	'98
$15	15	15	18	20	20	25

WINTER PLAYGROUND

ITEM #	INTRO	RETIRED	OSRP	GBTRU	↓
5436-4	1992	1995	$20	$30	17%

Two swings and a playground slide. Two trees and two birds complete the piece.

DATE: _____ $ _____
○ WISH   ○ HAVE

'92	'93	'94	'95	'96	'97	'98
$20	20	20	20	35	30	36

SPIRIT OF SNOW VILLAGE AIRPLANE

ITEM #	INTRO	RETIRED	OSRP	GBTRU	↓
5440-2	1992	1996	$32.50	$42	7%

Red prop biplane. Metal strap spring on three tree base allows positioning.

DATE: _____ $ _____
○ WISH   ○ HAVE

'92	'93	'94	'95	'96	'97	'98
$32.50	32.50	32.50	32.50	32.50	45	45

SAFETY PATROL

ITEM #	INTRO	RETIRED	OSRP	GBTRU	↓
5449-6	1993	1997	$27.50	$30	19%

Set of 4. Older children are safety guards at street crossing for two younger children.

DATE: _____ $ _____
○ WISH   ○ HAVE

'93	'94	'95	'96	'97	'98
$27.50	27.50	27.50	27.50	27.50	37

CHRISTMAS AT THE FARM

Item #	Intro	Retired	OSRP	GBTRU	↑
5450-0	1993	1996	$16	**$30**	11%

Set of 2. Calf and lamb greet girl carrying a pail of feed.

Date: ____ $ ____	'93	'94	'95	'96	'97	'98
○ Wish ○ Have	$16	16	16	16	28	27

CHECK IT OUT BOOKMOBILE

Item #	Intro	Retired	OSRP	GBTRU	↓
5451-8	1993	1995	$25	**$28**	15%

Set of 3. Bookmobile van carries library books to children in villages and farms. Boys and girls select the ones they want to borrow.

Date: ____ $ ____	'93	'94	'95	'96	'97	'98
○ Wish ○ Have	$25	25	25	28	35	33

TOUR THE VILLAGE

Item #	Intro	Retired	OSRP	GBTRU	↓
5452-6	1993	1997	$12.50	**$18**	10%

Tourist information booth with clerk to assist visitors new to the Village.
Notable: "Bayport" is misspelled. Has "q" instead of "p".

Date: ____ $ ____	'93	'94	'95	'96	'97	'98
○ Wish ○ Have	$12.50	12.50	12.50	12.50	12.50	20

PINT-SIZE PONY RIDES

Item #	Intro	Retired	OSRP	GBTRU	↓
5453-4	1993	1996	$37.50	**$40**	11%

Set of 3. One child waits to buy a pony ride as another rides and one offers a carrot to the pony. A stable building, bench and snow-covered tree complete the scene.

Date: ____ $ ____	'93	'94	'95	'96	'97	'98
○ Wish ○ Have	$37.50	37.50	37.50	37.50	45	45

PICK-UP AND DELIVERY

ITEM #	INTRO	RETIRED	OSRP	GBTRU	NO
5454-2	1993	CURRENT	$10	**$10**	CHANGE

Pick-up truck carries Christmas trees. **St. Nick's Promotional Piece: GBTru$ is $20.**

DATE: ____ $ ____		'93	'94	'95	'96	'97	'98
○ WISH ○ HAVE		$10	10	10	10	10	10

A HERD OF HOLIDAY HEIFERS

ITEM #	INTRO	RETIRED	OSRP	GBTRU	↓
5455-0	1993	1997	$18	**$25**	7%

Set of 3 Holstein cows.

DATE: ____ $ ____		'93	'94	'95	'96	'97	'98
○ WISH ○ HAVE		$18	18	18	18	18	27

CLASSIC CARS

ITEM #	INTRO	RETIRED	OSRP	GBTRU	↑
5457-7	1993	1998	$22.50	**$30**	33%

Set of 3. Station wagon with roof rack, two-tone green sedan with tail fins, sedan with spare tire mounted outside trunk.

DATE: ____ $ ____		'93	'94	'95	'96	'97	'98
○ WISH ○ HAVE		$22.50	22.50	22.50	22.50	22.50	22.50

SPIRIT OF SNOW VILLAGE AIRPLANE

ITEM #	INTRO	RETIRED	OSRP	GBTRU	↓
5458-5	1993	1996	$12.50	**$25**	11%

2 Assorted–blue or yellow. Propeller double strut winged planes.

DATE: ____ $ ____		'93	'94	'95	'96	'97	'98
○ WISH ○ HAVE		$12.50	12.50	12.50	12.50	22	28

VILLAGE NEWS DELIVERY

ITEM #	INTRO	RETIRED	OSRP	GBTru	↓
5459-3	1993	1996	$15	**$18**	36%

Set of 2. Driver carries newspapers from van to stores and home-delivery children carriers.

DATE: ____ $ ____	'93	'94	'95	'96	'97	'98
○ Wish ○ Have	$15	15	15	15	27	28

SUNDAY SCHOOL SERENADE

ITEM #	INTRO	RETIRED	OSRP	GBTru
5462-3*	1994	1996	*	*

Three children sing from a song book.
Notable: *This accessory is part of The Original Snow Village® *Starter Set*, 1994 Item #5462-3. It is not usually individually available on the secondary market.

DATE: ____ $ ____
○ Wish   ○ Have

CAROLING AT THE FARM

ITEM #	INTRO	RETIRED	OSRP	GBTru	NO
5463-1	1994	CURRENT	$35	**$35**	CHANGE

Midyear release. Farmer drives tractor pulling carolers on hay-covered wagon. One child pulls another onto the wagon.
Notable: First ceramic accessory to be a midyear release.

DATE: ____ $ ____	'94	'95	'96	'97	'98
○ Wish ○ Have	$35	35	35	35	35

STUCK IN THE SNOW

ITEM #	INTRO	RETIRED	OSRP	GBTru	↑
5471-2	1994	1998	$30	**$38**	27%

Set of 3. Dad pushes car, Mom watches while son holds shovel and sand.

DATE: ____ $ ____	'94	'95	'96	'97	'98
○ Wish ○ Have	$30	30	30	30	30

PETS ON PARADE

ITEM #	INTRO	RETIRED	OSRP	GBTRU	↑
5472-0	1994	1998	$16.50	**$20**	21%

Set of 2. Two children walk dogs on cold wintry day.

DATE: _____ $ _____
○ WISH   ○ HAVE

'94	'95	'96	'97	'98
$16.50	16.50	16.50	16.50	16.50

FEEDING THE BIRDS

ITEM #	INTRO	RETIRED	OSRP	GBTRU	↑
5473-9	1994	1997	$25	**$35**	25%

Set of 3. Woman and children are feeding birds as other birds sit on frozen birdbath.

DATE: _____ $ _____
○ WISH   ○ HAVE

'94	'95	'96	'97	'98
$25	25	25	25	28

MUSH!

ITEM #	INTRO	RETIRED	OSRP	GBTRU	↓
5474-7	1994	1997	$20	**$25**	11%

Set of 2. A small child sits on a sled that is harnessed to a St. Bernard. An older child shouts to them from behind the mailbox.

DATE: _____ $ _____
○ WISH   ○ HAVE

'94	'95	'96	'97	'98
$20	20	20	20	28

SKATERS & SKIERS

ITEM #	INTRO	RETIRED	OSRP	GBTRU	NO
5475-5	1994	CURRENT	$27.50	**$27.50**	CHANGE

Set of 3. One child laces up her skates while another is happy to be able to stand. As one skier looks on, another goes BOOM!

DATE: _____ $ _____
○ WISH   ○ HAVE

'94	'95	'96	'97	'98
$27.50	27.50	27.50	27.50	27.50

The Original Snow Village® Accessories

GOING TO THE CHAPEL

ITEM #	INTRO	RETIRED	OSRP	GBT RU	NO
5476-3	1994	CURRENT	$20	**$20**	CHANGE

Set of 2. Family walks to the chapel with gifts and a wreath as a clergyman waits to greet them.

DATE: ____ $ ____
○ WISH ○ HAVE

'94	'95	'96	'97	'98
$20	20	20	20	20

SANTA COMES TO TOWN, 1995

ITEM #	INTRO	RETIRED	OSRP	GBT RU	↓
5477-1	1994	1995 ANNUAL	$30	**$40**	15%

1st in a Series of Dated Annual Santa pieces. Children circle Santa as he passes out presents. He is holding a sack of toys and a book dated "1995."

DATE: ____ $ ____
○ WISH ○ HAVE

'94	'95	'96	'97	'98
$30	30	34	42	47

MARSHMALLOW ROAST

ITEM #	INTRO	RETIRED	OSRP	GBT RU	NO
5478-0	1994	CURRENT	$32.50	**$32.50**	CHANGE

Set of 3. Fire glows when lighted. Children take skating rest, roasting marshmallows over log fire.
Notable: Battery operated or can be used with Adapter, Item #5225-6.

DATE: ____ $ ____
○ WISH ○ HAVE

'94	'95	'96	'97	'98
$32.50	32.50	32.50	32.50	32.50

COCA–COLA® BRAND DELIVERY TRUCK

ITEM #	INTRO	RETIRED	OSRP	GBT RU	↑
5479-8	1994	1998	$15	**$25**	67%

Red and white Coca-Cola delivery truck with large wreath on the back.

DATE: ____ $ ____
○ WISH ○ HAVE

'94	'95	'96	'97	'98
$15	15	15	15	15

COCA–COLA® BRAND DELIVERY MEN

ITEM #	INTRO	RETIRED	OSRP	GBTRU	↑
5480-1	1994	1998	$25	$32	28%

Set of 2. One man carries crates to truck as another stops to enjoy a Coke.

DATE: _____ $ _____
○ WISH ○ HAVE

	'94	'95	'96	'97	'98
	$25	25	25	25	25

COCA–COLA® BRAND BILLBOARD

ITEM #	INTRO	RETIRED	OSRP	GBTRU	↑
5481-0	1994	1997	$18	$27	8%

Three lights "shine" on a billboard featuring Santa enjoying a Coke. Trees grow in the shade of the sign.

DATE: _____ $ _____
○ WISH ○ HAVE

	'94	'95	'96	'97	'98
	$18	18	18	18	25

A VISIT WITH SANTA

ITEM #	INTRO	RETIRED	OSRP	GBTRU	NO
VARIOUS	1995	PROMO	$25	$45	CHANGE

Mother and children meet Santa on the street. Mother has shopping bag. Gifts are stacked on the snow. Piece was crafted for specific stores. The store's logo is on the shopping bag. The retailers chose the colors for the gift packages.

The stores and individual Item Numbers are as follows:

Bachman's®	#754-4
Fortunoff	#767-6
Pine Cone Christmas Shop	#773-0
Stat's	#765-0
The Lemon Tree	#768-4
The Limited Edition	#764-1
William Glen	#766-8
Young's Ltd.	#769-2

DATE: _____ $ _____
○ WISH ○ HAVE

	'97	'98
	$60	45

FROSTY PLAYTIME

ITEM #	INTRO	RETIRED	OSRP	GBTRU	↑
54860	1995	1997	$30	**$45**	22%

Set of 3. Child rides on playground bouncing deer as another holds a hula hoop. Boys make snow and ice houses.

DATE: _____ $ _____
○ WISH ○ HAVE

'95	'96	'97	'98
$30	30	30	37

POINSETTIAS FOR SALE

ITEM #	INTRO	RETIRED	OSRP	GBTRU	↑
54861	1995	1998	$30	**$40**	33%

Set of 3. Vendor offers choice of plants to shoppers. Plants are made of felt rather than ceramic.

DATE: _____ $ _____
○ WISH ○ HAVE

'95	'96	'97	'98
$30	30	30	30

SANTA COMES TO TOWN, 1996

ITEM #	INTRO	RETIRED	OSRP	GBTRU	↓
54862	1995	1996 ANNUAL	$32.50	**$40**	11%

2nd in a Series of Dated Annual Santa pieces. Santa pulls sleigh loaded with gifts as children catch a ride.

DATE: _____ $ _____
○ WISH ○ HAVE

'95	'96	'97	'98
$32.50	32.50	40	45

CHOPPING FIREWOOD

ITEM #	INTRO	RETIRED	OSRP	GBTRU	NO CHANGE
54863	1995	CURRENT	$16.50	**$16.50**	

Set of 2. Father chops wood as son stacks into ventilated cords. Materials are ceramic and wood.

DATE: _____ $ _____
○ WISH ○ HAVE

'95	'96	'97	'98
$16.50	16.50	16.50	16.50

FIREWOOD DELIVERY TRUCK

ITEM #	INTRO	RETIRED	OSRP	GBTRU	NO
54864	1995	CURRENT	$15	**$15**	CHANGE

Holiday Farms truck loaded with firewood held in place by slatted wood panels.

DATE: ____ $ ____		'95	'96	'97	'98
○ WISH ○ HAVE		$15	15	15	15

SERVICE WITH A SMILE

ITEM #	INTRO	RETIRED	OSRP	GBTRU	↑
54865	1995	1998	$25	**$32**	28%

Set of 2. One attendant at car service station cleans windshield as other holds new tire.

DATE: ____ $ ____		'95	'96	'97	'98
○ WISH ○ HAVE		$25	25	25	25

PIZZA DELIVERY

ITEM #	INTRO	RETIRED	OSRP	GBTRU	↑
54866	1995	1998	$20	**$30**	50%

Set of 2. Pisa Pizza green VW bug auto used for home delivery of fresh pizzas. Delivery person carries stacked boxed pies plus additional take-out.

DATE: ____ $ ____		'95	'96	'97	'98
○ WISH ○ HAVE		$20	20	20	20

GRAND OLD OPRY CAROLERS

ITEM #	INTRO	RETIRED	OSRP	GBTRU	↑
54867	1995	1997	$25	**$36**	20%

Singer and musicians present carols country-style.

DATE: ____ $ ____		'95	'96	'97	'98
○ WISH ○ HAVE		$25	25	25	30

SNOW CARNIVAL ICE SCULPTURES

ITEM #	INTRO	RETIRED	OSRP	GBTRU	↑
54868	1995	1998	$27.50	**$36**	31%

Set of 2. Mother and child get set to photograph an ice angel sculpture as the artist puts the final touches on penguins and snowflakes sculpture.

DATE: _____ $ _____
○ WISH ○ HAVE

'95	'96	'97	'98
$27.50	27.50	27.50	27.50

SNOW CARNIVAL KING & QUEEN

ITEM #	INTRO	RETIRED	OSRP	GBTRU	↑
54869	1995	1998	$35	**$45**	29%

Snow King and Queen arrive in sled dog-drawn sleigh. King's scepter was often broken.

DATE: _____ $ _____
○ WISH ○ HAVE

'95	'96	'97	'98
$35	35	35	35

STARBUCKS® COFFEE CART

ITEM #	INTRO	RETIRED	OSRP	GBTRU	NO
54870	1995	CURRENT	$27.50	**$27.50**	CHANGE

Set of 2. Woman stops to purchase hot coffee from vendor with mobile cart.

DATE: _____ $ _____
○ WISH ○ HAVE

'95	'96	'97	'98
$27.50	27.50	27.50	27.50

JUST MARRIED

ITEM #	INTRO	RETIRED	OSRP	GBTRU	NO
54879	1995	CURRENT	$25	**$25**	CHANGE

Set of 2. Groom carries bride. Car is decorated in congratulatory balloons, tin cans and banner.

DATE: _____ $ _____
○ WISH ○ HAVE

'95	'96	'97	'98
$25	25	25	25

ITEM #	INTRO	RETIRED	OSRP	GBTru	↓
VARIOUS	1996	PROMO	$25	**$35**	22%

Three children follow Santa; one carries a gift wrapped present.

The following retailers had this piece personalized for their store:

Bachman's® .... #07744
Bronner's Wonderland .... #07745
Broughton Christmas Shoppe .... #07748
Calabash Nautical Gifts .... #07753
Carson Pirie Scott .... #07763
Dickens' Gift Shoppe .... #07750
European Imports .... #07762
Fibber Magee's .... #07747
Fortunoff .... #07741
Gustaf's .... #07759
Ingle's Nook .... #07754
North Pole City .... #07742
Pine Cone Christmas Shop .... #07740
Royal Dutch Collectibles .... #07760
Russ Country Gardens .... #07756
St. Nick's .... #07757
Seventh Avenue .... #07758
Stat's .... #07749 ($45)
The Cabbage Rose .... #07752
The Calico Butterfly .... #07751
The Christmas Loft .... #07755
The Limited Edition .... #07746
William Glen .... #07743
Young's Ltd. .... #07761

DATE: ____ $ ____
O WISH   O HAVE

'98
$45

ITEM #	INTRO	RETIRED	OSRP	GBTru	↓
54875	1996	1997	$35	**$40**	20%

Midyear release. Set of 3. Family ready to depart for the holidays. Child and Bus Driver and Reindeer Line Bus with racing deer on front and sides complete with large chrome bumper, wipers, and windows all around.

DATE: ____ $ ____
O WISH   O HAVE

'96	'97	'98
$35	35	50

TREETOP TREE HOUSE

ITEM #	INTRO	RETIRED	OSRP	GBTRU	NO
54890	1996	CURRENT	$35	**$35**	CHANGE

Children's tree playhouse nestles in branches of a Jack Pine tree. A wooden ladder allows entry/exit and a mailbox is attached to the base of the tree. A tire swing hangs from a bare branch. Material is resin.

DATE: _____ $ _____
○ WISH ○ HAVE

'97	'98
$35	35

ON THE ROAD AGAIN

ITEM #	INTRO	RETIRED	OSRP	GBTRU	NO
54891	1996	CURRENT	$20	**$20**	CHANGE

Set of 2. Station wagon carrying a canoe on roof rack hauls a trailer.

DATE: _____ $ _____
○ WISH ○ HAVE

'97	'98
$20	20

MOVING DAY

ITEM #	INTRO	RETIRED	OSRP	GBTRU	↑
54892	1996	1998	$32.50	**$40**	23%

Set of 3. New owners help moving men carry household goods from the moving van into their new home in the Village.

DATE: _____ $ _____
○ WISH ○ HAVE

'97	'98
$32.50	32.50

HOLIDAY HOOPS

ITEM #	INTRO	RETIRED	OSRP	GBTRU	NO
54893	1996	CURRENT	$20	**$20**	CHANGE

Set of 3. Two students play one-on-one basketball.

DATE: _____ $ _____
○ WISH ○ HAVE

'97	'98
$20	20

MEN AT WORK

ITEM #	INTRO	RETIRED	OSRP	GBTʀᴜ	↑
54894	1996	1998	$27.50	**$36**	31%

Set of 5. Village street and road repairs are handled by work crew and road vehicle.

DATE: ____ $ ____
○ WISH ○ HAVE

'97	'98
$27.50	27.50

TERRY'S TOWING

ITEM #	INTRO	RETIRED	OSRP	GBTʀᴜ	NO
54895	1996	CURRENT	$20	**$20**	CHANGE

Set of 2. Track Compatible. Yellow tow truck hauls non-working cars to a service center.

DATE: ____ $ ____
○ WISH ○ HAVE

'97	'98
$20	20

CAROLING THROUGH THE SNOW

ITEM #	INTRO	RETIRED	OSRP	GBTʀᴜ	NO
54896	1996	CURRENT	$15	**$15**	CHANGE

Track Compatible. Boy pushes carolers in sleigh.

DATE: ____ $ ____
○ WISH ○ HAVE

'97	'98
$15	15

HEADING FOR THE HILLS

ITEM #	INTRO	RETIRED	OSRP	GBTʀᴜ	NO
54897	1996	CURRENT	$8.50	**$8.50**	CHANGE

Set of 2. Track Compatible. Car with ski carriers mounted to the car roof.

DATE: ____ $ ____
○ WISH ○ HAVE

'97	'98
$8.50	8.50

A HARLEY-DAVIDSON® HOLIDAY

ITEM #	INTRO	RETIRED	OSRP	GBTRU	NO
54898	1996	CURRENT	$22.50	**$22.50**	CHANGE

Set of 2. Father and child carry family presents to Harley-Davidson® motorcycle and sidecar for trip home.

DATE: _____ $ _____
○ WISH   ○ HAVE

'97	'98
$22.50	22.50

SANTA COMES TO TOWN, 1997

ITEM #	INTRO	RETIRED	OSRP	GBTRU	↓
54899	1996	1997 ANNUAL	$35	**$40**	5%

3rd in a Series of Dated Annual Santa pieces. Mayor presents Santa with a key to the Village as a children's band strikes up a tune.

DATE: _____ $ _____
○ WISH   ○ HAVE

'97	'98
$35	42

HARLEY-DAVIDSON® FAT BOY & SOFTAIL

ITEM #	INTRO	RETIRED	OSRP	GBTRU	NO
54900	1996	CURRENT	$16.50	**$16.50**	CHANGE

Set of 2. Two different popular motorcycle design.

DATE: _____ $ _____
○ WISH   ○ HAVE

'97	'98
$16.50	16.50

HARLEY-DAVIDSON® SIGN

ITEM #	INTRO	RETIRED	OSRP	GBTRU	NO
54901	1996	CURRENT	$18	**$18**	CHANGE

Motorcycle mounted on a sign advertises the location of Harley-Davidson® Motor Sales, Parts and Service business.

DATE: _____ $ _____
○ WISH   ○ HAVE

'97	'98
$18	18

SATURDAY MORNING DOWNTOWN

ITEM #	INTRO	RETIRED	OSRP	GBTRU
54902*	1997	1998	*	*

Set of 2. A little girl sips a mug of hot chocolate while a boy pulls a sled of presents.
Notable: *This accessory is part of The Original Snow Village® *Start A Tradition Set*, 1997 Item #54902. It is not usually individually available on the secondary market.

DATE: _____ $ _____
O WISH   O HAVE

WHOLE FAMILY GOES SHOPPING, THE

ITEM #	INTRO	RETIRED	OSRP	GBTRU	NO
54905	1997	CURRENT	$25	$25	CHANGE

Set of 3. Midyear release. Dad, Mom and children on a busy holiday shopping spree. Family Dalmatian joins in, hoping for a trip to the feed store for biscuits.

DATE: _____ $ _____
O WISH   O HAVE

'97	'98
$25	25

A HOLIDAY SLEIGH RIDE TOGETHER

ITEM #	INTRO	RETIRED	OSRP	GBTRU	NO
54921	1997	CURRENT	$32.50	$32.50	CHANGE

Track Compatible. Family goes for a sleigh ride in old-fashioned sleigh pulled by a horse with bell trimmed harness.

DATE: _____ $ _____
O WISH   O HAVE

'98
$32.50

CHRISTMAS KIDS

ITEM #	INTRO	RETIRED	OSRP	GBTRU	NO
54922	1997	CURRENT	$27.50	$27.50	CHANGE

Set of 5. Children carry gifts, shopping bags and holiday trim.

DATE: _____ $ _____
O WISH   O HAVE

'98
$27.50

LET IT SNOW, LET IT SNOW

ITEM #	INTRO	RETIRED	OSRP	GBTRU	NO
54923	1997	CURRENT	$20	**$20**	CHANGE

Track Compatible. Father uses snow blower to clear sidewalk and little boy sweeps away blown snow.

DATE: _____ $ _____
O WISH   O HAVE

'98
$20

KIDS LOVE HERSHEY'S™!

ITEM #	INTRO	RETIRED	OSRP	GBTRU	NO
54924	1997	CURRENT	$30	**$30**	CHANGE

Set of 2. Boy and girl wave at the Hershey's™ delivery truck.

DATE: _____ $ _____
O WISH   O HAVE

'98
$30

McDONALD'S® ... LIGHTS UP THE NIGHT

ITEM #	INTRO	RETIRED	OSRP	GBTRU	NO
54925	1997	CURRENT	$30	**$30**	CHANGE

15¢ hamburgers? Curbside Golden Arch lights up to let drivers know a fast-food restaurant is open for business.

DATE: _____ $ _____
O WISH   O HAVE

'98
$30

KIDS, CANDY CANES ... & RONALD McDONALD®

ITEM #	INTRO	RETIRED	OSRP	GBTRU	NO
54926	1997	CURRENT	$30	**$30**	CHANGE

Set of 3. Ronald and children with sled carrying candy canes.

DATE: _____ $ _____
O WISH   O HAVE

'98
$30

HE LED THEM DOWN THE STREETS OF TOWN

ITEM #	INTRO	RETIRED	OSRP	GBTRU	NO
54927	1997	CURRENT	$30	**$30**	CHANGE

Set of 3. Snow Puff Marshmallow man carries store signboard as children dance around in delight.

DATE: _____ $ _____
O WISH O HAVE

'98
$30

EVERYBODY GOES SKATING AT ROLLERAMA

ITEM #	INTRO	RETIRED	OSRP	GBTRU	NO
54928	1997	CURRENT	$25	**$25**	CHANGE

Set of 2. Girls wearing '50's poodle skirts and boy in jeans carry skates and head to roller rink.

DATE: _____ $ _____
O WISH O HAVE

'98
$25

AT THE BARN DANCE, IT'S ALLEMANDE LEFT

ITEM #	INTRO	RETIRED	OSRP	GBTRU	NO
54929	1997	CURRENT	$30	**$30**	CHANGE

Set of 2. Hound dog keeps eye on fiddler as children do intricate square dance step.

DATE: _____ $ _____
O WISH O HAVE

'98
$30

HITCH-UP THE BUCKBOARD

ITEM #	INTRO	RETIRED	OSRP	GBTRU	NO
54930	1997	CURRENT	$40	**$40**	CHANGE

Track Compatible. Rancher drives horse-drawn carriage for holiday visitors.

DATE: _____ $ _____
O WISH O HAVE

'98
$40

FARM ACCESSORY SET

Item #	Intro	Retired	OSRP	GBTru	NO
54931	1997	Current	$75	**$75**	CHANGE

Set of 35. Trees, fences, hay, farm animals, watering trough & pump.

Date: _____ $ _____
○ Wish ○ Have

'98
$75

SAY IT WITH FLOWERS

Item #	Intro	Retired	OSRP	GBTru	↑
2204	1998	Promo	$30	**$40**	33%

Set of 3. Includes Bachman's® employee with purple wheelbarrow, a father and daughter with purple packages and a woman with purple wrapped flowers and wreath. Real paper is used on both packages. **Notable:** Created for Bachman's® Village Gathering. Companion accessory to Bachman's® Flower Shop and Bachman's® Greenhouse. Re-issued as Christmas Visit To The Florist, 1998 Item #54957.

Date: _____ $ _____
○ Wish ○ Have

'98
$30

SANTA COMES TO TOWN, 1998

Item #	Intro	Retired	OSRP	GBTru	↑
54920	1998	1998 Annual	$30	**$40**	33%

4th in a Series of Dated Annual Santa pieces. Santa and children decorate a Santa Snowman for the Village.

Date: _____ $ _____
○ Wish ○ Have

'98
$30

DECORATE THE TREE

Item #	Intro	Retired	OSRP	GBTru
54934*	1998	Event G/S Acc.	*	*

Set of 2. Children add tinsel garland to a tree.
Notable: *This accessory is part of the Original Snow Village® Snowy Pines Inn Gift Set, 1998 Item #54934. It is not usually individually available on the secondary market.

Date: _____ $ _____
○ Wish ○ Have

First Round Of The Year

Item #	Intro	Retired	OSRP	GBTru	NO
54936	1998	Current	$30	**$30**	CHANGE

Set of 3. Midyear release. Track Compatible. Coordinates with Linden Hills Country Club. Man and woman golfers with golf cart.

Date: _____ $ _____
○ Wish ○ Have

'98
$30

Trick Or Treat Kids

Item #	Intro	Retired	OSRP	GBTru	NO
54937	1998	Current	$33	**$33**	CHANGE

Set of 3. Midyear release. Children dressed in costumes for Halloween festivities.

Date: _____ $ _____
○ Wish ○ Have

'98
$33

Carnival Tickets & Cotton Candy

Item #	Intro	Retired	OSRP	GBTru	NO
54938	1998	Current	$30	**$30**	CHANGE

Set of 3. Midyear release. Vendor sells cotton candy and carousel tickets. Children buy cotton candy and balloons.

Date: _____ $ _____
○ Wish ○ Have

'98
$30

Two For The Road

Item #	Intro	Retired	OSRP	GBTru	NO
54939	1998	Current	$20/ea	**$20/ea**	CHANGE

3 Assorted. Midyear release. Softail Harley-Davidson® motorcycle with double riders offered in three different colors; blue, red or yellow.

Date: _____ $ _____
○ Wish ○ Have

'98
$20

| **UPTOWN MOTORS FORD®** | ITEM # | INTRO | RETIRED | OSRP | GBTRU |
| **BILLBOARD** | 52780 | 1998 | CURRENT | $20 | **$20** |

Similar to the Village's other billboard, 1994 Item #5481-0, this billboard features three lanterns and two ceramic trees.

DATE: _____ $ _____
O WISH   O HAVE

| **1955 FORD® AUTOMOBILES** | ITEM # | INTRO | RETIRED | OSRP | GBTRU |
| | 54950 | 1998 | CURRENT | $10/EA | **$10/EA** |

6 assorted, with 6 signs. Track Compatible. There are 6 to choose from, two each of an eight-passenger Country Squire, Fairlane Club Sedan, and Thunderbird. The signs have the model name of each vehicle.
Notable: Decals are on the license plates and side panels.

DATE: _____ $ _____
O WISH   O HAVE

| **1964-1/2 FORD®** | ITEM # | INTRO | RETIRED | OSRP | GBTRU |
| **MUSTANG** | 54951 | 1998 | CURRENT | $10/EA | **$10/EA** |

3 assorted, with 3 signs. These replicas of the "Pony" offer a little free spirit to the Village. The signs feature the names of the cars.

DATE: _____ $ _____
O WISH   O HAVE

| **VILLAGE FIRE TRUCK** | ITEM # | INTRO | RETIRED | OSRP | GBTRU |
| | 54952 | 1998 | CURRENT | $22.50 | **$22.50** |

This, the first fire truck for the Village, is also the first vehicle to offer working headlights and a lighted beacon.

DATE: _____ $ _____
O WISH   O HAVE

FIREMAN TO THE RESCUE

ITEM #	INTRO	RETIRED	OSRP	GBTRU
54953	1998	CURRENT	$30	**$30**

Set of 3. A little girl watches as her hero descends a ladder with her kitten.

DATE: _____ $ _____
O WISH   O HAVE

FUN AT THE FIREHOUSE

ITEM #	INTRO	RETIRED	OSRP	GBTRU
54954	1998	CURRENT	$27.50	**$27.50**

Set of 2. A child tries on a fireman's helmet as he and a Dalmatian watch two other children try to get another helmet away from a second Dalmatian.

DATE: _____ $ _____
O WISH   O HAVE

FARMER'S FLATBED

ITEM #	INTRO	RETIRED	OSRP	GBTRU
54955	1998	CURRENT	$17.50	**$17.50**

A truck with wooden side rails delivers bags of Rock Creek Mill grain and hay.

DATE: _____ $ _____
O WISH   O HAVE

CATCH OF THE DAY, THE

ITEM #	INTRO	RETIRED	OSRP	GBTRU
54956	1998	CURRENT	$30	**$30**

A novice angler reels in the big one as a grandfather looks on with pride.

DATE: _____ $ _____
O WISH   O HAVE

CHRISTMAS VISIT TO THE FLORIST

ITEM #	INTRO	RETIRED	OSRP	GBTRU
54957	1998	CURRENT	$30	**$30**

Set of 3. A family carries flowers while a man transports trees in a wheelbarrow.
Notable: The silk flowers and potted plant are wrapped in paper. The landscaping supplies are separate from the wheelbarrow.

DATE: _____ $ _____
○ WISH   ○ HAVE

SANTA COMES TO TOWN, 1999

ITEM #	INTRO	RETIRED	OSRP	GBTRU
54958	1998	1999 ANNUAL	$30	**$30**

5th in a Series of Dated Annual Santa pieces. Children tempt a reindeer with apples as Santa watches.

DATE: _____ $ _____
○ WISH   ○ HAVE

VILLAGE SERVICE VEHICLES

ITEM #	INTRO	RETIRED	OSRP	GBTRU
54959	1998	CURRENT	$45	**$45**

Set of 3. Track Compatible. This accessory includes the Village sanitation truck, Village snowplow, and AAA tow truck.

DATE: _____ $ _____
○ WISH   ○ HAVE

QUALITY SERVICE AT FORD®

ITEM #	INTRO	RETIRED	OSRP	GBTRU
54970	1998	CURRENT	$27.50	**$27.50**

Set of 2. A serviceman readies to fill tires with air. A lift is prepared to support a vehicle being worked on.

DATE: _____ $ _____
○ WISH   ○ HAVE

PATROLLING THE ROAD

ITEM #	INTRO	RETIRED	OSRP	GBTRU
54971	1998	CURRENT	$20	**$20**

A motorcycle policeman rides aboard his Harley-Davidson® while patrolling the city.

DATE: _____ $ _____
○ WISH ○ HAVE

COULDN'T WAIT UNTIL CHRISTMAS

ITEM #	INTRO	RETIRED	OSRP	GBTRU
54972	1998	CURRENT	$17	**$17**

Not being able to handle the excitement, a father and son take a look at their newest train.

DATE: _____ $ _____
○ WISH ○ HAVE

COSTUMES FOR SALE

ITEM #	INTRO	RETIRED	OSRP	GBTRU
54973	1998	CURRENT	$60	**$60**

Set of 2. A little trick-or-treater slips into a costume at the local costume shop. The proprietor is also a fortune teller. **Notable:** The pumpkin lights are battery operated and adapter compatible.

DATE: _____ $ _____
○ WISH ○ HAVE

UNCLE SAM'S FIREWORKS STAND

ITEM #	INTRO	RETIRED	OSRP	GBTRU
54974	1998 EVENT PIECE 1999		$45	**$45**

Set of 2. A youngster waves a sparkler and a flag as Uncle Sam tends his booth. **Notable:** This accessory available during the 1999 July event.

DATE: _____ $ _____
○ WISH ○ HAVE

HARLEY-DAVIDSON® WATER TOWER	ITEM # 54975	INTRO 1998	RETIRED CURRENT	OSRP $37.50	GBTRU $37.50

This tower supplies water to the Harley-Davidson® Manufacturing plant.
Notable: This water tower is similar to the Village's two previous towers, 1988 Item #5133-0, and Item #2510-4.

DATE: ____ $ ____
○ WISH   ○ HAVE

...ANOTHER MAN'S TREASURE ACCESSORIES	ITEM # 54976	INTRO 1998	RETIRED CURRENT	OSRP $27.50	GBTRU $27.50

Set of 3. "Treasure" hunters claim their prizes as they search through the items for sale.

DATE: ____ $ ____
○ WISH   ○ HAVE

Get Free Updates For This Guide

The 1999 midyear introductions have been announced since this guide was printed. Yet you can still include them and all their information in this edition.

Look for the updates in the July-August 1999 issue of the Village Chronicle magazine. They will be on pages that you can remove from the magazine and insert in the appropriate locations within this Guide.

For more information, or to subscribe to the magazine, contact:

the Village Chronicle
757 Park Ave.
Cranston, RI 02910

the **Village Chronicle.**

401-467-9343
401-467-9359 Fax

www.villagechronicle.com

Subscription rate is $27 for one year. Mention GREENBOOK when subscribing, and you'll receive a free bonus issue.

(R.I. residents: add 7% sales tax. International residents: $32 U.S. funds.)

Item#	Name	Intro	Retired	OSRP$	GBTru$	Wish	Have	Date	Qty	Paid Each	Total
6515-3	ORIGINAL SHOPS OF DICKENS' VILLAGE, THE, SET/7	1984	1988	175	1115	○	○				
6515-3	Crowntree Inn	1984	1988	25	235	○	○				
6515-3	Candle Shop	1984	1988	25	160	○	○				
6515-3	Green Grocer	1984	1988	25	165	○	○				
6515-3	Golden Swan Baker	1984	1988	25	150	○	○				
6515-3	Bean And Son Smithy Shop	1984	1988	25	165	○	○				
6515-3	Abel Beesley Butcher	1984	1988	25	120	○	○				
6515-3	Jones & Co. Brush & Basket Shop	1984	1988	25	245	○	○				
6516-1	Dickens' Village Church—"White"	1985	1989	35	435	○	○				
6516-1	Dickens' Village Church—"Cream"	1985	1989	35	175	○	○				
6516-1	Dickens' Village Church—"Green"	1985	1989	35	335	○	○				
6516-1	Dickens' Village Church—"Tan"	1985	1989	35	145	○	○				
6516-1	Dickens' Village Church—"Dark"	1985	1989	35	125	○	○				
6518-8	Dickens' Cottages, Set/3	1985	1988	75	865	○	○				
6518-8	Thatched Cottage	1985	1988	25	170	○	○				
6518-8	Stone Cottage—"Tan"	1985	1988	25	395	○	○				
6518-8	Stone Cottage—"Green"	1985	1988	25	320	○	○				
6518-8	Tudor Cottage	1985	1988	25	285	○	○				
6519-6	Dickens' Village Mill	1985	Ltd Ed 2,500	35	4755	○	○				
6500-5	Christmas Carol Cottages, Set/3	1986	1995	75	95	○	○				
6500-5	Fezziwig's Warehouse	1986	1995	25	40	○	○				
6500-5	Scrooge & Marley Counting House	1986	1995	25	45	○	○				
6500-5	Cottage of Bob Cratchit & Tiny Tim, The	1986	1995	25	60	○	○				
6502-1	Norman Church	1986	Ltd Ed 3,500	40	3350	○	○				
6507-2	Dickens' Lane Shops, Set/3	1986	1989	80	505	○	○				
6507-2	Thomas Kersey Coffee House	1986	1989	27	155	○	○				
6507-2	Cottage Toy Shop	1986	1989	27	160	○	○				
6507-2	Tuttle's Pub	1986	1989	27	205	○	○				
6508-0	Blythe Pond Mill House—"Correct"	1986	1990	37	195	○	○				
6508-0	Blythe Pond Mill House—"By The Pond"	1986	1990	37	85	○	○				
6528-5	Chadbury Station And Train	1986	1989	65	325	○	○				

DV Page 1 Totals: 1,225.00   15,580.00

Item#	Name	Intro	Retired	OSRP$	GBTru$	Wish	Have	Date	Qty	Paid Each	Total
5900-5	BARLEY BREE, SET/2	1987	1989	60	325	○	○				
5900-5	FARMHOUSE	1987	1989	30	*NE	○	○				
5900-5	BARN	1987	1989	30	*NE	○	○				
5905-6	OLD CURIOSITY SHOP, THE	1987	CURRENT	32	45	○	○				
5916-1	KENILWORTH CASTLE	1987	1988	70	555	○	○				
6549-8	BRICK ABBEY	1987	1989	33	300	○	○				
6568-4	CHESTERTON MANOR HOUSE	1987	LTD ED 7,500	45	1385	○	○				
5902-1	COUNTING HOUSE & SILAS THIMBLETON BARRISTER	1988	1990	32	80	○	○				
5904-8	C. FLETCHER PUBLIC HOUSE	1988	LTD ED 12,500*	35	465	○	○				
5924-2	COBBLESTONE SHOPS, SET/3	1988	1990	95	305	○	○				
5924-2	WOOL SHOP, THE	1988	1990	32	150	○	○				
5924-2	BOOTER AND COBBLER	1988	1990	32	85	○	○				
5924-2	T. WELLS FRUIT & SPICE SHOP	1988	1990	32	80	○	○				
5925-0	NICHOLAS NICKLEBY, SET/2	1988	1991	72	150	○	○				
5925-0	NICHOLAS NICKLEBY COTTAGE	1988	1991	36	80	○	○				
5925-0	NIC"K"OLAS NICKLEBY COTTAGE	1988	1991	36	100	○	○				
5925-0	WACKFORD SQUEERS BOARDING SCHOOL	1988	1991	36	90	○	○				
5926-9	MERCHANT SHOPS, SET/5	1988	1993	150	205	○	○				
5926-9	POULTERER	1988	1993	32.50	50	○	○				
5926-9	GEO. WEETON WATCHMAKER	1988	1993	32.50	45	○	○				
5926-9	MERMAID FISH SHOPPE, THE	1988	1993	32.50	60	○	○				
5926-9	WHITE HORSE BAKERY	1988	1993	32.50	60	○	○				
5926-9	WALPOLE TAILORS	1988	1993	32.50	40	○	○				
5927-7	IVY GLEN CHURCH	1988	1991	35	70	○	○				
5550-6	DAVID COPPERFIELD, SET/3	1989	1992	125	170	○	○				
5550-6	MR. WICKFIELD SOLICITOR	1989	1992	42.50	80	○	○				
5550-6	BETSY TROTWOOD'S COTTAGE	1989	1992	42.50	65	○	○				
5550-6	PEGGOTTY'S SEASIDE COTTAGE—"TAN"	1989	1992	42.50	95	○	○				
5550-6	PEGGOTTY'S SEASIDE COTTAGE—"GREEN"	1989	1992	42.50	60	○	○				
5574-3	VICTORIA STATION	1989	1998	100	120	○	○				
5582-4	KNOTTINGHILL CHURCH	1989	1995	50	55	○	○				
5583-2	COBLES POLICE STATION	1989	1991	37.50	125	○	○				
5584-0	THEATRE ROYAL	1989	1992	45	65	○	○				
5585-9	RUTH MARION SCOTCH WOOLENS	1989	LTD ED 17,500*	65	360	○	○				

DV PAGE 2 TOTALS: 1,678.00   5,920.00

Item#	Name	Intro	Retired	OSRP$	GBTru$	Wish	Have	Date	Qty	Paid Each	Total
5586-7	Green Gate Cottage	1989	Ltd Ed 22,500*	65	225	○	○				
5587-5	Flat Of Ebenezer Scrooge, The—"Taiwan/Panes"	1989	Variation		90	○	○				
5587-5	Flat Of Ebenezer Scrooge, The—"Taiwan/No Panes"	1989	Variation	37.50	65	○	○				
5587-5	Flat Of Ebenezer Scrooge, The	1989	Current	37.50	37.50	○	○				
5567-0	Bishops Oast House	1990	1992	45	65	○	○				
5568-9	King's Road, Set/2	1990	1996	72	85	○	○				
55690	Tutbury Printer	1990	1996	36	45	○	○				
55691	C.H. Watt Physician	1990	1996	36	50	○	○				
5552-2	Fagin's Hide-A-Way	1991	1995	68	60	○	○				
5553-0	Oliver Twist, Set/2	1991	1993	75	95	○	○				
5553-0	Brownlow House	1991	1993	37.50	60	○	○				
5553-0	Maylie Cottage	1991	1993	37.50	50	○	○				
5555-7	Ashbury Inn	1991	1995	55	65	○	○				
5557-3	Nephew Fred's Flat	1991	1994	35	85	○	○				
5750-9	Crown & Cricket Inn	1991	1992 Annual	100	150	○	○				
5562-0	Old Michaelchurch	1992	1996	42	50	○	○				
5751-7	Pied Bull Inn, The	1992	1993 Annual	100	140	○	○				
5800-9	Hembleton Pewterer	1992	1995	72	75	○	○				
5801-7	King's Road Post Office	1992	1998	45	50	○	○				
5809-2	Boarding & Lodging School (#18)	1992	1993 Annual	48	90	○	○				
5752-5	Dedlock Arms	1993	1994 Annual	100	105	○	○				
5808-4	Pump Lane Shoppes, Set/3	1993	1996	112	110	○	○				
58085	Bumpstead Nye Cloaks & Canes	1993	1996	37.50	40	○	○				
58086	Lomas Ltd. Molasses	1993	1996	37.50	45	○	○				
58087	W.M. Wheat Cakes & Puddings	1993	1996	37.50	50	○	○				
5811-4	Kingsford's Brew House	1993	1996	45	50	○	○				
5812-2	Great Denton Mill	1993	1997	50	45	○	○				
5753-3	Sir John Falstaff Inn	1994	1995 Annual	100	105	○	○				
5810-6	Boarding & Lodging School (#43)	1994	1998	48	55	○	○				
5821-1	Whittlesbourne Church	1994	1998	85	90	○	○				
5822-0	Giggelswick Mutton & Ham	1994	1997	48	55	○	○				
5823-8	Hather Harness	1994	1997	48	45	○	○				

DV Page 3 Totals: 1,830.00   2,427.50

Item#	Name	Intro	Retired	OSRP$	GBTru$	Wish	Have	Date	Qty	Paid Each	Total
5824-6	PORTOBELLO ROAD THATCHED COTTAGES, SET/3	1994	1997	120	135	○	○				
58247	MR. & MRS. PICKLE	1994	1997	40	45	○	○				
58248	COBB COTTAGE	1994	1997	40	50	○	○				
58249	BROWNING COTTAGE	1994	1997	40	45	○	○				
57534	GRAPES INN, THE	1995	1996 ANNUAL	120	125	○	○				
5832-7	DICKENS' VILLAGE START A TRADITION SET	1995	1996	85	90	○	○				
	FAVERSHAM LAMPS & OIL										
	MORSTON STEAK AND KIDNEY PIE										
58328	J.D. NICHOLS TOY SHOP	1995	1998	48	55	○	○				
58329	DURSLEY MANOR	1995	CURRENT	50	55	○	○				
58330	BLENHAM STREET BANK	1995	1998	60	70	○	○				
58331	WRENBURY SHOPS, SET/3	1995	1997 &1998	100	125	○	○				
58332	WRENBURY BAKER	1995	1997	35	45	○	○				
58333	CHOP SHOP, THE	1995	1997	35	40	○	○				
58334	T. PUDDLEWICK SPECTACLE SHOP	1995	1998	35	45	○	○				
5833-5	MALTINGS, THE	1995	1998	50	50	○	○				
5834-3	DUDDEN CROSS CHURCH	1995	1997	45	55	○	○				
57535	GAD'S HILL PLACE	1996	1997 ANNUAL	98	120	○	○				
58336	RAMSFORD PALACE	1996	LTD ED 27,500	175	425	○	○				
58337	BUTTER TUB FARMHOUSE	1996	CURRENT	40	40	○	○				
58338	BUTTER TUB BARN	1996	CURRENT	48	48	○	○				
58339	CHRISTMAS CAROL COTTAGE, THE (REVISITED)	1996	CURRENT	60	60	○	○				
58344	NETTIE QUINN PUPPETS & MARIONETTES	1996	CURRENT	50	50	○	○				
58345	MULBERRIE COURT BROWNSTONES	1996	CURRENT	90	90	○	○				
58346	OLDE CAMDEN TOWN CHURCH, THE (REVISITED)	1996	CURRENT	55	55	○	○				
58347	MELANCHOLY TAVERN, THE (REVISITED)	1996	CURRENT	45	45	○	○				
58348	QUILLY'S ANTIQUES	1996	CURRENT	46	46	○	○				
58322	DICKENS' VILLAGE START A TRADITION SET	1997	1998	75*	100	○	○				
	SUDBURY CHURCH										
	OLD EAST RECTORY										
58323	J. LYTES COAL MERCHANT	1997	CURRENT	50	50	○	○				
58324	BARMBY MOOR COTTAGE	1997	CURRENT	48	48	○	○				
58500	TOWER OF LONDON	1997	SEE HISTORICAL LANDMARK SERIES™								

DV PAGE 4 TOTALS: 1,783.00 2,207.00

Item#	Name	Intro	Retired	OSRP$	GBTru$	Wish	Have	Date	Qty	Paid Each	Total
58301	Manchester Square	1997	Current	250	250	O	O				
	G. Choir's Weights & Scales										
	Frogmore Chemist										
	Custom House										
	Lydby Trunk & Satchel Shop										
58302	East Indies Trading Co.	1997	Current	65	65	O	O				
58303	Leacock Poulterer (Revisited)	1997	Current	48	48	O	O				
58304	Crooked Fence Cottage	1997	Current	60	60	O	O				
58305	Ashwick Lane Hose & Ladder	1997	Current	54	54	O	O				
58306	Canadian Trading Co.	1997	1998	65	150	O	O				
58501	Old Globe Theatre, The	1997	See Historical Landmark Series™								
58307	Thomas Mudge Timepieces	1998	Current	60	60	O	O				
58308	Seton Morris Spice Merchant Gift Set	1998	Event Gift Set	65	90	O	O				
58309	Kensington Palace	1998	Event Piece	195	245	O	O				
58310	Great Expectations Satis Manor	1998	Current	110	110	O	O				
58311	Tattyeave Knoll	1998	Current	55	55	O	O				
58313	Heathmoor Castle	1998	1999 Annual	90	90	O	O				
58314	Teaman & Crupp China Shop	1998	Current	64	64	O	O				
58315	Lynton Point Tower	1998	Current	80	80	O	O				
58316	North Eastern Sea Fisheries Ltd.	1998	Current	70	70	O	O				
58340	Horse And Hounds Pub, The	1998	Current	70	70	O	O				
58341	Big Ben	1998	See Historical Landmark Series™								
	DV Page 5 Totals:			1,401.00	1,561.00						
	DV Page 1 Totals:			1,225.00	15,580.00						
	DV Page 2 Totals:			1,678.00	5,920.00						
	DV Page 3 Totals:			1,830.00	2,427.50						
	DV Page 4 Totals:			1,783.00	2,207.00						
	DV Page 5 Totals:			1,401.00	1,561.00						
	DV Grand Totals:			7,917.00	27,695.50						

𝔇ickens' 𝔙illage 𝔖eries® 𝔊𝔅 𝔥istory 𝔏ist

ORIGINAL SHOPS OF DICKENS' VILLAGE, THE

ITEM #	INTRO	RETIRED	OSRP	GBTRU	↓
6515-3	1984	1988	$175	**$1115**	12%

Set of 7 includes *Crowntree Inn, Candle Shop, Green Grocer, Golden Swan Baker, Bean And Son Smithy Shop, Abel Beesley Butcher, Jones & Co. Brush & Basket Shop.*

see below

DATE: ____ $ ____		'91	'92	'93	'94	'95	'96	'97	'98
○ WISH ○ HAVE		$1200	1375	1295	1325	1295	1325	1310	1265

CROWNTREE INN

ITEM #	INTRO	RETIRED	OSRP	GBTRU	↓
6515-3	1984	1988	$25	**$235**	15%

1 of the 7-piece set—THE ORIGINAL SHOPS OF DICKENS' VILLAGE. Large multi-paned windows run length of front of Inn with entry door decorated by wreath, second story stone, attic dormer.

DATE: ____ $ ____		'91	'92	'93	'94	'95	'96	'97	'98
○ WISH ○ HAVE		$375	350	335	320	300	305	300	275

CANDLE SHOP

ITEM #	INTRO	RETIRED	OSRP	GBTRU	↓
6515-3	1984	1988	$25	**$160**	14%

1 of the 7-piece set—THE ORIGINAL SHOPS OF DICKENS' VILLAGE. Timber framed windows, plaster on stone small house/store. Attic rental rooms, light over front entry.
Notable: Variation in roof color—first ones shipped were gray followed by blue.

DATE: ____ $ ____		'91	'92	'93	'94	'95	'96	'97	'98
○ WISH ○ HAVE		$235	210	210	190	190	195	195	185

GREEN GROCER

ITEM #	INTRO	RETIRED	OSRP	GBTRU	↓
6515-3	1984	1988	$25	**$165**	20%

1 of the 7-piece set—THE ORIGINAL SHOPS OF DICKENS' VILLAGE. Thatched roof over timber two-story grocery/provisions store. Bay window for display. Attached storage room on side of store.

DATE: ____ $ ____		'91	'92	'93	'94	'95	'96	'97	'98
○ WISH ○ HAVE		$220	200	190	185	185	185	195	205

Golden Swan Baker

Item #	Intro	Retired	OSRP	GBTru	↓
6515-3	1984	1988	$25	**$150**	19%

1 of the 7-piece set—THE ORIGINAL SHOPS OF DICKENS' VILLAGE. Painted sign with gold swan hangs above large bay window for display. Timbered building, brick chimney, light above entry door.

DATE: ____ $ ____   ○ WISH   ○ HAVE

'91	'92	'93	'94	'95	'96	'97	'98
$170	155	180	180	180	180	175	185

Bean And Son Smithy Shop

Item #	Intro	Retired	OSRP	GBTru	↓
6515-3	1984	1988	$25	**$165**	15%

1 of the 7-piece set—THE ORIGINAL SHOPS OF DICKENS' VILLAGE. Double wood door, stone first story, second story set on stone with overhang. Steep curved roof with brick chimney.

DATE: ____ $ ____   ○ WISH   ○ HAVE

'91	'92	'93	'94	'95	'96	'97	'98
$185	185	185	190	195	190	195	195

Abel Beesley Butcher

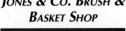

Item #	Intro	Retired	OSRP	GBTru	↓
6515-3	1984	1988	$25	**$120**	11%

1 of the 7-piece set—THE ORIGINAL SHOPS OF DICKENS' VILLAGE. Timbered bottom half, second story plaster over stone, two chimneys.

DATE: ____ $ ____   ○ WISH   ○ HAVE

'91	'92	'93	'94	'95	'96	'97	'98
$175	145	130	120	125	130	130	135

Jones & Co. Brush & Basket Shop

Item #	Intro	Retired	OSRP	GBTru	↓
6515-3	1984	1988	$25	**$245**	16%

1 of the 7-piece set—THE ORIGINAL SHOPS OF DICKENS' VILLAGE. Cellar shop is a cobbler with small sign by his door to advertise, rest of building is for basketry, mats, and brush. Narrow staircase leads to entry.

DATE: ____ $ ____   ○ WISH   ○ HAVE

'91	'92	'93	'94	'95	'96	'97	'98
$325	355	355	335	300	290	300	290

DICKENS' VILLAGE CHURCH—"WHITE"

	ITEM #	INTRO	RETIRED	OSRP	GBTRU	↑
	6516-1	1985	1989	$35	**$435**	2%

Notable: There are Five Versions of the *Village Church:* "White," "Cream," "Green," "Tan" and "Dark." The variations in color affect GBTru$. "White" Church has off white to cream walls and brown roof matches brown cornerstones.

DATE: ____ $ ____
○ WISH ○ HAVE

'91	'92	'93	'94	'95	'96	'97	'98
$250	-	-	425	375	385	400	425

DICKENS' VILLAGE CHURCH—"CREAM"

GBTRU	↓
$175	22%

Notable: "Cream" or "Yellow" Church has cream walls with light yellow coloring in mortar between stones and a butterscotch roof.

DATE: ____ $ ____
○ WISH ○ HAVE

'91	'92	'93	'94	'95	'96	'97	'98
$145	285	350	295	225	275	285	225

DICKENS' VILLAGE CHURCH—"GREEN"

GBTRU	↓
$335	6%

Notable: "Green" Church has very light green tone on walls and a butterscotch roof.

DATE: ____ $ ____
○ WISH ○ HAVE

'91	'92	'93	'94	'95	'96	'97	'98
$225	350	415	350	330	325	385	355

DICKENS' VILLAGE CHURCH—"TAN"

GBTRU	↓
$145	26%

Notable: "Tan" Church has tan walls and a butterscotch roof.

DATE: ____ $ ____
○ WISH ○ HAVE

'91	'92	'93	'94	'95	'96	'97	'98
$100	170	195	205	190	175	200	195

DICKENS' VILLAGE CHURCH—"DARK"

GBT**RU** ↓
$125 14%

Notable: "Dark" Church or sometimes called "Butterscotch" has walls that are or nearly are the same color as the roof. This is the only sleeve to read "Village Church." All others read "Shops Of Dickens' Village."

DATE: ____ $ ____	'91	'92	'93	'94	'95	'96	'97	'98
○ WISH ○ HAVE	$-	155	160	155	155	150	160	145

DICKENS' COTTAGES

ITEM #	INTRO	RETIRED	OSRP	GBT**RU**	↓
6518-8	1985	1988	$75	$865	6%

Set of 3 includes *Thatched Cottage, Stone Cottage, Tudor Cottage.*
Notable: Early release to Gift Creations Concepts (GCC).

see below

DATE: ____ $ ____	'91	'92	'93	'94	'95	'96	'97	'98
○ WISH ○ HAVE	$875	1015	1015	1050	950	915	965	925

THATCHED COTTAGE

ITEM #	INTRO	RETIRED	OSRP	GBT**RU**	↓
6518-8	1985	1988	$25	$170	6%

1 of the 3-piece set—DICKENS' COTTAGES. Double chimneys rise from thatched roof, two-story plastered/timbered home with second story extending out on sides.
Notable: Early release to Gift Creations Concepts (GCC).

DATE: ____ $ ____	'91	'92	'93	'94	'95	'96	'97	'98
○ WISH ○ HAVE	$210	210	200	200	200	185	195	180

NOTES: _____
_____
_____
_____
_____
_____

STONE COTTAGE—"TAN"

ITEM #	INTRO	RETIRED	OSRP	GBTRU	↓
6518-8	1985	1988	$25	**$395**	15%

1 of the 3-piece set—DICKENS' COTTAGES.
Notable: There are Two Versions of the *Stone Cottage:* "Tan" and "Green." Tan variation is considered the first color shipped. The color change affects GBTru$. Early release to Gift Creations Concepts (GCC).

DATE: ___ $ ___		'91	'92	'93	'94	'95	'96	'97	'98
○ WISH ○ HAVE		$425	465	450	425	400	400	455	465

STONE COTTAGE—"GREEN"

	GBTRU	↓
	$320	11%

Notable: The "Green" version of the *Stone Cottage* is considered to be later shipments. Cottage has variegated fieldstone walls and roughhewn shingle roof.

DATE: ___ $ ___		'91	'92	'93	'94	'95	'96	'97	'98
○ WISH ○ HAVE		$425	380	375	425	400	400	395	360

TUDOR COTTAGE

ITEM #	INTRO	RETIRED	OSRP	GBTRU	↓
6518-8	1985	1988	$25	**$285**	26%

1 of the 3-piece set—DICKENS' COTTAGES. Stone foundation with timbered/plastered walls forming a small house. Two chimneys for heating/cooking.
Notable: Early release to Gift Creations Concepts (GCC).

DATE: ___ $ ___		'91	'92	'93	'94	'95	'96	'97	'98
○ WISH ○ HAVE		$400	455	450	450	400	375	385	385

DICKENS' VILLAGE MILL

ITEM #	INTRO	RETIRED	OSRP	GBTRU	↓
6519-6	1985	LTD ED 2,500	$35	**$4755**	5%

Roughhewn stone makes up 3-section mill with large wooden mill wheel. Two sets double doors—one large set to allow carriage to be brought directly into building, smaller doors open into silo area.
Notable: Early release to Gift Creations Concepts (GCC). Some sleeves read "Dickens' Village Cottage."

DATE: ___ $ ___		'91	'92	'93	'94	'95	'96	'97	'98
○ WISH ○ HAVE		$5550	5550	5550	5150	5000	4850	4995	5025

CHRISTMAS CAROL COTTAGES	ITEM #	INTRO	RETIRED	OSRP	GBTRU	↓
	6500-5	1986	1995	$75	**$95**	24%

Set of 3 includes *Fezziwig's Warehouse, Scrooge & Marley Counting House, The Cottage Of Bob Cratchit & Tiny Tim.*

see below

DATE: ____ $ ____	'91	'92	'93	'94	'95	'96	'97	'98
○ WISH ○ HAVE	$90	90	90	90	90	115	125	125

FEZZIWIG'S WAREHOUSE	ITEM #	INTRO	RETIRED	OSRP	GBTRU	NO
	6500-5	1986	1995	$25	**$40**	CHANGE

1 of the 3-piece set—CHRISTMAS CAROL COTTAGES. In *A Christmas Carol*, Fezziwig was young Scrooge's employer. On one day a year, Christmas Eve, Fezziwig held a high-spirited party for his staff and family in the warehouse.
Notable: Early pieces have panes cut out of front door (photo). Later pieces have a solid front door. This does not affect secondary market value.

DATE: ____ $ ____	'91	'92	'93	'94	'95	'96	'97	'98
○ WISH ○ HAVE	$30	30	30	30	30	40	40	40

SCROOGE & MARLEY COUNTING HOUSE	ITEM #	INTRO	RETIRED	OSRP	GBTRU	NO
	6500-5	1986	1995	$25	**$45**	CHANGE

1 of the 3-piece set—CHRISTMAS CAROL COTTAGES. The office of Scrooge and his departed partner, Jacob Marley, in *A Christmas Carol*. A Counting House kept books and transacted business for different accounts–you would go to a Counting House to borrow money or repay a loan. Building is simple rectangular shape. Bottom brick, second story plastered with shuttered windows.

DATE: ____ $ ____	'91	'92	'93	'94	'95	'96	'97	'98
○ WISH ○ HAVE	$30	30	30	30	30	40	45	45

COTTAGE OF BOB CRATCHIT & TINY TIM, THE	ITEM #	INTRO	RETIRED	OSRP	GBTRU	NO
	6500-5	1986	1995	$25	**$60**	CHANGE

1 of the 3-piece set—CHRISTMAS CAROL COTTAGES. This is the tiny home in which Bob & Mary Cratchit raised their children—most notably Tiny Tim.
Notable: Many scholars believe that Dickens modeled the home after his own childhood home on Bayham Street in Camden Town.

DATE: ____ $ ____	'91	'92	'93	'94	'95	'96	'97	'98
○ WISH ○ HAVE	$30	30	30	30	30	50	60	60

NORMAN CHURCH

ITEM #	INTRO	RETIRED	OSRP	GBTRU	↓
6502-1	1986	LTD ED 3,500	$40	**$3350**	1%

Solid four-sided tower used as both watch and bell tower. Doors and windows reflect the Romanesque rounded arches.
Notable: The first pieces are light gray, the later pieces are darker gray. This does not affect secondary market value. Early release to Gift Creations Concepts (GCC).

DATE: ____ $ ____		'91	'92	'93	'94	'95	'96	'97	'98
○ WISH ○ HAVE		$3500	3500	3500	3600	3000	3250	3325	3400

DICKENS' LANE SHOPS

ITEM #	INTRO	RETIRED	OSRP	GBTRU	↓
6507-2	1986	1989	$80	**$505**	13%

Set of 3 includes *Thomas Kersey Coffee House, Cottage Toy Shop, Tuttle's Pub.*

see below

DATE: ____ $ ____		'91	'92	'93	'94	'95	'96	'97	'98
○ WISH ○ HAVE		$475	490	565	650	595	615	620	580

THOMAS KERSEY COFFEE HOUSE

ITEM #	INTRO	RETIRED	OSRP	GBTRU	↓
6507-2	1986	1989	$27	**$155**	9%

1 of the 3-piece set—DICKENS' LANE SHOPS. Unique roof set upon simple rectangular building rises up to central chimney with four flue pipes. Brick, plaster, and timber with tile or slate roof. Large multi-paned windows predominate front walls.

DATE: ____ $ ____		'91	'92	'93	'94	'95	'96	'97	'98
○ WISH ○ HAVE		$145	150	175	165	165	170	190	170

COTTAGE TOY SHOP

ITEM #	INTRO	RETIRED	OSRP	GBTRU	↓
6507-2	1986	1989	$27	**$160**	18%

1 of the 3-piece set—DICKENS' LANE SHOPS. Small thatched roof cottage. Shop has large bay windows for light and display. Outside side stair/entry for family to living quarters.

DATE: ____ $ ____		'91	'92	'93	'94	'95	'96	'97	'98
○ WISH ○ HAVE		$175	215	265	250	225	235	225	195

TUTTLE'S PUB

ITEM #	INTRO	RETIRED	OSRP	GBTRU	↓
6507-2	1986	1989	$27	$205	9%

1 of the 3-piece set—DICKENS' LANE SHOPS. Building rises three stories, ground level has pub for refreshments plus stable area for horse and carriages, second and third story jut out in step fashion. Travelers could rent rooms.

DATE: ____ $ ____	'91	'92	'93	'94	'95	'96	'97	'98
○ WISH ○ HAVE	$185	220	240	245	225	225	220	225

BLYTHE POND MILL HOUSE—"CORRECT"

ITEM #	INTRO	RETIRED	OSRP	GBTRU	↓
6508-0	1986	1990	$37	$195	29%

Three-story timber house, fieldstone wing holds water wheel gears. Grinding stones rest next to house.
Notable: Commonly referred to as the "correct" version, "Blythe Pond" is inscribed correctly on the bottom of the building. (The "Blythe Pond" sign above the door is correct in both versions.)

DATE: ____ $ ____	'91	'92	'93	'94	'95	'96	'97	'98
○ WISH ○ HAVE	$170	215	255	305	315	280	295	275

BLYTHE POND MILL HOUSE—"BY THE POND"

	GBTRU	↓
	$85	32%

Notable: Commonly referred to as the "By The Pond" version because this is inscribed, in error, on the bottom of the building. (The "Blythe Pond" sign above the door is correct in both versions.) The error is more common than the correct piece.

DATE: ____ $ ____	'91	'92	'93	'94	'95	'96	'97	'98
○ WISH ○ HAVE	$95	105	125	135	135	135	130	125

CHADBURY STATION AND TRAIN

ITEM #	INTRO	RETIRED	OSRP	GBTRU	↓
6528-5	1986	1989	$65	$325	16%

Set of 4. Three-car train. Station built of rough stone base and fieldstone. Columns support overhang. Wooden benches for waiting area.
Notable: Early version of the station is 1/2" smaller than later version. Its sleeve read "Train And Lighted Station." The latter version had a sleeve that read "Chadbury Station And Train." This has no affect on secondary market value.

DATE: ____ $ ____	'91	'92	'93	'94	'95	'96	'97	'98
○ WISH ○ HAVE	$315	385	385	385	375	385	380	385

BARLEY BREE

	Item #	Intro	Retired	OSRP	GBTru	↓
	5900-5	1987	1989	$60	**$325**	13%

Set of 2. Includes *Farmhouse* and *Barn*. Unlike many sets, it is very unusual for *Barley Bree* to be sold or sought-after as individual pieces.
Notable: Early versions have dark roofs, later versions have lighter roofs.

see below

Date: ___ $ ___	'91	'92	'93	'94	'95	'96	'97	'98
○ Wish ○ Have	$285	370	380	395	395	375	380	375

FARMHOUSE

	Item #	Intro	Retired	OSRP	GBTru
	5900-5	1987	1989	$30	*NE

1 of the 2-piece set—BARLEY BREE. Thatched roof on small farmhouse with centralized chimney. Half-story tucked into steeply pitched roof. *Secondary market value not established for individual pieces in the set.

Date: ___ $ ___	'91	'92	'93	'94	'95	'96	'97	'98
○ Wish ○ Have	NE	NE	NE	NE	NE	NE	NE	NE

BARN

	Item #	Intro	Retired	OSRP	GBTru
	5900-5	1987	1989	$30	*NE

1 of the 2-piece set—BARLEY BREE. Stone foundation, thatched roof, for livestock. *Secondary market value not established for individual pieces in the set.

Date: ___ $ ___	'91	'92	'93	'94	'95	'96	'97	'98
○ Wish ○ Have	NE	NE	NE	NE	NE	NE	NE	NE

OLD CURIOSITY SHOP, THE

	Item #	Intro	Retired	OSRP	GBTru	NO
	5905-6	1987	Current	$32	**$45**	CHANGE

Antiques corner shop is adjacent to rare book store. Curiosity shop has large display window and two chimneys. Book shop is taller and narrower.
Notable: Generally thought to be designed after the Old Curiosity Shop on Portsmouth St. in London, as stated on the front of the actual building. However, many historians believe that this is not the building Dickens used for a model when writing *The Old Curiosity Shop*.

Date: ___ $ ___	'91	'92	'93	'94	'95	'96	'97	'98
○ Wish ○ Have	$37.50	37.50	40	40	42	42	45	45

KENILWORTH CASTLE

ITEM #	INTRO	RETIRED	OSRP	GBTru	↓
5916-1	1987	1988	$70	**$555**	18%

Inspired by the remains of Kenilworth Castle, Warwickshire, England. A stronghold for Kings and Lords, it began in 1122 as a fortress. With living quarters it became a Medieval Palace, a favorite of Elizabeth I.
Notable: Early pieces are larger. It's not unusual for the Castle to have concave walls. Relatively straight walls can be found and are generally considered to be more valuable.

Date: ____ $ ____	'91	'92	'93	'94	'95	'96	'97	'98
○ Wish ○ Have	$375	440	495	540	675	695	675	675

BRICK ABBEY

ITEM #	INTRO	RETIRED	OSRP	GBTru	↓
6549-8	1987	1989	$33	**$300**	12%

Two spires flank front doors, rose window above entry oak doors. Example of a stage of Gothic architecture. An abbey is a church that belongs or once belonged to a monastery or convent.
Notable: Many pieces have spires that lean inward. Those with straight spires are considered to be premiere pieces and usually command a higher price.

Date: ____ $ ____	'91	'92	'93	'94	'95	'96	'97	'98
○ Wish ○ Have	$350	400	380	405	395	375	375	340

CHESTERTON MANOR HOUSE

ITEM #	INTRO	RETIRED	OSRP	GBTru	↓
6568-4	1987	LTD ED 7,500	$45	**$1385**	4%

Known as a Great House, a countryside home with many acres of land. Stone facade, slate roof, plaster and half timber, open pediment above wood entry door with double gable roof design.
Notable: Early release to Gift Creations Concepts (GCC). Box and bottomstamp read "Manor."

Date: ____ $ ____	'91	'92	'93	'94	'95	'96	'97	'98
○ Wish ○ Have	$1800	1875	1825	1725	1650	1665	1575	1445

COUNTING HOUSE & SILAS THIMBLETON BARRISTER

ITEM #	INTRO	RETIRED	OSRP	GBTru	↓
5902-1	1988	1990	$32	**$80**	11%

Square, three-story, 3-chimney, offices. Equal angle gables create 4-section roof. Attached plaster/timbered three-story building is smaller and narrower.
Notable: Lamps in initial shipments had natural porcelain panes. Lamps in later shipments had yellow panes. Box reads "Silas Thimbleton Barrister," bottomstamp reads "Counting House."

Date: ____ $ ____	'91	'92	'93	'94	'95	'96	'97	'98
○ Wish ○ Have	$95	95	90	90	85	90	90	90

C. FLETCHER PUBLIC HOUSE

	ITEM #	INTRO	RETIRED	OSRP	GBTRU	↓
	5904-8	1988 LTD ED 12,500*		$35	**$465**	11%

Pub windows wrap around corner. Wood ribs support wider/longer second story. Sweet Shop tucks in next to pub, is plaster/timber design.
Notable: Early release to Gift Creations Concepts (GCC).
*Plus Proof Editions. Market Price for Proofs is not established.

DATE: ___ $ ___		'91	'92	'93	'94	'95	'96	'97	'98
○ WISH ○ HAVE		$725	700	645	590	575	545	580	525

COBBLESTONE SHOPS

	ITEM #	INTRO	RETIRED	OSRP	GBTRU	↓
	5924-2	1988	1990	$95	**$305**	16%

Set of 3 includes *The Wool Shop, Booter And Cobbler, T. Wells Fruit & Spice Shop.*

see below

DATE: ___ $ ___		'91	'92	'93	'94	'95	'96	'97	'98
○ WISH ○ HAVE		$245	300	310	355	365	380	375	365

WOOL SHOP, THE

	ITEM #	INTRO	RETIRED	OSRP	GBTRU	↓
	5924-2	1988	1990	$32	**$150**	14%

1 of the 3-piece set—COBBLESTONE SHOPS. Low turret rounds out one front corner of shop. Wood framing of three front windows and lattice design. Light by front door.

DATE: ___ $ ___		'91	'92	'93	'94	'95	'96	'97	'98
○ WISH ○ HAVE		$120	140	170	170	180	175	175	175

BOOTER AND COBBLER

	ITEM #	INTRO	RETIRED	OSRP	GBTRU	↓
	5924-2	1988	1990	$32	**$85**	29%

1 of the 3-piece set—COBBLESTONE SHOPS. Shoes made and repaired in this stone building with entry via Tannery where leather is cured and dyed.
Notable: Some box sleeves picture the *T. Wells Fruit & Spice Shop.*

DATE: ___ $ ___		'91	'92	'93	'94	'95	'96	'97	'98
○ WISH ○ HAVE		$85	90	115	105	115	125	125	120

T. WELLS FRUIT & SPICE SHOP

	ITEM #	INTRO	RETIRED	OSRP	GBTRU	↓
	5924-2	1988	1990	$32	**$80**	16%

1 of the 3-piece set—COBBLESTONE SHOPS. White washed brick and timbered building. Front window has stone ledge. Outdoor covered produce bin for food.
Notable: Some box sleeves picture *Booter And Cobbler*.

DATE: ____ $ ____	'91	'92	'93	'94	'95	'96	'97	'98
○ WISH ○ HAVE	$85	90	95	95	95	100	95	95

NICHOLAS NICKLEBY

ITEM #	INTRO	RETIRED	OSRP	GBTRU	↓
5925-0	1988	1991	$72	**$150**	14%
			W/ERROR	**$175**	↓19%

Set of 2. Includes *Nicholas Nickleby Cottage, Wackford Squeers Boarding School*.

see below

Nic"k"olas error:	'91	'92	'93	'94	'95	'96	'97	'98
	$90	210	195	195	185	200	200	215

DATE: ____ $ ____	'91	'92	'93	'94	'95	'96	'97	'98
○ WISH ○ HAVE	$82	170	155	155	155	160	175	175

NICHOLAS NICKLEBY COTTAGE

ITEM #	INTRO	RETIRED	OSRP	GBTRU	NO
5925-0	1988	1991	$36	**$80**	CHANGE

1 of the 2-piece set—NICHOLAS NICKLEBY. This is the cottage where Nicholas Nickleby lived as the main character in Dickens' work by the same name.
Notable: On this piece the name on the sign and bottom inscription are spelled correctly.

DATE: ____ $ ____	'91	'92	'93	'94	'95	'96	'97	'98
○ WISH ○ HAVE	$41	90	80	80	80	85	85	80

NIC"K"OLAS NICKLEBY COTTAGE

	GBTRU	↓
	$100	13%

Notable: The error in spelling—Nic"k"olas rather than Nicholas—appears only on the bottom of the piece (see photo). The sign over the window is correct.

DATE: ____ $ ____	'91	'92	'93	'94	'95	'96	'97	'98
○ WISH ○ HAVE	$90	120	120	120	100	120	125	115

WACKFORD SQUEERS BOARDING SCHOOL

ITEM #	INTRO	RETIRED	OSRP	GBTRU	NO
5925-0	1988	1991	$36	**$90**	CHANGE

1 of the 2-piece set—NICHOLAS NICKLEBY. In *Nicholas Nickleby* headmaster Wackford Squeers "employs" students as farm hands. Due to its size, the building's roof sags in the middle. One with a flat roof commands a higher value.
Notable: Dickens based his version of the school on the Bowes Academy that once stood in Yorkshire.

DATE: ___ $ ___		'91	'92	'93	'94	'95	'96	'97	'98
○ WISH ○ HAVE		$41	92	85	85	85	85	85	90

MERCHANT SHOPS

ITEM #	INTRO	RETIRED	OSRP	GBTRU	↓
5926-9	1988	1993	$150	**$205**	25%

Set of 5 includes *Poulterer, Geo. Weeton Watchmaker, The Mermaid Fish Shoppe, White Horse Bakery, Walpole Tailors.*

see below

DATE: ___ $ ___		'91	'92	'93	'94	'95	'96	'97	'98
○ WISH ○ HAVE		$175	175	180	230	255	245	260	275

POULTERER

ITEM #	INTRO	RETIRED	OSRP	GBTRU	↓
5926-9	1988	1993	$32.50	**$50**	17%

1 of the 5-piece set—MERCHANT SHOPS. Three-story stone block and timber, fresh geese hang outside front door.

DATE: ___ $ ___		'91	'92	'93	'94	'95	'96	'97	'98
○ WISH ○ HAVE		$35	35	36	60	55	55	60	60

GEO. WEETON WATCHMAKER

ITEM #	INTRO	RETIRED	OSRP	GBTRU	↓
5926-9	1988	1993	$32.50	**$45**	18%

1 of the 5-piece set—MERCHANT SHOPS. All brick, rounded bay window, slate roof, fan light window in oak front door.

DATE: ___ $ ___		'91	'92	'93	'94	'95	'96	'97	'98
○ WISH ○ HAVE		$35	35	36	60	55	55	55	55

MERMAID FISH SHOPPE, THE

ITEM #	INTRO	RETIRED	OSRP	GBTRU	↓
5926-9	1988	1993	$32.50	$60	14%

1 of the 5-piece set—MERCHANT SHOPS. Roadside fish bins, bay windows, angled doors and walls, wooden trap door in roof.

DATE: _____ $ _____
○ WISH   ○ HAVE

'91	'92	'93	'94	'95	'96	'97	'98
$35	35	36	70	65	70	75	70

WHITE HORSE BAKERY

ITEM #	INTRO	RETIRED	OSRP	GBTRU	NO
5926-9	1988	1993	$32.50	$60	CHANGE

1 of the 5-piece set—MERCHANT SHOPS. Two large windows to display baked goods, roof is hipped and gabled with scalloped shingles.

DATE: _____ $ _____
○ WISH   ○ HAVE

'91	'92	'93	'94	'95	'96	'97	'98
$35	35	36	55	55	55	70	60

WALPOLE TAILORS

ITEM #	INTRO	RETIRED	OSRP	GBTRU	↓
5926-9	1988	1993	$32.50	$40	27%

1 of the 5-piece set—MERCHANT SHOPS. Stone and brick covered by stucco. Large first-floor windows have wood panels under sills. Second floor has bow window.

DATE: _____ $ _____
○ WISH   ○ HAVE

'91	'92	'93	'94	'95	'96	'97	'98
$35	35	36	55	55	55	55	55

IVY GLEN CHURCH

ITEM #	INTRO	RETIRED	OSRP	GBTRU	↓
5927-7	1988	1991	$35	$70	13%

Square-toothed parapet tops stone turret by front entry of a thatched roof church. Curved timber design above door is repeated on bell chamber of turret. Arched windows. This church has a chimney.

DATE: _____ $ _____
○ WISH   ○ HAVE

'91	'92	'93	'94	'95	'96	'97	'98
$37.50	80	85	80	85	80	85	80

DAVID COPPERFIELD

ITEM #	INTRO	RETIRED	OSRP	GBTRU	↓
5550-6	1989	1992	$125	**$170**	13%
		w/TAN PEGOTTY'S		**$210**	↓16%

Set of 3 includes *Mr. Wickfield Solicitor, Betsy Trotwood's Cottage, Peggotty's Seaside Cottage.*
Notable: Early release to Showcase Dealers, 1989.

see below

Set w/original Tan Pegotty's	'91	'92	'93	'94	'95	'96	'97	'98
	$220	220	310	250	225	230	235	250
DATE: ____ $ ____	'91	'92	'93	'94	'95	'96	'97	'98
○ WISH ○ HAVE	$125	125	230	190	175	165	180	195

MR. WICKFIELD SOLICITOR

ITEM #	INTRO	RETIRED	OSRP	GBTRU	↓
5550-6	1989	1992	$42.50	**$80**	16%

1 of the 3-piece set—DAVID COPPERFIELD. This is the home and office of Mr. Wickfield in *David Copperfield.* He resides in Canterbury and is a friend of Betsy Trotwood.
Notable: It's thought that Dickens used the house at 71 St. Dunstan's Street in Canterbury as the model for Mr. Wickfield's residence. Early release to Showcase Dealers, 1989.

DATE: ____ $ ____	'91	'92	'93	'94	'95	'96	'97	'98
○ WISH ○ HAVE	$42.50	42.50	90	96	95	95	95	95

BETSY TROTWOOD'S COTTAGE

ITEM #	INTRO	RETIRED	OSRP	GBTRU	↑
5550-6	1989	1992	$42.50	**$65**	8%

1 of the 3-piece set—DAVID COPPERFIELD. This cottage is the home of David Copperfield's aunt, Betsy Trotwood.
Notable: Though the story places the cottage in Dover, historians believe that Dickens based the cottage on the one owned by Mary Strong in Broadstairs. It's now a Dickens museum. Early release to Showcase Dealers, 1989.

DATE: ____ $ ____	'91	'92	'93	'94	'95	'96	'97	'98
○ WISH ○ HAVE	$42.50	42.50	78	65	65	60	60	60

NOTES: _____

_____

_____

_____

_____

_____

PEGGOTTY'S SEASIDE COTTAGE—"TAN"

ITEM #	INTRO	RETIRED	OSRP	GBTRU	↓
5550-6	1989	1992	$42.50	**$95**	21%

1 of the 3-piece set—DAVID COPPERFIELD.
Notable: The hull of the boat was actually unpainted.
Department 56, Inc. stated that the particular green paint
they intended to use would not adhere to the porcelain, so
they shipped them unpainted until the problem could be
corrected. Early release to Showcase Dealers, 1989.

		'91	'92	'93	'94	'95	'96	'97	'98
DATE: ___ $ ___									
○ WISH ○ HAVE		$155	155	175	150	150	125	135	120

PEGGOTTY'S SEASIDE COTTAGE—"GREEN"

	GBTRU	NO
	$60	CHANGE

1 of the 3-piece set—DAVID COPPERFIELD. This
overturned boat converted into a cottage belongs to
Daniel Peggotty in *David Copperfield*.
Notable: Though a similar cottage was located in
Yarmouth, it's strongly believed that Dickens based his
Peggotty's Cottage on an actual boat-turned-dwelling on
the bank of the canal at Gravesend.

		'91	'92	'93	'94	'95	'96	'97	'98
DATE: ___ $ ___									
○ WISH ○ HAVE		$42.50	42.50	70	60	60	55	55	60

VICTORIA STATION

ITEM #	INTRO	RETIRED	OSRP	GBTRU	↑
5574-3	1989	1998	$100	**$120**	7%

Designed after Victoria Station in London. Brownstone
with granite pillars and facings—central section with
domed red tile roof, two side wings, covered front drive-
through, gold clock above entry.
Notable: Early release to Showcase Dealers and National
Association Of Limited Edition Dealers (NALED), 1990.

		'91	'92	'93	'94	'95	'96	'97	'98
DATE: ___ $ ___									
○ WISH ○ HAVE		$100	105	105	110	112	112	112	112

KNOTTINGHILL CHURCH

ITEM #	INTRO	RETIRED	OSRP	GBTRU	↓
5582-4	1989	1995	$50	**$55**	27%

Beige/honey stone with gray slate roof, arched windows.
Turret bell chamber rises where church wings intersect.

		'91	'92	'93	'94	'95	'96	'97	'98
DATE: ___ $ ___									
○ WISH ○ HAVE		$50	50	52	52	55	65	75	75

Dickens' And Department 56®'s England

This is the last article to be written before heading to tour Dickens' England with three dozen other Department 56® collectors. I thought I'd write about one of the things that has been streaming through my mind for the last week or so as I eagerly anticipate the adventure—what's where.

Some of the many places on our itinerary are buildings that Charles Dickens used as models for locations in his works, those that Department 56, Inc. has replicated in Dickens' Village Series®, or both. Knowing that this is a highlight, I thought that you might want this information in case you ever have the opportunity to visit the area.

If the time comes and you do visit these places, remember that just because Dickens used a particular building as a model, it's not necessarily true that Department 56, Inc. used the same building for one. Many of the buildings in our villages are actually composites of various buildings and styles or simply something from the artist's imagination.

Quite possibly the most popular building for "collector visits" is the Old Curiosity Shop. It's located on Portsmouth Street in London. Though this building has been known for generations as the building used by Dickens for the title of his novel, many historians believe it may actually have been another Old Curiosity Shop that was standing at that time. In either case, the porcelain version has become the best-selling building for Department 56, Inc.

Here are a few locations for *A Christmas Carol* fans. In the story, the cottage of Bob, Tiny Tim, and the rest of the Cratchit family was inspired by a house that once stood on Bayham Street in Camden Town. It has since been demolished. St. Stephen's in Camden Town was most likely the church where Bob Cratchit and Tiny Tim worshiped. Baker's Chop Shop was the inspiration for the Melancholy Tavern where Scrooge stopped to eat his melancholy dinner. The shop once stood in Change Alley in London.

Did you collect the Charles Dickens' Signature Series? Would you like to visit them? If so, a trip to England will be an exciting one. *Crown & Cricket Inn* is based on the style of building where Dickens first lived as an adult in London. Located at Tavistock Square, the row houses are very familiar. *Dedlock Arms* was a tavern in Dickens' *Bleak House*. Dickens, it's believed, based this building on the Sondes Arms in Rockingham. Sir John Falstaff Inn stands diagonally across the street from Dickens' home in Kent, Gad's Hill. *The Grapes Inn* sits along the Thames in Limehouse. It's said that it was used as the model for the building featured in *Our Mutual Friend*. *Gad's Hill Place* was, of course, based on the actual Gad's Hill Place. This was the only home that Dickens ever owned. It was also his last. You may have noticed that I skipped over the Pied Bull Inn. This is because I haven't been able to confirm where, if anywhere, its model is located.

Other novels have been "rebuilt" in our villages too. *Wackford Squeers Boarding School* of *Nicholas Nickleby* fame was inspired by an infamous school that once stood in Yorkshire, Bowes Academy.

The house belonging to the Wickfields in *David Copperfield* was modeled after one standing at 71 St. Dunstan's Street in Canterbury. It closely resembles Dickens' description, but is nothing like the house by Department 56, Inc. Another house featured in *David Copperfield* was the one belonging to Betsy Trotwood. Dickens used Mary Strong's house in Broadstairs for inspiration. Now a Dickens museum, you would recognize it as the Trotwood cottage in Dickens' Village Series®. The third building in *David Copperfield* that is also in the village is *Peggotty's Cottage.* There were two known boats made into homes in Dickens' time. One was in Yarmouth, the other in Gravesend. It's believed that the latter was used by Dickens.

Brownlow's house in *Oliver Twist* was re-created by Dickens from a house at 39 Craven Street in London.

A building that certainly exists in London and in our villages is *Victoria Station.* Though the shape we know in the village can be seen in the actual structure, there are a number of other buildings that now make up the station, so it is somewhat different.

Oast houses dot the countryside of Kent. Many of these roasting houses are now private homes.

Though I haven't located the three cottages of Portobello Road, a visit to the street on a Saturday morning is an experience you won't soon forget.

The area of Yorkshire has provided Department 56, Inc. with a number of designs. *Giggelswick Mutton & Ham* is named after the town of Giggelswick. *Barmby Moor Cottage* is named after the town of Barmby Moor. And *Ramsford Palace* is styled after Castle Howard in York. *Butter Tub Farmhouse* and *Barn* derive their name from the Buttertub region in Yorkshire.

Of course three of the buildings in the Historical Landmark Series™ are based on actual buildings. *The Tower Of London* that we have in our villages is actually the White Tower within the Tower of London. *The Globe Theatre* is a close reproduction of the Globe Theatre where Shakespeare performed and the replica that now stands in its place. *Big Ben* is a replica of the tower that houses one of the most famous bells in the world.

With all the thoughts of these buildings fresh in mind, I can't wait to see how many I can visit.

the **Village Chronicle.**

COBLES POLICE STATION

ITEM #	INTRO	RETIRED	OSRP	GBTRU	↓
5583-2	1989	1991	$37.50	**$125**	22%

Two-story brick, stone outlines front entry and upper windows. Two watch turrets on second-story corners.

DATE: ____ $ ____		'91	'92	'93	'94	'95	'96	'97	'98
○ WISH ○ HAVE		$37.50	85	85	90	125	145	150	160

THEATRE ROYAL

ITEM #	INTRO	RETIRED	OSRP	GBTRU	↓
5584-0	1989	1992	$45	**$65**	19%

Double set of doors fill theatre frontage. Garlands and gold bells add festive touch. Second-floor rounded arch windows are separated by pilasters.
Notable: Inspired by the Theatre Royal in Rochester, England where Charles Dickens saw his first Shakespearean play.

DATE: ____ $ ____		'91	'92	'93	'94	'95	'96	'97	'98
○ WISH ○ HAVE		$45	48	80	80	80	85	80	80

RUTH MARION SCOTCH WOOLENS

ITEM #	INTRO	RETIRED	OSRP	GBTRU	NO
5585-9	1989	LTD ED 17,500*	$65	**$360**	CHANGE

Herringbone brick design between timbers decorates front of 1 1/2-story shops and home. Small flower shop tucked onto one side.
Notable: Named for the wife of Department 56, Inc. artist, Neilan Lund. Early release to Gift Creations Concepts (GCC). *Plus Proof Editions. Proofs have "Proof" stamped on the bottom of the piece instead of a number. **GBTru$ for Proof is $325.**

DATE: ____ $ ____		'91	'92	'93	'94	'95	'96	'97	'98
○ WISH ○ HAVE		$350	405	380	405	385	390	395	360

GREEN GATE COTTAGE

ITEM #	INTRO	RETIRED	OSRP	GBTRU	↓
5586-7	1989	LTD ED 22,500*	$65	**$225**	10%

Three-story home. Repeated vault design on chimney, dormers, and 3rd-story windows. Balcony above door. Fenced courtyard and 2 doors give impression of 2 homes. Small part has steep roof, crooked chimney, and ornamental molding.
Notable: *Plus Proof Editions. Proofs have "Proof" stamped on the bottom of the piece instead of a number. **GBTru$ for Proof is $200.**

DATE: ____ $ ____		'91	'92	'93	'94	'95	'96	'97	'98
○ WISH ○ HAVE		$300	340	280	275	275	270	275	250

FLAT OF EBENEZER SCROOGE, THE—"TAIWAN/PANES"

ITEM #	INTRO	RETIRED	OSRP	GBTRU	NO
5587-5	1989	VARIATION	$37.50	**$90**	CHANGE

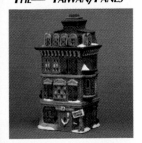

Addition to *Christmas Carol* grouping.
Notable: There are Three Variations of *The Flat Of Ebenezer Scrooge* that affect secondary market value. The First Version was made in Taiwan, has yellow panes in the windows and the far left shutter on the 4th floor is slightly open allowing light to shine through. Early release to National Association Of Limited Edition Dealers (NALED), 1989.

DATE: ___ $ ___	'91	'92	'93	'94	'95	'96	'97	'98
○ WISH ○ HAVE	$-	-	-	135	100	95	85	90

FLAT OF EBENEZER SCROOGE, THE—"TAIWAN/NO PANES"

	GBTRU	↓
	$65	19%

Notable: The Second Version was made in Taiwan but doesn't have panes in the windows.

DATE: ___ $ ___	'91	'92	'93	'94	'95	'96	'97	'98
○ WISH ○ HAVE	$-	115	-	85	60	65	75	80

FLAT OF EBENEZER SCROOGE, THE

	GBTRU	NO
	$37.50	CHANGE

Notable: The Third Version is back to panes in the windows and is made in the Philippines or China.

DATE: ___ $ ___	'91	'92	'93	'94	'95	'96	'97	'98
○ WISH ○ HAVE	$-	-	-	37.50	37.50	37.50	37.50	37.50

BISHOPS OAST HOUSE

ITEM #	INTRO	RETIRED	OSRP	GBTRU	↓
5567-0	1990	1992	$45	**$65**	19%

Large attached barn, round cobblestone oasts contain a kiln for drying malt or hops to produce ale. Exterior finished as a roughcast surface over brick. Oast houses are located throughout the Kent countryside. Many, however, have been converted to private homes.

DATE: ___ $ ___	'91	'92	'93	'94	'95	'96	'97	'98
○ WISH ○ HAVE	$45	48	85	85	75	80	75	80

KING'S ROAD

	Item #	Intro	Retired	OSRP	GBTʀᴜ	↓
	5568-9	1990	1996	$72	**$85**	23%

Set of 2 includes *Tutbury Printer,* and *C.H. Watt Physician.*

see below

Date: ____ $ ____		'91	'92	'93	'94	'95	'96	'97	'98
○ Wish ○ Have		$72	75	80	80	80	80	100	110

TUTBURY PRINTER

	Item #	Intro	Retired	OSRP	GBTʀᴜ	↓
	55690	1990	1996	$36	**$45**	10%

1 of the 2-piece set—KING'S ROAD. Timbered/plaster design with decorative molding between first and second story. Ground floor bay window with smaller bays on second floor. Steeply pitched roof with a dormer.

Date: ____ $ ____		'91	'92	'93	'94	'95	'96	'97	'98
○ Wish ○ Have		$36	37.50	40	40	40	40	50	50

C.H. WATT PHYSICIAN

	Item #	Intro	Retired	OSRP	GBTʀᴜ	↓
	55691	1990	1996	$36	**$50**	17%

1 of the 2-piece set—KING'S ROAD. Doctor's office on ground floor, outside staircase leads to family residence, bricks used above most windows as decorative arch, exposed stone edges on four corners of house walls.

Date: ____ $ ____		'91	'92	'93	'94	'95	'96	'97	'98
○ Wish ○ Have		$36	37.50	40	40	36	40	50	60

FAGIN'S HIDE-A-WAY

	Item #	Intro	Retired	OSRP	GBTʀᴜ	↓
	5552-2	1991	1995	$68	**$60**	29%

Two attached buildings in disrepair. Broken shutters, cracks in wall. Barrel warehouse with step roof, gate across doors.
Notable: In *Oliver Twist,* this is the hide-out for Fagin and his gang of young criminals. Dickens based many of the characters on people who frequented a series of underground passages in London.

Date: ____ $ ____		'91	'92	'93	'94	'95	'96	'97	'98
○ Wish ○ Have		$68	68	72	72	72	80	85	85

OLIVER TWIST

ITEM #	INTRO	RETIRED	OSRP	GBTRU	↓
5553-0	1991	1993	$75	**$95**	30%

Set of 2 includes *Brownlow House* and *Maylie Cottage*.

see below

DATE: ____ $ ____		'91	'92	'93	'94	'95	'96	'97	'98
○ WISH ○ HAVE		$75	75	80	140	130	135	135	135

BROWNLOW HOUSE

ITEM #	INTRO	RETIRED	OSRP	GBTRU	↓
5553-0	1991	1993	$37.50	**$60**	20%

1 of the 2-piece set—OLIVER TWIST. Two-story stone house with two brick chimneys and three front gables. Double doors. The gentleman living in this house befriends Oliver and later adopts him.
Notable: The house at 39 Craven Street in London is thought to be Dickens' model for the house.

DATE: ____ $ ____		'91	'92	'93	'94	'95	'96	'97	'98
○ WISH ○ HAVE		$37.50	37.50	40	75	70	75	75	75

MAYLIE COTTAGE

ITEM #	INTRO	RETIRED	OSRP	GBTRU	↓
5553-0	1991	1993	$37.50	**$50**	17%

1 of the 2-piece set—OLIVER TWIST. Oliver was forced to burglarize Mrs. Maylie's cottage and was wounded. He recuperated under her care at the cottage. This cottage has a pronounced roof ridge, curved cone roof shape repeated on dormers and front door. One chimney rises up the front facade, a second chimney on side of house.

DATE: ____ $ ____		'91	'92	'93	'94	'95	'96	'97	'98
○ WISH ○ HAVE		$37.50	37.50	40	75	65	65	65	60

ASHBURY INN

ITEM #	INTRO	RETIRED	OSRP	GBTRU	↓
5555-7	1991	1995	$55	**$65**	13%

Tudor timbered Inn for coach travelers. Food, lodging, and drink. Double chimneys, two roof dormers, and double peaks over multi-paned windows by entry.

DATE: ____ $ ____		'91	'92	'93	'94	'95	'96	'97	'98
○ WISH ○ HAVE		$55	55	60	60	60	70	75	75

NEPHEW FRED'S FLAT

ITEM #	INTRO	RETIRED	OSRP	GBTRU	↑
5557-3	1991	1994	$35	**$85**	13%

Christmas Carol Four-story home with three-story turret-like bow windows. Planters flank front door. Overhang window above side door with crowstepped coping in gable rising to two chimneys. Ivy grows up corner area—garlands, wreath, and Christmas greetings decorate facade.
Notable: Taiwan piece is darker in color and approx. 1/4" shorter than pieces from China.

DATE: ____ $ ____		'91	'92	'93	'94	'95	'96	'97	'98
○ WISH ○ HAVE		$35	35	36	36	65	65	70	75

CROWN & CRICKET INN

ITEM #	INTRO	RETIRED	OSRP	GBTRU	↓
5750-9	1991	1992 ANNUAL	$100	**$150**	9%

Three-story brick and stone with pillars flanking covered formal entry. Curved canopy roof on Golden Lion Arms Pub. Wrought iron balustrade outlines triple window on second floor. Dressed stone edges walls. Mansard roof with decorative trim and molding.
Notable: Charles Dickens' Signature Series. Special collector box and hang tag. The trim on the early pieces was light; later pieces had a darker gray trim.

DATE: ____ $ ____	'92	'93	'94	'95	'96	'97	'98
○ WISH ○ HAVE	$100	165	175	175	145	170	165

OLD MICHAELCHURCH

ITEM #	INTRO	RETIRED	OSRP	GBTRU	↓
5562-0	1992	1996	$42	**$50**	17%

Stone base with lath and plaster filling space between timbered upper portion. Tower rises up front facade with heavy solid look, a simple four-sided structure. Double wood doors at rear of church.
Notable: Early release to Showcase Dealers and Gift Creations Concepts (GCC).

DATE: ____ $ ____	'92	'93	'94	'95	'96	'97	'98
○ WISH ○ HAVE	$42	46	46	48	48	60	60

PIED BULL INN, THE

ITEM #	INTRO	RETIRED	OSRP	GBTRU	↓
5751-7	1992	1993 ANNUAL	$100	**$140**	7%

Elizabethan style with wood and plaster upper stories and stone and brick lower levels. Front entry at side of Inn allows public rooms to be of good size to service guests and local folk.
Notable: Charles Dickens' Signature Series. Special collector box and hang tag.

DATE: ____ $ ____	'93	'94	'95	'96	'97	'98
○ WISH ○ HAVE	$100	160	145	150	150	150

HEMBLETON PEWTERER

ITEM #	INTRO	RETIRED	OSRP	GBTRU	NO
5800-9	1992	1995	$72	**$75**	CHANGE

Timber framed with plaster in Elizabethan style. Bay windows create two-story front facade. Chimney Sweep shop with steep pitched roof hugs one side of the pewterer.
Notable: Early issue has two small additions on right side, later issue has one large addition.

DATE: ____ $ ____	'92	'93	'94	'95	'96	'97	'98
○ Wish ○ Have	$72	72	72	72	75	80	75

KING'S ROAD POST OFFICE

ITEM #	INTRO	RETIRED	OSRP	GBTRU	↑
5801-7	1992	1998	$45	**$50**	11%

Simple four-sided stone three-story building with semicircular turret-like two-story rise out of window area. Entrance door surmounted by pediment just below post office sign. Triple flue chimney rises off back of building.

DATE: ____ $ ____	'92	'93	'94	'95	'96	'97	'98
○ Wish ○ Have	$45	45	45	45	45	45	45

BOARDING & LODGING SCHOOL (#18)

ITEM #	INTRO	RETIRED	OSRP	GBTRU	↓
5809-2	1992	1993 ANNUAL	$48	**$90**	36%

This is the school Scrooge attended as a youngster.
Notable: Charles Dickens' Signature Series. Special collector box and hang tag. Bottomstamp of the Charles Dickens Heritage Foundation commemorates the 150th Anniversary of *A Christmas Carol*. Address is #18. Early release to Showcase Dealers & select buying groups. Building also available (1994-1998) as Item #5810-6, w/o the commemorative stamp & an address of #43.

DATE: ____ $ ____	'93	'94	'95	'96	'97	'98
○ Wish ○ Have	$48	200	200	160	165	140

DEDLOCK ARMS

ITEM #	INTRO	RETIRED	OSRP	GBTRU	↓
5752-5	1993	1994 ANNUAL	$100	**$105**	16%

Stone wall courtyard has metal gate and 2 lanterns. Three-story Inn is brightly lit with Inn sign above front window.
Notable: Charles Dickens' Signature Series. Special collector box and hang tag. A tavern in Dickens' *Bleak House*, Dickens based his description on Sondes Arms in Rockingham.

DATE: ____ $ ____	'94	'95	'96	'97	'98
○ Wish ○ Have	$100	150	135	140	125

PUMP LANE SHOPPES

	ITEM #	INTRO	RETIRED	OSRP	GBTRU	↓
	5808-4	1993	1996	$112	**$110**	19%

Set of 3 includes *Bumpstead Nye Cloaks & Canes, Lomas Ltd. Molasses,* and *W.M. Wheat Cakes & Puddings.*

see below

DATE: ____ $ ____		'93	'94	'95	'96	'97	'98
○ WISH ○ HAVE		$112	112	112	112	145	135

BUMPSTEAD NYE CLOAKS & CANES

	ITEM #	INTRO	RETIRED	OSRP	GBTRU	↓
	58085	1993	1996	$37.50	**$40**	20%

1 of the 3-piece set—PUMP LANE SHOPPES. Tall narrow shop with timbered second story. Front gable has design etched into trim. Shop was noted for cloaks and capes as well as canes and walking sticks.

DATE: ____ $ ____		'93	'94	'95	'96	'97	'98
○ WISH ○ HAVE		$37.50	37.50	27.50	37.50	45	50

LOMAS LTD. MOLASSES

	ITEM #	INTRO	RETIRED	OSRP	GBTRU	NO
	58086	1993	1996	$37.50	**$45**	CHANGE

1 of the 3-piece set—PUMP LANE SHOPPES. Steps lead up to store above stone lower level where molasses and treacles are refined and stored. Double chimneys rise above thatched roof.

DATE: ____ $ ____		'93	'94	'95	'96	'97	'98
○ WISH ○ HAVE		$37.50	37.50	37.50	37.50	45	45

W.M. WHEAT CAKES & PUDDINGS

	ITEM #	INTRO	RETIRED	OSRP	GBTRU	NO
	58087	1993	1996	$37.50	**$50**	CHANGE

1 of the 3-piece set—PUMP LANE SHOPPES. Baking chimney rises from center of main shop roof. Second-story rooms are dormered with additional chimney at rear. Wreath hangs above curved front door and arched design is repeated above front windows.

DATE: ____ $ ____		'93	'94	'95	'96	'97	'98
○ WISH ○ HAVE		$37.50	37.50	37.50	37.50	45	50

KINGSFORD'S BREW HOUSE

	ITEM #	INTRO	RETIRED	OSRP	GBTRU	↓
	5811-4	1993	1996	$45	**$50**	17%

Stone three-story building with slate roof. Grain was processed into ale by fermentation. Chimneys rise from both sides from ovens & vats where the beverages were brewed. Banner with tankard hangs outside.

DATE:____ $ ____ ○ WISH ○ HAVE

'93	'94	'95	'96	'97	'98
$45	45	45	45	60	60

GREAT DENTON MILL

	ITEM #	INTRO	RETIRED	OSRP	GBTRU	↓
	5812-2	1993	1997	$50	**$45**	18%

Both grinding of grain for baking and animal feed as well as preparation of wool combed into yarn took place at Mill. Narrow three-story wood structure with water wheel for power to turn wheels.

DATE:____ $ ____ ○ WISH ○ HAVE

'93	'94	'95	'96	'97	'98
$50	50	50	50	50	55

SIR JOHN FALSTAFF INN

	ITEM #	INTRO	RETIRED	OSRP	GBTRU	↓
	5753-3	1994	1995 ANNUAL	$100	**$105**	16%

This building is based on the inn still located across the street from Gad's Hill Place, Dickens' last home. Three-story Inn of stucco, timber and brick with slate roof. Two-story bay windows frame front entry.
Notable: Charles Dickens' Signature Series. Special collector box and hang tag.

DATE:____ $ ____ ○ WISH ○ HAVE

'95	'96	'97	'98
$100	130	130	125

BOARDING & LODGING SCHOOL (#43)

	ITEM #	INTRO	RETIRED	OSRP	GBTRU	↑
	5810-6	1994	1998	$48	**$55**	15%

Notable: Original release, Item #5809-2 was a commemorative version with #18 as address. This building has #43 as the address. When both Boarding Schools are side-by-side, the addresses create 1843, the year that *A Christmas Carol* was published.

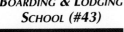

DATE:____ $ ____ ○ WISH ○ HAVE

'94	'95	'96	'97	'98
$48	48	48	48	48

WHITTLESBOURNE CHURCH

ITEM #	INTRO	RETIRED	OSRP	GBTRU	↑
5821-1	1994	1998	$85	**$90**	6%

Midyear release. Stone church with a single fortress-like tower rising off front right side. A masonry brace built against left side supports massive stone wall and provides a walkway.

DATE: ____ $ ____
○ WISH ○ HAVE

'94	'95	'96	'97	'98
$85	85	85	85	85

GIGGELSWICK MUTTON & HAM

ITEM #	INTRO	RETIRED	OSRP	GBTRU	NO
5822-0	1994	1997	$48	**$55**	CHANGE

Midyear release. The town of Giggleswick is located in North Yorkshire. Butcher shop concentrates on meats from sheep and pigs. Smokehouse on side cures meat and adds special flavoring. Shop has corner wraparound windows.

DATE: ____ $ ____
○ WISH ○ HAVE

'94	'95	'96	'97	'98
$48	48	48	48	55

HATHER HARNESS

ITEM #	INTRO	RETIRED	OSRP	GBTRU	↓
5823-8	1994	1997	$48	**$45**	18%

Stone, brick and stucco three-story shop and family home. Double doors allow entry of horses, oxen, carriages and wagons to be fixed.

DATE: ____ $ ____
○ WISH ○ HAVE

'94	'95	'96	'97	'98
$48	48	48	48	55

PORTOBELLO ROAD THATCHED COTTAGES

ITEM #	INTRO	RETIRED	OSRP	GBTRU	↑
5824-6	1994	1997	$120	**$135**	4%

Set of 3 includes *Mr. & Mrs. Pickle, Cobb Cottage,* and *Browning Cottage.*

see next page

DATE: ____ $ ____
○ WISH ○ HAVE

'94	'95	'96	'97	'98
$120	120	120	120	130

Mr. & Mrs. Pickle

Item #	Intro	Retired	OSRP	GBTru	NO
58247	1994	1997	$40	**$45**	CHANGE

1 of the 3-piece set—PORTOBELLO ROAD THATCHED COTTAGES. Timbered stucco home with attached Antique Store. Home sign highlights a pickle.

Date: ____ $ ____
○ Wish ○ Have

'94	'95	'96	'97	'98
$40	40	40	40	45

Cobb Cottage

Item #	Intro	Retired	OSRP	GBTru	↑
58248	1994	1997	$40	**$50**	11%

1 of the 3-piece set—PORTOBELLO ROAD THATCHED COTTAGES. The thatched roof is being completed on a stucco, timber and brick home. Unique L-shape with ornate roof ridges.
Notable: First Heritage Village Collection® house without snow on the roof.

Date: ____ $ ____
○ Wish ○ Have

'94	'95	'96	'97	'98
$40	40	40	40	45

Browning Cottage

Item #	Intro	Retired	OSRP	GBTru	NO
58249	1994	1997	$40	**$45**	CHANGE

1 of the 3-piece set—PORTOBELLO ROAD THATCHED COTTAGES. Two-story brick, timber and stucco home. Original thatch roof replaced by slate to denote increase in family's wealth. Dutch door entry.

Date: ____ $ ____
○ Wish ○ Have

'94	'95	'96	'97	'98
$40	40	40	40	45

Grapes Inn, The

Item #	Intro	Retired	OSRP	GBTru	↓
57534	1995	1996 Annual	$120	**$125**	7%

Inn on the waterfront supplies food, drink and lodging for weary travelers. Rowboats are tied up to rear unloading dock. Two staircases outside lead to inn or to pub and dining areas.
Notable: Charles Dickens' Signature Series. Special collector box and hang tag. Located in Limehouse, this Inn is said to be used as the model for the "Porters" in *Our Mutual Friend*.

Date: ____ $ ____
○ Wish ○ Have

'96	'97	'98
$120	135	135

DICKENS' VILLAGE START A TRADITION SET

ITEM #	INTRO	RETIRED	OSRP	GBTRU	↓
5832-7	1995	1996	$85	**$90**	22%

Set of 13. Midyear release. Set includes: *Faversham Lamps & Oil*—Two-story shop/home w/stone trim on arched door/windows. Crowstepped roof edges. *Morston Steak And Kidney Pie*—Meat pies prepared in small 1 1/2-story shop/home. *Town Square Carolers* accessory, 6 assorted sisal trees, a Cobblestone Road, and bag of Real Plastic Snow.
Notable: Was featured at Department 56, Inc.'s National Homes For The Holidays Open House Event—Oct/Nov, 1995. Special packaging for promotion. Set was also available during Event week of November 7–11, 1996.

DATE: ____ $ ____
○ WISH   ○ HAVE

'95	'96	'97	'98
$85	85	120	115

J.D. NICHOLS TOY SHOP

ITEM #	INTRO	RETIRED	OSRP	GBTRU	↑
58328	1995	1998	$48	**$55**	10%

Brightly lit front window, topped by ledge carrying store name and trimmed with 3 potted trees, highlights toy shop. Tall front gables feature timber design. Brick chimneys rise from steeply pitched roof.

DATE: ____ $ ____
○ WISH   ○ HAVE

'95	'96	'97	'98
$48	50	50	50

DURSLEY MANOR

ITEM #	INTRO	RETIRED	OSRP	GBTRU	NO
58329	1995	CURRENT	$50	**$55**	CHANGE

Two plaques above entry state building name and year cornerstone placed. Brick with stone trim at windows, carriage portico, roof edging and the 3 chimneys.

DATE: ____ $ ____
○ WISH   ○ HAVE

'95	'96	'97	'98
$50	50	55	55

BLENHAM STREET BANK

ITEM #	INTRO	RETIRED	OSRP	GBTRU	↑
58330	1995	1998	$60	**$70**	17%

Many windows bring light and openness to squared building design. Strength and fortress-like solidarity promoted by use of stone, columns, and arches above windows. Double entry doors topped by fanlight window arch.

DATE: ____ $ ____
○ WISH   ○ HAVE

'95	'96	'97	'98
$60	60	60	60

WRENBURY SHOPS

ITEM #	INTRO	RETIRED	OSRP	GBTRU
58331	1995	1997 &1998	$100	**$125**

Set of 3 includes *Wrenbury Baker, The Chop Shop,* and *T. Puddlewick Spectacle Shop.*

see below

DATE: ____ $ ____	'95	'96	'97	'98
○ WISH ○ HAVE	$100	100	100	*

WRENBURY BAKER

ITEM #	INTRO	RETIRED	OSRP	GBTRU	↑
58332	1995	1997	$35	**$45**	13%

1 of the 3-piece set—WRENBURY SHOPS. Cottage shop houses baker. 1 1/2-story with roof line coming down to first floor. Single chimney rises through hand-hewn roof. Sign outside by entry.

DATE: ____ $ ____	'95	'96	'97	'98
○ WISH ○ HAVE	$35	35	35	40

CHOP SHOP, THE

ITEM #	INTRO	RETIRED	OSRP	GBTRU	↓
58333	1995	1997	$35	**$40**	5%

1 of the 3-piece set—WRENBURY SHOPS. Large chimney with 4 flue pots rises through rough shingle roof. Sign outside entry advertises wares. Stucco facade.

DATE: ____ $ ____	'95	'96	'97	'98
○ WISH ○ HAVE	$35	35	35	42

T. PUDDLEWICK SPECTACLE SHOP

ITEM #	INTRO	RETIRED	OSRP	GBTRU	↑
58334	1995	1998	$35	**$45**	29%

1 of the 3-piece set—WRENBURY SHOPS. Ornate timber Tudor style shop selling glasses, lorgnettes, looking glasses, monocles, and spyglasses. Sign outside advertises product.

DATE: ____ $ ____	'95	'96	'97	'98
○ WISH ○ HAVE	$35	35	35	35

MALTINGS, THE

ITEM #	INTRO	RETIRED	OSRP	GBTRU	NO
5833-5	1995	1998	$50	**$50**	CHANGE

Midyear release. Home, shop and bridge in one construct of stone, stucco and wood. Large doors allow carts to enter.
Notable: A malting is a building used to roast or malt barley for brewing beer and ale.

DATE: ____ $ ____
○ WISH ○ HAVE

'95	'96	'97	'98
$50	50	50	50

DUDDEN CROSS CHURCH

ITEM #	INTRO	RETIRED	OSRP	GBTRU	NO
5834-3	1995	1997	$45	**$55**	CHANGE

Midyear release. Brick church with stone coping. Bell tower rises on one side through roof. Stone archway to courtyard on other side near entry door.

DATE: ____ $ ____
○ WISH ○ HAVE

'95	'96	'97	'98
$45	45	45	55

GAD'S HILL PLACE

ITEM #	INTRO	RETIRED	OSRP	GBTRU	NO
57535	1996	1997 ANNUAL	$98	**$120**	CHANGE

Three-story red brick home in Queen Anne period style. Balance established by center hall entry highlighted by pediment. Each side of home equals the other in rooms and window treatment. One chimney, bell tower, and an attached gazebo displaying Christmas tree.
Notable: Charles Dickens' Signature Series. Special collector box and hang tag. Located in Kent, this was the last home of Dickens and the only one he ever owned.

DATE: ____ $ ____
○ WISH ○ HAVE

'97	'98
$98	120

RAMSFORD PALACE

ITEM #	INTRO	RETIRED	OSRP	GBTRU	↓
58336	1996	LTD ED 27,500	$175	**$425**	11%

Midyear release. Set of 17 includes *Ramsford Palace* and Accessories: *Palace Guards*, Set/2, *Palace Gate, Palace Fountain, Wall Hedge*, Set/8, *Corner Wall Topiaries*, Set/4. The south facade comprises a central block surmounted by a dome, between two wings. Corinthian pilasters accentuate the height.
Notable: The building is modeled after Castle Howard in York. The mansion, built by the Earl of Carlisle, was begun in 1700.

DATE: ____ $ ____
○ WISH ○ HAVE

'96	'97	'98
$175	495	475

BUTTER TUB FARMHOUSE

ITEM #	INTRO	RETIRED	OSRP	GBTru	NO
58337	1996	CURRENT	$40	**$40**	CHANGE

Midyear release. Three steeply pitched red roof heights set off tall narrow chimneys. Door and windows have wood frames. High gables match roof heights on front facade. **Notable:** Butter Tub refers to a pass in Yorkshire where cool pools of water known as buttertubs form in potholes.

DATE: ____ $ ____	'96	'97	'98
○ WISH ○ HAVE	$40	40	40

BUTTER TUB BARN

ITEM #	INTRO	RETIRED	OSRP	GBTru	NO
58338	1996	CURRENT	$48	**$48**	CHANGE

Midyear release. Two separate barn areas share one steep roof. Wagons can enter through double wood doors or into central loading area.

DATE: ____ $ ____	'96	'97	'98
○ WISH ○ HAVE	$48	48	48

CHRISTMAS CAROL COTTAGE, THE (REVISITED)

ITEM #	INTRO	RETIRED	OSRP	GBTru	NO
58339	1996	CURRENT	$60	**$60**	CHANGE

"Smoking House." Midyear release. *Christmas Carol Revisited Series.* A new expanded version of home of Bob and Mary Cratchit. Roof has 2 dormer windows. Two fireplaces now heat the house. A log pile against a large chimney holds a built-in Magic Smoking Element powered by a separate transformer that heats a supplied nontoxic liquid allowing smoke to rise out of the chimney.

DATE: ____ $ ____	'96	'97	'98
○ WISH ○ HAVE	$60	60	60

NETTIE QUINN PUPPETS & MARIONETTES

ITEM #	INTRO	RETIRED	OSRP	GBTru	NO
58344	1996	CURRENT	$50	**$50**	CHANGE

Front of store features a puppet/marionette stage for performances to passing village folk. Decorations on stage and front facade of three-story building advertise the woodcarving craftsman's talents.
Notable: This is the first Heritage Village Collection® building to feature multiple weathervanes.

DATE: ____ $ ____	'97	'98
○ WISH ○ HAVE	$50	50

MULBERRIE COURT BROWNSTONES

ITEM #	INTRO	RETIRED	OSRP	GBTRU	NO
58345	1996	CURRENT	$90	**$90**	CHANGE

Three identical attached town houses, #5, #6, #7 are three-story brick residences. Each entry door features a glass fanlight and each has a bow window on first and second story. Individual room fireplace chimneys are grouped into one roof structure. Railing with gate separates home from passing strollers.

DATE: ____ $ ____
○ WISH ○ HAVE

'97	'98
$90	90

OLDE CAMDEN TOWN CHURCH, THE (REVISITED)

ITEM #	INTRO	RETIRED	OSRP	GBTRU	NO
58346	1996	CURRENT	$55	**$55**	CHANGE

Christmas Carol Revisited Series. This is the church where Bob Cratchit and Tiny Tim spent Christmas morning in *A Christmas Carol.* Piece comes with a miniature storybook created and written by designers which sets scene for piece.
Notable: Dickens may have used St. Stephen's Church in Camden as a model.

DATE: ____ $ ____
○ WISH ○ HAVE

'97	'98
$55	55

MELANCHOLY TAVERN, THE (REVISITED)

ITEM #	INTRO	RETIRED	OSRP	GBTRU	NO
58347	1996	CURRENT	$45	**$45**	CHANGE

Christmas Carol Revisited Series. Tavern where Scrooge ate in *A Christmas Carol.* Tall narrow timbered tavern offers brew and meals. Piece comes with a miniature storybook created and written by designers which sets scene for piece.
Notable: It is believed that Dickens developed his idea for the tavern from Baker's Chop Shop that once stood along Change Alley in London.

DATE: ____ $ ____
○ WISH ○ HAVE

'97	'98
$45	45

QUILLY'S ANTIQUES

ITEM #	INTRO	RETIRED	OSRP	GBTRU	NO
58348	1996	CURRENT	$46	**$46**	CHANGE

Small town shop with entry and display window built out from front wall. Family lives in cramped upper-floor quarters. Walkway crowded with antique objects and small items. Access to side yard through wood door.

DATE: ____ $ ____
○ WISH ○ HAVE

'97	'98
$46	46

DICKENS' VILLAGE START A TRADITION SET

ITEM #	INTRO	RETIRED	OSRP	GBTru	NO
58322	1997	1998	$75*	**$100**	CHANGE

Set of 13. Midyear release. Includes 2 lighted buildings: *Sudbury Church* and *Old East Rectory*. An Accessory Set of 3, *The Spirit Of Giving*, a young lady and girl giving gift baskets of food for the poor to the Rector, a Cobblestone Road, 6 sisal trees and Real Plastic Snow complete the set.

Notable: Set was featured at Department 56, Inc.'s National Homes For The Holidays Open House Event, November 1–9, 1997. *SRP reduced to $75 for the Event.

				'97	'98
DATE: ____ $ ____				$100	100
○ WISH ○ HAVE					

J. LYTES COAL MERCHANT

ITEM #	INTRO	RETIRED	OSRP	GBTru	NO
58323	1997	CURRENT	$50	**$50**	CHANGE

Midyear release. A very tall building housing a coal merchant. Coverings for the upper windows are metal plates hinged to the window instead of glass panes.
Notable: Original shipments had bottomstamps that read "Dickens' Vallage."

				'97	'98
DATE: ____ $ ____				$50	50
○ WISH ○ HAVE					

BARMBY MOOR COTTAGE

ITEM #	INTRO	RETIRED	OSRP	GBTru	NO
58324	1997	CURRENT	$48	**$48**	CHANGE

Midyear release. House is 1 1/2-story built of stones from the moor. Front of home has one large gable highlighted by a carved barge-board. Above front door are two small gabled dormer windows.
Notable: Barmby Moor is a village located east of York.

				'97	'98
DATE: ____ $ ____				$48	48
○ WISH ○ HAVE					

TOWER OF LONDON

ITEM #	INTRO
58500	1997

See Historical Landmark Series™.

MANCHESTER SQUARE

ITEM #	INTRO	RETIRED	OSRP	GBTru	NO
58301	1997	CURRENT	$250	**$250**	CHANGE

Set of 25. Four lighted buildings: *G. Choir's Weights & Scales, Frogmore Chemist, Custom House, Lydby Trunk & Satchel Shop.* Also included: *Manchester Square Accessory Set* (7 pieces), 12 trees, Road and Snow. The *Custom House* features the first circular staircase with detailed metal rails.

Notable: Early shipments had a bottomstamp that read "Dickens' Village Seires."

DATE: ____ $ ____
○ WISH ○ HAVE

'98
$250

EAST INDIES TRADING CO.

ITEM #	INTRO	RETIRED	OSRP	GBTru	NO
58302	1997	CURRENT	$65	**$65**	CHANGE

Three-story brick and plaster trading company plus attached warehouse. Features an acrylic skylight. The original East India Company was a British trading company incorporated in 1600. Their primary business was exporting English woolen cloth and importing the products of the East Indies.

Notable: Similar to 1997 *Canadian Trading Co.,* Item #58306, with a change of color and name, a variation only available in Canada.

DATE: ____ $ ____
○ WISH ○ HAVE

'98
$65

LEACOCK POULTERER (REVISITED)

ITEM #	INTRO	RETIRED	OSRP	GBTru	NO
58303	1997	CURRENT	$48	**$48**	CHANGE

Christmas Carol Revisited Series. Fresh game hangs outside front window to advertise shop. Stone chimneys rise on sides of Tudor timber and plaster building.

DATE: ____ $ ____
○ WISH ○ HAVE

'98
$48

CROOKED FENCE COTTAGE

ITEM #	INTRO	RETIRED	OSRP	GBTru	NO
58304	1997	CURRENT	$60	**$60**	CHANGE

Thatched cottage with large stone fireplace chimney. Hanging metal birdcage and kitten are featured. Small crooked fence gave cottage its name. Before towns used a numbering system, houses and buildings were known by their unique architectural details.

Notable: Early shipments had bottomstamp that read "Dickens' Village Seires."

DATE: ____ $ ____
○ WISH ○ HAVE

'98
$60

	ITEM #	INTRO	RETIRED	OSRP	GBTRU	NO
ASHWICK LANE HOSE & LADDER	58305	1997	CURRENT	$54	**$54**	CHANGE

Brick and stone 2 1/2-story firehouse has ornate coping design on front tower turret. Rails designed to have a swayed look surround top of tower and second-story building area.

DATE: ____ $ ____
○ WISH   ○ HAVE

'98
$54

	ITEM #	INTRO	RETIRED	OSRP	GBTRU	↑
CANADIAN TRADING CO.	58306	1997	1998	$65	**$150**	131%

Three-story brick and plaster trading company plus attached warehouse. Features an acrylic skylight.
Notable: This was only available in Canada. Similar to 1997 *East Indies Trading Co.*, Item #58302, with a change of color and name.

DATE: ____ $ ____
○ WISH   ○ HAVE

'98
$65

	ITEM #	INTRO
OLD GLOBE THEATRE, THE	58501	1997

See Historical Landmark Series™.

	ITEM #	INTRO	RETIRED	OSRP	GBTRU	NO
THOMAS MUDGE TIMEPIECES	58307	1998	CURRENT	$60	**$60**	CHANGE

Midyear release. Stone two-story shop with timepiece advertisement sign hanging off corner turret extension. Steep copperplated roof caps this turret. Wrought iron railing is part of decorative building front. Watches made in the 1700's by Englishman Thomas Mudge are on display at Windsor Castle.
Notable: The name N. Lund stands for Department 56, Inc. Master Architect, Neilan Lund.

DATE: ____ $ ____
○ WISH   ○ HAVE

'98
$60

SETON MORRIS SPICE MERCHANT GIFT SET

ITEM #	INTRO	RETIRED	OSRP	GBTRU	↑
58308	1998	EVENT GIFT SET	$65	**$90**	38%

Set of 10. Midyear release. Lighted building is slate roofed, plaster and timber shop selling spices and condiments. Accessory Set of 3 is entitled *Christmas Apples* and is boy and girl with an apple seller. Also included are 4 sisal trees, Cobblestone Road, and 1.5 oz. bag of Village Fresh Fallen Snow.

Notable: One of three Gift Sets featured at Department 56 , Inc.'s National Homes For The Holidays Open House Event, November 5–9, 1998.

DATE: _____ $ _____
○ WISH ○ HAVE

'98
$65

KENSINGTON PALACE

ITEM #	INTRO	RETIRED	OSRP	GBTRU	↑
58309	1998	EVENT PIECE	$195	**$245**	26%

Included are Palace Gates, Statue of William III, Flag of Great Britain, 4 sisal trees, 4 sisal hedges and Camden Park Cobblestone Road. Will always be remembered as a residence of Princess Diana. As a tribute to her love for children, a portion of the proceeds from each piece will be given to the Ronald McDonald Houses® across the U.S. and Canada. **Notable:** A Special Edition Piece, it was introduced during the 1998 International Collectible Exposition in Rosemont, Illinois and was available exclusively at Department 56, Inc.'s National Homes For The Holidays Open House Event, November 5–9, 1998.

DATE: _____ $ _____
○ WISH ○ HAVE

'98
$195

GREAT EXPECTATIONS SATIS MANOR

ITEM #	INTRO	RETIRED	OSRP	GBTRU
58310	1998	CURRENT	$110	**$110**

Set of 4 plus book.
Notable: The first of the Literary Classics, this "snowless" building comes with a three-piece accessory and a 528-page specially printed copy of *Great Expectations*.

DATE: _____ $ _____
○ WISH ○ HAVE

TATTYEAVE KNOLL

ITEM #	INTRO	RETIRED	OSRP	GBTRU
58311	1998	CURRENT	$55	**$55**

Built in 1749, this fieldstone cottage shows its age, thus getting its name.

DATE: _____ $ _____
○ WISH ○ HAVE

Heathmoor Castle

Item #	Intro	Retired	OSRP	GBTru
58313	1998	1999 Annual	$90	**$90**

Gargoyles, a coat of arms, tartan banners, and an outside staircase are four characteristics of this realistic looking castle.
Notable: Limited to year of production 1999.

Date: _____ $ _____
○ Wish   ○ Have

Teaman & Crupp China Shop

Item #	Intro	Retired	OSRP	GBTru
58314	1998	Current	$64	**$64**

Fine china fills windows of this three-story shop.

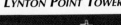

Date: _____ $ _____
○ Wish   ○ Have

Lynton Point Tower

Item #	Intro	Retired	OSRP	GBTru
58315	1998	Current	$80	**$80**

The light tower stands alongside the keeper's cottage on a rocky coastline. Comes with two light bulbs.

Date: _____ $ _____
○ Wish   ○ Have

North Eastern Sea Fisheries Ltd.

Item #	Intro	Retired	OSRP	GBTru
58316	1998	Current	$70	**$70**

A waterfront building, it accepts the fishermen's daily catch and also sells it to the area's mongers.

Date: _____ $ _____
○ Wish   ○ Have

HORSE AND HOUNDS PUB, THE

ITEM #	INTRO	RETIRED	OSRP	GBTRU
58340	1998	CURRENT	$70	$70

The entrance to this pub is at the corner. The windows appear to be made of antique leaded glass.

DATE: _____ $ _____
○ WISH   ○ HAVE

BIG BEN

ITEM #	INTRO
58341	1998

See Historical Landmark Series™.

OTHER GUIDES FROM GREENBOOK

GREENBOOK Guide to
    Precious Moments® by Enesco

GREENBOQK Guide to
    The Cherished Teddies®
    Collection

GREENBOOK Guide to
    Department 56® Snowbabies™

GREENBOOK Guide to
    Hallmark Keepsake Ornaments

GREENBOOK Guide to
    Hallmark Kiddie Car Classics

GREENBOOK Guide to
    The Walt Disney Classics
    Collection

GREENBOOK Guide to
    Harbour Lights™

Coming in 1999:

GREENBOOK Guide to
    The Boyds Collection Ltd. Plush

GREENBOOK Guide to
    The Boyds Collection Ltd. Resin

GREENBOOK Guide to
    Charming Tails

GREENBOOK Guide to
    Harmony Kingdom

GREENBOOK Guide to
    Shelia's Collectibles ... AND
    MORE!

Item#	Name	Intro	Retired	OSRP$	GBTru$	Wish	Have	Date	Qty	Paid Each	Total
	NEW ENGLAND VILLAGE, SET/7	1986	1989	170	1050						
6530-7	APOTHECARY SHOP	1986	1989	25	110	○	○				
6530-7	GENERAL STORE	1986	1989	25	310	○	○				
6530-7	NATHANIEL BINGHAM FABRICS	1986	1989	25	125	○	○				
6530-7	LIVERY STABLE & BOOT SHOP	1986	1989	25	120	○	○				
6530-7	STEEPLE CHURCH—"FIRST VERSION"	1986	1989	25	140	○	○				
6530-7	STEEPLE CHURCH—"SECOND VERSION"	1986	1989	25	105	○	○				
6530-7	BRICK TOWN HALL	1986	1989	25	165	○	○				
6530-7	RED SCHOOLHOUSE	1986	1989	25	245	○	○				
6538-2	JACOB ADAMS FARMHOUSE	1986	1989	65	465	○	○				
6538-2	JACOB ADAMS BARN	1986	1989			○	○				
5930-7	CRAGGY COVE LIGHTHOUSE	1987	1994	35	50	○	○				
5931-5	WESTON TRAIN STATION	1987	1989	42	255	○	○				
5543-9	SMYTHE WOOLEN MILL	1987	LTD ED 7,500	42	1025	○	○				
6544-7	TIMBER KNOLL LOG CABIN	1987	1990	28	160	○	○				
5932-3	OLD NORTH CHURCH	1988	1998	40	50	○	○				
5939-0	CHERRY LANE SHOPS, SET/3	1988	1990	80	275	○	○				
5939-0	BEN'S BARBERSHOP	1988	1990	27	95	○	○				
5939-0	OTIS HAYES BUTCHER SHOP	1988	1990	27	80	○	○				
5939-0	ANNE SHAW TOYS	1988	1990	27	160	○	○				
5940-4	ADA'S BED AND BOARDING HOUSE—SAMPLE	1988	1991	36	750	○	○				
5940-4	ADA'S BED AND BOARDING HOUSE—"VERSION 1"	1988	1991	36	240	○	○				
5940-4	ADA'S BED AND BOARDING HOUSE—"VERSION 2"	1988	1991	36	125	○	○				
5940-4	ADA'S BED AND BOARDING HOUSE—"VERSION 3"	1988	1991	36	110	○	○				
5942-0	BERKSHIRE HOUSE—"ORIGINAL BLUE"	1989	1991	40	115	○	○				
5942-0	BERKSHIRE HOUSE—"TEAL"	1989	1991	40	100	○	○				
5942-0	BERKSHIRE HOUSE—"FOREST GREEN"	1989	1991	40	100	○	○				
5943-9	JANNES MULLET AMISH FARM HOUSE	1989	1992	32	100	○	○				
5944-7	JANNES MULLET AMISH BARN	1989	1992	48	95	○	○				
6539-0	STEEPLE CHURCH	1989	1990	30	90	○	○				
5946-3	SHINGLE CREEK HOUSE	1990	1994	37.50	55	○	○				
5947-1	CAPTAIN'S COTTAGE	1990	1996	40	50	○	○				

NE PAGE 1 TOTALS: 1,234.50   6,915.00

NEW ENGLAND VILLAGE® GB HISTORY LIST

Item#	Name	Intro	Retired	OSRP$	GBTru$	Wish	Have	Date	Qty	Paid Each	Total
5954-4	SLEEPY HOLLOW, SET/3	1990	1993	96	160	○	○				
5954-4	SLEEPY HOLLOW SCHOOL	1990	1993	32	80	○	○				
5954-4	VAN TASSEL MANOR	1990	1993	32	45	○	○				
5954-4	ICHABOD CRANE'S COTTAGE	1990	1993	32	45	○	○				
5955-2	SLEEPY HOLLOW CHURCH	1990	1993	36	45	○	○				
5640-5	MCGREBE-CUTTERS & SLEIGHS	1991	1995	45	50	○	○				
5642-1	BLUEBIRD SEED AND BULB	1992	1996	48	50	○	○				
5643-0	YANKEE JUD BELL CASTING	1992	1995	44	50	○	○				
5644-8	STONEY BROOK TOWN HALL	1992	1995	42	50	○	○				
5647-2	BLUE STAR ICE CO.	1993	1997	45	55	○	○				
5648-0	A. BIELER FARM, SET/2	1993	1996	92	100	○	○				
56481	PENNSYLVANIA DUTCH FARMHOUSE	1993	1996	42	55	○	○				
56482	PENNSYLVANIA DUTCH BARN	1993	1996	50	55	○	○				
5651-0	ARLINGTON FALLS CHURCH	1994	1997	40	50	○	○				
5652-9	CAPE KEAG FISH CANNERY	1994	1998	48	55	○	○				
5653-7	PIGEONHEAD LIGHTHOUSE	1994	1998	50	55	○	○				
1657-0	BREWSTER BAY COTTAGES, SET/2	1995	1997	90	105	○	○				
56568	JEREMIAH BREWSTER HOUSE	1995	1997	45	50	○	○				
56569	THOMAS T. JULIAN HOUSE	1995	1997	45	60	○	○				
56571	CHOWDER HOUSE	1995	1998	40	50	○	○				
56572	WOODBRIDGE POST OFFICE	1995	1998	40	50	○	○				
56573	PIERCE BOAT WORKS	1995	CURRENT	55	55	○	○				
56172	APPLE VALLEY SCHOOL	1996	CURRENT	35	35	○	○				
56574	J. HUDSON STOVEWORKS	1996	1998	60	70	○	○				
56575	NAVIGATIONAL CHARTS & MAPS	1996	CURRENT	48	48	○	○				
56576	BOBWHITE COTTAGE	1996	CURRENT	50	50	○	○				
56577	VAN GUILDER'S ORNAMENTAL IRONWORKS	1997	CURRENT	50	50	○	○				
56578	EAST WILLET POTTERY	1997	CURRENT	45	45	○	○				
56579	STEEN'S MAPLE HOUSE	1997	CURRENT	60	60	○	○				
56580	SEMPLE'S SMOKEHOUSE	1997	CURRENT	45	45	○	○				

NE PAGE 2 TOTALS: 1,482.00   1,773.00

Item#	Name	Intro	Retired	OSRP$	GBTru$	Wish	Have	Date	Qty	Paid Each	Total
56581	Emily Louise, The	1998	Current	70	70	O	O				
56601	Franklin Hook & Ladder Co.	1998	Current	55	55	O	O				
56602	Moggin Falls General Store	1998	Current	60	60	O	O				
56604	Deacon's Way Chapel	1998	Current	68	68	O	O				
56605	Harper's Farm	1998	Current	65	65	O	O				
	NE Page 3 Totals:			318.00	318.00						
	NE Page 1 Totals:			1,234.50	6,915.00						
	NE Page 2 Totals:			1,482.00	1,773.00						
	NE Page 3 Totals:			318.00	318.00						
	NE Grand Totals:			3,034.50	9,006.00						

NEW ENGLAND VILLAGE® GB HISTORY LIST

NEW ENGLAND VILLAGE

	ITEM #	INTRO	RETIRED	OSRP	GBTRU	↓
	6530-7	1986	1989	$170	**$1050**	9%

Set of 7 includes *Apothecary Shop, General Store, Nathaniel Bingham Fabrics, Livery Stable & Boot Shop, Steeple Church, Brick Town Hall* and *Red Schoolhouse.*

see below

DATE: ____ $ ____	'91	'92	'93	'94	'95	'96	'97	'98
○ WISH ○ HAVE	$650	950	1125	*	1250	1225	1275	1150

APOTHECARY SHOP

	ITEM #	INTRO	RETIRED	OSRP	GBTRU	↑
	6530-7	1986	1989	$25	**$110**	10%

1 of the 7-piece set—NEW ENGLAND VILLAGE. Variegated fieldstone with white wood bay window. Gable and lean-to are blue clapboard.

DATE: ____ $ ____	'91	'92	'93	'94	'95	'96	'97	'98
○ WISH ○ HAVE	$70	80	88	92	100	100	105	100

GENERAL STORE

	ITEM #	INTRO	RETIRED	OSRP	GBTRU	↑
	6530-7	1986	1989	$25	**$310**	5%

1 of the 7-piece set—NEW ENGLAND VILLAGE. Round columns support full length covered porch. Two small dormers on roof with central chimney.

DATE: ____ $ ____	'91	'92	'93	'94	'95	'96	'97	'98
○ WISH ○ HAVE	$185	250	360	360	350	325	345	295

NATHANIEL BINGHAM FABRICS

	ITEM #	INTRO	RETIRED	OSRP	GBTRU	↓
	6530-7	1986	1989	$25	**$125**	26%

1 of the 7-piece set—NEW ENGLAND VILLAGE. Clapboard saltbox design fabric store and Post Office. Each shop has own chimney. Living quarters above larger fabric store.

DATE: ____ $ ____	'91	'92	'93	'94	'95	'96	'97	'98
○ WISH ○ HAVE	$85	125	150	150	150	160	160	170

NEW ENGLAND VILLAGE®

LIVERY STABLE & BOOT SHOP

Item #	Intro	Retired	OSRP	GBTru	↓
6530-7	1986	1989	$25	**$120**	20%

1 of the 7-piece set—NEW ENGLAND VILLAGE. Two-story painted clapboard house with wood planked wing contains tannery and livery stable. Stable has stone chimney, double doors.

DATE: _____ $ _____

	'91	'92	'93	'94	'95	'96	'97	'98
○ Wish ○ Have	$70	105	112	142	145	150	155	150

STEEPLE CHURCH— "FIRST VERSION"

Item #	Intro	Retired	OSRP	GBTru	↓
6530-7	1986	1989	$25	**$140**	20%

1 of the 7-piece set—NEW ENGLAND VILLAGE.
Notable: Variations in this piece affect GBTru$. This is the First Version where the tree is attached with porcelain slip. Re-issued in 1989 as Item #6539-0 when Item #6530-7 retired with the rest of the Original NEW ENGLAND VILLAGE Set.

DATE: _____ $ _____

	'91	'92	'93	'94	'95	'96	'97	'98
○ Wish ○ Have	$65	130	155	175	175	185	180	175

STEEPLE CHURCH— "SECOND VERSION"

GBTru	NO
$105	CHANGE

1 of the 7-piece set—NEW ENGLAND VILLAGE. This is the Second Version where the tree is attached with glue. Building is a white clapboard church w/tier-2 steeple. Windows have molding above and below. Simple design.

DATE: _____ $ _____

	'91	'92	'93	'94	'95	'96	'97	'98
○ Wish ○ Have	$-	-	-	100	100	95	100	105

BRICK TOWN HALL

Item #	Intro	Retired	OSRP	GBTru	↓
6530-7	1986	1989	$25	**$165**	18%

1 of the 7-piece set—NEW ENGLAND VILLAGE. Mansard roof over two-story Town Hall. Cupola is centered on roof ridge between two brick chimneys. Windows trimmed with ornamental molding.

DATE: _____ $ _____

	'91	'92	'93	'94	'95	'96	'97	'98
○ Wish ○ Have	$150	190	212	215	210	220	225	200

NEW ENGLAND VILLAGE®

RED SCHOOLHOUSE

ITEM #	INTRO	RETIRED	OSRP	GBTru	↓
6530-7	1986	1989	$25	**$245**	16%

1 of the 7-piece set—NEW ENGLAND VILLAGE. Red one-room wood school with stone chimney and open belfry. Generally heated by wood stove. Hand powered water pump by front door.

DATE: ____ $ ____		'91	'92	'93	'94	'95	'96	'97	'98
○ WISH ○ HAVE		$150	210	240	270	260	255	280	290

JACOB ADAMS FARMHOUSE

ITEM #	INTRO	RETIRED	OSRP	GBTru	↓
6538-2	1986	1989	$65	**$465**	16%

Set of 5. Two buildings–Farmhouse and Barn, 3 animals. Buildings light. Red multilevel wood barn atop a stone foundation with silo attached. Home features front porch, small front bay window, simple design.
Notable: It is very unusual for these buildings to be sold separately. Because the animals were simply wrapped and placed in the box with **no** separate compartments, they are often damaged. Sleeves on early shipments read "New England Village Farm." Those on later shipments read "Jacob Adams Farmhouse And Barn."

JACOB ADAMS BARN

DATE: ____ $ ____		'91	'92	'93	'94	'95	'96	'97	'98
○ WISH ○ HAVE		$250	375	510	575	575	525	565	555

CRAGGY COVE LIGHTHOUSE

ITEM #	INTRO	RETIRED	OSRP	GBTru	↓
5930-7	1987	1994	$35	**$50**	29%

Keeper lives in small white clapboard home attached to lighthouse. Front porch of home features holiday decorated columns. Stone house foundation, whitewashed brick light tower.

DATE: ____ $ ____		'91	'92	'93	'94	'95	'96	'97	'98
○ WISH ○ HAVE		$44	45	45	45	60	60	70	70

NEW ENGLAND VILLAGE®

WESTON TRAIN STATION

ITEM #	INTRO	RETIRED	OSRP	GBTRU	↓
5931-5	1987	1989	$42	**$255**	7%

Luggage ramps lead to platform, where you purchase tickets and wait inside or on benches outside. Wheeled luggage cart stands on side of building.
Notable: This station looks very much like the now-dilapidated station in Weston, MA.

DATE: ___ $ ___		'91	'92	'93	'94	'95	'96	'97	'98
○ WISH	○ HAVE	$165	215	248	265	275	260	280	275

SMYTHE WOOLEN MILL

ITEM #	INTRO	RETIRED	OSRP	GBTRU	↓
6543-9	1987	LTD ED 7,500	$42	**$1025**	2%

Fabric woven for manufacturing into clothing, yard goods. Hydro powered by water wheel. Stone base with wood upper stories. Bales of wool stacked outside office door. Lower windows each with shutter.

DATE: ___ $ ___		'91	'92	'93	'94	'95	'96	'97	'98
○ WISH	○ HAVE	$1100	1235	1255	1255	1150	1050	1085	1050

TIMBER KNOLL LOG CABIN

ITEM #	INTRO	RETIRED	OSRP	GBTRU	↓
6544-7	1987	1990	$28	**$160**	11%

Two stone chimneys and fireplace provide heat and cooking facilities for rustic log cabin. Wood shakes comprise roof. One wing rises two stories.

DATE: ___ $ ___		'91	'92	'93	'94	'95	'96	'97	'98
○ WISH	○ HAVE	$75	95	130	150	165	165	175	180

OLD NORTH CHURCH

ITEM #	INTRO	RETIRED	OSRP	GBTRU	↑
5932-3	1988	1998	$40	**$50**	4%

Red brick church. First- and second-floor windows feature sunburst and/or spoke tops. Steeple rises from main entry. Belfry has tiered design.
Notable: This design is based on the famous historic landmark, Christ Church in Boston, where sexton Robert Newman hung lanterns in its steeple to warn colonists in Charlestown that the British were on their way to Lexington and Concord.

DATE: ___ $ ___		'91	'92	'93	'94	'95	'96	'97	'98
○ WISH	○ HAVE	$42	44	45	45	45	45	48	48

NEW ENGLAND VILLAGE®

Get Me To The Church On Time

Churches are everywhere in our villages. If you collect Dickens' Village Series®, I'm sure you've noticed. If you collect The Original Snow Village®, you have no choice but to notice. New England Village® collectors, however, haven't had a reason to feel this way.

In its eleven-plus years, New England Village® has only had five churches. Contrast that with Dickens' Village Series'® 10 buildings of worship in only two more years. Neither can compare to the 30 that have been part of The Original Snow Village® during its more than 21 years.

Even with only five churches in New England Village®, there is some history—both figuratively and literally. The first church to be introduced was the *Steeple Church* which was included in the set of original seven buildings. A modest white clapboard building, the church was first introduced with Item Number 6530-7.

Before it retired in 1989, the church sported a second version. The second church still had 6530-7 as its Item Number, but the tree attached to the front, lefthand corner differed in the manner in which it was applied. Where the tree on the first version was adhered with porcelain slip (a liquefied porcelain), the tree on the second version was applied with glue. Also, the tree on the first version was raised slightly.

In 1989, Department 56, Inc. re-introduced the building with Item Number 6539-0. The company simply replaced the Item Number because it wanted to keep the church current, but retired the church's previous Item Number and with the original set of buildings. In retrospect, it seems a bit odd, not that the number was changed, but that the building was kept at all.

You might think that the church was continued because Department 56, Inc. didn't want the village to be "churchless." But it was more likely that the company thought that the Village should maintain a white church. This thinking is confirmed by the fact that in 1988 *Old North Church* was introduced.

Old North Church is a replica of the historical church in Boston, Massachusetts, Christ Church. More famous than the church itself is its steeple. It was there that sexton Robert Newman placed lanterns to signal Paul Revere that British troops were approaching Lexington and Concord. Christ Church still exists and is open to the public.

The next church to appear in New England Village® wasn't situated in the six-state region. Its locale was high on a hill overlooking the Hudson River. *Sleepy Hollow Church*, though not part of the Sleepy Hollow set, was introduced along with the set of three as a companion piece. Like the *Steeple Church*, it was a simple design, though yellow siding was the artist's choice this time. Again like the set, it retired in 1993, leaving *Old North Church* as the Village's only place of worship.

In 1994, *Arlington Falls Church* was introduced. Another white clapboard building, it included two garland-wrapped pillars supporting the portico above the front door. It retired in 1997, leaving *Old North Church* to be the lone current church.

The logical question to this series of introductions and retirements is why has Department 56, Inc. kept *Old North Church* current while two others came and went? Though the company is not likely to offer a reason, the most logical one is that it has outsold the others. Another, but less likely, reason could be that the company enjoys having a replica of an actual building in the village.

the **Village Chronicle.**

The *Old North Church* retired in November 1998, ending its reign at ten years. When it did, it was almost certain that Department 56, Inc. would introduce another church shortly after. A month later, *Deacon's Way Chapel* became the newest church in the New England Village®.

CHERRY LANE SHOPS

Item #	Intro	Retired	OSRP	GBTru	↓
5939-0	1988	1990	$80	**$275**	11%

Set of 3 includes *Ben's Barbershop, Otis Hayes Butcher Shop* and *Anne Shaw Toys*.

see below

Date: ____ $ ____	'91	'92	'93	'94	'95	'96	'97	'98
○ Wish ○ Have	$175	215	275	NE	325	330	345	310

BEN'S BARBERSHOP

Item #	Intro	Retired	OSRP	GBTru	↓
5939-0	1988	1990	$27	**$95**	14%

1 of the 3-piece set—CHERRY LANE SHOPS. A barber pole hangs from front house corner next to a bench for customers. Water tower on roof supplies the shop's needs. Upstairs office used by a lawyer.

Date: ____ $ ____	'91	'92	'93	'94	'95	'96	'97	'98
○ Wish ○ Have	$60	75	85	85	95	110	115	110

OTIS HAYES BUTCHER SHOP

Item #	Intro	Retired	OSRP	GBTru	↓
5939-0	1988	1990	$27	**$80**	16%

1 of the 3-piece set—CHERRY LANE SHOPS. Dutch door entry, stone side walls, brick front. Small size and thick walls plus river/lake ice helped keep meat fresh.

Date: ____ $ ____	'91	'92	'93	'94	'95	'96	'97	'98
○ Wish ○ Have	$55	65	68	75	75	80	90	95

ANNE SHAW TOYS

Item #	Intro	Retired	OSRP	GBTru	↓
5939-0	1988	1990	$27	**$160**	6%

1 of the 3-piece set—CHERRY LANE SHOPS. Large front windows with window boxes allow a look at toys for sale. Molding beneath floor edge and squared shape give roof a turret look and feel.

Date: ____ $ ____	'91	'92	'93	'94	'95	'96	'97	'98
○ Wish ○ Have	$80	115	125	150	160	155	175	170

ADA'S BED AND BOARDING HOUSE—SAMPLE

ITEM #	INTRO	RETIRED	OSRP	GBTRU	
5940-4	1988	1991	$36	$750	NO CHANGE

Notable: This wine color version was the sample that was first shown at the various Department 56® showrooms. It was never available at dealers. Not long after being shown in this color, it was changed to the yellow production version.

DATE: ___ $ ___	'91	'92	'93	'94	'95	'96	'97	'98
○ WISH ○ HAVE								$750

ADA'S BED AND BOARDING HOUSE—"VERSION 1"

GBTRU ↓
$240 19%

Building is a large family home converted to a bed and breakfast for travelers. Double chimneys. Central cupola and wraparound front porch.
Notable: There are Three Variations in color and mold that affect GBTru$. The First Version is lemon yellow in color, the rear steps are part of the building's mold, and there are alternating yellow panes on the second-story windows.

DATE: ___ $ ___	'91	'92	'93	'94	'95	'96	'97	'98
○ WISH ○ HAVE	$37.50	310	300	300	325	310	285	295

ADA'S BED AND BOARDING HOUSE—"VERSION 2"

GBTRU ↓
$125 11%

Notable: The Second Version is a paler yellow but the same mold as Version 1–the rear steps are part of the building's mold.

DATE: ___ $ ___	'91	'92	'93	'94	'95	'96	'97	'98
○ WISH ○ HAVE	$37.50	150	160	195	150	165	155	140

ADA'S BED AND BOARDING HOUSE—"VERSION 3"

GBTRU ↓
$110 12%

Notable: The Third Version is pale yellow in color and a different mold where the rear steps are an add on—not part of the the building's mold. In this version the second-story windows have yellow panes in the top half only.

DATE: ___ $ ___	'91	'92	'93	'94	'95	'96	'97	'98
○ WISH ○ HAVE	$37.50	85	105	125	125	125	130	125

the *Village Chronicle*

The Magazine for Department 56 Collectors

All The News That's Lit To Print

Subscribe to the Village Chronicle® today and begin enjoying your Dept 56® collection more than ever!

Have the world of Department 56® delivered to your door! Each issue is packed with:

◆ articles and information about each village

◆ late-breaking news

◆ display-making articles and tips

◆ history of the pieces and the buildings that inspired them

◆ product highlights featuring items you'll want to have

◆ Department 56® events

◆ information every collector should know

◆ and always much more.

Subscribe today, and join the thousands of collectors who consider the Village Chronicle® to be the premier publication about Dept 56®!

BERKSHIRE HOUSE— "ORIGINAL BLUE"

ITEM #	INTRO	RETIRED	OSRP	GBTRU	↓
5942-0	1989	1991	$40	**$115**	26%

Building is a Dutch colonial inn with two front entries, half porch, five dormered windows on front, second-story mansard roof.
Notable: Variations in color affect GBTru$: "Original Blue," "Teal," or "Forest Green." This is the "Original Blue."

		'91	'92	'93	'94	'95	'96	'97	'98
○ WISH	○ HAVE	$40	125	140	150	150	160	160	155

BERKSHIRE HOUSE—"TEAL"

	GBTRU	NO
	$100	CHANGE

This is the "Teal" house.

		'91	'92	'93	'94	'95	'96	'97	'98
○ WISH	○ HAVE	$40	95	95	95	100	110	110	100

BERKSHIRE HOUSE— "FOREST GREEN"

	GBTRU	↑
	$100	11%

This is the "Forest Green" house.

		'91	'92	'93	'94	'95	'96	'97	'98
○ WISH	○ HAVE	-	-	-	-	NE	NE	NE	$90

JANNES MULLET AMISH FARM HOUSE

ITEM #	INTRO	RETIRED	OSRP	GBTRU	↓
5943-9	1989	1992	$32	**$100**	9%

White frame house, fenced yard on side, two chimneys, gutter and leader to barrel to collect rain water.
Notable: Along with the *Jannes Mullet Amish Barn,* this is the first "non-New England" building to be added to the New England Village®.

		'91	'92	'93	'94	'95	'96	'97	'98
○ WISH	○ HAVE	$32	32	85	100	110	110	115	110

JANNES MULLET AMISH BARN

Item #	Intro	Retired	OSRP	GBTru	NO
5944-7	1989	1992	$48	**$95**	CHANGE

Wood and fieldstone with attached sheds and silo, Amish family black buggy stands at barn entrance.
Notable: Along with the *Jannes Mullet Amish Farm House,* this is the first "non-New England" building to be added to the New England Village®.

Date: ____ $ ____	'91	'92	'93	'94	'95	'96	'97	'98
○ Wish ○ Have	$48	48	86	98	90	90	95	95

STEEPLE CHURCH

Item #	Intro	Retired	OSRP	GBTru	↓
6539-0	1989	1990	$30	**$90**	5%

Re-issue—see 1986 *Steeple Church,* Item #6530-7. White clapboard church with steeple. Windows have molding above and below. Simple design.

Date: ____ $ ____	'91	'92	'93	'94	'95	'96	'97	'98
○ Wish ○ Have	$65	85	85	85	90	90	80	95

SHINGLE CREEK HOUSE

Item #	Intro	Retired	OSRP	GBTru	NO
5946-3	1990	1994	$37.50	**$55**	CHANGE

Saltbox design with chimney rising from mid-roof. Windows have shutters and molding on top and base. Attached shed on one side, with storm cellar doors and fenced side entrance.
Notable: Early release to Showcase Dealers and National Association Of Limited Edition Dealers (NALED).

Date: ____ $ ____	'91	'92	'93	'94	'95	'96	'97	'98
○ Wish ○ Have	$37.50	40	40	40	45	55	60	55

CAPTAIN'S COTTAGE

Item #	Intro	Retired	OSRP	GBTru	↓
5947-1	1990	1996	$40	**$50**	17%

2 1/2-story has balcony full length of second story. Enclosed staircase on house side to second floor. A connected double dormer is centered on front roof between two ridge chimneys.

Date: ____ $ ____	'91	'92	'93	'94	'95	'96	'97	'98
○ Wish ○ Have	$40	40	42	42	44	45	55	60

SLEEPY HOLLOW

	Item #	Intro	Retired	OSRP	GBTru	↓
	5954-4	1990	1993	$96	**$160**	22%

see below

Set of 3 includes *Sleepy Hollow School, Van Tassel Manor,* and *Ichabod Crane's Cottage.*
Notable: This set was inspired by Washington Irving's classic, *The Legend of Sleepy Hollow.* The story takes place along the Hudson River in N. Tarrytown, NY.

Date: ___ $ ___	'91	'92	'93	'94	'95	'96	'97	'98
○ Wish ○ Have	$96	96	96	180	170	175	195	205

SLEEPY HOLLOW SCHOOL

Item #	Intro	Retired	OSRP	GBTru	↓
5954-4	1990	1993	$32	**$80**	16%

1 of the 3-piece set—SLEEPY HOLLOW. Framed stone chimney warms log cabin school. Brick and wood belfry houses bell. Wood pile and bench with bucket near front door. School teacher Ichabod Crane taught in this one-room schoolhouse.

Date: ___ $ ___	'91	'92	'93	'94	'95	'96	'97	'98
○ Wish ○ Have	$32	32	32	78	80	90	90	95

VAN TASSEL MANOR

Item #	Intro	Retired	OSRP	GBTru	↓
5954-4	1990	1993	$32	**$45**	18%

1 of the 3-piece set—SLEEPY HOLLOW. Yellow house with mansard roof with two front dormers. Wood corner posts support porch. Stone lean-to on one side. Double chimneys rise off roof ridge. Four ears of corn decorate front entry. After attending a party at the Van Tassel residence, Ichabod Crane set out for home but never got there.

Date: ___ $ ___	'91	'92	'93	'94	'95	'96	'97	'98
○ Wish ○ Have	$32	32	32	65	60	60	60	55

ICHABOD CRANE'S COTTAGE

Item #	Intro	Retired	OSRP	GBTru	↓
5954-4	1990	1993	$32	**$45**	18%

1 of the 3-piece set—SLEEPY HOLLOW. Stone first story topped by wood second story. Rough shingled roof with dip in the middle between two brick chimneys. This is the modest home provided for the village school master.

Date: ___ $ ___	'91	'92	'93	'94	'95	'96	'97	'98
○ Wish ○ Have	$32	32	32	60	55	55	65	55

NEW ENGLAND VILLAGE®

SLEEPY HOLLOW CHURCH

ITEM #	INTRO	RETIRED	OSRP	GBTRU	↓
5955-2	1990	1993	$36	**$45**	25%

Wood church with steeple rising off front. Arched windows with prominent sills. Front steps lead to double doors with ornate hinges and molding.

		'91	'92	'93	'94	'95	'96	'97	'98
DATE: ____ $ ____		$36	36	36	65	60	60	65	60
○ WISH ○ HAVE									

McGREBE-CUTTERS & SLEIGHS

ITEM #	INTRO	RETIRED	OSRP	GBTRU	↓
5640-5	1991	1995	$45	**$50**	17%

Builders of carriages, sleighs, and sleds to move people and goods in snowy New England. A cutter is a small sleigh that seats one person. Stone and wood building. Large doors in front and side to allow movement of vehicles. Stone half has short tower atop roof. Large loft doors above entry.

		'91	'92	'93	'94	'95	'96	'97	'98
DATE: ____ $ ____		$45	45	48	48	48	65	65	60
○ WISH ○ HAVE									

BLUEBIRD SEED AND BULB

ITEM #	INTRO	RETIRED	OSRP	GBTRU	↓
5642-1	1992	1996	$48	**$50**	9%

Covered storage area near entry door has open storage bins. Small shuttered arched window adjacent to door. Outside stairs lead to other storage areas. Two stories with stone block lower level and fieldstone chimney.

		'92	'93	'94	'95	'96	'97	'98
DATE: ____ $ ____		$48	48	48	48	48	55	55
○ WISH ○ HAVE								

YANKEE JUD BELL CASTING

ITEM #	INTRO	RETIRED	OSRP	GBTRU	↓
5643-0	1992	1995	$44	**$50**	9%

Red brick foundry with steeply pitched gable roof. Projecting side doors on second and third story for lifting large, heavy castings. Tall circular brick chimney rises off rear of foundry.

		'92	'93	'94	'95	'96	'97	'98
DATE: ____ $ ____		$44	44	44	44	60	55	55
○ WISH ○ HAVE								

STONEY BROOK TOWN HALL

Item #	Intro	Retired	OSRP	GBTru	↓
5644-8	1992	1995	$42	**$50**	17%

Rectangular brick building serves as meeting hall for town governance. Side entry with a latch gate, cellar windows with shutters, roof dormers and two chimneys, and many windows on long sides of building complete structure.

DATE: ____ $ ____
○ Wish ○ Have

'92	'93	'94	'95	'96	'97	'98
$42	42	42	42	60	60	60

BLUE STAR ICE CO.

Item #	Intro	Retired	OSRP	GBTru	NO
5647-2	1993	1997	$45	**$55**	CHANGE

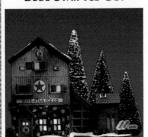

Stone first story with insulated wood upper storage level. Wooden chute enabled ice block to be pulled up where sawdust or salt hay insulated each block.

DATE: ____ $ ____
○ Wish ○ Have

'93	'94	'95	'96	'97	'98
$45	45	48	48	48	55

A. BIELER FARM

Item #	Intro	Retired	OSRP	GBTru	↓
5648-0	1993	1996	$92	**$100**	9%

Set of 2 includes *Pennsylvania Dutch Farmhouse,* and *Pennsylvania Dutch Barn.*

see below

DATE: ____ $ ____
○ Wish ○ Have

'93	'94	'95	'96	'97	'98
$92	92	95	95	115	110

PENNSYLVANIA DUTCH FARMHOUSE

Item #	Intro	Retired	OSRP	GBTru	↓
56481	1993	1996	$42	**$55**	8%

1 of the 2-piece set—A. BIELER FARM. Two-story clapboard home. Many-windowed to let in light, colorful trim on all windows, roof and wall moldings.

DATE: ____ $ ____
○ Wish ○ Have

'93	'94	'95	'96	'97	'98
$42	42	43.50	43.50	65	60

NEW ENGLAND VILLAGE®

PENNSYLVANIA DUTCH BARN

ITEM #	INTRO	RETIRED	OSRP	GBTRU	↓
56482	1993	1996	$50	**$55**	15%

1 of the 2-piece set—A. BIELER FARM. Red barn with green mansard roof. Two stone silos on one corner. Double door entry reached by stone supported ramp. Hex signs hung on barn outer walls.

DATE: _____ $ _____
○ WISH ○ HAVE

	'93	'94	'95	'96	'97	'98
	$50	50	51.50	51.50	65	65

ARLINGTON FALLS CHURCH

ITEM #	INTRO	RETIRED	OSRP	GBTRU	NO
5651-0	1994	1997	$40	**$50**	CHANGE

Midyear release. Wood church with steeple rising in tiers above main entry. Pillars at front doors are wrapped in garlands. Double tier of windows on side of church to let in daylight. Simple structure with a country look.

DATE: _____ $ _____
○ WISH ○ HAVE

	'94	'95	'96	'97	'98
	$40	42	42	42	50

CAPE KEAG FISH CANNERY

ITEM #	INTRO	RETIRED	OSRP	GBTRU	↑
5652-9	1994	1998	$48	**$55**	15%

Lobster pots, buoys are stacked on wharf along building front. Brick tower rising on side of factory cannery allows visual check of fishing boats.

DATE: _____ $ _____
○ WISH ○ HAVE

	'95	'96	'97	'98
	$48	48	48	48

PIGEONHEAD LIGHTHOUSE

ITEM #	INTRO	RETIRED	OSRP	GBTRU	↑
5653-7	1994	1998	$50	**$55**	10%

Light shines from porthole windows. Tower connects to keeper's home. Steps lead down from rocks to water.

DATE: _____ $ _____
○ WISH ○ HAVE

	'95	'96	'97	'98
	$50	50	50	50

NEW ENGLAND VILLAGE®

BREWSTER BAY COTTAGES	ITEM #	INTRO	RETIRED	OSRP	GBTRU	↓
	5657-0	1995	1997	$90	**$105**	9%

Set of 2 includes *Jeremiah Brewster House,* and *Thomas T. Julian House.*

see below

			'95	'96	'97	'98
DATE: ____ $ ____			$90	90	90	115
○ Wish ○ Have						

JEREMIAH BREWSTER HOUSE

	ITEM #	INTRO	RETIRED	OSRP	GBTRU	↓
	56568	1995	1997	$45	**$50**	17%

1 of the 2-piece set—BREWSTER BAY COTTAGES. Midyear release. Shed roof side addition attached to main square two-story house. Shuttered windows, widow's walk on roof.
Notable: The boxes of the first pieces shipped read "Thomas T. Julian House." When the mistake was noticed, Department 56, Inc. applied a sticker with the correct name over the incorrect one. Later shipments have the correct name printed directly on the box.

			'95	'96	'97	'98
DATE: ____ $ ____			$45	45	45	60
○ Wish ○ Have						

THOMAS T. JULIAN HOUSE

	ITEM #	INTRO	RETIRED	OSRP	GBTRU	
	56569	1995	1997	$45	**$60**	NO CHANGE

1 of the 2-piece set—BREWSTER BAY COTTAGES. Midyear release. Central chimney rises where 4 gabled roof meets. Two-story bay windowed turret next to covered porch entry. The boxes of the first pieces shipped read "Jeremiah Brewster House." When the mistake was noticed, Department 56, Inc. applied a sticker with the correct name over the incorrect one. Later shipments have the correct name printed directly on the box.

			'95	'96	'97	'98
DATE: ____ $ ____			$45	45	45	60
○ Wish ○ Have						

CHOWDER HOUSE

	ITEM #	INTRO	RETIRED	OSRP	GBTRU	↑
	56571	1995	1998	$40	**$50**	25%

Small cozy eating establishment sits on fieldstone base. Small boats can tie up to one side while another entry serves walk-ins. Blue clapboard with a mansard roof.

			'95	'96	'97	'98
DATE: ____ $ ____			$40	40	40	40
○ Wish ○ Have						

NEW ENGLAND VILLAGE®

Woodbridge Post Office

Item #	Intro	Retired	OSRP	GBTru	↑
56572	1995	1998	$40	**$50**	25%

Two-story brick post office serves village for mail, stamps, parcels and postal cards. Windows flank double entry doors.

		'95	'96	'97	'98
Date: ____ $ ____		$40	40	40	40
○ Wish ○ Have					

Pierce Boat Works

Item #	Intro	Retired	OSRP	GBTru	
56573	1995	Current	$55	**$55**	NO CHANGE

Boats for lobstermen and fishermen are built at the boat works. Wooden building with double doors allow boats to be pulled or rolled down ramp. Rowboat held on winch and pulley rig on side of building.

		'95	'96	'97	'98
Date: ____ $ ____		$55	55	55	55
○ Wish ○ Have					

Apple Valley School

Item #	Intro	Retired	OSRP	GBTru	
56172	1996	Current	$35	**$35**	NO CHANGE

Midyear release. Small squared brick and stone Village school. Tall central chimney connects to stove to keep schoolrooms heated. Bell tower in front gable.

		'96	'97	'98
Date: ____ $ ____		$35	35	35
○ Wish ○ Have				

J. Hudson Stoveworks

Item #	Intro	Retired	OSRP	GBTru	↑
56574	1996	1998	$60	**$70**	17%

Manufacturer of stoves combines shop and foundry. Stone and brick factory attached to office. Stoves are on display outside front door. Foundry is powered by coal and wood furnaces.

		'97	'98
Date: ____ $ ____		$60	60
○ Wish ○ Have			

NEW ENGLAND VILLAGE®

NAVIGATIONAL CHARTS & MAPS

ITEM #	INTRO	RETIRED	OSRP	GBTRU	
56575	1996	CURRENT	$48	**$48**	NO CHANGE

Business provides information for sea and river vessels to travel the waterways safely. 2 1/2-story with stone base and clapboard upper levels. Double stairs hug front facade with door entry on second story. Seagulls rest on roof which also has weathervane.

DATE: ____ $ ____
○ WISH ○ HAVE

	'97	'98
	$48	48

BOBWHITE COTTAGE

ITEM #	INTRO	RETIRED	OSRP	GBTRU	
56576	1996	CURRENT	$50	**$50**	NO CHANGE

1 1/2-story home with front and side porches. Porch design features square and octagonal fretwork. Steep pitched roof has front dormer. Upper side bedroom has door to sun porch protected by balustrade railing.
Notable: The house is named for a North American quail or partridge native to this area.

DATE: ____ $ ____
○ WISH ○ HAVE

	'97	'98
	$50	50

VAN GUILDER'S ORNAMENTAL IRONWORKS

ITEM #	INTRO	RETIRED	OSRP	GBTRU	
56577	1997	CURRENT	$50	**$50**	NO CHANGE

Midyear release. Third building in the Village that pertains to metal craftsmanship. A sign on the front of the building announces that weathervanes are available.
Notable: It is the first New England Village® building with multiple weathervanes.

DATE: ____ $ ____
○ WISH ○ HAVE

	'97	'98
	$50	50

EAST WILLET POTTERY

ITEM #	INTRO	RETIRED	OSRP	GBTRU	
56578	1997	CURRENT	$45	**$45**	NO CHANGE

Shop with an attached kiln to fire pottery. Assorted pottery containers are displayed on ground in front of shop windows.

DATE: ____ $ ____
○ WISH ○ HAVE

	'98
	$45

NEW ENGLAND VILLAGE®

STEEN'S MAPLE HOUSE

ITEM #	INTRO	RETIRED	OSRP	GBTᴿᴜ	NO
56579	1997	CURRENT	$60	**$60**	CHANGE

"Smoking building." Shop sells products made from maple tree sap boiled into syrup on the premises. Stone foundation supports a clapboard building. Cast iron burner produces the valued product. With Magic Smoking Element to produce smoke.

DATE: ____ $ ____
○ WISH   ○ HAVE

'98
$60

SEMPLE'S SMOKEHOUSE

ITEM #	INTRO	RETIRED	OSRP	GBTᴿᴜ	NO
56580	1997	CURRENT	$45	**$45**	CHANGE

Stone and wood shop that specializes in slow cooking and curing of meats by burning different woods to create special smoky flavors in the finished product. Cords of firewood stacked outside.

DATE: ____ $ ____
○ WISH   ○ HAVE

'98
$45

EMILY LOUISE, THE

ITEM #	INTRO	RETIRED	OSRP	GBTᴿᴜ	NO
56581	1998	CURRENT	$70	**$70**	CHANGE

Set of 2. Midyear release. Ship is inspired by cargo-carrying packet ships popular in the 1800's. Double masted with tiny rope used to create the rigging. Dock is second piece of the set. (Ship is lighted.)

DATE: ____ $ ____
○ WISH   ○ HAVE

'98
$70

FRANKLIN HOOK & LADDER CO.

ITEM #	INTRO	RETIRED	OSRP	GBTᴿᴜ
56601	1998	CURRENT	$55	**$55**

This "stone and wooden" structure features a metal bell in its tower, a water tower, and large barn doors in front.

DATE: ____ $ ____
○ WISH   ○ HAVE

MOGGIN FALLS GENERAL STORE

ITEM #	INTRO	RETIRED	OSRP	GBTRU
56602	1998	CURRENT	$60	**$60**

A twenty star American flag flies from the right side of this "wooden" general store.
Notable: It houses New England Village®'s third post office.

DATE: _____ $ _____
○ WISH ◐ HAVE

DEACON'S WAY CHAPEL

ITEM #	INTRO	RETIRED	OSRP	GBTRU
56604	1998	CURRENT	$68	**$68**

This brightly colored church has a stained glass-like window in the front, known as a rose window, and a partially opened front door. The year it was built, 1849, is above the door.

DATE: _____ $ _____
○ WISH ◐ HAVE

HARPER'S FARM

ITEM #	INTRO	RETIRED	OSRP	GBTRU
56605	1998	CURRENT	$65	**$65**

This reliable old barn shows its age with a sagging roof and its unhinged door.

DATE: _____ $ _____
○ WISH ◐ HAVE

NOTES: _____

_____

_____

_____

_____

NEW ENGLAND VILLAGE®

Item#	Name	Intro	Retired	OSRP$	GBTru$	Wish	Have	Date	Qty	Paid Each	Total
6540-4	ALPINE VILLAGE, SET/5	1986	1996 & 1997	150	180	○	○				
65405	BESSON BIERKELLER	1986	1996	25	35	○	○				
65406	GASTHOF EISL	1986	1997	25	35	○	○				
65407	APOTHEKE	1986	1997	25	35	○	○				
65408	E. STAUBR BACKER	1986	1997	25	35	○	○				
65409	MILCH-KASE	1986	1996	25	40	○	○				
5952-8	JOSEF ENGEL FARMHOUSE	1987	1989	33	865	○	○				
6541-2	ALPINE CHURCH—"WHITE TRIM"	1987	1991	32	210	○	○				
6541-2	ALPINE CHURCH—"DARK TRIM"	1987	1991	32	150	○	○				
5953-6	GRIST MILL	1988	1997	42	40	○	○				
5615-4	BAHNHOF	1990	1993	42	70	○	○				
5617-0	ST. NIKOLAUS KIRCHE	1991	CURRENT	37.50	37.50	○	○				
5618-9	ALPINE SHOPS, SET/2	1992	1997 & 1998	75	85	○	○				
56190	METTERNICHE WURST	1992	1997	37.50	45	○	○				
56191	KUKUCK UHREN	1992	1998	37.50	40	○	○				
5612-0	SPORT LADEN	1993	1998	50	55	○	○				
5614-6	BAKERY & CHOCOLATE SHOP	1994	1998	37.50	40	○	○				
56171	KAMM HAUS	1995	CURRENT	42	42	○	○				
56173	DANUBE MUSIC PUBLISHER	1996	CURRENT	55	55	○	○				
56174	BERNHARDINER HUNDCHEN	1997	CURRENT	50	50	○	○				
56192	SPIELZEUG LADEN	1997	CURRENT	65	65	○	○				
56176	FEDERBETTEN UND STEPPDECKEN	1998	CURRENT	48	48	○	○				
56177	HEIDI'S GRANDFATHER'S HOUSE	1998	CURRENT	64	64	○	○				
56178	SOUND OF MUSIC® VON TRAPP VILLA, THE	1998	CURRENT	130	130	○	○				
	AV GRAND TOTALS:			1,185.00	2,451.50						

ALPINE VILLAGE

	Item #	Intro	Retired	OSRP	GBTru	↓
	6540-4	1986	1996 & 1997	$150	**$180**	14%

Set of 5 includes *Besson Bierkeller, Gasthof Eisl, Apotheke, E. Staubr Backer, Milch-Kase.* Early release to National Association Of Limited Edition Dealers (NALED), 1987. In 1996, three of the five buildings were retired. The remaining two were retired in 1997.

see below

Date: ____ $ ____	'91	'92	'93	'94	'95	'96	'97	'98
○ Wish ○ Have	$185	185	185	185	195	195	*	210

BESSON BIERKELLER

	Item #	Intro	Retired	OSRP	GBTru	↓
	65405	1986	1996	$25	**$35**	22%

1 of the 5-piece set—ALPINE VILLAGE. (Beer Cellar) Window boxes on second story hung with colorful banners. Third-story rustic timbered enclosed balcony has garland decoration.
Notable: Early release to National Association Of Limited Edition Dealers (NALED), 1987.

Date: ____ $ ____	'91	'92	'93	'94	'95	'96	'97	'98
○ Wish ○ Have	$37	37	37	37	39	39	45	45

GASTHOF EISL

	Item #	Intro	Retired	OSRP	GBTru	↓
	65406	1986	1996	$25	**$35**	13%

1 of the 5-piece set—ALPINE VILLAGE. (Guest House) Rustic inn, fieldstone first floor with two stories of stucco topped by orange/red roof. A third-story balcony is decorated with greenery and banners. Window boxes also decorate other rooms.
Notable: Early release to National Association Of Limited Edition Dealers (NALED), 1987.

Date: ____ $ ____	'91	'92	'93	'94	'95	'96	'97	'98
○ Wish ○ Have	$37	37	37	37	39	39	45	40

APOTHEKE

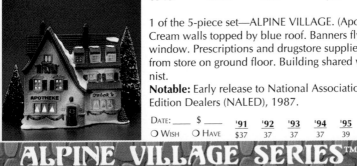

	Item #	Intro	Retired	OSRP	GBTru	↓
	65407	1986	1997	$25	**$35**	22%

1 of the 5-piece set—ALPINE VILLAGE. (Apothecary) Cream walls topped by blue roof. Banners flying from attic window. Prescriptions and drugstore supplies available from store on ground floor. Building shared with tobacconist.
Notable: Early release to National Association Of Limited Edition Dealers (NALED), 1987.

Date: ____ $ ____	'91	'92	'93	'94	'95	'96	'97	'98
○ Wish ○ Have	$37	37	37	37	39	39	39	45

E. STAUBR BACKER

ITEM #	INTRO	RETIRED	OSRP	GBTRU	↓
65408	1986	1997	$25	**$35**	22%

1 of the 5-piece set—ALPINE VILLAGE. (Bakery) Only building in which bulb is inserted in the side. Three stories with bakery on ground level. Third story has some timbering design and an oriel window. Tiled roof and two chimneys.
Notable: Early release to National Association Of Limited Edition Dealers (NALED), 1987.

DATE: ___ $ ___	'91	'92	'93	'94	'95	'96	'97	'98
○ WISH ○ HAVE	$37	37	37	37	39	39	39	45

MILCH-KASE

ITEM #	INTRO	RETIRED	OSRP	GBTRU	↓
65409	1986	1996	$25	**$40**	11%

1 of the 5-piece set—ALPINE VILLAGE. (Milk & Cheese Shop) Milk cans by door denotes shop that sells milk and cheese. Rough slate roof tops blue walls and wood planking exterior. Double wood doors allow wagons to bring supplies in/out.
Notable: Early release to National Association Of Limited Edition Dealers (NALED), 1987.

DATE: ___ $ ___	'91	'92	'93	'94	'95	'96	'97	'98
○ WISH ○ HAVE	$37	37	37	37	39	39	45	45

JOSEF ENGEL FARMHOUSE

ITEM #	INTRO	RETIRED	OSRP	GBTRU	↓
5952-8	1987	1989	$33	**$865**	13%

House and barn are connected. Stucco over stone. Barn has hayloft above animal and equipment area. Shutters swing overhead. Home has balcony above front entry with herringbone planking. Red roof, capped chimneys.

DATE: ___ $ ___	'91	'92	'93	'94	'95	'96	'97	'98
○ WISH ○ HAVE	$225	450	610	960	975	925	970	995

NOTES: _____
_____
_____
_____
_____
_____

ALPINE CHURCH— "WHITE TRIM"

ITEM #	INTRO	RETIRED	OSRP	GBTRU	↓
6541-2	1987	1991	$32	**$210**	44%

Onion dome tops steeple which also features a clock on all sides of the tower.
Notable: Variations in color affect GBTru$—"White Trim" or "Dark Trim." This is the "White Trim."

DATE: ___ $ ___	'91	'92	'93	'94	'95	'96	'97	'98
○ WISH ○ HAVE	$36	85	112	155	295	350	385	375

ALPINE CHURCH— "DARK TRIM"

	GBTRU	↓
	$150	14%

This is the "Dark Trim."

DATE: ___ $ ___	'91	'92	'93	'94	'95	'96	'97	'98
○ WISH ○ HAVE	$36	85	112	155	165	155	160	175

GRIST MILL

ITEM #	INTRO	RETIRED	OSRP	GBTRU	↓
5953-6	1988	1997	$42	**$40**	11%

Stoder Grist Mill. Irregular shingle roofing tops the mill that grinds corn and wheat into meal and flour.

DATE: ___ $ ___	'91	'92	'93	'94	'95	'96	'97	'98
○ WISH ○ HAVE	$44	45	45	45	45	45	45	45

BAHNHOF

ITEM #	INTRO	RETIRED	OSRP	GBTRU	↓
5615-4	1990	1993	$42	**$70**	13%

(Train Station) Stucco upper wall atop tiled lower wall. Ticket window in base of tower rises through roof and repeats tile design.
Notable: The first pieces have gilded trim. Subsequent pieces have a yellow/mustard trim.

DATE: ___ $ ___	'91	'92	'93	'94	'95	'96	'97	'98
○ WISH ○ HAVE	$42	42	42	85	70	70	85	80

ST. NIKOLAUS KIRCHE

ITEM #	INTRO	RETIRED	OSRP	GBTRU	NO
5617-0	1991	CURRENT	$37.50	**$37.50**	CHANGE

Bell tower rises above front entry, topped by onion dome. Set-in rounded arched windows accent nave sides. Pebble-dash finish on surface walls.
Notable: Designed after Church Of St. Nikolaus in Oberndorf, Austria, the home of the Christmas hymn "Silent Night, Holy Night."

DATE: ____ $ ____
O WISH O HAVE

'91	'92	'93	'94	'95	'96	'97	'98
$37.50	37.50	37.50	37.50	37.50	37.50	37.50	37.50

ALPINE SHOPS

ITEM #	INTRO	RETIRED	OSRP	GBTRU	↑
5618-9	1992	1997 & 1998	$75	**$85**	13%

Set of 2 includes *Metterniche Wurst,* and *Kukuck Uhren.*

see below

DATE: ____ $ ____
O WISH O HAVE

'92	'93	'94	'95	'96	'97	'98
$75	75	75	75	75	75	75

METTERNICHE WURST

ITEM #	INTRO	RETIRED	OSRP	GBTRU	NO
56190	1992	1997	$37.50	**$45**	CHANGE

1 of the 2-piece set—ALPINE SHOPS. (Sausage Shop) Stucco over stone and brick with steeply pitched roof coming down to first floor on sides. Front facade framed by ornamental curved coping.

DATE: ____ $ ____
O WISH O HAVE

'92	'93	'94	'95	'96	'97	'98
$37.50	37.50	37.50	37.50	37.50	37.50	45

KUKUCK UHREN

ITEM #	INTRO	RETIRED	OSRP	GBTRU	↑
56191	1992	1998	$37.50	**$40**	7%

1 of the 2-piece set—ALPINE SHOPS. (Clock Shop) Franc Schiller displays his trademark clock on shop sign above recessed entry door. Small shop has wood timbers that outline the stone, brick and stucco exterior.

DATE: ____ $ ____
O WISH O HAVE

'92	'93	'94	'95	'96	'97	'98
$37.50	37.50	37.50	37.50	37.50	37.50	37.50

SPORT LADEN

ITEM #	INTRO	RETIRED	OSRP	GBTRU	↑
5612-0	1993	1998	$50	**$55**	10%

(Sports Shop) Shop for skiing and winter sports equipment. Smaller shop tucked away on one side. Roof overhangs protect facade and chimneys are capped to keep out snow, ice and rain.

DATE: ____ $ ____
○ WISH   ○ HAVE

'93	'94	'95	'96	'97	'98
$50	50	50	50	50	50

BAKERY & CHOCOLATE SHOP

ITEM #	INTRO	RETIRED	OSRP	GBTRU	↑
5614-6	1994	1998	$37.50	**$40**	7%

(Konditorei Schokolade) Garland and banners hang down from the second-story balcony. The extended eaves protect the building from heavy snows.

DATE: ____ $ ____
○ WISH   ○ HAVE

'94	'95	'96	'97	'98
$37.50	37.50	37.50	37.50	37.50

KAMM HAUS

ITEM #	INTRO	RETIRED	OSRP	GBTRU	
56171	1995	CURRENT	$42	**$42**	NO CHANGE

"House On The Crest" is the translation of this Alpine building's name. Long stairs lead up to the main balcony and front door of the skiers' inn. Roof overhangs offer protection from icing. Large fireplace at rear of roof has a cap to keep snow from falling in.

DATE: ____ $ ____
○ WISH   ○ HAVE

'95	'96	'97	'98
$42	42	42	42

DANUBE MUSIC PUBLISHER

ITEM #	INTRO	RETIRED	OSRP	GBTRU	
56173	1996	CURRENT	$55	**$55**	NO CHANGE

The Donau Musik Verlag continues onion dome roof motif on store facade and attached music studio which announces violin lessons. Dressed stone outlines windows, doorways and corners on main facade while pargeting carved in ornamental patterns highlights studio.

DATE: ____ $ ____
○ WISH   ○ HAVE

'97	'98
$55	55

ALPINE VILLAGE SERIES™

209

BERNHARDINER HUNDCHEN

ITEM #	INTRO	RETIRED	OSRP	GBTRU	NO
56174	1997	CURRENT	$50	**$50**	CHANGE

Midyear release. (St. Bernard Kennel) Kennels and training center for St. Bernard puppies and dogs. The breed is known for endurance and ability to track and rescue people lost or injured in snowy mountainous regions.

DATE: ____ $ ____
○ WISH ○ HAVE

'97	'98
$50	50

SPIELZEUG LADEN

ITEM #	INTRO	RETIRED	OSRP	GBTRU	NO
56192	1997	CURRENT	$65	**$65**	CHANGE

(Toy Shop) Two-story toy shop trimmed with gingerbread design cutouts on railing, door and clock tower.

DATE: ____ $ ____
○ WISH ○ HAVE

'98
$65

FEDERBETTEN UND STEPPDECKEN

ITEM #	INTRO	RETIRED	OSRP	GBTRU	NO
56176	1998	CURRENT	$48	**$48**	CHANGE

Midyear release. (Featherbeds and Quilts) Colorful bedcoverings are the products of this shop with some of the wares on display on the railings and front fence. Goose down and feathers are used in product design to provide toasty sleeping on wintry nights.

DATE: ____ $ ____
○ WISH ○ HAVE

'98
$48

HEIDI'S GRANDFATHER'S HOUSE

ITEM #	INTRO	RETIRED	OSRP	GBTRU
56177	1998	CURRENT	$64	**$64**

A quaint wooden house with antlers displayed above the second-floor window.

DATE: ____ $ ____
○ WISH ○ HAVE

	ITEM #	INTRO	RETIRED	OSRP	GBTRU
SOUND OF MUSIC® **VON TRAPP VILLA, THE**	56178	1998	CURRENT	$130	**$130**

Set of 5. Inspired by the famous story, this stately mansion includes a large gate and the family members.
Notable: First licensed piece in Alpine Village Series™.

DATE: ____ $ ____
○ WISH ○ HAVE

My, My, How Things Have Changed

I sat back one day to reminisce about the seven years we've been writing about Department 56® villages and the hobby of collecting them. I thought about the collectors we have had the honor of meeting, the retailers and secondary market dealers who have been a valuable part of our success, the pieces themselves, how collecting them has changed during that span, and how *the Village Chronicle* has reacted to those changes. It's when I got to this aspect that I realized how different things really are.

When we published the first issue of our then-newsletter in September 1991, we barely had enough information to fill eight pages. (I just looked through that issue…we didn't fill all eight pages.) Information was scarce; we hadn't yet developed the avenues that would later be crucial to obtaining timely, accurate data.

As time passed, we added a few retired items for sale in the newsletter, a little extra income to offset the cost of the newsletter, we thought. In time, as the demand for secondary market items grew, so grew that portion of our business. Not a bad situation to be in, it would seem. But that was not the business we had intended to be in. Certainly the brokerage was growing, but at what cost to the newsletter?

At that point, we decided to close the brokerage…cold turkey. Many of our associates in the collectible business questioned our sanity. Why give up a thriving business? We had to wonder if they were right. But the immediate drop in revenue was offset by the instantaneous increase in time, allowing us to focus on our love, *the Chronicle*.

Since then we have developed this publication to the point where we are beginning to near our original goals—a magazine format with a knowledgeable staff of writers offering informative and entertaining ideas. But approaching these goals means only one thing…raising the bar another notch or maybe even two.

Not only has *the Village Chronicle* changed, but what is contained in each issue has also changed. In the first half of the publication's life, the major topics focused on variations, the secondary market, and the Department 56®-related events that were taking place. Another often visited subject was (are you ready for this?) the collectors' desire and almost compelling nature to increase the number of buildings in their possession.

Can you believe that? Pertaining to that subject, articles covered the possibility of starting a new collection—perhaps beginning The Original Snow Village® if you had Dickens' Village Series® or New England Village® or vice versa. After all, you could never have too many. *continued page 227*

Item#	Name	Intro	Retired	OSRP$	GBTru$	Wish	Have	Date	Qty	Paid Each	Total
5961-7	Sutton Place Brownstones	1987	1989	80	785	○	○				
5962-5	Cathedral, The	1987	1990	60	325	○	○				
5963-3	Palace Theatre	1987	1989	45	825	○	○				
6512-9	Christmas In The City, Set/3	1987	1990	112	575	○	○				
6512-9	Toy Shop And Pet Store	1987	1990	37.50	255	○	○				
6512-9	Bakery	1987	1990	37.50	125	○	○				
6512-9	Tower Restaurant	1987	1990	37.50	255	○	○				
5968-4	Chocolate Shoppe	1988	1991	40	150	○	○				
5969-2	City Hall	1988	1991	65	165	○	○				
5970-6	Hank's Market	1988	1992	40	85	○	○				
5972-2	Variety Store	1988	1990	45	185	○	○				
5973-0	Ritz Hotel	1989	1994	55	70	○	○				
5974-9	Dorothy's Dress Shop	1989	Ltd Ed 12,500	70	345	○	○				
5977-3	5607 Park Avenue Townhouse	1989	1992	48	90	○	○				
5978-1	5609 Park Avenue Townhouse	1989	1992	48	90	○	○				
5536-0	Red Brick Fire Station	1990	1995	55	85	○	○				
5537-9	Wong's In Chinatown	1990	1994	55	85	○	○				
5534-4	Hollydale's Department Store	1991	1997	75	90	○	○				
5538-7	"Little Italy" Ristorante	1991	1995	50	70	○	○				
5542-5	All Saints Corner Church	1991	1998	96	115	○	○				
5543-3	Arts Academy	1991	1993	45	70	○	○				
5544-1	Doctor's Office, The	1991	1994	60	65	○	○				
5549-2	Cathedral Church Of St. Mark	1991	Ltd Ed 3,024*	120	1675	○	○				
5531-0	Uptown Shoppes, Set/3	1992	1996	150	165	○	○				
55311	Haberdashery	1992	1996	40	50	○	○				
55312	Music Emporium	1992	1996	54	65	○	○				
55313	City Clockworks	1992	1996	56	70	○	○				
5880-7	West Village Shops, Set/2	1993	1996	90	110	○	○				
58808	Potter's Tea Seller	1993	1996	45	50	○	○				
58809	Spring St. Coffee House	1993	1996	45	55	○	○				
5881-5	Brokerage House	1994	1997	48	60	○	○				
5882-3	First Metropolitan Bank	1994	1997	60	65	○	○				
5883-1	Heritage Museum Of Art	1994	1998	96	105	○	○				

CIC Page 1 Totals: 2,060.50   7,375.00

CHRISTMAS IN THE CITY® GB HISTORY LIST

Item#	Name	Intro	Retired	OSRP$	GBTru$	Wish	Have	Date	Qty	Paid Each	Total
5887-4	Ivy Terrace Apartments	1995	1997	60	65	○	○				
58875	Holy Name Church	1995	Current	96	96	○	○				
58876	Brighton School	1995	1998	52	60	○	○				
58877	Brownstones on the Square, Set/2	1995	*	90	90	○	○				
58878	Beekman House	1995	Current	45	45	○	○				
58879	Pickford Place	1995	1998	45	50	○	○				
58880	Washington Street Post Office	1996	1998	52	65	○	○				
58881	Grand Central Railway Station	1996	Current	90	90	○	○				
58882	Cafe Caprice French Restaurant	1996	Current	45	45	○	○				
58883	City Globe, The	1997	Current	65	65	○	○				
58884	Hi-De-Ho Nightclub	1997	Current	52	52	○	○				
58886	Johnson's Grocery & Deli	1997	Current	60	60	○	○				
58887	Capitol, The	1997	1998	110	115	○	○				
58888	Riverside Row Shops	1997	Current	52	52	○	○				
58870	Grand Movie Theater, The	1998	Current	50	50	○	○				
58871	Scottie's Toy Shop Exclusive Gift Set	1998	Event Gift Set	65	95	○	○				
58940	Old Trinity Church	1998	Current	96	96	○	○				
58941	Precinct 25 Police Station	1998	Current	56	56	○	○				
58943	Wedding Gallery, The	1998	Current	60	60	○	○				
58945	University Club, The	1998	Current	60	60	○	○				
			CIC Page 2 Totals:	1,301.00	1,367.00						
			CIC Page 1 Totals:	2,060.50	7,375.00						
			CIC Page 2 Totals:	1,301.00	1,367.00						
			CIC Grand Totals:	3,361.50	8,742.00						

SUTTON PLACE BROWNSTONES

ITEM #	INTRO	RETIRED	OSRP	GBTRU	↓
5961-7	1987	1989	$80	**$785**	12%

Three multistoried homes, attached via shared common walls. Three shops occupy semi-below ground-level space. Attic dormer windows have iron grillwork.
Notable: "Sutton Place Rowhouse" is inscribed on the bottom, not "Sutton Place Brownstones." It's common for a piece to have a concave back wall; however, one with a relatively straight wall can be found and is generally considered to be more valuable.

DATE: ____	$ ____	'91	'92	'93	'94	'95	'96	'97	'98
○ WISH	○ HAVE	$425	760	775	825	825	845	875	895

CATHEDRAL, THE

ITEM #	INTRO	RETIRED	OSRP	GBTRU	↓
5962-5	1987	1990	$60	**$325**	7%

Twin spires, early Gothic design and decorated windows set this Cathedral apart. Stone church incorporates a fortress-like solidness.
Notable: The First Version is smaller, darker, and has snow on the steps. The Second Version is larger, lighter, and has **no** snow on the steps.

DATE: ____	$ ____	'91	'92	'93	'94	'95	'96	'97	'98
○ WISH	○ HAVE	$220	285	305	330	335	340	355	350

PALACE THEATRE

ITEM #	INTRO	RETIRED	OSRP	GBTRU	↓
5963-3	1987	1989	$45	**$825**	12%

Mask of Comedy & Tragedy are bas-reliefs on brick building featuring Christmas Show of Nutcracker. Stage entrance on side of building. The First Version is smaller and has more snow on the roof.
Notable: The First Version has gilded trim; the Second Version has yellow/mustard trim. It's not unusual for a piece to have concave or convex walls; however, a piece with relatively straight walls can be found and is generally considered to be more valuable.

DATE: ____	$ ____	'91	'92	'93	'94	'95	'96	'97	'98
○ WISH	○ HAVE	$450	1100	1025	925	925	890	935	940

CHRISTMAS IN THE CITY

ITEM #	INTRO	RETIRED	OSRP	GBTRU	↓
6512-9	1987	1990	$112	**$575**	8%

Set of 3 includes *Toy Shop And Pet Store, Bakery* and *Tower Restaurant.*

see next page

DATE: ____	$ ____	'91	'92	'93	'94	'95	'96	'97	'98
○ WISH	○ HAVE	$250	290	335	375	475	565	590	625

TOY SHOP AND PET STORE

ITEM #	INTRO	RETIRED	OSRP	GBTRU	↑
6512-9	1987	1990	$37.50	**$255**	2%

1 of the 3-piece set—CHRISTMAS IN THE CITY. Side by side Pet Store and Toy Shop. Tucked in at side is Tailor Shop. Ground floor has extra high ceiling with half-circle windows.
Notable: Individual pieces may vary in color. The earlier pieces are very dark, later ones are lighter.

DATE: ___ $ ___		'91	'92	'93	'94	'95	'96	'97	'98
○ WISH ○ HAVE		$85	115	120	150	220	235	275	250

BAKERY

ITEM #	INTRO	RETIRED	OSRP	GBTRU	NO
6512-9	1987	1990	$37.50	**$125**	CHANGE

1 of the 3-piece set—CHRISTMAS IN THE CITY. Four-story building with Bakery on first two levels. Iron grill work for safety and decor on smaller windows.
Notable: Two different height chimneys. Individual pieces may vary in color. The earlier pieces are light, later ones are darker.

DATE: ___ $ ___		'91	'92	'93	'94	'95	'96	'97	'98
○ WISH ○ HAVE		$80	80	95	95	95	100	115	125

TOWER RESTAURANT

ITEM #	INTRO	RETIRED	OSRP	GBTRU	↓
6512-9	1987	1990	$37.50	**$255**	11%

1 of the 3-piece set—CHRISTMAS IN THE CITY. Multi-sided tower structure is integral part of residential building. Double door entry to restaurant/cafe. Iron grillwork on upper tower windows.
Notable: Individual pieces may vary in color. The earlier pieces are very dark, later ones are lighter. Box reads "Tower Cafe," bottom has **no** name.

DATE: ___ $ ___		'91	'92	'93	'94	'95	'96	'97	'98
○ WISH ○ HAVE		$110	130	165	175	200	235	275	285

CHOCOLATE SHOPPE

ITEM #	INTRO	RETIRED	OSRP	GBTRU	NO
5968-4	1988	1991	$40	**$150**	CHANGE

Paneled roof between first and second story extends to shop signs. Building over Shoppe rises three stories plus attic. Above Brown Brothers Bookstore is one short story plus attic. Stone facade has heart panels at base while bookstore has sign and canopy over window.
Notable: Individual pieces may vary in color. The earlier pieces are dark, later ones are lighter. The roof of the attached bookstore is most often not level. None of the variations affect GBTru$.

DATE: ___ $ ___		'91	'92	'93	'94	'95	'96	'97	'98
○ WISH ○ HAVE		$45	90	90	110	100	135	150	150

CHRISTMAS IN THE CITY®

CITY HALL

ITEM #	INTRO	RETIRED	OSRP	GBTRU	↓
5969-2	1988	1991	$65	**$165**	11%

Imposing fortress with four towers at corners plus repeat design on clock tower. Broad steps plus large columns establish entry doors. Stone arches accent first-floor windows plus tower window. Planters with evergreens on either side of steps. **Notable:** The City Hall "Proof" is smaller than the regular City Hall edition. It came in a foam box with **no** sleeve or light cord. **GBTru$ for Proof is $135.**

DATE: ____ $ ____	'91	'92	'93	'94	'95	'96	'97	'98
○ WISH ○ HAVE	$75	150	150	150	155	160	170	185

HANK'S MARKET

ITEM #	INTRO	RETIRED	OSRP	GBTRU	↓
5970-6	1988	1992	$40	**$85**	6%

Boxes and barrels of produce are on display. Rolled awnings over sign. Brick building with painted brick on upper sections of second story. Two upper windows are multi-paned with half-circle sunburst, other window has awning. Two chimneys on steeply pitched roof. **Notable:** This piece is also referred to as "Corner Grocer."

DATE: ____ $ ____	'91	'92	'93	'94	'95	'96	'97	'98
○ WISH ○ HAVE	$45	45	78	78	80	85	85	90

VARIETY STORE

ITEM #	INTRO	RETIRED	OSRP	GBTRU	NO CHANGE
5972-2	1988	1990	$45	**$185**	

Corner store in two-story brick building. Garland-decorated awnings extend out to shelter display windows and shoppers. Separate door for upper story. Next door shop is barbershop with striped pole outside. Small eyeglass shop completes trio. **Notable:** The mold used for this building is the same one used for the *Drugstore,* Item #672-6, in the Bachman's® Hometown Series. The design was based on a building in Stillwater, MN.

DATE: ____ $ ____	'91	'92	'93	'94	'95	'96	'97	'98
○ WISH ○ HAVE	$100	105	108	135	150	165	180	185

RITZ HOTEL

ITEM #	INTRO	RETIRED	OSRP	GBTRU	↓
5973-0	1989	1994	$55	**$70**	13%

Red doors complete columned entryway, red window canopy over each second-story French window. Stone, block, and brick building. Cupola on attic window. Slate roof.

DATE: ____ $ ____	'91	'92	'93	'94	'95	'96	'97	'98
○ WISH ○ HAVE	$55	55	55	55	65	75	80	80

DOROTHY'S DRESS SHOP

ITEM #	INTRO	RETIRED	OSRP	GBTRU	↓
5974-9	1989	LTD ED 12,500	$70	**$345**	12%

Bright green door and awning, bay windows on first and second floor, mansard roof.

DATE: ____ $ ____	'91	'92	'93	'94	'95	'96	'97	'98
○ Wish ○ Have	$350	355	370	370	350	375	380	390

5607 PARK AVENUE TOWNHOUSE

ITEM #	INTRO	RETIRED	OSRP	GBTRU	NO
5977-3	1989	1992	$48	**$90**	CHANGE

Four stories with ground floor card and gift shop, curved corner turret, blue canopy over double French door entry. **Notable:** Earlier pieces had gilded trim at top of building, later production had dull gold colored paint. This does not affect secondary market value.

DATE: ____ $ ____	'91	'92	'93	'94	'95	'96	'97	'98
○ Wish ○ Have	$48	50	78	81	80	80	85	90

5609 PARK AVENUE TOWNHOUSE

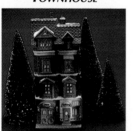

ITEM #	INTRO	RETIRED	OSRP	GBTRU	NO
5978-1	1989	1992	$48	**$90**	CHANGE

Four stories with ground floor art gallery, double wood doors lead to apartments, blue canopy over entry. **Notable:** Earlier pieces had gilded trim at top of building, later production has dull gold colored paint. This does not affect secondary market value.

DATE: ____ $ ____	'91	'92	'93	'94	'95	'96	'97	'98
○ Wish ○ Have	$48	50	78	82	80	80	85	90

RED BRICK FIRE STATION

ITEM #	INTRO	RETIRED	OSRP	GBTRU	NO
5536-0	1990	1995	$55	**$85**	CHANGE

Brick Station House for Hook & Ladder Company. Large wood doors lead to equipment with separate door for upper level. Stone block detailing on turret and above upper floor windows. Formal pediment at front gate.

DATE: ____ $ ____	'91	'92	'93	'94	'95	'96	'97	'98
○ Wish ○ Have	$55	55	55	55	55	75	80	85

WONG'S IN CHINATOWN

ITEM #	INTRO	RETIRED	OSRP	GBTRU	↑
5537-9	1990	1994	$55	**$85**	6%

Chinese restaurant and a laundry in brick building. Canopy over entry and at roof feature pagoda shape. Fire escape for second- and third-story tenants. Chinese writing: Above the door –"Good Luck," on right side of the building–"Cantonese Cuisine," on left side of building–"Laundry," and on the Wong's sign–"Restaurant."
Notable: In the First Version the top window is red. In the Second Version the top window is gold.

DATE: ____ $ ____		'91	'92	'93	'94	'95	'96	'97	'98
○ WISH ○ HAVE		$55	55	55	55	70	70	80	80

HOLLYDALE'S DEPARTMENT STORE

ITEM #	INTRO	RETIRED	OSRP	GBTRU	NO
5534-4	1991	1997	$75	**$90**	CHANGE

Building has corner curved front with awnings on windows, domed cupola, skylights on roof, and carved balustrade design on second-story windows highlight store.
Notable: First Version shipments are from Taiwan and have holly on the first-floor canopies only. The Second Version is from China and has holly on all canopies. The Third Version is from the Philippines.

DATE: ____ $ ____		'91	'92	'93	'94	'95	'96	'97	'98
○ WISH ○ HAVE		$75	75	85	85	85	85	85	90

"LITTLE ITALY" RISTORANTE

ITEM #	INTRO	RETIRED	OSRP	GBTRU	↓
5538-7	1991	1995	$50	**$70**	18%

Tall, narrow three-story building with stucco finish on upper level above brick street-level entry. Outdoor cafe serving pizza is on side.

DATE: ____ $ ____		'91	'92	'93	'94	'95	'96	'97	'98
○ WISH ○ HAVE		$50	50	52	52	52	75	85	85

ALL SAINTS CORNER CHURCH

ITEM #	INTRO	RETIRED	OSRP	GBTRU	↑
5542-5	1991	1998	$96	**$115**	5%

Gothic style. Carved support frame arched windows, tall steeple with corners capped by small steeple design. Large windows exhibit tracery pattern.

DATE: ____ $ ____		'91	'92	'93	'94	'95	'96	'97	'98
○ WISH ○ HAVE		$96	96	105	105	110	110	110	110

ARTS ACADEMY

	ITEM # 5543-3	INTRO 1991	RETIRED 1993	OSRP $45	GBTRU **$70**	↓ 13%

Two-story brick building has classrooms and practice halls. Curved canopy over entrance repeats design of arched triple window, skylight & small tower window.

		'91	'92	'93	'94	'95	'96	'97	'98
DATE: ____ $ ____ ○ WISH ○ HAVE		$45	45	46	80	75	75	80	80

DOCTOR'S OFFICE, THE

	ITEM # 5544-1	INTRO 1991	RETIRED 1994	OSRP $60	GBTRU **$65**	↓ 19%

Four-story brick building for Doctor, Dentist, and office space. Bow window is first level Doctor. Dentist windows have broad awning.

		'91	'92	'93	'94	'95	'96	'97	'98
DATE: ____ $ ____ ○ WISH ○ HAVE		$60	60	60	60	75	75	80	80

CATHEDRAL CHURCH OF ST. MARK

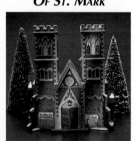

	ITEM # 5549-2	INTRO 1991	RETIRED LTD ED 3,024*	OSRP $120	GBTRU **$1675**	↓ 18%

Front has look of fortification with two towers rising next to entry. Moldings are richly carved above double doors. Stone and brick with accented stone work framing walls and towers. Triple windows on each upper tower side. **Notable:** Commonly referred to as "St. Mark's." *Announced Edition of 17,500—closed at 3,024 pieces due to production problems. Early release to Gift Creations Concepts (GCC), Fall 1992. This building is subject to firing cracks and should be inspected closely while lighted.

		'91	'92	'93	'94	'95	'96	'97	'98
DATE: ____ $ ____ ○ WISH ○ HAVE		$120	120	2900	2850	2300	1860	1850	2050

UPTOWN SHOPPES

	ITEM # 5531-0	INTRO 1992	RETIRED 1996	OSRP $150	GBTRU **$165**	↓ 11%

Set of 3 includes *Haberdashery,* Music Emporium, *and* City Clockworks.

see next page

		'92	'93	'94	'95	'96	'97	'98
DATE: ____ $ ____ ○ WISH ○ HAVE		$150	150	150	150	150	175	185

HABERDASHERY

Item #	Intro	Retired	OSRP	GBTru	↓
55311	1992	1996	$40	**$50**	17%

1 of the 3-piece set—UPTOWN SHOPPES. Squared corner of three-story building is men's clothier entry. First-level front window topped by canopy and store sign. Second-story triple windows topped by ornamental molding and side windows have triangular canopies. Brick, stone, and roughcast pepple-dash facade.

DATE: ____ $ ____	'92	'93	'94	'95	'96	'97	'98
○ Wish ○ Have	$40	40	40	40	40	55	60

MUSIC EMPORIUM

Item #	Intro	Retired	OSRP	GBTru	↓
55312	1992	1996	$54	**$65**	7%

1 of the 3-piece set—UPTOWN SHOPPES. Brick store decorates side wall with a musical score. Store name is superimposed and trimmed for holidays. Other signs advertise violins, flutes, and horns. Tallest of the three shops, building has 3 floors and attic dormer.
Notable: The music on the side of the building was inspired by a similar idea on the side of Schmitt Music Center in Minneapolis, MN.

DATE: ____ $ ____	'92	'93	'94	'95	'96	'97	'98
○ Wish ○ Have	$54	54	54	54	54	65	70

CITY CLOCKWORKS

Item #	Intro	Retired	OSRP	GBTru	
55313	1992	1996	$56	**$70**	NO CHANGE

1 of the 3-piece set—UPTOWN SHOPPES. Triangular shaped building. Front angle blunted by semicircular windows above entry to shop. Large clock hangs at right angles to store between sign and windows. Second clock next to entrance.

DATE: ____ $ ____	'92	'93	'94	'95	'96	'97	'98
○ Wish ○ Have	$56	56	56	56	56	70	70

WEST VILLAGE SHOPS

Item #	Intro	Retired	OSRP	GBTru	↓
5880-7	1993	1996	$90	**$110**	8%

Set of 2 includes *Potter's Tea Seller*, and *Spring St. Coffee House*.

see next page

DATE: ____ $ ____	'93	'94	'95	'96	'97	'98
○ Wish ○ Have	$90	90	90	90	120	120

POTTER'S TEA SELLER

	ITEM #	INTRO	RETIRED	OSRP	GBTRU	↓
	58808	1993	1996	$45	**$50**	23%

1 of the 2-piece set—WEST VILLAGE SHOPS. Stone 3-story shop serves tea by the cup or pot. Stone arches decorate windows. Green awing covers upper window above entry. Sign hangs in front of door to alert shoppers.

DATE: _____ $ _____
○ WISH ○ HAVE

'93	'94	'95	'96	'97	'98
$45	45	45	45	60	65

SPRING ST. COFFEE HOUSE

	ITEM #	INTRO	RETIRED	OSRP	GBTRU	↓
	58809	1993	1996	$45	**$55**	15%

1 of the 2-piece set—WEST VILLAGE SHOPS. Four-story narrow building. Steps lead to entry door covered by small pillared portico. Buy beans ground to order & blended for taste, or have a cup at the shop. Lower level is brick, upper stories are stucco.

DATE: _____ $ _____
○ WISH ○ HAVE

'93	'94	'95	'96	'97	'98
$45	45	45	45	65	65

BROKERAGE HOUSE

	ITEM #	INTRO	RETIRED	OSRP	GBTRU	
	5881-5	1994	1997	$48	**$60**	NO CHANGE

Stone building gives impression of invincibility. Four pillars support large entry pediment which has name of Exchange carved into stone. Feeling of wealth is reinforced by gold embellishments.

Notable: "18" is symbolic of initial Department 56, Inc. stock offering at $18.00. "Price & Price" is in honor of Mr. & Mrs. Price. Judith Price is Department 56, Inc.'s Ms. Lit Town.

DATE: _____ $ _____
○ WISH ○ HAVE

'94	'95	'96	'97	'98
$48	48	48	48	60

FIRST METROPOLITAN BANK

	ITEM #	INTRO	RETIRED	OSRP	GBTRU	↓
	5882-3	1994	1997	$60	**$65**	13%

Domed, three-story building presents solid edifice. Four columns reach to third story and create covered entry and area for name inscription. Bank has gilt trim on dome, windows and door.

DATE: _____ $ _____
○ WISH ○ HAVE

'94	'95	'96	'97	'98
$60	60	60	60	75

HERITAGE MUSEUM OF ART

ITEM #	INTRO	RETIRED	OSRP	GBTRU	↑
5883-1	1994	1998	$96	**$105**	9%

A stately, symmetrical structure with large windows. Names of famous artists are displayed around the top of the building and Thomas Nast's rendition of Santa Claus is on display above the entrance.

DATE: _____ $ _____
○ WISH ○ HAVE

'94	'95	'96	'97	'98
$96	96	96	96	96

IVY TERRACE APARTMENTS

ITEM #	INTRO	RETIRED	OSRP	GBTRU	↓
5887-4	1995	1997	$60	**$65**	7%

Midyear release. Three-story brick building with two canopy covered entries. Third-floor apartment has terrace with wrought iron enclosure.

DATE: _____ $ _____
○ WISH ○ HAVE

'95	'96	'97	'98
$60	60	60	70

HOLY NAME CHURCH

ITEM #	INTRO	RETIRED	OSRP	GBTRU	NO
58875	1995	CURRENT	$96	**$96**	CHANGE

Brick church with entry and steeple with ornate pediment and molding topped by golden dome and cross. Stained glass fills rose window and lancet windows. Niche for statuary in steeple. Ribbed roof with carved design in ridge edging.
Notable: Design adaptation—Cathedral of the Immaculate Conception, Kansas City, MO.

DATE: _____ $ _____
○ WISH ○ HAVE

'95	'96	'97	'98
$96	96	96	96

BRIGHTON SCHOOL

ITEM #	INTRO	RETIRED	OSRP	GBTRU	↑
58876	1995	1998	$52	**$60**	15%

Brick school with small flag flying atop clock tower. Stone foundation with steps that lead to front doors. School name above doors. Banner over windows tells children date of winter recess.

DATE: _____ $ _____
○ WISH ○ HAVE

'95	'96	'97	'98
$52	52	52	52

CHRISTMAS IN THE CITY®

BROWNSTONES ON THE SQUARE

ITEM #	INTRO	RETIRED	OSRP	GBTRU	NO
58877	1995	*	$90	**$90**	CHANGE

Set of 2 includes *Beekman House,* and *Pickford Place.*
**Pickford Place* retired in 1998, *Beekman House* is current.

see below

DATE: ____ $ ____					
○ WISH ○ HAVE					

'95	'96	'97	'98
$90	90	90	90

BEEKMAN HOUSE

ITEM #	INTRO	RETIRED	OSRP	GBTRU	NO
58878	1995	CURRENT	$45	**$45**	CHANGE

1 of the 2-piece set—BROWNSTONES ON THE SQUARE. Four-story walkup with entry canopy, decorated with script "B." Building name above paned first level window with lamp close by. Second-story arched window has wrought iron ornamentation, while other front windows are canopied. Date appears on ornate roof molding.

DATE: ____ $ ____
○ WISH ○ HAVE

'95	'96	'97	'98
$45	45	45	45

PICKFORD PLACE

ITEM #	INTRO	RETIRED	OSRP	GBTRU	↑
58879	1995	1998	$45	**$50**	11%

1 of the 2-piece set—BROWNSTONES ON THE SQUARE. Four-story walkup with entry canopy, decorated with script "P." Building name above paned first-level window with lamp close by. Second-story arched window has potted plant while other front windows have wrought iron ornamentation. Date appears on ornate roof molding.

DATE: ____ $ ____
○ WISH ○ HAVE

'95	'96	'97	'98
$45	45	45	45

WASHINGTON STREET POST OFFICE

ITEM #	INTRO	RETIRED	OSRP	GBTRU	↑
58880	1996	1998	$52	**$65**	25%

Midyear release. Three-story brick with roof and edges of building finished in dressed stone. This office can receive and send letters, packages and airmail as well as sell stamps.

DATE: ____ $ ____
○ WISH ○ HAVE

'96	'97	'98
$52	52	52

CHRISTMAS IN THE CITY®

GRAND CENTRAL RAILWAY STATION

ITEM #	INTRO	RETIRED	OSRP	GBTRU	NO
58881	1996	CURRENT	$90	**$90**	CHANGE

Two-story rendition of New York City's Grand Central Terminal. Arched colonnade entry topped by balustrade. Access to platforms from side entrances. Brick building with formal elegant trim topped by clock.

DATE: ____ $ ____
○ WISH   ○ HAVE

'97	'98
$90	90

CAFE CAPRICE FRENCH RESTAURANT

ITEM #	INTRO	RETIRED	OSRP	GBTRU	NO
58882	1996	CURRENT	$45	**$45**	CHANGE

Blue roof and shutters trim three-story building housing French restaurant. Onion dome tower rises at front. French/English tutor lives and works on third floor.

DATE: ____ $ ____
○ WISH   ○ HAVE

'97	'98
$45	45

CITY GLOBE, THE

ITEM #	INTRO	RETIRED	OSRP	GBTRU	NO
58883	1997	CURRENT	$65	**$65**	CHANGE

Midyear release. Newspaper publishing company for the City. Globe that tops the tower actually spins.

DATE: ____ $ ____
○ WISH   ○ HAVE

'97	'98
$65	65

HI-DE-HO NIGHTCLUB

ITEM #	INTRO	RETIRED	OSRP	GBTRU	NO
58884	1997	CURRENT	$52	**$52**	CHANGE

Midyear release. Posters on three-story red brick nightclub highlight present and future club acts. Marquee over double door entry. Club name highlights a Cab Calloway jazz riff.

DATE: ____ $ ____
○ WISH   ○ HAVE

'97	'98
$52	52

JOHNSON'S GROCERY & DELI

ITEM #	INTRO	RETIRED	OSRP	GBTRU	NO
58886	1997	CURRENT	$60	**$60**	CHANGE

Corner store typical of NY's Soho district for groceries, produce, baked goods and prepared ready-to-eat take-out. Combination of three shops create a one-stop shop. Brick construction with awnings over windows and produce bins. Some second-story windows have ornamental ironwork.

DATE: ____ $ ____
○ WISH   ○ HAVE

'98
$60

CAPITOL, THE

ITEM #	INTRO	RETIRED	OSRP	GBTRU	↑
58887	1997	1998	$110	**$115**	5%

Fortress-like formal edifice is softened by the domes on the four corners and the central gold trimmed rotunda. Golden lions guard the rotunda. Broad steps lead up to the main entrance.

DATE: ____ $ ____
○ WISH   ○ HAVE

'98
$110

RIVERSIDE ROW SHOPS

ITEM #	INTRO	RETIRED	OSRP	GBTRU	NO
58888	1997	CURRENT	$52	**$52**	CHANGE

Clustered together tightly along the riverside, these three shops include the North Branch of the National Bank, the Riverside Barber Shop and the Crosby & Smith Stationers. Made of red brick, each shop has its own facade design.

DATE: ____ $ ____
○ WISH   ○ HAVE

'98
$52

GRAND MOVIE THEATER, THE

ITEM #	INTRO	RETIRED	OSRP	GBTRU	NO
58870	1998	CURRENT	$50	**$50**	CHANGE

Midyear release. Colorful design of movie theater is fashioned after early movie houses in the cities. Ticket stall is designed as an attachment and painted with 18 karat gold. Double entry doors flank ticket booth.

DATE: ____ $ ____
○ WISH   ○ HAVE

'98
$50

SCOTTIE'S TOY SHOP EXCLUSIVE GIFT SET

ITEM #	INTRO	RETIRED	OSRP	GBTRU	↑
58871	1998	EVENT GIFT SET	$65	**$95**	46%

Set of 10. Midyear release. This 3-story toy emporium has a large bay window to display toys. Accessory Set of 3, *5¢ Pony Rides* features children and a pony on a spring and metal base. Also included are 4 sisal trees, Cobblestone Road, and 1.5 oz. bag of Village Fresh Fallen Snow.
Notable: This Gift Set was one of three featured at Department 56, Inc.'s National Homes For The Holidays Open House Event, November 5–9, 1998.

DATE: _____ $ _____
○ WISH   ○ HAVE

'98
$65

OLD TRINITY CHURCH

ITEM #	INTRO	RETIRED	OSRP	GBTRU
58940	1998	CURRENT	$96	**$96**

Trimmed in gold, this church has twin spires, each containing a bell. The windows resemble actual stained glass.

DATE: _____ $ _____
○ WISH   ○ HAVE

PRECINCT 25 POLICE STATION

ITEM #	INTRO	RETIRED	OSRP	GBTRU
58941	1998	CURRENT	$56	**$56**

Molded metal railings adorn the roof, center window, and front doors. There are separate entrances for the chief of police and chief detective.

DATE: _____ $ _____
○ WISH   ○ HAVE

WEDDING GALLERY, THE

ITEM #	INTRO	RETIRED	OSRP	GBTRU
58943	1998	CURRENT	$60	**$60**

Bridal attire is displayed in the front window.
Notable: Included with this piece is a brass plaque that can be personalized.

DATE: _____ $ _____
○ WISH   ○ HAVE

UNIVERSITY CLUB, THE	ITEM # 58945	INTRO 1998	RETIRED CURRENT	OSRP $60	GBTRU $60

This stone building features a pool and lockers in its third-floor glassed-in terrace.

DATE: _____ $ _____
○ WISH   ○ HAVE

My, My, How Things Have Changed

continued from page 211

Another idea was to "adopt" pieces from other villages and include them in the one you collected. *McGrebe—Cutters & Sleighs* certainly fit well in a Dickens' Village Series® collection. Likewise, *Bean & Son Smithy* could be placed in a New England Village® collection. A surprising "relocation" concerned The Original Snow Village® *Greenhouse.* Christmas In The City® collectors were more than happy to break tradition and include a ceramic piece in their City collections.

Very seldom was there an article about display making—the thrust of the hobby was collecting them. Even more rare was the mention of miniatures. In fact, I wouldn't be surprised if we never wrote about them in any depth. It only made sense. If collectors weren't craving an abundance of information on displays, they certainly weren't knocking down doors to get any about miniatures to put in displays.

But oh, how times change. Display making is now a major part of the hobby, and, therefore, a major part of our magazine. This fact led me to write an article in this column stating that collecting Department 56® pieces had surpassed mere collecting and become a full-fledged hobby based on display making. Sure, collectors still view variations as being important, but I believe their relevance has slipped a bit.

The secondary market doesn't dominate pages the way it did from time-to-time. Yes, it's still a very viable aspect of the collection, but perhaps not as powerful as it once was. The void created by this seems to have filled with interest in miniatures. Where there was little interest in these before, there is a huge amount of interest now.

If asked when *the Village Chronicle* began if I could predict what collectors would be interested in now, I never would have imagined it to be what it is. If you ask me now what will be on the minds of collectors seven years from now, I could only guess. But I am looking forward to finding out. If it's anywhere nearly as interesting as the past seven years have been, it's going to be a blast!

the Village Chronicle.

Item#	Name	Intro	Retired	OSRP$	GBTru$	Wish Have	Date	Qty	Paid Each	Total
5975-7	Little Town Of Bethlehem	1987	Current	150	150	○ ○	___			___
	LTB Grand Totals:			$150.00	$150.00					

228 *Little Town Of Bethlehem™ GB History List*

LITTLE TOWN OF BETHLEHEM

ITEM #	INTRO	RETIRED	OSRP	GBT	RU	NO
5975-7	1987	CURRENT	$150	**$150**		CHANGE

Set of 12. Replica of Holy Family Manger Scene with Three Wise Men and Shepherd. Stone and sun-dried brick homes and shelters add Mideast simplicity. Animals attentive to Holy Family. The First Version has snow on the manger. The Second Version does not.

DATE: ____ $ ____	'91	'92	'93	'94	'95	'96	'97	'98
○ WISH ○ HAVE	$150	150	150	150	150	150	150	150

Item#	Name	Intro	Retired	OSRP$	GBTru$	Wish	Have	Date	Qty	Paid Each	Total
5600-6	Santa's Workshop	1990	1993	72	345	O	O				
5601-4	North Pole, Set/2	1990	*	70	*	O	O				
56015	Reindeer Barn	1990	Current	35	40	O	O				
56016	Elf Bunkhouse	1990	1996	35	45	O	O				
5620-0	NeeNee's Dolls and Toys	1991	1995	36	55	O	O				
5621-9	North Pole Shops, Set/2	1991	1995	75	130	O	O				
5621-9	Orly's Bell & Harness Supply	1991	1995	37.50	55	O	O				
5621-9	Rimpy's Bakery	1991	1995	37.50	75	O	O				
5622-7	Tassy's Mittens & Hassel's Woolies	1991	1995	50	70	O	O				
5623-5	Post Office	1992	Current	45	50	O	O				
5624-3	Obbie's Books & Letrinka's Candy	1992	1996	70	90	O	O				
5625-1	Elfie's Sleds & Skates	1992	1996	48	55	O	O				
5626-0	North Pole Chapel	1993	Current	45	45	O	O				
5627-8	North Pole Express Depot	1993	1998	48	55	O	O				
5628-6	Santa's Woodworks	1993	1996	42	60	O	O				
5629-4	Santa's Lookout Tower	1993	Current	45	48	O	O				
5633-2	Elfin Snow Cone Works	1994	1997	40	50	O	O				
5634-0	Beard Barber Shop	1994	1997	27.50	40	O	O				
5635-9	North Pole Dolls & Santa's Bear Works	1994	1997	96	115	O	O				
5638-3	Tin Soldier Shop	1995	1997	42	55	O	O				
56384	Elfin Forge & Assembly Shop	1995	1998	65	70	O	O				
56385	Weather & Time Observatory	1995	Current	50	50	O	O				
56386	Santa's Rooming House	1995	Current	50	50	O	O				
56387	Elves' Trade School	1995	1998	50	55	O	O				
56388	Popcorn & Cranberry House	1996	1997	45	85	O	O				
56389	Santa's Bell Repair	1996	1998	45	55	O	O				
56390	North Pole Start A Tradition Set Candy Cane Lane, Set/2 Candy Cane & Peppermint Shop Gift Wrap & Ribbons	1996	1996	85	90	O	O				
56391	Route 1, North Pole, Home Of Mr. & Mrs. Claus	1996	Current	110	110	O	O				

NP Page 1 Totals: 1,496.50 2,043.00

ITEM#	NAME	INTRO	RETIRED	OSRP$	GBTRU$	WISH	HAVE	DATE	QTY	PAID EACH	TOTAL
56392	HALL OF RECORDS	1996	CURRENT	50	50	○	○	——	——	——	——
56393	CHRISTMAS BREAD BAKERS	1996	CURRENT	55	55	○	○	——	——	——	——
56394	GLACIER GAZETTE, THE	1997	CURRENT	48	48	○	○	——	——	——	——
56395	MRS. CLAUS' GREENHOUSE	1997	CURRENT	68	68	○	○	——	——	——	——
56396	GLASS ORNAMENT WORKS	1997	CURRENT	60	60	○	○	——	——	——	——
56397	SANTA'S LIGHT SHOP	1997	CURRENT	52	52	○	○	——	——	——	——
56398	ELSIE'S GINGERBREAD	1997	1998 ANNUAL	65	110	○	○	——	——	——	——
56400	CUSTOM STITCHERS	1998	CURRENT	37.50	37.50	○	○	——	——	——	——
56401	TILLIE'S TINY CUP CAFÉ	1998	CURRENT	37.50	37.50	○	○	——	——	——	——
56402	ELF SPA, THE	1998	CURRENT	40	40	○	○	——	——	——	——
56403	REAL PLASTIC SNOW FACTORY	1998	CURRENT	80	80	○	○	——	——	——	——
56404	REINDEER FLIGHT SCHOOL	1998	CURRENT	55	55	○	○	——	——	——	——
			NP PAGE 2 TOTALS:	648.00	693.00						
			NP PAGE 1 TOTALS:	1,496.50	2,043.00						
			NP PAGE 2 TOTALS:	648.00	693.00						
			NP GRAND TOTALS:	2,144.50	2,736.00						

SANTA'S WORKSHOP

ITEM #	INTRO	RETIRED	OSRP	GBTRU	↓
5600-6	1990	1993	$72	**$345**	13%

Multi-chimnied, many-gabled home and workshop. Stone foundation with stucco and timber upper stories. Balconies extend off windows and hold garlands. Mailbox by front door.

DATE: ____	$ ____	'91	'92	'93	'94	'95	'96	'97	'98
○ WISH	○ HAVE	$72	75	75	150	375	485	420	395

NORTH POLE

ITEM #	INTRO	RETIRED	OSRP	GBTRU
5601-4	1990	*	$70	*

Set of 2 includes *Reindeer Barn,* and *Elf Bunkhouse.* *Set is split between Current and Retired—the *Elf Bunkhouse* was retired in 1996.

see below

DATE: ____	$ ____	'91	'92	'93	'94	'95	'96	'97	'98
○ WISH	○ HAVE	$70	75	80	80	80	80	*	*

REINDEER BARN

ITEM #	INTRO	RETIRED	OSRP	GBTRU	NO
56015	1990	CURRENT	$35	**$40**	CHANGE

1 of the 2-piece set—NORTH POLE. Stone and stucco has stalls for all reindeer. Steeply pitched roof has cupola on ridge and step design on front of dormers. Roof vents and Dutch stall doors provide ventilation.
Notable: A common variation is a name duplicated, another omitted, on reindeer stalls.

DATE: ____	$ ____	'91	'92	'93	'94	'95	'96	'97	'98
○ WISH	○ HAVE	$35	37.50	40	40	40	40	40	40

ELF BUNKHOUSE

ITEM #	INTRO	RETIRED	OSRP	GBTRU	↓
56016	1990	1996	$35	**$45**	25%

1 of the 2-piece set—NORTH POLE. Home for Santa's helpers, 3 stories with steeply pitched roof and protected chimney. Made of wood, stone and stucco featuring bay windows, dormers, and a balcony.
Notable: The box and bottomstamp both read "Elf Bunkhouse," while the sign on the front of the building reads "Elves Bunkhouse."

DATE: ____	$ ____	'91	'92	'93	'94	'95	'96	'97	'98
○ WISH	○ HAVE	$35	37.50	40	40	40	40	60	60

NeeNee's Dolls And Toys

Item #	Intro	Retired	OSRP	GBTru	↓
5620-0	1991	1995	$36	$55	8%

Rough finish stucco and stone house. Steeply pitched rear roof, red shuttered lattice-paned front second-story windows. "N" monogram within wreath begins spelling out of N-O-R-T-H P-O-L-E.
Notable: Early release to Showcase Dealers and Gift Creations Concepts (GCC).

Date: ___ $ ___	'91	'92	'93	'94	'95	'96	'97	'98
○ Wish ○ Have	$36	37.50	37.50	37.50	37.50	55	60	60

NORTH POLE SHOPS

Item #	Intro	Retired	OSRP	GBTru	↓
5621-9	1991	1995	$75	$130	4%

Set of 2 includes *Orly's Bell & Harness Supply* and *Rimpy's Bakery*.

see below

Date: ___ $ ___	'91	'92	'93	'94	'95	'96	'97	'98
○ Wish ○ Have	$75	75	75	75	75	105	130	135

ORLY'S BELL & HARNESS SUPPLY

Item #	Intro	Retired	OSRP	GBTru	↓
5621-9	1991	1995	$37.50	$55	21%

1 of the 2-piece set—NORTH POLE SHOPS. Stone steps lead to bell shop doorway with brick work design to frame it. Sleigh strap with bells above sign. Harness area has large wood doors that open to allow horse-drawn carriage or wagon to enter. Window with balcony above, on second story. "O" monogram within wreath, part of spelling out of N-O-R-T-H P-O-L-E.

Date: ___ $ ___	'91	'92	'93	'94	'95	'96	'97	'98
○ Wish ○ Have	$37.50	37.50	37.50	37.50	37.50	55	65	70

RIMPY'S BAKERY

Item #	Intro	Retired	OSRP	GBTru	
5621-9	1991	1995	$37.50	$75	NO CHANGE

1 of the 2-piece set—NORTH POLE SHOPS. Three-storied, half wood timbered narrow building. Hipped roof with gable on facade. Large eight-paned front window with wood crib in front and on side. "R" monogram within wreath, part of spelling out of N-O-R-T-H P-O-L-E.

Date: ___ $ ___	'91	'92	'93	'94	'95	'96	'97	'98
○ Wish ○ Have	$37.50	37.50	37.50	37.50	37.50	55	70	75

TASSY'S MITTENS & HASSEL'S WOOLIES

ITEM #	INTRO	RETIRED	OSRP	GBTRu	↓
5622-7	1991	1995	$50	**$70**	13%

Two shops in connected buildings. Hassel's has corner turret window and oriel turret upper window. Tassy's has angled front window at ground and three arched windows on overhang second story. Gable has carved bough and berry design—roof angles steeply pitched. "T" and "H" monograms within wreaths, part of spelling out of N-O-R-T-H P-O-L-E.

DATE: ____ $ ____	'91	'92	'93	'94	'95	'96	'97	'98
○ WISH ○ HAVE	$50	50	50	50	50	75	80	80

POST OFFICE

ITEM #	INTRO	RETIRED	OSRP	GBTRu	NO
5623-5	1992	CURRENT	$45	**$50**	CHANGE

Basis for building is turret with what appears to be a half-house on one side of main tower. Second floor features multi-paned windows, small curved turret between second and third floor could hold staircase. Third floor has low balcony outside windows. "P" monogram within wreath, part of spelling out of N-O-R-T-H P-O-L-E. **Notable:** Early release to Showcase Dealers.

DATE: ____ $ ____	'92	'93	'94	'95	'96	'97	'98
○ WISH ○ HAVE	$45	50	50	50	50	50	50

OBBIE'S BOOKS & LETRINKA'S CANDY

ITEM #	INTRO	RETIRED	OSRP	GBTRu	↑
5624-3	1992	1996	$70	**$90**	6%

The tall, narrow book and toy shop contrasts sharply with the shorter, wider, candy shop. Both shops have steep pitched roofs. A bay window on Obbie's side wall plus a number of dormer windows reinforce the angular look of the shop. Onion dome-shaped chimney and cupola on roof ridge are unique to Letrinka's which also has a vertical timbered ground level design. "O" and "L" monograms within wreaths, part of spelling out of N-O-R-T-H P-O-L-E.

DATE: ____ $ ____	'92	'93	'94	'95	'96	'97	'98
○ WISH ○ HAVE	$70	70	70	70	70	90	85

ELFIE'S SLEDS & SKATES

ITEM #	INTRO	RETIRED	OSRP	GBTRu	↓
5625-1	1992	1996	$48	**$55**	8%

Distinctive roof design with chimneys that are only visible outside from the second story. Roof hood projects out from walls to protect windows on house sides as well as sweeping down to help form large front window. "E" monogram within wreath, part of spelling out of N-O-R-T-H P-O-L-E.

DATE: ____ $ ____	'92	'93	'94	'95	'96	'97	'98
○ WISH ○ HAVE	$48	48	48	48	48	60	60

NORTH POLE SERIES™

NORTH POLE CHAPEL

	ITEM #	INTRO	RETIRED	OSRP	GBTRU	
	5626-0	1993	CURRENT	$45	**$45**	NO CHANGE

Spire, containing brass bell, rises at rear of Chapel. Fieldstone topped by timbered upper story. Double door front entry flanked by evergreens. Side chimney rises through roof with flue pipe capped by onion cap. Large wreath-encircled clock above entry.
Notable: Early release to Showcase Dealers and select buying groups.

DATE: ____ $ ____
○ WISH ○ HAVE

'93	'94	'95	'96	'97	'98
$45	45	45	45	45	45

NORTH POLE EXPRESS DEPOT

	ITEM #	INTRO	RETIRED	OSRP	GBTRU	↑
	5627-8	1993	1998	$48	**$55**	15%

Receiving area for people and deliveries in and out of North Pole not going by Santa's sled. Roof line at lowest point is pagoda-like with an A-frame gable transversing a ridge. Stone chimney rises at rear of roof. Separate doors for passengers and freight.

DATE: ____ $ ____
○ WISH ○ HAVE

'93	'94	'95	'96	'97	'98
$48	48	48	48	48	48

SANTA'S WOODWORKS

	ITEM #	INTRO	RETIRED	OSRP	GBTRU	↓
	5628-6	1993	1996	$42	**$60**	8%

Lower level contains heavy equipment for sawing, debarking and trimming wood. Main level reached by wood stairs at side of open porch. Structure is a log house.

DATE: ____ $ ____
○ WISH ○ HAVE

'93	'94	'95	'96	'97	'98
$42	42	45	45	60	65

SANTA'S LOOKOUT TOWER

	ITEM #	INTRO	RETIRED	OSRP	GBTRU	
	5629-4	1993	CURRENT	$45	**$48**	NO CHANGE

Pennants fly above door and top of tower which rises above trees to give Santa a clear picture of flight conditions. Balcony around highest story lets Santa check wind velocity.

DATE: ____ $ ____
○ WISH ○ HAVE

'93	'94	'95	'96	'97	'98
$45	45	48	48	48	48

NORTH POLE SERIES™

ELFIN SNOW CONE WORKS

ITEM #	INTRO	RETIRED	OSRP	GBTRU	↓
5633-2	1994	1997	$40	**$50**	9%

Snow cones on shutters and sign of steep-roofed shop. Roof molding trim resembles icing. Oriole window extends from third floor to rooftop.

DATE: _____ $ _____
○ WISH ○ HAVE

'94	'95	'96	'97	'98
$40	40	40	40	55

BEARD BARBER SHOP

ITEM #	INTRO	RETIRED	OSRP	GBTRU	NO
5634-0	1994	1997	$27.50	**$40**	CHANGE

Small shop with 3 tall front windows allowing light to enter. Barber pole at entry and banner of shears establish function of shop.

DATE: _____ $ _____
○ WISH ○ HAVE

'94	'95	'96	'97	'98
$27.50	27.50	27.50	27.50	40

NORTH POLE DOLLS & SANTA'S BEAR WORKS

ITEM #	INTRO	RETIRED	OSRP	GBTRU	NO
5635-9	1994	1997	$96	**$115**	CHANGE

Set of 3. Consists of *North Pole Dolls, Santa's Bear Works* and *Entrance.* Entrance is non-lit. Two 3-story mirror image buildings with 2-story center connecting entrance way. Shops have signs by doors. A "NP" pennant flies from the cupola in the center.

DATE: _____ $ _____
○ WISH ○ HAVE

'94	'95	'96	'97	'98
$96	96	96	96	115

TIN SOLDIER SHOP

ITEM #	INTRO	RETIRED	OSRP	GBTRU	↓
5638-3	1995	1997	$42	**$55**	8%

Midyear release. Tall, narrow shop with garland-draped balcony. Toy soldiers decorate base of two-story turret at side of entry.

DATE: _____ $ _____
○ WISH ○ HAVE

'95	'96	'97	'98
$42	42	42	60

ELFIN FORGE & ASSEMBLY SHOP

ITEM #	INTRO	RETIRED	OSRP	GBTRU	↑
56384	1995	1998	$65	**$70**	8%

North Pole folks make all the necessary iron works at the forge. Steps lead up to entry that connects two building wings. The forge furnaces are housed in the three-story building with the tall furnace pipes. Design and assembly takes place in attached turret, with finished product exiting through large double doors.

DATE: _____ $ _____
○ WISH   ○ HAVE

'95	'96	'97	'98
$65	65	65	65

WEATHER & TIME OBSERVATORY

ITEM #	INTRO	RETIRED	OSRP	GBTRU	
56385	1995	CURRENT	$50	**$50**	NO CHANGE

Santa has to know all time zones and prevailing climate to plan his big sleigh trip as well as conditions for visiting folk, elves and animals. Telescope located in rooftop observatory, clocks are set for all time zones. Satellite dish brings in news on weather. Fortress-like turret for astronomy and smaller attached areas for offices.

DATE: _____ $ _____
○ WISH   ○ HAVE

'95	'96	'97	'98
$50	50	50	50

SANTA'S ROOMING HOUSE

ITEM #	INTRO	RETIRED	OSRP	GBTRU	
56386	1995	CURRENT	$50	**$50**	NO CHANGE

Visitors to the North Pole stay at this red clapboard inn. Stairs lead up to entry door for bedrooms. Lower level houses kitchen, dining and sitting rooms, as well as the cloak room.

DATE: _____ $ _____
○ WISH   ○ HAVE

'95	'96	'97	'98
$50	50	50	50

ELVES' TRADE SCHOOL

ITEM #	INTRO	RETIRED	OSRP	GBTRU	↑
56387	1995	1998	$50	**$55**	10%

All Toy Workshop, Forge & Assembly, Astronomy and Charting skills are taught at the school for elves. Stone pillars form part of sturdy base to support wood structure. Hammer holds school sign above red door.
Notable: Some buildings had signs that read "Evles Trade School."

DATE: _____ $ _____
○ WISH   ○ HAVE

'95	'96	'97	'98
$50	50	50	50

POPCORN & CRANBERRY HOUSE

ITEM #	INTRO	RETIRED	OSRP	GBTru	↑
56388	1996	1997	$45	**$85**	6%

Midyear release. Tall chimney separates front part of house from rear work area. Elves work on the berries and corn preparing them for stringing into garlands and creation of holiday trim. Berries trim front sign accented by red roof, door and windows.

DATE: ____ $ ____
○ WISH ○ HAVE

'96	'97	'98
$45	45	80

SANTA'S BELL REPAIR

ITEM #	INTRO	RETIRED	OSRP	GBTru	↑
56389	1996	1998	$45	**$55**	22%

Midyear release. Bells that no longer ring, chime or jingle are sent to the repair shop to be fixed and shined. Brass bells over entry, tall fieldstone chimney, and combination bell tower dormer set this design apart.

DATE: ____ $ ____
○ WISH ○ HAVE

'96	'97	'98
$45	45	45

NORTH POLE START A TRADITION SET

ITEM #	INTRO	RETIRED	OSRP	GBTru	↓
56390	1996	1996	$85	**$90**	18%

Set of 12. Midyear release. Includes CANDY CANE LANE, Set of 2—*Candy Cane & Peppermint Shop* and *Gift Wrap & Ribbons*. Accessory Set of 2—*Candy Cane Elves*, 6 trees, Brick Road, and a bag of Snow. **Notable:** Starter Set was featured at Department 56, Inc.'s National Homes For The Holidays Open House Event, November 7–11, 1996. Special packaging for promotion. Starter Set was priced at $65.00 during the Event.

DATE: ____ $ ____
○ WISH ○ HAVE

'96	'97	'98
$85	105	110

ROUTE 1, NORTH POLE, HOME OF MR. & MRS. CLAUS

ITEM #	INTRO	RETIRED	OSRP	GBTru	NO
56391	1996	CURRENT	$110	**$110**	CHANGE

Steep red rooftop, double turrets flank entry door. Rear turret flies a North Pole banner. Mailbox on front stone wall. The first shipments came with the green gates separate in the box. A short time later, the pieces arrived with the gates already inserted into the fence.

DATE: ____ $ ____
○ WISH ○ HAVE

'97	'98
$110	110

HALL OF RECORDS

ITEM #	INTRO	RETIRED	OSRP	GBTRU	
56392	1996	CURRENT	$50	**$50**	NO CHANGE

Central fortress-like tower with clock provides record-keeping on naughty and nice files for Santa and elves. Side wings of building have bright red rooftops with green struts and saw-toothed trim. Staff out for hot chocolate break.

DATE: ____ $ ____
○ WISH   ○ HAVE

'97	'98
$50	50

CHRISTMAS BREAD BAKERS

ITEM #	INTRO	RETIRED	OSRP	GBTRU	
56393	1996	CURRENT	$55	**$55**	NO CHANGE

Bright blue curved roof with wheat grain symbols on red trim. Domed awnings cover front windows and door. Special treats listed on facade above bay window.

DATE: ____ $ ____
○ WISH   ○ HAVE

'97	'98
$55	55

GLACIER GAZETTE, THE

ITEM #	INTRO	RETIRED	OSRP	GBTRU	
56394	1997	CURRENT	$48	**$48**	NO CHANGE

Midyear release. North Pole newspaper and telegraph office.

DATE: ____ $ ____
○ WISH   ○ HAVE

'97	'98
$48	48

MRS. CLAUS' GREENHOUSE

ITEM #	INTRO	RETIRED	OSRP	GBTRU	
56395	1997	CURRENT	$68	**$68**	NO CHANGE

Poinsettias, holly and evergreens are available at the greenhouse. The flowering plants are visible through the "glass" of the growing area.

DATE: ____ $ ____
○ WISH   ○ HAVE

'98
$68

NORTH POLE SERIES™

GLASS ORNAMENT WORKS

ITEM #	INTRO	RETIRED	OSRP	GBTRU	
56396	1997	CURRENT	$60	**$60**	NO CHANGE

Glass blown, silvered and painted ornaments are made in this special shop. They also decorate the front of the building creating a festive design. The bright red and green painted trim of the shop is enhanced by the garlands and evergreen boughs.

DATE: _____ $ _____
O WISH   O HAVE

'98
$60

SANTA'S LIGHT SHOP

ITEM #	INTRO	RETIRED	OSRP	GBTRU	
56397	1997	CURRENT	$52	**$52**	NO CHANGE

Shop produces strings of brightly colored lights for holiday trim. Lights surround Santa's building sign and decorate the make-believe trees out front.

DATE: _____ $ _____
O WISH   O HAVE

'98
$52

ELSIE'S GINGERBREAD

ITEM #	INTRO	RETIRED	OSRP	GBTRU	↑
56398	1997	1998 ANNUAL	$65	**$110**	69%

"Smoking house." Magic Smoke used smells like cinnamon. Bake shop specializes in Mrs. Claus' secret gingerbread recipe. Steep tiled roof, large gingerbread baking oven on side of building, main entrance plus a special on-sale location in side section of shop.

DATE: _____ $ _____
O WISH   O HAVE

'98
$65

CUSTOM STITCHERS

ITEM #	INTRO	RETIRED	OSRP	GBTRU
56400	1998	CURRENT	$37.50	**$37.50**

Elf Land. Three outfits hang on the outside of this building. Its bell is atop its onion dome.

DATE: _____ $ _____
O WISH   O HAVE

TILLIE'S TINY CUP CAFÉ

ITEM #	INTRO	RETIRED	OSRP	GBTru
56401	1998	CURRENT	$37.50	**$37.50**

Elf Land. This building has a open panel to illuminate the sign and teacup cutouts for windows.

DATE: ____ $ ____
O WISH O HAVE

ELF SPA, THE

ITEM #	INTRO	RETIRED	OSRP	GBTru
56402	1998	CURRENT	$40	**$40**

Elf Land. This double onion domed building has a separate spa, sauna and outdoor pool.

DATE: ____ $ ____
O WISH O HAVE

REAL PLASTIC SNOW FACTORY

ITEM #	INTRO	RETIRED	OSRP	GBTru
56403	1998	CURRENT	$80	**$80**

Department 56, Inc. pokes fun at itself with this colorful building. It features a plastic freezing tower containing Real Plastic Snow.

DATE: ____ $ ____
O WISH O HAVE

REINDEER FLIGHT SCHOOL

ITEM #	INTRO	RETIRED	OSRP	GBTru
56404	1998	CURRENT	$55	**$55**

This Quonset hut shaped building includes a flight tower and reindeer flight school.

DATE: ____ $ ____
O WISH O HAVE

NORTH POLE SERIES™

Item#	Name	Intro	Retired	OSRP$	GBTru$	Wish	Have	Date	Qty	Paid Each	Total
5350-3	Mickey's Christmas Carol—"10 Points"	1994	1996	144	175	O	O				
5350-3	Mickey's Christmas Carol—"6 Points"	1994	1996	144	155	O	O				
5351-1	Olde World Antiques Shops, Set/2	1994	1996	90	95	O	O				
5351-1	Olde World Antiques I	1994	1996	45	50	O	O				
5351-1	Olde World Antiques II	1994	1996	45	50	O	O				
5352-0	Disneyland Fire Department #105	1994	1996	45	55	O	O				
53521	Silversmith	1995	1996	50	235	O	O				
53522	Tinker Bell's Treasures	1995	1996	60	235	O	O				
	DPV Grand Totals:			**$623.00**	**$1,050.00**						

Disney Parks Village™ GB History List

MICKEY'S CHRISTMAS CAROL—"10 POINTS"

ITEM #	INTRO	RETIRED	OSRP	GBTRU	NO
5350-3	1994	1996	$144	$175	CHANGE

Set of 2. This is the First Version with small gold spires at the lower corners of the roof dormers as well as at their peaks. Replica of the building in Fantasyland at Disney World in Orlando, Florida. Gold trim and blue roof along with multiple turrets and gables make this a very distinctive building.
Notable: Item #742-0, sold by the Disney Theme Parks, has the **"Holiday Collection"** bottomstamp and a **GBTru$ of $245**.

DATE: ____ $ ____
O Wish O Have

'94	'95	'96	'97	'98
$144	144	144	144	175

MICKEY'S CHRISTMAS CAROL—"6 POINTS"

ITEM #	INTRO	RETIRED	OSRP	GBTRU	↑
5350-3	1994	1996	$144	$155	7%

Set of 2. This is the Second Version—small gold spires are no longer at the lower corners of the roof dormers.
Notable: Item #742-0, sold by the Disney Theme Parks, has the **"Holiday Collection"** bottomstamp and a **GBTru$ of $195**.

DATE: ____ $ ____
O Wish O Have

'94	'95	'96	'97	'98
$144	144	144	144	145

OLDE WORLD ANTIQUES SHOPS

ITEM #	INTRO	RETIRED	OSRP	GBTRU	↑
5351-1	1994	1996	$90	$95	6%

Set of 2 includes *Olde World Antiques I* and *Olde World Antiques II*.
Notable: Item #743-9, sold by the Disney Theme Parks, has the **"Holiday Collection"** bottomstamp and a **GBTru$ of $130**.

see below

DATE: ____ $ ____
O Wish O Have

'94	'95	'96	'97	'98
$90	90	90	90	90

OLDE WORLD ANTIQUES I

ITEM #	INTRO	RETIRED	OSRP	GBTRU	↑
5351-1	1994	1996	$45	$50	11%

1 of the 2-piece set—OLDE WORLD ANTIQUES SHOPS. Similar building can be seen in Disney World's Liberty Square. Windows vary from arched to rectangular.
Notable: Item #743-9, sold by the Disney Theme Parks, has the **"Holiday Collection"** bottomstamp and a **GBTru$ of $65**.

DATE: ____ $ ____
O Wish O Have

'94	'95	'96	'97	'98
$45	45	45	45	45

OLDE WORLD ANTIQUES II

Item #	Intro	Retired	OSRP	GBTru	↑
5351-1	1994	1996	$45	**$50**	11%

1 of the 2-piece set—OLDE WORLD ANTIQUES SHOPS. Replica of the building in Liberty Square in Orlando's Disney World. Long staircase in front leads to second floor.

Notable: Item #743-9, sold by the Disney Theme Parks, has the **"Holiday Collection"** bottomstamp and a **GBTru$ of $65**.

Date: ____ $ ____
○ Wish ○ Have

'94	'95	'96	'97	'98
$45	45	45	45	45

DISNEYLAND FIRE DEPARTMENT #105

Item #	Intro	Retired	OSRP	GBTru	↑
5352-0	1994	1996	$45	**$55**	22%

Inspired by the fire station on Main Street in Disneyland. Brick station's large front doors allow fire equipment in and out.

Notable: Item #744-7, sold by the Disney Theme Parks, has the **"Holiday Collection"** bottomstamp and a **GBTru$ of $75**.

Date: ____ $ ____
○ Wish ○ Have

'94	'95	'96	'97	'98
$45	45	45	45	45

SILVERSMITH

Item #	Intro	Retired	OSRP	GBTru	↓
53521	1995	1996	$50	**$235**	11%

Five-sided building of fieldstone. Many windows on all sides. Dormers in each roof section. Hanging sign above double entry doors. Potted trees flank door.

Notable: Item #7448, sold by the Disney Theme Parks, has the **"Holiday Collection"** bottomstamp and a **GBTru$ of $275**.

Date: ____ $ ____
○ Wish ○ Have

'95	'96	'97	'98
$50	50	225	265

TINKER BELL'S TREASURES

Item #	Intro	Retired	OSRP	GBTru	↓
53522	1995	1996	$60	**$235**	11%

Timbered and stucco building with twin chimneys. Porcelain trees in raised stone garden beds flank front and sides. Roof line slopes down to trees to frame front entry.

Notable: Item #7449, sold by the Disney Theme Parks has the **"Holiday Collection"** bottomstamp and a **GBTru$ of $275**.

Date: ____ $ ____
○ Wish ○ Have

'95	'96	'97	'98
$60	60	245	265

#	Name	Intro	Retired	OSRP $	Sec'd ROS	Wish	Have	Date	Qty	Paid Each	Total
6526-9	Carolers—"White Post"-DV	1984	1990	10	80	O	O				
6526-9	Carolers—"Black Post"-DV	1984	1990	10	30	O	O				
6527-7	Village Train-DV	1985	1986	12	395	O	O				
6501-3	Christmas Carol Figures-DV	1986	1990	12.50	75	O	O				
6510-2	Lighted Tree W/Children & Ladder-CIC	1986	1989	35	215	O	O				
6511-0	Sleighride-DV, NE	1986	1990	19.50	42	O	O				
6531-5	Covered Wooden Bridge-NE	1986	1990	10	35	O	O				
6532-3	New England Winter Set-NE	1986	1990	18	38	O	O				
6542-0	Alpine Villagers-ALP	1986	1992	13	28	O	O				
5901-3	Farm People & Animals-DV	1987	1989	24	70	O	O				
5934-0	Blacksmith-DV	1987	1990	20	80	O	O				
5950-1	Silo & Hay Shed-DV	1987	1989	18	165	O	O				
5951-0	Ox Sled—"Tan Pants"-DV	1987	1989	20	190	O	O				
5951-0	Ox Sled—"Blue Pants"-DV	1987	1989	20	115	O	O				
5951-0	Ox Sled—"Blue Pants/Mold Change"-DV	1987	1989	20	125	O	O				
5960-9	Christmas In The City Sign-CIC	1987	1993	6	10	O	O				
5964-1	Automobiles-CIC	1987	1996	15	25	O	O				
5965-0	City People-CIC	1987	1990	27.50	50	O	O				
5966-8	Shopkeepers -DV	1987	1988	15	32	O	O				
5967-6	City Workers-DV	1987	1988	15	30	O	O				
6545-5	Skating Pond-DV	1987	1990	24	55	O	O				
6546-3	Stone Bridge	1987	1990	12	55	O	O				
6547-1	Village Well & Holy Cross-DV	1987	1989	13	125	O	O				
6569-2	Dickens' Village Sign-DV	1987	1993	6	12	O	O				
6570-6	New England Village Sign-NE	1987	1993	6	12	O	O				
6571-4	Alpine Village Sign-ALP	1987	1993	6	14	O	O				
6589-7	Maple Sugaring Shed-NE	1987	1989	19	210	O	O				
6590-0	Dover Coach—"First Version"-DV	1987	1990	18	80	O	O				
6590-0	Dover Coach—"Second Version"-DV	1987	1990	18	55	O	O				
6590-0	Dover Coach—"Third Version"-DV	1987	1990	18	50	O	O				
5903-0	Childe Pond And Skaters-DV	1988	1991	30	65	O	O				
5928-5	Fezziwig And Friends-DV	1988	1990	12.50	45	O	O				
5929-3	Nicholas Nickleby Characters-DV	1988	1991	20	30	O	O				

HVA Page 1 Totals: 543.00   2,638.00

Item#	Name	Intro	Retired	OSRP$	GBTru$	Wish	Have	Date	Qty	Paid Each	Total
5938-2	Snow Children	1988	1994	15	30	○	○				
5941-2	Village Harvest People-NE	1988	1991	27.50	40	○	○				
5971-4	City Newsstand-CIC	1988	1991	25	70	○	○				
5981-1	Village Train Trestle	1988	1990	17	50	○	○				
5982-0	One Horse Open Sleigh	1988	1993	20	35	○	○				
5983-8	City Bus & Milk Truck-CIC	1988	1991	15	30	○	○				
5985-4	Salvation Army Band-CIC	1988	1991	24	75	○	○				
5986-2	Woodcutter And Son-NE	1988	1990	10	38	○	○				
5987-0	Red Covered Bridge-NE	1988	1994	15	25	○	○				
5517-4	Mailbox & Fire Hydrant-CIC	1989	1990	5	18	○	○				
5551-4	David Copperfield Characters-DV	1989	1992	32.50	40	○	○				
5572-7	Village Sign With Snowman	1989	1994	10	18	○	○				
5577-8	Lamplighter With Lamp-DV	1989	Current	9	10	○	○				
5578-6	Royal Coach-DV	1989	1992	55	75	○	○				
5579-4	Constables-DV	1989	1991	17.50	65	○	○				
5580-8	Violet Vendor/Carolers/Chestnut Vendor-DV	1989	1992	23	34	○	○				
5581-6	King's Road Cab-DV	1989	1998	30	36	○	○				
5588-3	Christmas Carol Christmas Morning Figures-DV	1989	Current	18	18	○	○				
5589-1	Christmas Carol Christmas Spirits Figures-DV	1989	Current	27.50	27.50	○	○				
5945-5	Farm Animals-NE	1989	1991	15	35	○	○				
5957-9	Organ Grinder-CIC	1989	1991	21	32	○	○				
5958-7	Popcorn Vendor-CIC	1989	1992	22	30	○	○				
5959-5	River Street Ice House Cart-CIC	1989	1991	20	50	○	○				
5979-0	Central Park Carriage-CIC	1989	Current	30	30	○	○				
9953-8	Heritage Village Promotional Sign	1989	1990	5	20	○	○				
5214-0	Mailbox & Fire Hydrant-CIC	1990	1998	5	6	○	○				
5535-2	Busy Sidewalks-CIC	1990	1992	28	55	○	○				
5539-5	'Tis The Season-CIC	1990	1994	12.50	16	○	○				
5540-9	Rest Ye Merry Gentleman-CIC	1990	Current	12.50	13	○	○				
5569-7	Town Crier & Chimney Sweep-DV	1990	Current	15	16	○	○				
5570-0	Carolers On The Doorstep-DV	1990	1993	25	32	○	○				
5571-9	Holiday Travelers-DV	1990	Current	22.50	25	○	○				
5573-5	Flying Scot Train, The-DV	1990	1998	48	55	○	○				

HVA Page 2 Totals: 677.50 1,149.50

Item#	Name	Intro	Retired	OSRP$	GBTru$	Wish	Have	Date	Qty	Paid Each	Total
5575-1	Victoria Station Train Platform-DV	1990	Current	20	22	O	O				
5608-1	Trimming The North Pole-NP	1990	1993	10	37	O	O				
5609-0	Santa & Mrs. Claus-NP	1990	Current	15	15	O	O				
5610-3	Santa's Little Helpers-NP	1990	1993	28	65	O	O				
5611-1	Sleigh & Eight Tiny Reindeer-NP	1990	Current	40	42	O	O				
5616-2	Toy Peddler, The-ALP	1990	1998	22	32	O	O				
5948-0	Amish Family—"W/Mustache"-NE	1990	1992	20	44	O	O				
5948-0	Amish Family—"No Mustache"-NE	1990	1992	20	35	O	O				
5949-8	Amish Buggy-NE	1990	1992	22	55	O	O				
5956-1	Sleepy Hollow Characters-NE	1990	1992	27.50	45	O	O				
5523-9	Skating Party-NE	1991	Current	27.50	27.50	O	O				
5545-0	All Around The Town-CIC	1991	1993	18	24	O	O				
5546-8	Fire Brigade, The-CIC	1991	1995	20	25	O	O				
5547-6	"City Fire Dept." Fire Truck-CIC	1991	1995	18	28	O	O				
5548-4	Caroling Thru The City-CIC	1991	1998	27.50	30	O	O				
5554-9	Oliver Twist Characters-DV	1991	1993	35	38	O	O				
5558-1	Bringing Home The Yule Log-DV	1991	1998	27.50	32	O	O				
5559-0	Poultry Market-DV	1991	1995	30	36	O	O				
5560-3	Come Into The Inn-DV	1991	1994	22	27	O	O				
5561-1	Holiday Coach-DV	1991	1998	68	80	O	O				
5602-2	Toymaker Elves-NP	1991	1995	27.50	34	O	O				
5603-0	Baker Elves-NP	1991	1995	27.50	30	O	O				
5641-3	Market Day-NE	1991	1993	35	36	O	O				
5530-1	Gate House	1992	Event Piece 1992	22.50	35	O	O				
5532-8	Don't Drop The Presents!-CIC	1992	1995	25	30	O	O				
5533-6	Welcome Home-CIC	1992	1995	27.50	32	O	O				
5563-8	Churchyard Fence & Gate	1992	1992	15	65	O	O				
5604-9	Letters For Santa-NP	1992	1994	30	65	O	O				
5605-7	Testing The Toys-NP	1992	Current	16.50	16.50	O	O				
5619-7	Buying Bakers Bread-ALP	1992	1995	20	30	O	O				
5645-6	Harvest Seed Cart-DV	1992	1995	27.50	30	O	O				
5646-4	Town Tinker-DV	1992	1995	24	30	O	O				
5802-5	Old Puppeteer, The-DV	1992	1995	32	38	O	O				
5803-3	Bird Seller, The-DV	1992	1995	25	30	O	O				
	HVA Page 3 Totals:			873.00	1,241.00						

Item#	Name	Intro	Retired	OSRP$	GBTru$	Wish	Have	Date	Qty	Paid Each	Total
5804-1	Village Street Peddlers-DV	1992	1994	16	22	○	○				
5805-0	English Post Box-DV	1992	Current	4.50	4.50	○	○				
5806-8	Churchyard Gate And Fence	1992	1997	15	20	○	○				
5807-6	Churchyard Fence Extensions	1992	1997	16	18	○	○				
5865-3	Village Express Van-CIC	1992	1996	25	28	○	○				
9951-1	Village Express Van	1992	Promo	25	75	○	○				
5556-5	Playing In The Snow-CIC	1993	1996	25	35	○	○				
5564-6	Street Musicians-CIC	1993	1997	25	30	○	○				
5565-4	Town Tree-CIC	1993	Current	45	45	○	○				
5566-2	Town Tree Trimmers-CIC	1993	Current	32.50	32.50	○	○				
5613-8	Climb Every Mountain-ALP	1993	Current	27.50	27.50	○	○				
5630-8	Woodsmen Elves-NP	1993	1995	30	65	○	○				
5631-6	Sing A Song For Santa-NP	1993	1998	28	32	○	○				
5632-4	North Pole Gate-NP	1993	1998	32.50	35	○	○				
5649-9	Knife Grinder-NE	1993	1996	22.50	26	○	○				
5650-2	Blue Star Ice Harvesters-NE	1993	1997	27.50	28	○	○				
5813-0	Chelsea Market Fruit Monger & Cart-DV	1993	1997	25	35	○	○				
5814-9	Chelsea Market Fish Monger & Cart-DV	1993	1997	25	35	○	○				
5815-7	Chelsea Market Flower Monger & Cart-DV	1993	Current	27.50	27.50	○	○				
5816-5	Chelsea Lane Shoppers-DV	1993	Current	30	30	○	○				
5817-3	Vision Of A Christmas Past-DV	1993	1996	27.50	30	○	○				
5818-1	C. Bradford, Wheelwright & Son-DV	1993	1996	24	30	○	○				
5819-0	Bringing Fleeces To The Mill-DV	1993	1998	35	40	○	○				
5820-3	Dashing Through The Snow-DV	1993	Current	32.50	32.50	○	○				
5866-1	Christmas At The Park-CIC	1993	Current	27.50	27.50	○	○				
9977-5	Village Express Van—Gold	1993	Promo	25	675	○	○				
Various	Village Express Van For Gatherings	1994	Promo	25	50	○	○				
5353-8	Mickey & Minnie-DP	1994	1996	22.50	32	○	○				
5354-6	Disney Parks Family-DP	1994	1996	32.50	30	○	○				
5355-4	Olde World Antiques Gate-DP	1994	1996	15	18	○	○				
5607-3	Polka Fest-ALP	1994	Current	30	30	○	○				
5636-7	Last Minute Delivery-NP	1994	1998	35	40	○	○				
5637-5	Snow Cone Elves-NP	1994	1997	30	36	○	○				

HVA Page 4 Totals: 866.00 1,722.00

Item#	Name	Intro	Retired	OSRP$	GBTru$	Wish	Have	Date	Qty	Paid Each	Total
5654-5	Over The River And Through The Woods-NE	1994	1998	35	40	○	○				
5655-3	Old Man And The Sea, The-NE	1994	1998	25	38	○	○				
5656-1	Two Rivers Bridge-NE	1994	1997	35	38	○	○				
5825-4	Winter Sleighride-DV	1994	Current	18	18	○	○				
5826-2	Chelsea Market Mistletoe Monger & Cart-DV	1994	1998	25	35	○	○				
5827-0	Chelsea Market Curiosities Monger & Cart-DV	1994	1998	27.50	36	○	○				
5828-9	Portobello Road Peddlers-DV	1994	1998	27.50	30	○	○				
5829-7	Thatchers-DV	1994	1997	35	36	○	○				
5830-0	A Peaceful Glow On Christmas Eve-DV	1994	Current	30	30	○	○				
5831-9	Christmas Carol Holiday Trimming Set -DV	1994	1997	65	65	○	○				
5884-0	Chamber Orchestra-CIC	1994	1998	37.50	40	○	○				
5885-8	Holiday Field Trip-CIC	1994	1998	27.50	30	○	○				
5886-6	Hot Dog Vendor-CIC	1994	1997	27.50	30	○	○				
9871-0	Postern-DV	1994	1994 Annual	17.50	21	○	○				
Various	Promotional Village Express Vans	1995	Promo	*	*	○	○				
Various		1995				○	○				
Various		1995				○	○				
0753-6	Squash Cart-NE	1995	Promo	50	90	○	○				
53539	Balloon Seller-DP	1995	1996	25	40	○	○				
56180	"Silent Night" Music Box	1995	Current	32.50	32.50	○	○				
56182	"Alpenhorn Player" Alpine Village Sign-ALP	1995	Current	20	20	○	○				
56364	Charting Santa's Course-NP	1995	1997	25	32	○	○				
56365	I'll Need More Toys-NP	1995	1998	25	30	○	○				
56366	"A Busy Elf" North Pole Sign-NP	1995	Current	20	20	○	○				
56588	Farm Animals-NE	1995	Current	32.50	32.50	○	○				
56589	Lobster Trappers-NE	1995	Current	35	35	○	○				
56590	Lumberjacks-NE	1995	1998	30	36	○	○				
56591	Harvest Pumpkin Wagon-NE	1995	Current	45	45	○	○				
56592	"Fresh Paint" New England Village Sign-NE	1995	Current	20	20	○	○				
5832-7*	Town Square Carolers-DV	1995	1996	*	*	○	○				
5835-1	A Partridge In A Pear Tree—#I-DV	1995	Current	35	35	○	○				
5836-0	Two Turtle Doves—#II-DV	1995	Current	32.50	32.50	○	○				
58378	Three French Hens—#III-DV	1995	Current	32.50	32.50	○	○				
58379	Four Calling Birds—#IV-DV	1995	Current	32.50	32.50	○	○				
	HVA Page 5 Totals:			925.50	1,052.50						

Heritage Village Collection® Accessories GB History List　249

Item#	Name	Intro	Retired	OSRP$	GBTru$	Wish	Have	Date	Qty	Paid Each	Total
58381	Five Golden Rings—#V-DV	1995	Current	27.50	27.50	O	O				
58382	Six Geese A-Laying—#VI-DV	1995	Current	30	30	O	O				
58390	Brixton Road Watchman-DV	1995	Current	25	25	O	O				
58391	"Tallyho!"-DV	1995	1998	50	58	O	O				
58392	Chelsea Market Hat Monger & Cart-DV	1995	Current	27.50	27.50	O	O				
58393	"Ye Olde Lamplighter" Dickens' Village Sign-DV	1995	Current	20	20	O	O				
58394	Cobbler & Clock Peddler-DV	1995	1997	25	28	O	O				
58890	"Yes, Virginia..."-CIC	1995	Current	12.50	12.50	O	O				
58891	One-Man Band & The Dancing Dog-CIC	1995	1998	17.50	26	O	O				
58892	Choir Boys All-In-A-Row-CIC	1995	1998	20	28	O	O				
58893	"A Key To The City" Christmas In The City Sign-CIC	1995	Current	20	20	O	O				
52298	Elves On Ice-NP	1996	Current	7.50	7.50	O	O				
56183	Nutcracker Vendor & Cart-ALP	1996	Current	20	25	O	O				
56368	North Pole Express-NP	1996	Current	37.50	37.50	O	O				
56369	Early Rising Elves-NP	1996	Current	32.50	32.50	O	O				
56370	End Of The Line-NP	1996	Current	28	28	O	O				
56371	Holiday Deliveries-NP	1996	Current	16.50	16.50	O	O				
56390*	Candy Cane Elves-NP	1996	1996	*	*	O	O				
56593	A New Potbellied Stove For Christmas-NE	1996	1998	35	40	O	O				
56594	Christmas Bazaar: Handmade Quilts-NE	1996	Current	25	25	O	O				
56595	Christmas Bazaar: Woolens & Preserves-NE	1996	Current	25	25	O	O				
58383	Seven Swans-A-Swimming—#VII-DV	1996	Current	27.50	27.50	O	O				
58384	Eight Maids-A-Milking—#VIII-DV	1996	Current	25	25	O	O				
58395	Tending The New Calves-DV	1996	Current	30	30	O	O				
58396	Caroling W/The Cratchit Family (Revisited)-DV	1996	Current	37.50	37.50	O	O				
58397	Yeomen Of The Guard-DV	1996	1997	30	60	O	O				
58400	Fezziwig Delivery Wagon, The (Revisited)-DV	1996	Current	32.50	32.50	O	O				
58401	Red Christmas Sulky-DV	1996	Current	30	30	O	O				
58402	Gingerbread Vendor-DV	1996	Current	22.50	22.50	O	O				
58403	"A Christmas Carol" Reading By Charles Dickens-DV	1996	Current	45	45	O	O				

HVA Page 6 Totals: 782.00   849.50

Item#	Name	Intro	Retired	OSRP$	GBTru$	Wish	Have	Date	Qty	Paid Each	Total
58404	"A Christmas Carol" Reading By Charles Dickens-DV	1996	Ltd Ed 42,500	75	115	O	O				
58894	City Taxi-CIC	1996	Current	12.50	12.50	O	O				
58895	Family Tree, The-CIC	1996	Current	18	18	O	O				
58896	Going Home For The Holidays-CIC	1996	Current	27.50	27.50	O	O				
98711	Christmas Bells	1996	Event Piece	35	40	O	O				
8803	Bachman's® Wilcox Truck	1997	Promo	29.95	60	O	O				
56100	Holly & The Ivy, The	1997	Event Piece	17.50	20	O	O				
56175	A New Batch Of Christmas Friends-ALP	1997	Current	27.50	27.50	O	O				
56201	Heidi & Her Goats-ALP	1997	Current	30	30	O	O				
56372	Don't Break The Ornaments-NP	1997	Current	27.50	27.50	O	O				
56373	Delivering The Christmas Greens-NP	1997	Current	27.50	27.50	O	O				
56374	Untangle The Christmas Lights-NP	1997	Current	35	35	O	O				
56596	Christmas Bazaar... Flapjacks & Hot Cider-NE	1997	Current	27.50	27.50	O	O				
56597	Christmas Bazaar... Toy Vendor & Cart-NE	1997	Current	27.50	27.50	O	O				
56598	Christmas Bazaar... Sign-NE	1997	Current	16	16	O	O				
56599	Tapping The Maples-NE	1997	Current	75	75	O	O				
58301*	Manchester Square Accessory Set	1997	Current	*	*	O	O				
58322*	Spirit Of Giving, The-DV	1997	1998	*	*	O	O				
58326	Delivering Coal For The Hearth-DV	1997	Current	32.50	32.50	O	O				
58385	Nine Ladies Dancing—#IX-DV	1997	Current	30	30	O	O				
58386	Ten Pipers Piping—#X-DV	1997	Current	30	30	O	O				
58405	Ashley Pond Skating Party-DV	1997	Current	70	70	O	O				
58406	Fire Brigade Of London Town, The-DV	1997	Current	70	70	O	O				
58407	Father Christmas's Journey-DV	1997	Current	30	30	O	O				
58408	Christmas Pudding Costermonger-DV	1997	Current	32.50	32.50	O	O				
58885	Steppin' Out On The Town-CIC	1997	Current	35	35	O	O				
58897	Johnson's Grocery ... Holiday Deliveries-CIC	1997	Current	18	18	O	O				
58898	Spirit Of The Season-CIC	1997	Current	20	20	O	O				
58899	Let's Go Shopping In The City-CIC	1997	Current	35	35	O	O				
58900	Big Smile For The Camera-CIC	1997	Current	27.50	27.50	O	O				
59000	Poinsettia Delivery Truck	1997	Current	32.50	32.50	O	O				

HVA PAGE 7 TOTALS: 971.95   1,049.50

Heritage Village Collection® Accessories GB History List

Item#	Name	Intro	Retired	OSRP$	GBTru$	Wish	Have	Date	Qty	Paid Each	Total
Various	Our Own Village Park Bench	1998	Promo	10	12	○	○				
2208	Tending The Cold Frame	1998	Promo	35	60	○	○				
7880	Lord & Taylor Delivery Wagon	1998	Promo	32.50	95	○	○				
56363	Peppermint Skating Party-NP	1998	Current	64	64	○	○				
56587	Sea Captain & His Mates-NE	1998	Current	32.50	32.50	○	○				
58308*	Christmas Apples-DV	1998	Event G/S Acc.	*	*	○	○				
58871*	5¢ Pony Rides-CIC	1998	Event G/S Acc.	*	*	○	○				
52732	Loading The Sleigh-NP	1998	Current	125	125	○	○				
55501	Painting Our Own Village Sign	1998	Promo	12.50	12.50	○	○				
55502	Stars And Stripes Forever	1998	Event Piece	50	50	○	○				
56202	Trekking In The Snow-ALP	1998	Current	27.50	27.50	○	○				
56203	St. Nicholas-ALP	1998	Current	12	12	○	○				
56431	Welcome To Elf Land Gateway Entrance-NP	1998	Current	35	35	○	○				
56434	Christmas Fun Run-NP	1998	Current	35	35	○	○				
56435	Delivering Real Plastic Snow-NP	1998	Current	17	17	○	○				
56436	Reindeer Training Camp-NP	1998	Current	27.50	27.50	○	○				
56437	Have A Seat Elves-NP	1998	Current	30	30	○	○				
56438	Dash Away Delivery-NP	1998	Current	40	40	○	○				
56439	Downhill Elves-NP	1998	Current	9	9	○	○				
56630	Load Up The Wagon-NE	1998	Current	40	40	○	○				
56631	Under The Mistletoe-NE	1998	Current	16.50	16.50	○	○				
56633	Fly-casting In The Brook-NE	1998	Current	15	15	○	○				
56635	Volunteer Firefighters-NE	1998	Current	37.50	37.50	○	○				
56637	Farmer's Market-NE	1998	Current	55	55	○	○				
56638	An Artist's Touch-NE	1998	Current	17	17	○	○				
58410	Here We Come A-Wassailing-DV	1998	Current	45	45	○	○				
58411	Sitting In Camden Park-DV	1998	Current	35	35	○	○				
58413	Eleven Lords A-Leaping—XI-DV	1998	Current	27.50	27.50	○	○				
58414	Until We Meet Again-DV	1998	Current	27.50	27.50	○	○				
58415	Child's Play-DV	1998	Current	25	25	○	○				
58416	Tending The Cold Frame-DV	1998	Current	32.50	32.50	○	○				
58417	Ale Mates-DV	1998	Current	25	25	○	○				
58901	A Carriage Ride For The Bride-CIC	1998	Current	40	40	○	○				

HVA Page 8 Totals: 1,033.00   1,122.50

Item#	Name	Intro	Retired	OSRP$	GBTru$	Wish	Have	Date	Qty	Paid Each	Total
58902	To Protect And To Serve-CIC	1998	Current	32.50	32.50	○	○				
58903	City Police Car-CIC	1998	Current	16.50	16.50	○	○				
58906	1919 Ford® Model-T-CIC	1998	Current	20	20	○	○				
58907	Ready For The Road-CIC	1998	Current	20	20	○	○				
	HVA Page 9 Totals:			89.00	89.00						
	HVA Page 1 Totals:			543.00	2,638.00						
	HVA Page 2 Totals:			677.50	1,149.50						
	HVA Page 3 Totals:			873.00	1,241.00						
	HVA Page 4 Totals:			866.00	1,722.00						
	HVA Page 5 Totals:			925.50	1,052.50						
	HVA Page 6 Totals:			782.00	849.50						
	HVA Page 7 Totals:			971.95	1,049.50						
	HVA Page 8 Totals:			1,033.00	1,122.50						
	HVA Page 9 Totals:			89.00	89.00						
	HVA Grand Totals:			6,760.95	10,913.50						

CAROLERS—"WHITE POST"

	ITEM #	INTRO	RETIRED	OSRP	GBTRU	↓
	6526-9	1984	1990	$10	**$80**	27%

Dickens' Village Series® accessory. Set of 3. Group of Village people sing or listen to carols.

Notable: 3 Versions of set exist. Version 1—White post, viola is very light with dark brown trim, little detail in figures, made in Taiwan. This version is the most difficult version to find.

DATE: ____ $ ____	'91	'92	'93	'94	'95	'96	'97	'98
○ WISH ○ HAVE	$135	120	152	120	120	120	110	110

CAROLERS—"BLACK POST"

	GBTRU	↓
	$30	25%

Version 2—Black post, viola is one color, more detail in figures, made in Taiwan. Version 3—Black post, viola has dark trim, largest set, made in Philippines.

DATE: ____ $ ____	'91	'92	'93	'94	'95	'96	'97	'98
○ WISH ○ HAVE	$25	28	45	36	38	40	37	40

VILLAGE TRAIN

	ITEM #	INTRO	RETIRED	OSRP	GBTRU	
	6527-7	1985	1986	$12	**$395**	NO CHANGE

Dickens' Village Series® accessory. Set of 3. Three-car porcelain train, with engine, passenger car and caboose mail/freight car.

Notable: Also known as the "Brighton Train" because of the name on the side of the middle car.

DATE: ____ $ ____	'91	'92	'93	'94	'95	'96	'97	'98
○ WISH ○ HAVE	$450	475	455	455	475	395	410	395

CHRISTMAS CAROL FIGURES

	ITEM #	INTRO	RETIRED	OSRP	GBTRU	↓
	6501-3	1986	1990	$12.50	**$75**	6%

Dickens' Village Series® accessory. Set of 3. Ebenezer Scrooge, Bob Cratchit carrying Tiny Tim and young boy with poulterer/goose.

Notable: The sleeve shows Tiny Tim carrying a crutch, but there isn't one in the figurine.

DATE: ____ $ ____	'91	'92	'93	'94	'95	'96	'97	'98
○ WISH ○ HAVE	$20	28	42	65	80	85	85	80

LIGHTED TREE W/CHILDREN & LADDER

ITEM #	INTRO	RETIRED	OSRP	GBTRU	↓
6510-2	1986	1989	$35	**$215**	12%

Set of 3. Lighted. Christmas In The City® accessory. Children climb ladder to decorate tree. The tree is battery operated.

Notable: Many have been sold on the secondary market as defective, but it's usually just a matter of crossed wires. Once they are switched, the unit works nicely. Check the boy on the ladder carefully as he often falls off the ladder and gets damaged. The sleeve of the first shipments read "Christmas In The City" though that Village didn't make its debut for another year.

DATE: ___ $ ___	'91	'92	'93	'94	'95	'96	'97	'98
○ WISH ○ HAVE	$225	285	290	350	350	320	305	245

SLEIGHRIDE

ITEM #	INTRO	RETIRED	OSRP	GBTRU	↓
6511-0	1986	1990	$19.50	**$42**	24%

Dickens' Village Series® and New England Village® accessory. Couple enjoys ride in old-fashioned sleigh drawn by two horses. Inspired by a Nathaniel Currier print.

Notable: The Sleighride has Two Versions. Version 1—Original sleeve reads, "Dickens Sleighride"—man has narrow white scarf with red polka dots. Version 2—Man's scarf and lapels are white with red polka dots. Gray horse is more spotted.

DATE: ___ $ ___	'91	'92	'93	'94	'95	'96	'97	'98
○ WISH ○ HAVE	$35	38	50	58	50	50	50	55

COVERED WOODEN BRIDGE

ITEM #	INTRO	RETIRED	OSRP	GBTRU	↓
6531-5	1986	1990	$10	**$35**	17%

New England Village® accessory. Simple wooden bridge with shingle roof, protects travelers from weather while crossing river.

Notable: Variations in color from light to dark. Variations do not affect secondary market value.

DATE: ___ $ ___	'91	'92	'93	'94	'95	'96	'97	'98
○ WISH ○ HAVE	$25	28	32	32	35	38	40	42

NEW ENGLAND WINTER SET

ITEM #	INTRO	RETIRED	OSRP	GBTRU	↓
6532-3	1986	1990	$18	**$38**	21%

Set of 5. Stone well, man pushes sleigh as woman rides, snow-covered trees, man pulls cut tree.

Notable: Early shipments had box that read "Winter Village Accessories."

DATE: ___ $ ___	'91	'92	'93	'94	'95	'96	'97	'98
○ WISH ○ HAVE	$35	35	50	46	45	47	50	48

ALPINE VILLAGERS

ITEM #	INTRO	RETIRED	OSRP	GBTRU	↓
6542-0	1986	1992	$13	**$28**	20%

Set of 3. Seated man, walking woman carrying book, dog pulling wagon with milk cans.
Notable: Figurines got thinner in later years of production. This does not affect secondary market value.

DATE: ___ $ ___	'91	'92	'93	'94	'95	'96	'97	'98
○ WISH ○ HAVE	$15	15	36	36	35	38	38	35

FARM PEOPLE & ANIMALS

ITEM #	INTRO	RETIRED	OSRP	GBTRU	↓
5901-3	1987	1989	$24	**$70**	26%

Dickens' Village Series® accessory. Set of 5. Man hauling logs. Woman and girl feeding geese. Goat pulls wagon and deer eat winter hay.

DATE: ___ $ ___	'91	'92	'93	'94	'95	'96	'97	'98
○ WISH ○ HAVE	$55	60	72	80	90	94	100	95

BLACKSMITH

ITEM #	INTRO	RETIRED	OSRP	GBTRU	↓
5934-0	1987	1990	$20	**$80**	5%

Dickens' Village Series® accessory. Set of 3. One man tends fire while smithy shoes horse. Boy holds pail of nails.

DATE: ___ $ ___	'91	'92	'93	'94	'95	'96	'97	'98
○ WISH ○ HAVE	$35	42	46	55	70	75	80	84

SILO & HAY SHED

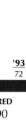
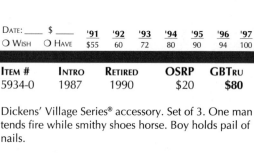

ITEM #	INTRO	RETIRED	OSRP	GBTRU	↓
5950-1	1987	1989	$18	**$165**	6%

Dickens' Village Series® accessory. Set of 2. Stone and stucco grain storage silo and elevated wood hay building.
Notable: There are Two Color Variations: 1st Version—silo roof has stripes of rust, gold and brown; 2nd Version—silo roof is almost solid brown. This does not affect secondary market value.

DATE: ___ $ ___	'91	'92	'93	'94	'95	'96	'97	'98
○ WISH ○ HAVE	$70	85	125	140	160	160	175	175

Ox Sled—"Tan Pants"

Item #	Intro	Retired	OSRP	GBTru	↓
5951-0	1987	1989	$20	**$190**	25%

Dickens' Village Series® accessory. Ox team pulls wood wagon on sled runners. Driver and a small boy holding a Christmas tree.
Notable: Variations in color affect GBTru$: "Tan Pants" or "Blue Pants." In this "Tan Pants" Version, the driver wears tan pants and sits on a green seat cushion. The mound of snow under the oxen is attached to the hind legs.

Date: ___ $ ___	'91	'92	'93	'94	'95	'96	'97	'98
○ Wish ○ Have	$65	85	112	225	250	250	250	255

Ox Sled—"Blue Pants"

	GBTru	↓
	$115	21%

In this version the driver has blue pants and sits on a black seat cushion. The mound of snow under the oxen is attached to the hind legs.

Date: ___ $ ___	'91	'92	'93	'94	'95	'96	'97	'98
○ Wish ○ Have	$65	85	112	135	145	140	160	145

Ox Sled—"Blue Pants/ Mold Change"

	GBTru	↓
	$125	24%

In this version the driver has blue pants and sits on a black seat cushion. The mound of snow under the oxen is not attached to the hind legs.

Date: ___ $ ___	'91	'92	'93	'94	'95	'96	'97	'98
○ Wish ○ Have	$65	85	112	135	145	140	160	165

Christmas In The City Sign

Item #	Intro	Retired	OSRP	GBTru	↓
5960-9	1987	1993	$6	**$10**	44%

Christmas In The City® Collection sign.

Date: ___ $ ___	'91	'92	'93	'94	'95	'96	'97	'98
○ Wish ○ Have	$6.50	6.50	8.50	12	15	15	18	18

AUTOMOBILES

ITEM #	INTRO	RETIRED	OSRP	GBT_{RU}	↓
5964-1	1987	1996	$15	**$25**	14%

Set of 3. Christmas In The City® accessory. City delivery truck, checkered taxi, and roadster. Size: 3".

DATE: ____ $ ____		'91	'92	'93	'94	'95	'96	'97	'98
○ WISH ○ HAVE		$20	20	22	22	22	22	27	29

CITY PEOPLE

ITEM #	INTRO	RETIRED	OSRP	GBT_{RU}	↓
5965-0	1987	1990	$27.50	**$50**	17%

Set of 5. Christmas In The City® accessory. Police officer, man walking dog, pretzel man with pushcart, mother and daughter with shopping bag, and woman collecting for the needy.

DATE: ____ $ ____		'91	'92	'93	'94	'95	'96	'97	'98
○ WISH ○ HAVE		$45	50	50	50	50	55	55	60

SHOPKEEPERS

ITEM #	INTRO	RETIRED	OSRP	GBT_{RU}	↓
5966-8	1987	1988	$15	**$32**	11%

Dickens' Village Series® accessory. Set of 4. Vendors of fruits, vegetables, breads, cakes.
Notable: *Shopkeepers* and *City Workers* are the only figures to have "snow" sprinkled on them.

DATE: ____ $ ____		'91	'92	'93	'94	'95	'96	'97	'98
○ WISH ○ HAVE		$35	30	35	35	38	38	40	36

CITY WORKERS

ITEM #	INTRO	RETIRED	OSRP	GBT_{RU}	↓
5967-6	1987	1988	$15	**$30**	38%

Dickens' Village Series® accessory. Set of 4. Police constable, nurse, driver, tradesman with packages.
Notable: *Shopkeepers* and *City Workers* are the only figures to have "snow" sprinkled on them. Some boxes read "City People."

DATE: ____ $ ____		'91	'92	'93	'94	'95	'96	'97	'98
○ WISH ○ HAVE		$35	35	38	38	40	35	45	48

SKATING POND

ITEM #	INTRO	RETIRED	OSRP	GBTRU	↓
6545-5	1987	1990	$24	**$55**	19%

Dickens' Village Series®, New England Village® & Christmas In The City® accessory. Low stone wall circles pond. One child watches another child skating. Two snowy trees.
Notable: There are Two Color Variations. Version 1 is made in Taiwan, the ice has generally very light blue streaks. Version 2 is made in the Philippines, blue covers most of ice surface. Variations do not affect secondary market value.

		'91	'92	'93	'94	'95	'96	'97	'98
DATE: ___ $ ___	O WISH O HAVE	$65	60	60	75	75	75	75	68

STONE BRIDGE

ITEM #	INTRO	RETIRED	OSRP	GBTRU	↓
6546-3	1987	1990	$12	**$55**	27%

Variegated fieldstone arches over river. Corner post has lamp.
Notable: Variations in color from light to dark do not affect secondary market value.

		'91	'92	'93	'94	'95	'96	'97	'98
DATE: ___ $ ___	O WISH O HAVE	$40	60	70	80	80	80	75	75

VILLAGE WELL & HOLY CROSS

ITEM #	INTRO	RETIRED	OSRP	GBTRU	↓
6547-1	1987	1989	$13	**$125**	17%

Dickens' Village Series® accessory. Set of 2. Old-fashioned hand pump for water housed in small gazebo. Cross upon pedestal on stone step base.
Notable: There are Two Variations in color. The First Version has blue water and dark birds. The Second Version has colorless water and the birds are light in color. Variations do not affect secondary market value.

		'91	'92	'93	'94	'95	'96	'97	'98
DATE: ___ $ ___	O WISH O HAVE	$70	98	145	130	160	165	150	150

DICKENS' VILLAGE SIGN

ITEM #	INTRO	RETIRED	OSRP	GBTRU	↓
6569-2	1987	1993	$6	**$12**	33%

Notable: The Village signs are the only pieces to identify the actual manufacturer of the piece. The bottomstamp reads "Handcrafted by Jiean Fung Porcelains, Taiwan." The early signs have a dark background. This does not affect secondary market value.

		'91	'92	'93	'94	'95	'96	'97	'98
DATE: ___ $ ___	O WISH O HAVE	$6.50	6.50	6.50	18	20	18	18	18

NEW ENGLAND VILLAGE SIGN

ITEM #	INTRO	RETIRED	OSRP	GBTRU	↓
6570-6	1987	1993	$6	**$12**	33%

Notable: The Village signs are the only pieces to identify the actual manufacturer of the piece. The bottomstamp reads "Handcrafted by Jiean Fung Porcelains, Taiwan." The early signs are more detailed and have richer colors. This does not affect secondary market value.

DATE: ____ $ ____

	'91	'92	'93	'94	'95	'96	'97	'98
○ WISH ○ HAVE	$6.50	6.50	6.50	14	15	16	17	18

ALPINE VILLAGE SIGN

ITEM #	INTRO	RETIRED	OSRP	GBTRU	↓
6571-4	1987	1993	$6	**$14**	22%

Notable: The Village signs are the only pieces to identify the actual manufacturer of the piece. The bottomstamp reads "Handcrafted by Jiean Fung Porcelains, Taiwan." The early signs are more detailed and have richer colors. This does not affect secondary market value.

DATE: ____ $ ____

	'91	'92	'93	'94	'95	'96	'97	'98
○ WISH ○ HAVE	$6.50	6.50	6.50	28	20	17	18	18

MAPLE SUGARING SHED

ITEM #	INTRO	RETIRED	OSRP	GBTRU	↓
6589-7	1987	1989	$19	**$210**	16%

New England Village® accessory. Set of 3. Two tapped trees, sled with bucket of syrup, and open walled shed with cooking vat.

DATE: ____ $ ____

	'91	'92	'93	'94	'95	'96	'97	'98
○ WISH ○ HAVE	$125	130	165	210	245	215	255	250

NOTES: _____

_____

_____

_____

_____

_____

DOVER COACH— "FIRST VERSION"

ITEM #	INTRO	RETIRED	OSRP	GBTRU	↓
6590-0	1987	1990	$18	**$80**	8%

Dickens' Village Series® accessory. Passenger coach with one horse, driver, and coachman.
Notable: There are 3 versions that affect GBTru$. This First Version is made in Taiwan, the coachman is clean shaven and the coach wheels are very crude.

DATE: ____ $ ____	'91	'92	'93	'94	'95	'96	'97	'98
O WISH O HAVE	$45	55	58	125	110	98	100	87

DOVER COACH— "SECOND VERSION"

ITEM #	INTRO	RETIRED	OSRP	GBTRU	↓
6590-0	1987	1990	$18	**$55**	19%

This Second Version is also made in Taiwan, the coachman has a mustache, the coach wheels are more round and there are two recesses on the underside of the base.

DATE: ____ $ ____	'91	'92	'93	'94	'95	'96	'97	'98
O WISH O HAVE	$45	55	58	65	65	60	75	68

DOVER COACH— "THIRD VERSION"

ITEM #	INTRO	RETIRED	OSRP	GBTRU	↓
6590-0	1987	1990	$18	**$50**	24%

This Third Version is made in Sri Lanka, the coachman has a mustache, and the coach wheels are round.

DATE: ____ $ ____	'91	'92	'93	'94	'95	'96	'97	'98
O WISH O HAVE	$45	55	58	75	75	64	60	66

CHILDE POND AND SKATERS

ITEM #	INTRO	RETIRED	OSRP	GBTRU	↓
5903-0	1988	1991	$30	**$65**	24%

Dickens' Village Series® accessory. Set of 4. Brick warming house, shutters latch against wind, wooden benches for skaters, birdhouse above door.
Notable: Color of warming hut varies. This does not affect secondary market value.

DATE: ____ $ ____	'91	'92	'93	'94	'95	'96	'97	'98
O WISH O HAVE	$32	65	72	85	80	80	80	85

FEZZIWIG AND FRIENDS

ITEM #	INTRO	RETIRED	OSRP	GBTRU	↓
5928-5	1988	1990	$12.50	**$45**	18%

Dickens' Village Series® accessory. Set of 3. *Christmas Carol*. Husband and wife bringing food to elderly neighbors.

DATE: ____ $ ____	'91	'92	'93	'94	'95	'96	'97	'98
○ WISH ○ HAVE	$30	30	42	48	50	52	50	55

NICHOLAS NICKLEBY CHARACTERS

ITEM #	INTRO	RETIRED	OSRP	GBTRU	↓
5929-3	1988	1991	$20	**$30**	21%

Dickens' Village Series® accessory. Set of 4. Nicholas and sister Kate, Wackford Squeers with schoolbook, three children playing, and four-wheeled wagon.
Notable: Misspelled as "Nicholas Nick**el**by" on sleeve.

DATE: ____ $ ____	'91	'92	'93	'94	'95	'96	'97	'98
○ WISH ○ HAVE	$20	45	40	35	36	32	38	38

SNOW CHILDREN

ITEM #	INTRO	RETIRED	OSRP	GBTRU	↓
5938-2	1988	1994	$15	**$30**	12%

Set of 3. Girl finishes snowman while dog watches. Two boys push off on sled, another belly flops on his sled.

DATE: ____ $ ____	'91	'92	'93	'94	'95	'96	'97	'98
○ WISH ○ HAVE	$16	16	17	17	22	28	30	34

VILLAGE HARVEST PEOPLE

ITEM #	INTRO	RETIRED	OSRP	GBTRU	↓
5941-2	1988	1991	$27.50	**$40**	20%

New England Village® accessory. Set of 4. Woman with butter churn, man loads pumpkins on cart, corn shocks, and pumpkins.
Notable: Sleeve reads "Harvest Time."

DATE: ____ $ ____	'91	'92	'93	'94	'95	'96	'97	'98
○ WISH ○ HAVE	$28	50	55	45	45	45	50	50

CITY NEWSSTAND

ITEM #	INTRO	RETIRED	OSRP	GBTRU	↑
5971-4	1988	1991	$25	**$70**	8%

Set of 4. Christmas In The City® accessory. News vendor, magazine and newspaper wooden stand, woman reading paper, newsboy showing headlines.

DATE: ___ $ ___	'91	'92	'93	'94	'95	'96	'97	'98
○ WISH ○ HAVE	$25	48	48	42	48	52	60	65

VILLAGE TRAIN TRESTLE

ITEM #	INTRO	RETIRED	OSRP	GBTRU	↓
5981-1	1988	1990	$17	**$50**	25%

Double arch trestle spans river. Single track on stone train overpass.
Notable: Sleeve reads "Stone Train Trestle."

DATE: ___ $ ___	'91	'92	'93	'94	'95	'96	'97	'98
○ WISH ○ HAVE	$35	42	60	60	60	70	70	67

ONE HORSE OPEN SLEIGH

ITEM #	INTRO	RETIRED	OSRP	GBTRU	↓
5982-0	1988	1993	$20	**$35**	8%

Couple out for a ride in sleigh with canopy. Lap robes protect against cold.

DATE: ___ $ ___	'91	'92	'93	'94	'95	'96	'97	'98
○ WISH ○ HAVE	$21	24	25	30	35	38	35	38

CITY BUS & MILK TRUCK

ITEM #	INTRO	RETIRED	OSRP	GBTRU	↓
5983-8	1988	1991	$15	**$30**	21%

Christmas In The City® accessory. Set of 2.
Notable: Box reads "Transport." Open back milk truck carries large milk cans. Old-fashioned city bus.

DATE: ___ $ ___	'91	'92	'93	'94	'95	'96	'97	'98
○ WISH ○ HAVE	$16	25	36	36	32	32	35	38

Heritage Village Collection® Accessories   263

SALVATION ARMY BAND

ITEM #	INTRO	RETIRED	OSRP	GBTRU	↓
5985-4	1988	1991	$24	**$75**	15%

Set of 6. Christmas In The City® accessory. Five uniformed musicians and conductor represent charitable organization.

DATE: ____ $ ____		'91	'92	'93	'94	'95	'96	'97	'98
○ Wish ○ Have		$24	40	42	50	65	75	90	88

WOODCUTTER AND SON

ITEM #	INTRO	RETIRED	OSRP	GBTRU	↓
5986-2	1988	1990	$10	**$38**	21%

New England Village® accessory. Set of 2. Father splits logs as son carries firewood.

DATE: ____ $ ____		'91	'92	'93	'94	'95	'96	'97	'98
○ Wish ○ Have		$25	25	32	50	40	42	45	48

RED COVERED BRIDGE

ITEM #	INTRO	RETIRED	OSRP	GBTRU	↓
5987-0	1988	1994	$15	**$25**	11%

New England Village® accessory. Wooden bridge spans Maple Creek supported by stone bases.

DATE: ____ $ ____		'91	'92	'93	'94	'95	'96	'97	'98
○ Wish ○ Have		$16	16	17	17	22	24	25	28

MAILBOX & FIRE HYDRANT

ITEM #	INTRO	RETIRED	OSRP	GBTRU	↓
5517-4	1989	1990	$5	**$18**	18%

Christmas In The City® accessory. U.S. Post Office colors of red, white and blue mailbox features "U.S. Mail" sign and eagle logo.
Notable: Replaced in 1990 by *Mailbox & Fire Hydrant*, Item #5214-0, a green and red HV mailbox.

DATE: ____ $ ____		'95	'96	'97	'98
○ Wish ○ Have		$20	22	20	22

DAVID COPPERFIELD CHARACTERS

ITEM #	INTRO	RETIRED	OSRP	GBTRU	↓
5551-4	1989	1992	$32.50	**$40**	11%

Dickens' Village Series® accessory. Set of 5. David Copperfield, Agnes, Mr. Wickfield, Peggotty with young David and Emily, Betsy Trotwood with Mr. Dick.

DATE: ___ $ ___	'91	'92	'93	'94	'95	'96	'97	'98
○ Wish ○ Have	$32.50	32.50	44	44	48	44	42	45

VILLAGE SIGN WITH SNOWMAN

ITEM #	INTRO	RETIRED	OSRP	GBTRU	↓
5572-7	1989	1994	$10	**$18**	10%

Snowman with top hat and scarf next to brick pillars and Heritage Village Collection® Sign.

DATE: ___ $ ___	'91	'92	'93	'94	'95	'96	'97	'98
○ Wish ○ Have	$10	10	10	10	12	20	17	20

LAMPLIGHTER WITH LAMP

ITEM #	INTRO	RETIRED	OSRP	GBTRU	
5577-8	1989	CURRENT	$9	**$10**	NO CHANGE

Dickens' Village Series® accessory. Set of 2. Man carries lit torch to light street lamps at dusk. Old-fashioned lamppost, small tree by post.

DATE: ___ $ ___	'91	'92	'93	'94	'95	'96	'97	'98
○ Wish ○ Have	$10	10	10	10	10	10	10	10

ROYAL COACH

ITEM #	INTRO	RETIRED	OSRP	GBTRU	↓
5578-6	1989	1992	$55	**$75**	4%

Dickens' Village Series® accessory. Gold filigree decorates red coach with Royal Coat Of Arms on door. Wheel base and undercarriage are cast metal, four gray horses have red and gold harnesses.
Notable: Early release to National Association Of Limited Edition Dealers (NALED).

DATE: ___ $ ___	'91	'92	'93	'94	'95	'96	'97	'98
○ Wish ○ Have	$55	56	86	75	75	75	75	78

CONSTABLES

ITEM #	INTRO	RETIRED	OSRP	GBTRU	NO
5579-4	1989	1991	$17.50	**$65**	CHANGE

Dickens' Village Series® accessory. Set of 3. One holds club, one with seated dog, one tips hat and stands by lamppost.

DATE: ___ $ ___	'91	'92	'93	'94	'95	'96	'97	'98
○ WISH ○ HAVE	$17.50	35	42	55	60	62	65	65

VIOLET VENDOR/CAROLERS/ CHESTNUT VENDOR

ITEM #	INTRO	RETIRED	OSRP	GBTRU	↓
5580-8	1989	1992	$23	**$34**	24%

Dickens' Village Series® accessory. Set of 3. Elderly woman sells bunches of violets from basket, man sells fresh roasted nuts, and two women singing carols.

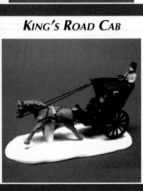

DATE: ___ $ ___	'91	'92	'93	'94	'95	'96	'97	'98
○ WISH ○ HAVE	$23	24	52	45	40	40	45	45

KING'S ROAD CAB

ITEM #	INTRO	RETIRED	OSRP	GBTRU	↑
5581-6	1989	1998	$30	**$36**	20%

Dickens' Village Series® accessory. Two-wheeled horse-drawn carriage. Driver sits high and behind cab. Passengers protected from weather.

DATE: ___ $ ___	'91	'92	'93	'94	'95	'96	'97	'98
○ WISH ○ HAVE	$30	30	30	30	30	30	30	30

CHRISTMAS CAROL CHRISTMAS MORNING FIGURES

ITEM #	INTRO	RETIRED	OSRP	GBTRU	NO
5588-3	1989	CURRENT	$18	**$18**	CHANGE

Dickens' Village Series® accessory. Set of 3. *Christmas Carol* Scrooge transformed—smiling, small boy by fence and lamppost—waving, couple carrying presents.
Notable: Early release to National Association Of Limited Edition Dealers (NALED).

DATE: ___ $ ___	'91	'92	'93	'94	'95	'96	'97	'98
○ WISH ○ HAVE	$18	18	18	18	18	18	18	18

CHRISTMAS CAROL CHRISTMAS SPIRITS FIGURES

ITEM #	INTRO	RETIRED	OSRP	GBTRU	NO
5589-1	1989	CURRENT	$27.50	**$27.50**	CHANGE

Dickens' Village Series® accessory. Set of 4. *Christmas Carol* Scrooge with Ghost of...1) Christmas Past, 2) Christmas Present, and 3) Future...&...Marley.

DATE: ___ $ ___	'91	'92	'93	'94	'95	'96	'97	'98
○ WISH ○ HAVE	$27.50	27.50	27.50	27.50	27.50	27.50	27.50	27.50

FARM ANIMALS

ITEM #	INTRO	RETIRED	OSRP	GBTRU	↓
5945-5	1989	1991	$15	**$35**	17%

New England Village® accessory. Set of 4. Chickens, geese, sheep, ewe and lamb.

DATE: ___ $ ___	'91	'92	'93	'94	'95	'96	'97	'98
○ WISH ○ HAVE	$15	25	33	36	40	40	45	42

ORGAN GRINDER

ITEM #	INTRO	RETIRED	OSRP	GBTRU	↓
5957-9	1989	1991	$21	**$32**	11%

Set of 3. Christmas In The City® accessory. Man turns handle to produce music for little monkey to dance. Woman and children watch monkey.

DATE: ___ $ ___	'91	'92	'93	'94	'95	'96	'97	'98
○ WISH ○ HAVE	$21	38	40	40	35	36	36	36

POPCORN VENDOR

ITEM #	INTRO	RETIRED	OSRP	GBTRU	↓
5958-7	1989	1992	$22	**$30**	17%

Set of 3. Christmas In The City® accessory. Truck with red and white striped top. Vendor fills red and white bag. Little girl has a full bag of popcorn.

DATE: ___ $ ___	'91	'92	'93	'94	'95	'96	'97	'98
○ WISH ○ HAVE	$22	22	40	35	40	32	38	36

RIVER STREET ICE HOUSE CART

ITEM #	INTRO	RETIRED	OSRP	GBTRU	↓
5959-5	1989	1991	$20	**$50**	9%

Christmas In The City® accessory. Horse pulls a blue and gray ice wagon for ice man.

DATE: ___ $ ___	'91	'92	'93	'94	'95	'96	'97	'98
○ WISH ○ HAVE	$20	40	45	45	50	50	55	55

CENTRAL PARK CARRIAGE

ITEM #	INTRO	RETIRED	OSRP	GBTRU	NO
5979-0	1989	CURRENT	$30	**$30**	CHANGE

Christmas In The City® accessory. Gray horse pulls red and black carriage. Driver has mother and child as passengers.

DATE: ___ $ ___	'91	'92	'93	'94	'95	'96	'97	'98
○ WISH ○ HAVE	$30	30	30	30	30	30	30	30

HERITAGE VILLAGE PROMOTIONAL SIGN

ITEM #	INTRO	RETIRED	OSRP	GBTRU	↓
9953-8	1989	1990	$5	**$20**	17%

Vertical sign with arched top and brick base. Gold lettering on white facade.
Notable: Variation exists of green lettering on green facade. This does not affect secondary market value. Earthenware.

DATE: ___ $ ___	'91	'92	'93	'94	'95	'96	'97	'98
○ WISH ○ HAVE	$-	-	-	18	20	25	28	24

MAILBOX & FIRE HYDRANT

ITEM #	INTRO	RETIRED	OSRP	GBTRU	↑
5214-0	1990	1998	$5	**$6**	20%

Christmas In The City® accessory. Set of 2. Red and green HV mailbox and red fire hydrant. Metal.
Notable: Replaced 1989 Mailbox & Fire Hydrant, Item #5517-4.

DATE: ___ $ ___	'91	'92	'93	'94	'95	'96	'97	'98
○ WISH ○ HAVE	$5	5	5	5	5	5	5	5

BUSY SIDEWALKS

ITEM #	INTRO	RETIRED	OSRP	GBTRU	↑
5535-2	1990	1992	$28	**$55**	10%

Set of 4. Christmas In The City® accessory. Delivery boy, doorman, two elderly ladies, mother with toddler and baby in carriage.

DATE: ____ $ ____	'91	'92	'93	'94	'95	'96	'97	'98
○ WISH ○ HAVE	$28	28	42	42	45	45	45	50

'TIS THE SEASON

ITEM #	INTRO	RETIRED	OSRP	GBTRU	↓
5539-5	1990	1994	$12.50	**$16**	27%

Christmas In The City® accessory. Santa with bell and iron kettle for Season donations. Little girl gives to the needy.

DATE: ____ $ ____	'91	'92	'93	'94	'95	'96	'97	'98
○ WISH ○ HAVE	$12.50	12.50	13	12.95	20	20	20	22

REST YE MERRY GENTLEMAN

ITEM #	INTRO	RETIRED	OSRP	GBTRU	NO
5540-9	1990	CURRENT	$12.50	**$13**	CHANGE

Christmas In The City® accessory. Man sits on bench reading newspaper with purchases all around him. Porcelain and Metal.

DATE: ____ $ ____	'91	'92	'93	'94	'95	'96	'97	'98
○ WISH ○ HAVE	$12.50	12.50	12.95	12.95	12.95	12.95	12.95	13

TOWN CRIER & CHIMNEY SWEEP

ITEM #	INTRO	RETIRED	OSRP	GBTRU	NO
5569-7	1990	CURRENT	$15	**$16**	CHANGE

Dickens' Village Series® accessory. Set of 2. Crier rings bell and reads out announcements. A Sweep in top hat and tails carries chimney brush.

DATE: ____ $ ____	'91	'92	'93	'94	'95	'96	'97	'98
○ WISH ○ HAVE	$15	15	16	16	16	16	16	16

CAROLERS ON THE DOORSTEP

	Item #	Intro	Retired	OSRP	GBTru	↓
	5570-0	1990	1993	$25	**$32**	16%

Dickens' Village Series® accessory. Set of 4. Four children sing carols to elderly man and woman, boys carry lanterns, girls have song books.

Date: ____ $ ____	'91	'92	'93	'94	'95	'96	'97	'98
○ Wish ○ Have	$25	25	25	36	40	40	40	38

HOLIDAY TRAVELERS

	Item #	Intro	Retired	OSRP	GBTru	NO
	5571-9	1990	Current	$22.50	**$25**	CHANGE

Dickens' Village Series® accessory. Set of 3. Train conductor, baggage handler, and man and woman passengers.

Date: ____ $ ____	'91	'92	'93	'94	'95	'96	'97	'98
○ Wish ○ Have	$22.50	24	25	25	25	25	25	25

FLYING SCOT TRAIN, THE

	Item #	Intro	Retired	OSRP	GBTru	↑
	5573-5	1990	1998	$48	**$55**	10%

Dickens' Village Series® accessory. Set of 4. Engine and wood supply car and two passenger cars with luggage carriers atop cars.

Date: ____ $ ____	'91	'92	'93	'94	'95	'96	'97	'98
○ Wish ○ Have	$48	50	50	50	50	50	50	50

VICTORIA STATION TRAIN PLATFORM

PLATFORM NO.2

	Item #	Intro	Retired	OSRP	GBTru	NO
	5575-1	1990	Current	$20	**$22**	CHANGE

Dickens' Village Series® accessory. Six-sided ticket booth with windows all around, long metal roof to protect passengers.

Date: ____ $ ____	'91	'92	'93	'94	'95	'96	'97	'98
○ Wish ○ Have	$20	20	22	22	22	22	22	22

TRIMMING THE NORTH POLE

ITEM #	INTRO	RETIRED	OSRP	GBTRU	↑
5608-1	1990	1993	$10	**$37**	3%

North Pole Series™ accessory. One elf holds another to hang greenery on North Pole sign while blue bird watches.

DATE: ____ $ ____	'91	'92	'93	'94	'95	'96	'97	'98
○ WISH ○ HAVE	$10	10	10	22	22	25	30	36

SANTA & MRS. CLAUS

ITEM #	INTRO	RETIRED	OSRP	GBTRU	NO
5609-0	1990	CURRENT	$15	**$15**	CHANGE

North Pole Series™ accessory. Set of 2. Mrs. Claus and elf wave good-bye to Santa as he does a final check of delivery book names before leaving North Pole.
Notable: Variation exists in title on book: "Good Boys" instead of "Good Kids." No secondary market value has been established for the "Good Boys" variation as very few have ever sold.

DATE: ____ $ ____	'91	'92	'93	'94	'95	'96	'97	'98
○ WISH ○ HAVE	$15	15	15	15	15	15	15	15

SANTA'S LITTLE HELPERS

ITEM #	INTRO	RETIRED	OSRP	GBTRU	↑
5610-3	1990	1993	$28	**$65**	5%

North Pole Series™ accessory. Set of 3. Elf stands on presents to hang wreath. Two elves move toy sack. One elf brings two reindeer to sleigh.

DATE: ____ $ ____	'91	'92	'93	'94	'95	'96	'97	'98
○ WISH ○ HAVE	$28	28	28	40	48	52	55	62

SLEIGH & EIGHT TINY REINDEER

ITEM #	INTRO	RETIRED	OSRP	GBTRU	NO
5611-1	1990	CURRENT	$40	**$42**	CHANGE

North Pole Series™ accessory. Set of 5. Toys fill sleigh harnessed to Santa's eight reindeer.

DATE: ____ $ ____	'91	'92	'93	'94	'95	'96	'97	'98
○ WISH ○ HAVE	$40	42	42	42	42	42	42	42

TOY PEDDLER, THE

ITEM #	INTRO	RETIRED	OSRP	GBTRU	↑
5616-2	1990	1998	$22	**$32**	45%

Alpine Village Series™ accessory. Set of 3. Toy peddler carries tray with toys. Mother and son look at toy horse. Little girl holds top.

DATE: ___ $ ___	'91	'92	'93	'94	'95	'96	'97	'98
○ WISH ○ HAVE	$22	22	22	22	22	22	22	22

AMISH FAMILY— "W/MUSTACHE"

ITEM #	INTRO	RETIRED	OSRP	GBTRU	↓
5948-0	1990	1992	$20	**$44**	6%

New England Village® accessory. Set of 3. Mother w/apples in apron, father stacks boxes, children sort apples.
Notable: Two Versions produced. In the First Version, the father has a mustache. Realizing that this is against Amish custom, Department 56, Inc. stopped production and redesigned the piece. Early release to Showcase Dealers and National Association Of Limited Edition Dealers (NALED).

DATE: ___ $ ___	'92	'93	'94	'95	'96	'97	'98
○ WISH ○ HAVE	$40	46	40	50	55	55	47

AMISH FAMILY— "NO MUSTACHE"

GBTRU	NO
$35	CHANGE

In this Second Version, the father has no mustache, as is the Amish custom.

DATE: ___ $ ___	'97	'98
○ WISH ○ HAVE	$40	35

AMISH BUGGY

ITEM #	INTRO	RETIRED	OSRP	GBTRU	↓
5949-8	1990	1992	$22	**$55**	11%

New England Village® accessory. Amish man feeds brown horse harnessed to privacy curtained family carriage.

DATE: ___ $ ___	'91	'92	'93	'94	'95	'96	'97	'98
○ WISH ○ HAVE	$22	22.50	50	50	50	50	60	62

SLEEPY HOLLOW CHARACTERS

Item #	Intro	Retired	OSRP	GBTRU	↑
5956-0	1990	1992	$27.50	**$45**	7%

New England Village® accessory. Set of 3. Man carving pumpkin. Squire and Mrs. Van Tassel, Ichabod Crane with children.

Date: ____ $ ____	'91	'92	'93	'94	'95	'96	'97	'98
○ Wish ○ Have	$27.50	27.50	48	45	45	42	45	42

SKATING PARTY

Item #	Intro	Retired	OSRP	GBTRU	NO
5523-9	1991	Current	$27.50	**$27.50**	CHANGE

New England Village® accessory. Set of 3. Skating couple, boy, and girl.

Date: ____ $ ____	'91	'92	'93	'94	'95	'96	'97	'98
○ Wish ○ Have	$27.50	27.50	27.50	27.50	27.50	27.50	27.50	27.50

ALL AROUND THE TOWN

Item #	Intro	Retired	OSRP	GBTRU	NO
5545-0	1991	1993	$18	**$24**	CHANGE

Christmas In The City® accessory. Set of 2. Man with "sandwich boards" as a walking ad for "White Christmas." Man with packages stops to get a shoeshine from young boy.

Date: ____ $ ____	'91	'92	'93	'94	'95	'96	'97	'98
○ Wish ○ Have	$18	18	18	30	30	28	28	24

FIRE BRIGADE, THE

Item #	Intro	Retired	OSRP	GBTRU	↓
5546-8	1991	1995	$20	**$25**	17%

Christmas In The City® accessory. Set of 2. Two firemen carry ladder and ax. Fireman with pail takes a moment to pet mascot Dalmatian.

Date: ____ $ ____	'91	'92	'93	'94	'95	'96	'97	'98
○ Wish ○ Have	$20	20	20	20	20	24	32	30

"CITY FIRE DEPT." FIRE TRUCK

ITEM #	INTRO	RETIRED	OSRP	GBTRU	↓
5547-6	1991	1995	$18	**$28**	22%

Christmas In The City® accessory. Ladder attached to side, hose and nozzle assembly on top and rear of red fire truck.

DATE: ___ $ ___	'91	'92	'93	'94	'95	'96	'97	'98
○ WISH ○ HAVE	$18	18	18	18	18	22	32	36

CAROLING THRU THE CITY

ITEM #	INTRO	RETIRED	OSRP	GBTRU	↑
5548-4	1991	1998	$27.50	**$30**	9%

Set of 3. Christmas In The City® accessory. Singing man pulls sled with two boys, two women with young girl, man (alone), all with song books.

DATE: ___ $ ___	'91	'92	'93	'94	'95	'96	'97	'98
○ WISH ○ HAVE	$27.50	27.50	27.50	27.50	27.50	27.50	27.50	27.50

OLIVER TWIST CHARACTERS

ITEM #	INTRO	RETIRED	OSRP	GBTRU	↓
5554-9	1991	1993	$35	**$38**	10%

Dickens' Village Series® accessory. Set of 3. Mr. Brownlow in long coat, stovepipe hat, walks with cane. Oliver in rags next to food cart as another boy reaches to steal food, third boy holds sack.

DATE: ___ $ ___	'91	'92	'93	'94	'95	'96	'97	'98
○ WISH ○ HAVE	$35	35	35	58	45	45	45	42

BRINGING HOME THE YULE LOG

ITEM #	INTRO	RETIRED	OSRP	GBTRU	↑
5558-1	1991	1998	$27.50	**$32**	14%

Dickens' Village Series® accessory. Set of 3. Two boys pull on ropes to haul log. One girl holds lantern to light way and another walks alongside.

DATE: ___ $ ___	'91	'92	'93	'94	'95	'96	'97	'98
○ WISH ○ HAVE	$27.50	27.50	28	28	28	28	28	28

POULTRY MARKET

ITEM #	INTRO	RETIRED	OSRP	GBTRU	↓
5559-0	1991	1995	$30	**$36**	20%

Dickens' Village Series® accessory. Set of 3. An aproned poulterer holds game bird. Covered stand with display of turkeys and geese. Woman holds purchase as child watches.
Notable: Early samples had patches on left hand side of the green drape. No secondary market value has been established for the proof as very few have ever sold.

DATE: ___ $ ___	'91	'92	'93	'94	'95	'96	'97	'98
○ WISH ○ HAVE	$30	30	32	32	32	37	40	45

COME INTO THE INN

ITEM #	INTRO	RETIRED	OSRP	GBTRU	↓
5560-3	1991	1994	$22	**$27**	25%

Dickens' Village Series® accessory. Set of 3. Innkeeper's wife pauses to read note as she sweeps snow from the entry. Young boy with lantern lights way for coach driver. Gentleman stands by luggage.

DATE: ___ $ ___	'91	'92	'93	'94	'95	'96	'97	'98
○ WISH ○ HAVE	$22	22	22	22	26	27	30	36

HOLIDAY COACH

ITEM #	INTRO	RETIRED	OSRP	GBTRU	↑
5561-1	1991	1998	$68	**$80**	14%

Dickens' Village Series® accessory. Four horses pull coach full of travelers who ride inside and on topside seats. Coachman blows horn on arrival as driver guides horses. The First Version had gold chains, the Second Version has silver chains.

DATE: ___ $ ___	'91	'92	'93	'94	'95	'96	'97	'98
○ WISH ○ HAVE	$68	68	70	70	70	70	70	70

TOYMAKER ELVES

ITEM #	INTRO	RETIRED	OSRP	GBTRU	↓
5602-2	1991	1995	$27.50	**$34**	6%

North Pole Series™ accessory. Set of 3. Two elves carry trunk of toys. One elf balances stack of toys. One elf has apron filled with toys.

DATE: ___ $ ___	'91	'92	'93	'94	'95	'96	'97	'98
○ WISH ○ HAVE	$27.50	27.50	27.50	27.50	27.50	42	40	36

BAKER ELVES

ITEM #	INTRO	RETIRED	OSRP	GBTRU	↓
5603-0	1991	1995	$27.50	**$30**	25%

North Pole Series™ accessory. Set of 3. One elf holds piece of belled harness from sleigh. One elf holds tray of baked goods. One elf takes a cookie from sweets cart.

DATE: ___ $ ___	'91	'92	'93	'94	'95	'96	'97	'98
○ WISH ○ HAVE	$27.50	27.50	27.50	27.50	27.50	43	40	40

MARKET DAY

ITEM #	INTRO	RETIRED	OSRP	GBTRU	↓
5641-3	1991	1993	$35	**$36**	5%

New England Village® accessory. Set of 3. Mother carries baby and basket. Daughter holds bread basket. Merchant tips hat as he pushes sledge with bagged food. Man and boy rest on goat cart while standing boy holds bag.

DATE: ___ $ ___	'91	'92	'93	'94	'95	'96	'97	'98
○ WISH ○ HAVE	$35	35	35	48	45	45	45	38

GATE HOUSE

ITEM #	INTRO	RETIRED	OSRP	GBTRU	↓
5530-1	1992 EVENT PIECE 1992		$22.50	**$35**	24%

Available at 1992 Village Gatherings and select Showcase Dealer Open Houses. Walled castle fortified entry is brick and stone archway. Guards check soldiers, carriages, carts and villagers. Narrow, shuttered windows protect against weather and attack.
Notable: Variations in color between shades of gray or blue do not affect the secondary market value.

DATE: ___ $ ___	'92	'93	'94	'95	'96	'97	'98
○ WISH ○ HAVE	$22.50	72	65	55	60	50	46

DON'T DROP THE PRESENTS!

ITEM #	INTRO	RETIRED	OSRP	GBTRU	↓
5532-8	1992	1995	$25	**$30**	9%

Christmas In The City® accessory. Set of 2. Mother cautions father to take care as dog jumps up to sniff presents. Daughter peeks out from mother's skirt as shopping bag rests on snow. Son slips and tumbles in snow.

DATE: ___ $ ___	'92	'93	'94	'95	'96	'97	'98
○ WISH ○ HAVE	$25	25	25	25	36	36	33

WELCOME HOME

ITEM #	INTRO	RETIRED	OSRP	GBTRU	↓
5533-6	1992	1995	$27.50	**$32**	16%

Set of 3. Christmas In The City® accessory. Boy reaches to hug Grandmother visiting for holiday as girl and Grandfather reach out to hug each other. Family pet joins the greeting.

DATE: ____ $ ____		'92	'93	'94	'95	'96	'97	'98
○ WISH ○ HAVE		$27.50	27.50	27.50	27.50	34	37	38

CHURCHYARD FENCE & GATE

ITEM #	INTRO	RETIRED	OSRP	GBTRU	↑
5563-8	1992	1992	$15	**$65**	8%

Set of 3.
Notable: Early release to Gift Creations Concepts (GCC). There were two different sets of *Churchyard Fence & Gate* introduced in 1992:
First Version—*Churchyard Fence & Gate* (1992–1992), Set of 3, Item #5563-8 was a midyear release and a GCC Exclusive. It included one gate, one wall, and one corner. The *Quarterly* pictured it in gray, but it was shipped in brown.
Second Version—*Churchyard Gate & Fence* (1992–1997), Set of 3, Item #5806-8, included one gate and two corners.
In addition, there was *Churchyard Fence Extensions* (1992–1997), Item #5807-6, which was 4 straight wall pieces.

DATE: ____ $ ____		'92	'93	'94	'95	'96	'97	'98
○ WISH ○ HAVE		$15	25	40	40	45	55	60

LETTERS FOR SANTA

ITEM #	INTRO	RETIRED	OSRP	GBTRU	NO
5604-9	1992	1994	$30	**$65**	CHANGE

North Pole Series™ accessory. Set of 3. One elf carries bundles of letters, as another elf tries to lift sack of letters. Two additional elves arrive with reindeer cart filled with mailbags of letters for Santa.

DATE: ____ $ ____		'92	'93	'94	'95	'96	'97	'98
○ WISH ○ HAVE		$30	30	30	50	50	60	65

Heritage Village Collection® Accessories   277

TESTING THE TOYS

ITEM #	INTRO	RETIRED	OSRP	GBTRU	NO
5605-7	1992	CURRENT	$16.50	**$16.50**	CHANGE

North Pole Series™ accessory. Set of 2. One elf rides downhill on a sled as two others try out a toboggan.

DATE: ____ $ ____
○ WISH ○ HAVE

'92	'93	'94	'95	'96	'97	'98
$16.50	16.50	16.50	16.50	16.50	16.50	16.50

BUYING BAKERS BREAD

ITEM #	INTRO	RETIRED	OSRP	GBTRU	↓
5619-7	1992	1995	$20	**$30**	12%

Alpine Village Series™ accessory. Set of 2. Man and woman lift basket together to carry loaves, plus she carries basket on arm. Another man carries basket tray of bread while rest of loaves are carried in his basket backpack.

DATE: ____ $ ____
○ WISH ○ HAVE

'92	'93	'94	'95	'96	'97	'98
$20	20	20	20	32	30	34

HARVEST SEED CART

ITEM #	INTRO	RETIRED	OSRP	GBTRU	↓
5645-6	1992	1995	$27.50	**$30**	17%

Dickens' Village Series® and New England Village® accessory. Set of 3. Boy lifts sack of corn onto wheelbarrow. Man lifts barrow filled with corn sacks as a chicken pecks at sack. Another chicken walks next to him. Girl holds white rooster and has basket on ground by her feet.

DATE: ____ $ ____
○ WISH ○ HAVE

'92	'93	'94	'95	'96	'97	'98
$27.50	27.50	27.50	27.50	42	40	36

TOWN TINKER

ITEM #	INTRO	RETIRED	OSRP	GBTRU	↓
5646-4	1992	1995	$24	**$30**	17%

Dickens' Village Series® and New England Village® accessory. Set of 2. Traveling peddler with cart he pushes, sells pots, pans, trinkets, and all odds and ends. He also repairs household items. He follows countryside roads and paths.

DATE: ____ $ ____
○ WISH ○ HAVE

'92	'93	'94	'95	'96	'97	'98
$24	24	24	24	25	38	36

OLD PUPPETEER, THE

ITEM #	INTRO	RETIRED	OSRP	GBTRU	↓
5802-5	1992	1995	$32	**$38**	16%

Dickens' Village Series® accessory. Set of 3. Children watch puppet show. Stage on wheels with man moving the stringed marionettes to tell stories to audiences of all ages.

DATE: ____ $ ____
○ WISH ○ HAVE

'92	'93	'94	'95	'96	'97	'98
$32	32	32	32	36	40	45

BIRD SELLER, THE

ITEM #	INTRO	RETIRED	OSRP	GBTRU	↓
5803-3	1992	1995	$25	**$30**	14%

Dickens' Village Series® accessory. Set of 3. Woman holds up two bird cages. Delighted child and mother with woman who has made a purchase.

DATE: ____ $ ____
○ WISH ○ HAVE

'92	'93	'94	'95	'96	'97	'98
$25	25	25	25	28	33	35

VILLAGE STREET PEDDLERS

ITEM #	INTRO	RETIRED	OSRP	GBTRU	↓
5804-1	1992	1994	$16	**$22**	12%

Dickens' Village Series® accessory. Set of 2. One man carries pole of fresh dressed rabbits. Second peddler wears wooden tray of spices to be sold in small pinches and ounces.

DATE: ____ $ ____
○ WISH ○ HAVE

'92	'93	'94	'95	'96	'97	'98
$16	16	16	22	25	25	25

ENGLISH POST BOX

ITEM #	INTRO	RETIRED	OSRP	GBTRU	
5805-0	1992	CURRENT	$4.50	**$4.50**	NO CHANGE

Dickens' Village Series® accessory. Red, six-sided, English-styled post box. Metal.

DATE: ____ $ ____
○ WISH ○ HAVE

'92	'93	'94	'95	'96	'97	'98
$4.50	4.50	4.50	4.50	4.50	4.50	4.50

Heritage Village Collection® Accessories

CHURCHYARD GATE & FENCE

ITEM #	INTRO	RETIRED	OSRP	GBTRU	↑
5806-8	1992	1997	$15	**$20**	11%

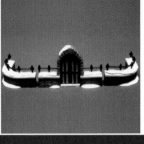

Set of 3. Two different *Churchyard Gate And Fence* sets were produced. This second set includes one gate and two corners. For original set, see Item #5563-8, 1992. See also 1992 *Churchyard Fence Extensions,* Item #5807-6.

DATE: ___ $ ___		'92	'93	'94	'95	'96	'97	'98
○ WISH ○ HAVE		$15	15	15	15	15	15	18

CHURCHYARD FENCE EXTENSIONS

ITEM #	INTRO	RETIRED	OSRP	GBTRU	NO
5807-6	1992	1997	$16	**$18**	CHANGE

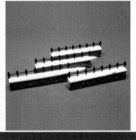

Set of 4. Stone base with wrought iron posts and connectors to extend fence around church and graveyard.

DATE: ___ $ ___		'92	'93	'94	'95	'96	'97	'98
○ WISH ○ HAVE		$16	16	16	16	16	16	18

VILLAGE EXPRESS VAN

ITEM #	INTRO	RETIRED	OSRP	GBTRU	↓
5865-3	1992	1996	$25	**$28**	7%

Christmas In The City® accessory. Green delivery van advertises On Time Service. Rack on van roof holds wrapped packages.
Notable: License plate is abbreviated address of Department 56, Inc. headquarters, 6436 City West Parkway.

DATE: ___ $ ___		'92	'93	'94	'95	'96	'97	'98
○ WISH ○ HAVE		$25	25	25	25	25	32	30

VILLAGE EXPRESS VAN

ITEM #	INTRO	RETIRED	OSRP	GBTRU	↓
9951-1	1992	PROMO	$25	**$75**	29%

Notable: This van was first given to Department 56, Inc. sales representatives as a gift at their National Sales Conference in December, 1992. It was later used as a special Event Piece at Bachman's® Village Gathering in 1993.

DATE: ___ $ ___		'92	'93	'94	'95	'96	'97	'98
○ WISH ○ HAVE		$25	-	-	125	185	135	105

PLAYING IN THE SNOW

ITEM #	INTRO	RETIRED	OSRP	GBTRU	NO
5556-5	1993	1996	$25	**$35**	CHANGE

Set of 3. Christmas In The City® accessory. Children build and dress a snowman.

DATE: ____ $ ____
○ WISH ○ HAVE

'93	'94	'95	'96	'97	'98
$25	25	25	25	33	35

STREET MUSICIANS

ITEM #	INTRO	RETIRED	OSRP	GBTRU	NO
5564-6	1993	1997	$25	**$30**	CHANGE

Set of 3. Christmas In The City® accessory. Girl gives coin to the street musicians.

DATE: ____ $ ____
○ WISH ○ HAVE

'93	'94	'95	'96	'97	'98
$25	25	25	25	25	30

TOWN TREE

ITEM #	INTRO	RETIRED	OSRP	GBTRU	NO
5565-4	1993	CURRENT	$45	**$45**	CHANGE

Set of 5. Lighted. Christmas In The City® accessory. Decorated town tree and stone sections to encircle tree.

DATE: ____ $ ____
○ WISH ○ HAVE

'93	'94	'95	'96	'97	'98
$45	45	45	45	45	45

TOWN TREE TRIMMERS

ITEM #	INTRO	RETIRED	OSRP	GBTRU	NO
5566-2	1993	CURRENT	$32.50	**$32.50**	CHANGE

Set of 4. Christmas In The City® accessory. Ladder and three helpers to decorate town tree.

DATE: ____ $ ____
○ WISH ○ HAVE

'93	'94	'95	'96	'97	'98
$32.50	32.50	32.50	32.50	32.50	32.50

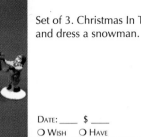

Heritage Village Collection® Accessories 281

CLIMB EVERY MOUNTAIN

ITEM #	INTRO	RETIRED	OSRP	GBTRU	NO
5613-8	1993	CURRENT	$27.50	**$27.50**	CHANGE

Alpine Village Series™ accessory. Set of 4. Three climbers and companion St. Bernard dog roped together for safety.

DATE: _____ $ _____
○ WISH ○ HAVE

'93	'94	'95	'96	'97	'98
$27.50	27.50	27.50	27.50	27.50	27.50

WOODSMEN ELVES

ITEM #	INTRO	RETIRED	OSRP	GBTRU	↑
5630-8	1993	1995	$30	**$65**	18%

North Pole Series™ accessory. Elves cut tree and wood to warm North Pole buildings.

DATE: _____ $ _____
○ WISH ○ HAVE

'93	'94	'95	'96	'97	'98
$30	30	30	47	55	55

SING A SONG FOR SANTA

ITEM #	INTRO	RETIRED	OSRP	GBTRU	↑
5631-6	1993	1998	$28	**$32**	14%

North Pole Series™ accessory. Set of 3. Caroling North Pole elves.

DATE: _____ $ _____
○ WISH ○ HAVE

'93	'94	'95	'96	'97	'98
$28	28	28	28	28	28

NORTH POLE GATE

ITEM #	INTRO	RETIRED	OSRP	GBTRU	↑
5632-4	1993	1998	$32.50	**$35**	8%

North Pole Series™ accessory. Entry gate to the North Pole.

DATE: _____ $ _____
○ WISH ○ HAVE

'93	'94	'95	'96	'97	'98
$32.50	32.50	32.50	32.50	32.50	32.50

KNIFE GRINDER

ITEM #	INTRO	RETIRED	OSRP	GBTRU	↓
5649-9	1993	1996	$22.50	**$26**	7%

New England Village® accessory. Set of 2. Man pedal-powered grinding wheel keeps sharp edges on knives and tools.

DATE: _____ $ _____
○ WISH   ○ HAVE

'93	'94	'95	'96	'97	'98
$22.50	22.50	22.50	22.50	28	28

BLUE STAR ICE HARVESTERS

ITEM #	INTRO	RETIRED	OSRP	GBTRU	↓
5650-2	1993	1997	$27.50	**$28**	15%

New England Village® accessory. Set of 2. Men cut up pond, lake and river ice to stack in icehouse for food storage and cooling. Early storage was dug into the ground which helped to insulate. Later wood and stone buildings were built to storehouse ice. Sawdust and straw were used to keep ice blocks from sticking together.

DATE: _____ $ _____
○ WISH   ○ HAVE

'93	'94	'95	'96	'97	'98
$27.50	27.50	27.50	27.50	27.50	33

CHELSEA MARKET FRUIT MONGER & CART

ITEM #	INTRO	RETIRED	OSRP	GBTRU	↑
5813-0	1993	1997	$25	**$35**	9%

Dickens' Village Series® accessory. Set of 2. Pushcart vendor of fresh fruit and vegetables.

DATE: _____ $ _____
○ WISH   ○ HAVE

'93	'94	'95	'96	'97	'98
$25	25	25	25	25	32

CHELSEA MARKET FISH MONGER & CART

ITEM #	INTRO	RETIRED	OSRP	GBTRU	↑
5814-9	1993	1997	$25	**$35**	6%

Dickens' Village Series® accessory. Set of 2. Pushcart vendor of fresh fish.

DATE: _____ $ _____
○ WISH   ○ HAVE

'93	'94	'95	'96	'97	'98
$25	25	25	25	25	33

CHELSEA MARKET FLOWER MONGER & CART

ITEM #	INTRO	RETIRED	OSRP	GBTRU	NO
5815-7	1993	CURRENT	$27.50	**$27.50**	CHANGE

Dickens' Village Series® accessory. Set of 2. Pushcart vendor of fresh cut flowers and nosegays.

DATE: ____ $ ____
○ WISH ○ HAVE

'93	'94	'95	'96	'97	'98
$27.50	27.50	27.50	27.50	27.50	27.50

CHELSEA LANE SHOPPERS

ITEM #	INTRO	RETIRED	OSRP	GBTRU	NO
5816-5	1993	CURRENT	$30	**$30**	CHANGE

Dickens' Village Series® accessory. Set of 4. Woman and girl, each with flowers. Couple walking with package and basket. Gentleman with walking stick.

DATE: ____ $ ____
○ WISH ○ HAVE

'93	'94	'95	'96	'97	'98
$30	30	30	30	30	30

VISION OF A CHRISTMAS PAST

ITEM #	INTRO	RETIRED	OSRP	GBTRU	↓
5817-3	1993	1996	$27.50	**$30**	6%

Dickens' Village Series® accessory. Set of 3. Innkeeper with coach dogs, traveling merchant, 2 young travelers.

DATE: ____ $ ____
○ WISH ○ HAVE

'93	'94	'95	'96	'97	'98
$28.50	27.50	27.50	27.50	35	32

C. BRADFORD, WHEELWRIGHT & SON

ITEM #	INTRO	RETIRED	OSRP	GBTRU	↑
5818-1	1993	1996	$24	**$30**	11%

Dickens' Village Series® accessory. Set of 2. Father and son wagon wheel makers and repairers.

DATE: ____ $ ____
○ WISH ○ HAVE

'93	'94	'95	'96	'97	'98
$24	24	24	24	30	27

BRINGING FLEECES TO THE MILL

	ITEM #	INTRO	RETIRED	OSRP	GBTRU	↑
	5819-0	1993	1998	$35	**$40**	14%

Dickens' Village Series® accessory. Set of 2. Shepherd takes wagon load of fleeces to market. Child stands with sheep.

DATE: _____ $ _____
○ WISH ○ HAVE

'93	'94	'95	'96	'97	'98
$35	35	35	35	35	35

DASHING THROUGH THE SNOW

	ITEM #	INTRO	RETIRED	OSRP	GBTRU	
	5820-3	1993	CURRENT	$32.50	**$32.50**	NO CHANGE

Dickens' Village Series® accessory. Horse-drawn sleigh takes couple for ride across snowy roads.

DATE: _____ $ _____
○ WISH ○ HAVE

'93	'94	'95	'96	'97	'98
$32.50	32.50	32.50	32.50	32.50	32.50

CHRISTMAS AT THE PARK

	ITEM #	INTRO	RETIRED	OSRP	GBTRU	
	5866-1	1993	CURRENT	$27.50	**$27.50**	NO CHANGE

Set of 3. Christmas In The City® accessory. Seated father, mother and child. Seated boy and girl with dog.

DATE: _____ $ _____
○ WISH ○ HAVE

'93	'94	'95	'96	'97	'98
$27.50	27.50	27.50	27.50	27.50	27.50

VILLAGE EXPRESS VAN—GOLD

	ITEM #	INTRO	RETIRED	OSRP	GBTRU	↓
	9977-5	1993	PROMO	$25	**$675**	20%

Notable: Gold "Road Show" Edition of the Village Express Van. Packed in a special gold box. Presented to potential investors before initial public offering.

DATE: _____ $ _____
○ WISH ○ HAVE

'95	'96	'97	'98
$1200	945	825	845

Heritage Village Collection® Accessories   285

VILLAGE EXPRESS VAN FOR GATHERINGS

ITEM #	INTRO	RETIRED	OSRP	GBTRU
VARIOUS	1994	PROMO	$25	**$50**

Black van for store delivery service. Right side is Department 56, Inc. logo and left side features specific Department 56, Inc. dealer name logo. 14 Vans were produced—The Lemon Tree received 1 Van to be sold to members of the store's Collector's Club; 13 were for dealer Department 56, Inc. sponsored Village Gatherings where the Van was sold:

Bachman's®	#729-3
Bronner's Christmas Wonderland	#737-4
European Imports	#739-0
Fortunoff	#735-8
Lemon Tree	#721-8
Lock, Stock & Barrel	#731-5
North Pole City	#736-6
Robert's Christmas Wonderland	$734-0
Stats	#741-2
The Christmas Dove	#730-7
The Incredible Christmas Place	#732-3
The Limited Edition	#733-1
The Windsor Shoppe	#740-4
William Glen	#738-2

DATE: _____ $ _____
O WISH   O HAVE

MICKEY & MINNIE

ITEM #	INTRO	RETIRED	OSRP	GBTRU	↓
5353-8	1994	1996	$22.50	**$32**	9%

Disney Parks Village™ accessory. Set of 2. Mickey and Minnie characters welcome guests to the Disney Theme Parks.

DATE: _____ $ _____
O WISH   O HAVE

'94	'95	'96	'97	'98
$22.50	22.50	22.50	35	35

DISNEY PARKS FAMILY

ITEM #	INTRO	RETIRED	OSRP	GBTRU	↓
5354-6	1994	1996	$32.50	**$30**	21%

Set of 3. Disney Parks Village™ accessory. Family of seven enjoys a day at a Disney Park. Mom photographs kids in Mouse ears as two others eat ice cream cones. One tot is seated on Dad's shoulders for best view.

DATE: _____ $ _____
O WISH   O HAVE

'94	'95	'96	'97	'98
$32.50	32.50	32.50	35	38

OLDE WORLD ANTIQUES GATE

ITEM #	INTRO	RETIRED	OSRP	GBTRU	↓
5355-4	1994	1996	$15	**$18**	10%

Disney Parks Village™ accessory. Entry gate with wooden door. Brick frames door and is base for wrought iron fencing.

DATE: ___ $ ___
O WISH   O HAVE

'94	'95	'96	'97	'98
$15	15	15	18	20

POLKA FEST

ITEM #	INTRO	RETIRED	OSRP	GBTRU	NO
5607-3	1994	CURRENT	$30	**$30**	CHANGE

Alpine Village Series™ accessory. Set of 3. Musicians play polka as a couple dances. Boy sings and yodels to the music.

DATE: ___ $ ___
O WISH   O HAVE

'94	'95	'96	'97	'98
$30	30	30	30	30

LAST MINUTE DELIVERY

ITEM #	INTRO	RETIRED	OSRP	GBTRU	↑
5636-7	1994	1998	$35	**$40**	14%

North Pole Series™ accessory. Elves hand-power a rail car pulling doll car and teddy car as another elf hangs onto rear bumper.
Notable: Shipping was delayed until 1996 due to production problems.

DATE: ___ $ ___
O WISH   O HAVE

'94	'95	'96	'97	'98
$35	35	35	35	35

SNOW CONE ELVES

ITEM #	INTRO	RETIRED	OSRP	GBTRU	NO
5637-5	1994	1997	$30	**$36**	CHANGE

North Pole Series™ accessory. Set of 4. Elves taste test new batch of snow cones. Cart holds more flavors. Icicles form on snow cone sign.

DATE: ___ $ ___
O WISH   O HAVE

'94	'95	'96	'97	'98
$30	30	30	30	36

Heritage Village Collection® Accessories

OVER THE RIVER AND THROUGH THE WOODS

Item #	Intro	Retired	OSRP	GBTru	↑
5654-5	1994	1998	$35	**$40**	14%

New England Village® accessory. After cutting tree for home, father and kids use horse-drawn sleigh to bring it in. Their dog runs along side.

Date: ____ $ ____
○ Wish ○ Have

'94	'95	'96	'97	'98
$35	35	35	35	35

OLD MAN AND THE SEA, THE

Item #	Intro	Retired	OSRP	GBTru	↑
5655-3	1994	1998	$25	**$38**	52%

New England Village® accessory. Set of 3. Two children listen closely as the man tells stories of the sea. Boy holds telescope.

Date: ____ $ ____
○ Wish ○ Have

'94	'95	'96	'97	'98
$25	25	25	25	25

TWO RIVERS BRIDGE

Item #	Intro	Retired	OSRP	GBTru	↓
5656-1	1994	1997	$35	**$38**	5%

New England Village® accessory. Wooden bridge on 3 sets of pilings spans 2 rivers. Horses, carriages and carts use center. Walkers use side passages. Porcelain and Resin.

Date: ____ $ ____
○ Wish ○ Have

'94	'95	'96	'97	'98
$35	35	35	35	40

WINTER SLEIGHRIDE

Item #	Intro	Retired	OSRP	GBTru	
5825-4	1994	Current	$18	**$18**	NO CHANGE

Dickens' Village Series® accessory. Ice-skating boys give a sleigh ride to a friend. In the proofs, the handle attached to the sleigh with wires that were curled at the ends.

Date: ____ $ ____
○ Wish ○ Have

'94	'95	'96	'97	'98
$18	18	18	18	18

CHELSEA MARKET MISTLE-TOE MONGER & CART

ITEM #	INTRO	RETIRED	OSRP	GBTRU	↑
5826-2	1994	1998	$25	**$35**	40%

Dickens' Village Series® accessory. Set of 2. Vendor sells greens from basket as wife sells from cart.

DATE: ____ $ ____
○ WISH   ○ HAVE

'94	'95	'96	'97	'98
$25	25	25	25	25

CHELSEA MARKET CURIOSITIES MONGER & CART

ITEM #	INTRO	RETIRED	OSRP	GBTRU	↑
5827-0	1994	1998	$27.50	**$36**	31%

Dickens' Village Series® accessory. Set of 2. Vendor stands next to cart playing concertina. He sells everything from toys to clocks to quilts.

DATE: ____ $ ____
○ WISH   ○ HAVE

'94	'95	'96	'97	'98
$27.50	27.50	27.50	27.50	27.50

PORTOBELLO ROAD PEDDLERS

ITEM #	INTRO	RETIRED	OSRP	GBTRU	↑
5828-9	1994	1998	$27.50	**$30**	9%

Dickens' Village Series® accessory. Set of 3. Peddlers sell toys and carol song sheets to passing villagers.

DATE: ____ $ ____
○ WISH   ○ HAVE

'94	'95	'96	'97	'98
$27.50	27.50	27.50	27.50	27.50

THATCHERS

ITEM #	INTRO	RETIRED	OSRP	GBTRU	↓
5829-7	1994	1997	$35	**$36**	5%

Dickens' Village Series® accessory. Set of 3. Workers gather up and place thatch bundles on cart.

DATE: ____ $ ____
○ WISH   ○ HAVE

'94	'95	'96	'97	'98
$35	35	35	35	38

Heritage Village Collection® Accessories 289

A PEACEFUL GLOW ON CHRISTMAS EVE

ITEM #	INTRO	RETIRED	OSRP	GBTRU	NO
5830-0	1994	CURRENT	$30	**$30**	CHANGE

Dickens' Village Series® accessory. Set of 3. Clergyman watches children sell candles for church service.

DATE: _____ $ _____
○ WISH   ○ HAVE

'94	'95	'96	'97	'98
$30	30	30	30	30

CHRISTMAS CAROL HOLIDAY TRIMMING SET

ITEM #	INTRO	RETIRED	OSRP	GBTRU	↓
5831-9	1994	1997	$65	**$65**	10%

Dickens' Village Series® accessory. Set of 21. Holiday trimming set with gate, fence, lamppost, trees, garlands, wreaths, and 3 figurine groupings.

DATE: _____ $ _____
○ WISH   ○ HAVE

'94	'95	'96	'97	'98
$65	65	65	65	72

CHAMBER ORCHESTRA

ITEM #	INTRO	RETIRED	OSRP	GBTRU	↑
5884-0	1994	1998	$37.50	**$40**	7%

Set of 4. Christmas In The City® accessory. Conductor and four musicians play outdoor holiday music concert.

DATE: _____ $ _____
○ WISH   ○ HAVE

'94	'95	'96	'97	'98
$37.50	37.50	37.50	37.50	37.50

HOLIDAY FIELD TRIP

ITEM #	INTRO	RETIRED	OSRP	GBTRU	↑
5885-8	1994	1998	$27.50	**$30**	9%

Set of 3. Christmas In The City® accessory. Five students walk with their teacher as they visit the City sights.

DATE: _____ $ _____
○ WISH   ○ HAVE

'94	'95	'96	'97	'98
$27.50	27.50	27.50	27.50	27.50

HOT DOG VENDOR

ITEM #	INTRO	RETIRED	OSRP	GBTRU	↓
5886-6	1994	1997	$27.50	**$30**	9%

Set of 3. Christmas In The City® accessory. Mother buys hot dog for son from a street vendor.

DATE: _____ $ _____
O WISH O HAVE

'94	'95	'96	'97	'98
$27.50	27.50	27.50	27.50	33

POSTERN

ITEM #	INTRO	RETIRED	OSRP	GBTRU	↓
9871-0	1994	1994 ANNUAL	$17.50	**$21**	22%

Dickens' Village Series® Ten Year Anniversary Piece. Cornerstone with dates. Arched, timbered entry connected to gatehouse. Flag flies at top of arch; Village sign hangs below it. Posterns were entrances to important places or village gathering areas.
Notable: Special commemorative imprint on bottom.

DATE: _____ $ _____
O WISH O HAVE

'94	'95	'96	'97	'98
$17.50	25	25	27	27

PROMOTIONAL VILLAGE EXPRESS VANS

ITEM #	INTRO	RETIRED	OSRP	GBTRU
VARIOUS	1995	PROMO	SEE BELOW	**SEE BELOW**

The Black Village Express Promotional Van design introduced in 1994 was continued in 1995 adding the following special pieces:
1) *St. Nick's Van,* #7560, was produced for St. Nick's in Littleton, CO. This van does not say Department 56, Inc. on the passenger door. Both doors read "1995."
GBTru$: $45
2) *Parkwest Van,* #7522, was produced for the NALED affiliated Parkwest Catalog Group to commemorate their 10th Anniversary. The group has 350 dealers. The panel of the van featured the symbol of a running deer, "Parkwest, 10th Anniversary" was printed below. **GBTru$: $565**
3) *Canadian Van,* #21637, was produced for Canadian dealers and distributed by Millard Lister Sales Ltd. The 10 Canadian Provinces were listed on the van's top rail. One side panel says "On-Time Delivery Since 1976: The Village Express." The other panel has a Red Maple Leaf, Canadian Event 1995. Doors have 1995. SRP was $40. **GBTru$: $32.**

DATE: _____ $ _____
O WISH O HAVE

SQUASH CART

ITEM #	INTRO	RETIRED	OSRP	GBTRU	↓
0753-6	1995	PROMO	$50	**$90**	10%

New England Village® accessory. Green squash are taken to market in horse-drawn burgundy wagon by Bachman's® workers.
Notable: Commemorates 110th Anniversary of Bachman's®. Special bottomstamp. Introduced at the Bachman's® Village Gathering, 1995. See 1995 *Harvest Pumpkin Wagon,* Item #56591, for the Heritage Village Collection® dealers piece with the orange pumpkins in place of green squash.

DATE: ____ $ ____
○ WISH ○ HAVE

'95	'96	'97	'98
$50	95	95	100

BALLOON SELLER

ITEM #	INTRO	RETIRED	OSRP	GBTRU	↓
53539	1995	1996	$25	**$40**	31%

Disney Parks Village™ accessory. Set of 2. Girl buys her brother a helium balloon from park vendor.

DATE: ____ $ ____
○ WISH ○ HAVE

'95	'96	'97	'98
$25	25	55	58

"SILENT NIGHT" MUSIC BOX

ITEM #	INTRO	RETIRED	OSRP	GBTRU	
56180	1995	CURRENT	$32.50	**$32.50**	NO CHANGE

Notable: This, the first music box in the Heritage Village Collection®, commemorates the Christmas song "Silent Night," and debuted at Bronner's Christmas Wonderland, Frankenmuth, MI, a Gold Key Dealer. It is based on Silent Night Memorial Chapel in Oberndorf, Austria. A replica of the Chapel is at Bronner's. Music box was available to all Heritage Village Collection® dealers as of 6/1/96.

DATE: ____ $ ____
○ WISH ○ HAVE

'95	'96	'97	'98
$32.50	32.50	32.50	32.50

"ALPENHORN PLAYER" ALPINE VILLAGE SIGN

ITEM #	INTRO	RETIRED	OSRP	GBTRU	
56182	1995	CURRENT	$20	**$20**	NO CHANGE

Alpine horn player in Tyrollean outfit plays long mountain horn.

DATE: ____ $ ____
○ WISH ○ HAVE

'95	'96	'97	'98
$20	20	20	20

CHARTING SANTA'S COURSE

ITEM #	INTRO	RETIRED	OSRP	GBTRU	↑
56364	1995	1997	$25	**$32**	7%

North Pole Series™ accessory. Set of 2. Elves plan Santa's sleigh ride. One checks skies with telescope as other checks constellation maps with globe of earth.

DATE: _____ $ _____
O WISH   O HAVE

'95	'96	'97	'98
$25	25	25	30

I'LL NEED MORE TOYS

ITEM #	INTRO	RETIRED	OSRP	GBTRU	↑
56365	1995	1998	$25	**$30**	20%

North Pole Series™ accessory. Set of 2. Santa tells elf that more toys are needed from the workshop.

DATE: _____ $ _____
O WISH   O HAVE

'95	'96	'97	'98
$25	25	25	25

"A BUSY ELF" NORTH POLE SIGN

ITEM #	INTRO	RETIRED	OSRP	GBTRU	NO
56366	1995	CURRENT	$20	**$20**	CHANGE

Red bird watches carver elf create village sign. Porcelain and Acrylic.

DATE: _____ $ _____
O WISH   O HAVE

'95	'96	'97	'98
$20	20	20	20

FARM ANIMALS

ITEM #	INTRO	RETIRED	OSRP	GBTRU	NO
56588	1995	CURRENT	$32.50	**$32.50**	CHANGE

New England Village® accessory. Set of 8 with 8 hay bales. Cows, horses, sheep, pig, goat, hen and rooster.

DATE: _____ $ _____
O WISH   O HAVE

'95	'96	'97	'98
$32.50	32.50	32.50	32.50

LOBSTER TRAPPERS

ITEM #	INTRO	RETIRED	OSRP	GBTRU	NO
56589	1995	CURRENT	$35	**$35**	CHANGE

New England Village® accessory. Set of 4. Boat at dock with lobster-filled traps (pots). Boy checks traps and lobsterman holds up a three pounder.

DATE: ____ $ ____
O WISH   O HAVE

'95	'96	'97	'98
$35	35	35	35

LUMBERJACKS

ITEM #	INTRO	RETIRED	OSRP	GBTRU	↑
56590	1995	1998	$30	**$36**	20%

New England Village® accessory. Set of 2. One man chops tree with ax as second worker saws trunk into logs. Porcelain and Wood.

DATE: ____ $ ____
O WISH   O HAVE

'95	'96	'97	'98
$30	30	30	30

HARVEST PUMPKIN WAGON

ITEM #	INTRO	RETIRED	OSRP	GBTRU	NO
56591	1995	CURRENT	$45	**$45**	CHANGE

New England Village® accessory. Farm workers gather pumpkins which are loaded onto green wagon. Driver and helper with horse-drawn wagon.
Notable: Though there are slight color modifications, this piece is based on the Bachman's® 110th Anniversary Squash Cart sold at the Bachman's® Village Gathering in 1995, Item #753-6.

DATE: ____ $ ____
O WISH   O HAVE

'95	'96	'97	'98
$45	45	45	45

"FRESH PAINT" NEW ENGLAND VILLAGE SIGN

ITEM #	INTRO	RETIRED	OSRP	GBTRU	NO
56592	1995	CURRENT	$20	**$20**	CHANGE

Sign maker completes lettering of Village sign.

DATE: ____ $ ____
O WISH   O HAVE

'95	'96	'97	'98
$20	20	20	20

TOWN SQUARE CAROLERS

ITEM #	INTRO	RETIRED	OSRP	GBTRU
5832-7*	1995	1996	*	*

Set of 3. The townspeople celebrate the season with song.
Notable: *This accessory is part of the Dickens' Village
Series® *Start A Tradition Set,* 1996 Item #5832-7. It is not
usually individually available on the secondary market.

DATE: ____ $ ____
O WISH   O HAVE

A PARTRIDGE IN A PEAR TREE—#I

ITEM #	INTRO	RETIRED	OSRP	GBTRU	NO
5835-1	1995	CURRENT	$35	**$35**	CHANGE

Dickens' Village Series® accessory. *The 12 Days Of
Dickens' Village.* Three children dance around tree as a
partridge sits on top.

DATE: ____ $ ____
O WISH   O HAVE

'95	'96	'97	'98
$35	35	35	35

TWO TURTLE DOVES—#II

ITEM #	INTRO	RETIRED	OSRP	GBTRU	NO
5836-0	1995	CURRENT	$32.50	**$32.50**	CHANGE

Dickens' Village Series® accessory. Set of 4. *The 12 Days
Of Dickens' Village.* Woman carries two turtle doves and
boy carries cage. Another woman and daughter watch.

DATE: ____ $ ____
O WISH   O HAVE

'95	'96	'97	'98
$32.50	32.50	32.50	32.50

THREE FRENCH HENS—#III

ITEM #	INTRO	RETIRED	OSRP	GBTRU	NO
58378	1995	CURRENT	$32.50	**$32.50**	CHANGE

Dickens' Village Series® accessory. Set of 3. *The 12 Days
Of Dickens' Village.* Farmyard with water pump, farm
worker collecting eggs, farm worker scattering grain feed
for hen and rooster.

DATE: ____ $ ____
O WISH   O HAVE

'95	'96	'97	'98
$32.50	32.50	32.50	32.50

Heritage Village Collection® Accessories

Four Calling Birds—#IV

Item #	Intro	Retired	OSRP	GBTru	NO
58379	1995	Current	$32.50	**$32.50** CHANGE

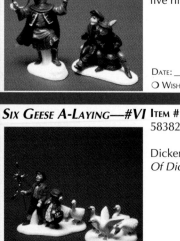

Dickens' Village Series® accessory. Set of 2. *The 12 Days Of Dickens' Village.* Street musicians play violin and bass as birds atop clock respond with song.

DATE: ____ $ ____
O WISH O HAVE

'95	'96	'97	'98
$32.50	32.50	32.50	32.50

Five Golden Rings—#V

Item #	Intro	Retired	OSRP	GBTru	NO
58381	1995	Current	$27.50	**$27.50** CHANGE

Dickens' Village Series® accessory. Set of 2. *The 12 Days Of Dickens' Village.* Townsfolk watch as juggler balances five rings.

DATE: ____ $ ____
O WISH O HAVE

'95	'96	'97	'98
$27.50	27.50	27.50	27.50

Six Geese A-Laying—#VI

Item #	Intro	Retired	OSRP	GBTru	NO
58382	1995	Current	$30	**$30** CHANGE

Dickens' Village Series® accessory. Set of 2. *The 12 Days Of Dickens' Village.* Six geese follow boy and girl.

DATE: ____ $ ____
O WISH O HAVE

'95	'96	'97	'98
$30	30	30	30

Brixton Road Watchman

Item #	Intro	Retired	OSRP	GBTru	NO
58390	1995	Current	$25	**$25** CHANGE

Dickens' Village Series® accessory. Set of 2. Early method of protection and enforcement of village rules and regulations. Watchman gave warnings, assistance and monitored activities. Guard house used for rest and foul weather.

DATE: ____ $ ____
O WISH O HAVE

'95	'96	'97	'98
$25	25	25	25

"TALLYHO!"

ITEM #	INTRO	RETIRED	OSRP	GBTRU	↑
58391	1995	1998	$50	**$58**	16%

Dickens' Village Series® accessory. Set of 5. Country aristocracy ride Hunters for the sport of following scent hounds as they pick up the trail of a fox. Jumping fences and hedges, they ride the countryside guided by the Whipper-in who sounds the tallyho.

DATE: ____ $ ____
O WISH O HAVE

'95	'96	'97	'98
$50	50	50	50

CHELSEA MARKET HAT MONGER & CART

ITEM #	INTRO	RETIRED	OSRP	GBTRU	
58392	1995	CURRENT	$27.50	**$27.50**	NO CHANGE

Dickens' Village Series® accessory. Set of 2. Hat maker seated on trunk holds up hats for sale for every occasion. Apprentice sits on hand cart with cat on lap.

DATE: ____ $ ____
O WISH O HAVE

'95	'96	'97	'98
$27.50	27.50	27.50	27.50

"YE OLDE LAMPLIGHTER" DICKENS' VILLAGE SIGN

ITEM #	INTRO	RETIRED	OSRP	GBTRU	
58393	1995	CURRENT	$20	**$20**	NO CHANGE

Lamplighter reaches up to light lamp wick in lantern on Village sign.

DATE: ____ $ ____
O WISH O HAVE

'95	'96	'97	'98
$20	20	20	20

COBBLER & CLOCK PEDDLER

ITEM #	INTRO	RETIRED	OSRP	GBTRU	
58394	1995	1997	$25	**$28**	NO CHANGE

Dickens' Village Series® accessory. Set of 2. Clock peddler sells and repairs clocks and timepieces while cobbler makes and repairs shoes.
Notable: Though designated as a Dickens' Village Series® accessory, many collectors believe it more appropriately fits the Alpine Village Series™.

DATE: ____ $ ____
O WISH O HAVE

'95	'96	'97	'98
$25	25	25	28

"Yes, Virginia..."

Item #	Intro	Retired	OSRP	GBTru	NO
58890	1995	Current	$12.50	**$12.50**	CHANGE

Christmas In The City® accessory. Set of 2. Young girl speaks to gentleman with close resemblance to Santa Claus. Famous letter to the editor once written by Virginia is remembered every holiday.

Date: ____ $ ____
○ Wish ○ Have

'95	'96	'97	'98
$12.50	12.50	12.50	12.50

One-Man Band & The Dancing Dog

Item #	Intro	Retired	OSRP	GBTru	↑
58891	1995	1998	$17.50	**$26**	49%

Christmas In The City® accessory. Set of 2. Man wears contraption to allow playing of 5 instruments as costumed dog dances to the music.

Date: ____ $ ____
○ Wish ○ Have

'95	'96	'97	'98
$17.50	17.50	17.50	17.50

Choir Boys All-In-A-Row

Item #	Intro	Retired	OSRP	GBTru	↑
58892	1995	1998	$20	**$28**	40%

Christmas In The City® accessory. Choir boys in red, white and gold robes sing Christmas service.

Date: ____ $ ____
○ Wish ○ Have

'95	'96	'97	'98
$20	20	20	20

"A Key To The City" Christmas In The City Sign

Item #	Intro	Retired	OSRP	GBTru	NO
58893	1995	Current	$20	**$20**	CHANGE

Mayor stands at city gate to welcome dignitary and give the key to the city. Porcelain and Metal.

Date: ____ $ ____
○ Wish ○ Have

'95	'96	'97	'98
$20	20	20	20

ELVES ON ICE

ITEM #	INTRO	RETIRED	OSRP	GBTRU	NO
52298	1996	CURRENT	$7.50	**$7.50**	CHANGE

North Pole Series™ accessory. Set of 4. Midyear release. Four skating elves. One skates as he rings bells. One pushes another on skates. One speeds on ice with stocking hat blown by wind. One hatless elf glides along ice. Resin.
Notable: Can be used on the 1994 *Village Animated Skating Pond*, Item #5229-9.

DATE: _____ $ _____
O WISH   O HAVE

'96	'97	'98
$7.50	7.50	7.50

NUTCRACKER VENDOR & CART

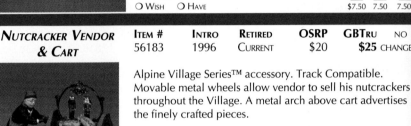

ITEM #	INTRO	RETIRED	OSRP	GBTRU	NO
56183	1996	CURRENT	$20	**$25**	CHANGE

Alpine Village Series™ accessory. Track Compatible. Movable metal wheels allow vendor to sell his nutcrackers throughout the Village. A metal arch above cart advertises the finely crafted pieces.

DATE: _____ $ _____
O WISH   O HAVE

'97	'98
$20	25

NORTH POLE EXPRESS

ITEM #	INTRO	RETIRED	OSRP	GBTRU	NO
56368	1996	CURRENT	$37.50	**$37.50**	CHANGE

North Pole Series™ accessory. Set of 3. Train brings vacationing elves and polar bear home to North Pole. Wood firebox engine, open freight car and passenger car topped with a gift carrier arrive at depot.

DATE: _____ $ _____
O WISH   O HAVE

'97	'98
$37.50	37.50

EARLY RISING ELVES

ITEM #	INTRO	RETIRED	OSRP	GBTRU	NO
56369	1996	CURRENT	$32.50	**$32.50**	CHANGE

North Pole Series™ accessory. Set of 5. Elves dressed in traditional costumes make early bakery deliveries.

DATE: _____ $ _____
O WISH   O HAVE

'97	'98
$32.50	32.50

Heritage Village Collection® Accessories

END OF THE LINE

ITEM #	INTRO	RETIRED	OSRP	GBTRU	NO
56370	1996	CURRENT	$28	**$28**	CHANGE

North Pole Series™ accessory. Set of 2. Elf in ticket booth welcomes home vacationers from Miami. Crate of oranges will fill many stockings with treats.

DATE: ____ $ ____
O WISH O HAVE

'97	'98
$28	28

HOLIDAY DELIVERIES

ITEM #	INTRO	RETIRED	OSRP	GBTRU	NO
56371	1996	CURRENT	$16.50	**$16.50**	CHANGE

North Pole Series™ accessory. Track Compatible. Elf pedals three-wheeled velocipede with rear basket filled with gifts to deliver.

DATE: ____ $ ____
O WISH O HAVE

'97	'98
$16.50	16.50

CANDY CANE ELVES

ITEM #	INTRO	RETIRED	OSRP	GBTRU
56390*	1996	1996	*	*

Set of 2. Two elves prepare candy canes in preparation for the busy season.
Notable: *This accessory is part of the North Pole Series™ *Start A Tradition Set,* 1996 Item #56390. It is not usually individually available on the secondary market.

DATE: ____ $ ____
O WISH O HAVE

A NEW POTBELLIED STOVE FOR CHRISTMAS

ITEM #	INTRO	RETIRED	OSRP	GBTRU	↑
56593	1996	1998	$35	**$40**	14%

New England Village® accessory to go with J. Hudson Stoveworks. Set of 2. Track Compatible. Two men lift a potbellied stove onto a horse-drawn wagon.

DATE: ____ $ ____
O WISH O HAVE

'97	'98
$35	35

CHRISTMAS BAZAAR: HANDMADE QUILTS

ITEM #	INTRO	RETIRED	OSRP	GBTRU	NO
56594	1996	CURRENT	$25	**$25**	CHANGE

New England Village® accessory. Set of 2. Woman holds up a quilt while child admires assortment piled on display table and shelves.

DATE: _____ $ _____
○ WISH ○ HAVE

'97	'98
$25	25

CHRISTMAS BAZAAR: WOOLENS & PRESERVES

ITEM #	INTRO	RETIRED	OSRP	GBTRU	NO
56595	1996	CURRENT	$25	**$25**	CHANGE

New England Village® accessory. Set of 2. Young boy at street stall sells preserves and pies while a woman and child sell knitted woolen items.
Notable: Early shipments read "Jame & Jellies" on the sign.

DATE: _____ $ _____
○ WISH ○ HAVE

'97	'98
$25	25

SEVEN SWANS-A-SWIMMING—#VII

ITEM #	INTRO	RETIRED	OSRP	GBTRU	NO
58383	1996	CURRENT	$27.50	**$27.50**	CHANGE

Dickens' Village Series® accessory. Set of 4. *The 12 Days Of Dickens' Village*. Dickensian couple watch swimming swans.

DATE: _____ $ _____
○ WISH ○ HAVE

'97	'98
$27.50	27.50

EIGHT MAIDS-A-MILKING—#VIII

ITEM #	INTRO	RETIRED	OSRP	GBTRU	NO
58384	1996	CURRENT	$25	**$25**	CHANGE

Dickens' Village Series® accessory. Set of 2. *The 12 Days Of Dickens' Village*. Maid carries milk pails on shoulder yoke after milking the cow.

DATE: _____ $ _____
○ WISH ○ HAVE

'97	'98
$25	25

TENDING THE NEW CALVES

ITEM #	INTRO	RETIRED	OSRP	GBTRU	NO
58395	1996	CURRENT	$30	**$30**	CHANGE

Dickens' Village Series® accessory. Set of 3. Midyear release. Boy leads calf. Girl churns butter from fresh milk. Small building to house young calves.

DATE: _____ $ _____
○ WISH ○ HAVE

'96	'97	'98
$30	30	30

CAROLING WITH THE CRATCHIT FAMILY (REVISITED)

ITEM #	INTRO	RETIRED	OSRP	GBTRU	NO
58396	1996	CURRENT	$37.50	**$37.50**	CHANGE

Dickens' Village Series® accessory. Set of 3. Midyear release. An addition to the *Christmas Carol Revisited Series.* Bob Cratchit pushes sleigh of family carolers as two sons lead the way, one with lantern and the other with songbook.

DATE: _____ $ _____
○ WISH ○ HAVE

'96	'97	'98
$37.50	37.50	37.50

YEOMEN OF THE GUARD

ITEM #	INTRO	RETIRED	OSRP	GBTRU	↓
58397	1996	1997	$30	**$60**	12%

Dickens' Village Series® accessory. Set of 5. Midyear release. Head Warder and Guards that protect royal buildings and residences.

DATE: _____ $ _____
○ WISH ○ HAVE

'96	'97	'98
$30	30	68

FEZZIWIG DELIVERY WAGON, THE (REVISITED)

ITEM #	INTRO	RETIRED	OSRP	GBTRU	NO
58400	1996	CURRENT	$32.50	**$32.50**	CHANGE

Dickens' Village Series® accessory. *Christmas Carol Revisited Series.* Track Compatible. Piece comes with a miniature storybook created and written by designers which sets scene for piece. Metal wheels turn on horse-drawn delivery wagon driven by Mr. Fezziwig.

DATE: _____ $ _____
○ WISH ○ HAVE

'97	'98
$32.50	32.50

RED CHRISTMAS SULKY

Item #	Intro	Retired	OSRP	GBTRU	NO
58401	1996	Current	$30	**$30**	CHANGE

Dickens' Village Series® accessory. Track Compatible. Horse-drawn carriage with two movable metal wheels carries driver and one passenger.

Date: ____ $ ____	'97	'98
○ Wish ○ Have	$30	30

GINGERBREAD VENDOR

Item #	Intro	Retired	OSRP	GBTRU	NO
58402	1996	Current	$22.50	**$22.50**	CHANGE

Dickens' Village Series® accessory. Set of 2. Track Compatible. Vendor sells large baked gingerbread cakes from a sleigh. Boy and girl hold their purchase as they nibble pieces.

Date: ____ $ ____	'97	'98
○ Wish ○ Have	$22.50	22.50

"A CHRISTMAS CAROL" READING BY CHARLES DICKENS

Item #	Intro	Retired	OSRP	GBTRU	NO
58403	1996	Current	$45	**$45**	CHANGE

Dickens' Village Series® accessory. Set of 4. *Christmas Carol Revisited Series.* Dickens reads his *A Christmas Carol* story to spectators in park setting.
Notable: This fewer piece set (than Item #58404) is non-limited and non-numbered. Color palette changes for all pieces except Dickens. Department 56, Inc. logo on bottomstamp.

Date: ____ $ ____	'97	'98
○ Wish ○ Have	$45	45

"A CHRISTMAS CAROL" READING BY CHARLES DICKENS

Item #	Intro	Retired	OSRP	GBTRU	↓
58404	1996	Ltd Ed 42,500	$75	**$115**	21%

Dickens' Village Series® accessory. Set of 7. *Christmas Carol Revisited Series.*
Notable: This limited edition set is based on the 4-piece set by the same name, Item #58403. Additional characters and ornaments make up the difference. The edition number is on the base of platform piece with Crest and Lion Badge of the Charles Dickens Heritage Ltd. Foundation. 6 pieces have Lion decal.

Date: ____ $ ____	'97	'98
○ Wish ○ Have	$75	145

Heritage Village Collection® Accessories | 303

CITY TAXI

ITEM #	INTRO	RETIRED	OSRP	GBTRU	NO
58894	1996	CURRENT	$12.50	**$12.50**	CHANGE

Christmas In The City® accessory. Track Compatible.
Green fender trim on brown cabs with metal wheels. Roof
rack holds packages and holiday tree.

DATE: ____ $ ____
O WISH O HAVE

'97	'98
$12.50	12.50

FAMILY TREE, THE

ITEM #	INTRO	RETIRED	OSRP	GBTRU	NO
58895	1996	CURRENT	$18	**$18**	CHANGE

Christmas In The City® accessory. Track Compatible.
Father pulls sled with evergreen tree as son, daughter and
family pet help bring it home to trim.

DATE: ____ $ ____
O WISH O HAVE

'97	'98
$18	18

GOING HOME FOR THE HOLIDAYS

ITEM #	INTRO	RETIRED	OSRP	GBTRU	NO
58896	1996	CURRENT	$27.50	**$27.50**	CHANGE

Set of 3. Christmas In The City® accessory. Mother, father
and two children carry gifts, family pet, and luggage. Train
porter with other luggage whistles for taxi.

DATE: ____ $ ____
O WISH O HAVE

'97	'98
$27.50	27.50

CHRISTMAS BELLS

ITEM #	INTRO	RETIRED	OSRP	GBTRU	↓
98711	1996	EVENT PIECE	$35	**$40**	20%

Gazebo with boy ringing town bell as one child holds ears
and another watches.
Notable: This is the Department 56, Inc. Homes For The
Holidays, November 1996 Event Piece.

DATE: ____ $ ____
O WISH O HAVE

'96	'97	'98
$35	50	50

	ITEM #	INTRO	RETIRED	OSRP	GBTRU	↓
BACHMAN'S® **WILCOX TRUCK**	8803	1997	PROMO	$29.95	**$60**	20%

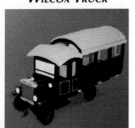

Notable: Replica of a Wilcox truck modeled after a 1919 Wilcox restored by the Bachman family. It was an exclusive created for the 1997 Bachman's® Village Gathering. It was re-issued as *Poinsettia Delivery Truck,* 1998 Item #59000.

DATE: ____ $ ____
O WISH O HAVE

'97	**'98**
$29.95	75

	ITEM #	INTRO	RETIRED	OSRP	GBTRU	↓
HOLLY & THE IVY, THE	56100	1997	EVENT PIECE	$17.50	**$20**	20%

Set of 2. Midyear release.
Notable: This was the Department 56, Inc. Homes For The Holiday, November 1997 Event Piece.

DATE: ____ $ ____
O WISH O HAVE

'97	**'98**
$17.50	25

	ITEM #	INTRO	RETIRED	OSRP	GBTRU	NO
A NEW BATCH OF **CHRISTMAS FRIENDS**	56175	1997	CURRENT	$27.50	**$27.50**	CHANGE

Alpine Village Series™ accessory. Set of 3. Midyear release. St. Bernard pup plays with little girl. Lederhosen dressed boy pulls pups on a sled.

DATE: ____ $ ____
O WISH O HAVE

'97	**'98**
$27.50	27.50

	ITEM #	INTRO	RETIRED	OSRP	GBTRU	NO
HEIDI & HER GOATS	56201	1997	CURRENT	$30	**$30**	CHANGE

Alpine Village Series™ accessory. Set of 4. Grandpa and Peter join Heidi and her goats. Characters, in traditional Alpine dress, based on a favorite children's book.

DATE: ____ $ ____
O WISH O HAVE

'98
$30

Heritage Village Collection® Accessories **305**

DON'T BREAK THE ORNAMENTS

ITEM #	INTRO	RETIRED	OSRP	GBTRU	NO
56372	1997	CURRENT	$27.50	**$27.50**	CHANGE

North Pole Series™ accessory. Set of 2. Elves carefully hang ornaments on display boughs.

DATE: ____ $ ____
○ WISH   ○ HAVE

'98
$27.50

DELIVERING THE CHRISTMAS GREENS

ITEM #	INTRO	RETIRED	OSRP	GBTRU	NO
56373	1997	CURRENT	$27.50	**$27.50**	CHANGE

North Pole Series™ accessory. Set of 2. Mrs. Santa sets plants on delivery tray so elves can deliver for the holidays.

DATE: ____ $ ____
○ WISH   ○ HAVE

'98
$27.50

UNTANGLE THE CHRISTMAS LIGHTS

ITEM #	INTRO	RETIRED	OSRP	GBTRU	NO
56374	1997	CURRENT	$35	**$35**	CHANGE

North Pole Series™ accessory. Elves check string of lights to make sure they are tangle-free.

DATE: ____ $ ____
○ WISH   ○ HAVE

'98
$35

CHRISTMAS BAZAAR ... FLAPJACKS & HOT CIDER

ITEM #	INTRO	RETIRED	OSRP	GBTRU	NO
56596	1997	CURRENT	$27.50	**$27.50**	CHANGE

New England Village® accessory. Set of 2. Just the treat for a cold wintry day, flapjacks plus a hot drink. Uniquely American, the griddlecake, johnnycake, hotcake, pancake or flapjack, is a popular food item that is fast and easy to make.

DATE: ____ $ ____
○ WISH   ○ HAVE

'98
$27.50

CHRISTMAS BAZAAR ... TOY VENDOR & CART

ITEM #	INTRO	RETIRED	OSRP	GBTRU	
56597	1997	CURRENT	$27.50	$27.50	NO CHANGE

New England Village® accessory. Set of 2. Children check out and choose toys and games sold by vendor from his wheeled cart.

DATE: ____ $ ____
O WISH O HAVE

'98
$27.50

CHRISTMAS BAZAAR ... SIGN

ITEM #	INTRO	RETIRED	OSRP	GBTRU	
56598	1997	CURRENT	$16	$16	NO CHANGE

New England Village® accessory. Set of 2. Handcrafted sign announces the street market is present and open for business.

DATE: ____ $ ____
O WISH O HAVE

'98
$16

TAPPING THE MAPLES

ITEM #	INTRO	RETIRED	OSRP	GBTRU	
56599	1997	CURRENT	$75	$75	NO CHANGE

New England Village® accessory. Set of 7. Taught by the Native Americans, early colonists learned to tap maple trees for the precious, sweet, syrupy treat. This set shows all phases of tapping and collecting the sap.

DATE: ____ $ ____
O WISH O HAVE

'98
$75

MANCHESTER SQUARE ACCESSORY SET

ITEM #	INTRO	RETIRED	OSRP	GBTRU
58301*	1997	CURRENT	*	*

Set of 7.
Notable: *This accessory is part of the Dickens' Village Series® *Manchester Square*, 1997 Item #58301. It is not usually individually available on the secondary market.

DATE: ____ $ ____
O WISH O HAVE

Heritage Village Collection® Accessories 307

SPIRIT OF GIVING, THE

ITEM #	INTRO	RETIRED	OSRP	GBTRU
58322*	1997	1998	*	*

Set of 3. A young lady and girl give baskets of food for the poor to the Rector.
Notable: *This accessory is part of the Dickens' Village Series® *Start A Tradition Set,* 1997 Item #58322. It is not usually individually available on the secondary market.

DATE: _____ $ _____
◯ WISH ◯ HAVE

DELIVERING COAL FOR THE HEARTH

ITEM #	INTRO	RETIRED	OSRP	GBTRU	NO
58326	1997	CURRENT	$32.50	$32.50	CHANGE

Dickens' Village Series® accessory. Set of 2. Midyear release. Horse-drawn coal cart comes with a small package of coal. Hanging from the rear is a coal scuttle. Coal merchant with broom and another scuttle completes set.
Notable: First shipments had maroon wheels and the coal buckets were attached permanently with silver hoops. The carts in subsequent shipments have red wheels and the buckets are hung on hooks.

DATE: _____ $ _____
◯ WISH ◯ HAVE

'97	'98
$32.50	32.50

NINE LADIES DANCING—#IX

ITEM #	INTRO	RETIRED	OSRP	GBTRU	NO
58385	1997	CURRENT	$30	$30	CHANGE

Dickens' Village Series® accessory. Set of 2. *The 12 Days Of Dickens' Village.* Girls dance as a young boy plays a tune.

DATE: _____ $ _____
◯ WISH ◯ HAVE

'98
$30

TEN PIPERS PIPING—#X

ITEM #	INTRO	RETIRED	OSRP	GBTRU	NO
58386	1997	CURRENT	$30	$30	CHANGE

Dickens' Village Series® accessory. Set of 3. *The 12 Days Of Dickens' Village.* Men playing the bagpipes led by a drum major.

DATE: _____ $ _____
◯ WISH ◯ HAVE

'98
$30

The Twelve Days Of Christmas
The Rhyme And Reason Of It All

Since the introduction of the ninth and tenth sets in the Twelve Days of Dickens' Village Series many collectors have asked me if Department 56, Inc. made a mistake. It seems that many of them were expecting Ten Lords-A-Leaping instead of Ten Pipers Piping, Department 56, Inc.'s version. Is it a mistake? Not necessarily.

Interestingly, there are various versions of this aged rhyme. According to Leigh Grant, author of *Twelve Days of Christmas, A Celebration and History*, there are three French versions, a Scottish version, and an English one. Though the French versions are thought to be the oldest, the rhyme was first published in England in 1780 in *Mirth Without Mischief*. Here it's used as a child's memory-and-forfeit game where one child begins and others add to it, then repeat all verses. If a child forgets or skips a verse, that child must forfeit something of "value" such as a kiss or sweet.

In her book, Ms. Grant explains the origin of the twelve **the Village Chronicle.** themes. For instance, the partridge—the most often mentioned subject in the rhyme—wasn't brought to England until 1770, yet the verse predates that. This is further proof that the rhyme originated in France.

Four calling birds, you say. Actually four colly birds—black birds. Did you ever notice that the first four items are birds, the fifth is jewelry, and the sixth and seventh are birds again? Not quite. The five golden rings aren't the 18 or 24 karat variety. They are, in fact, a reference to five "gold" ring-necked pheasants.

In her book, Ms. Grant agrees with Department 56, Inc. that there should be Ten Pipers Piping. But she differs with a common version we sing today as well as Department 56, Inc. on numbers nine, eleven, and twelve. She cites Nine Drummers Drumming, Eleven Ladies Dancing, and Twelve Lords-A-Leaping. This demonstrates that Department 56, Inc. was not wrong when it designed its porcelain version of the rhyme.

The book, published by Harry N. Abrams, Inc. of New York, is well illustrated and a fine insight to the background of one of the world's most recognized holiday songs. It's available at amazon.com as well as other book sellers.

How They Compare

Today's Commonly Sung Version	Department 56®'s Porcelain Version	Twelve Days Of Christmas, A Celebration And History, by Leigh Grant
A Partridge in a Pear Tree	A Partridge in a Pear Tree	A Partridge in a Pear Tree
Two Turtle Doves	Two Turtle Doves	Two Turtle Doves
Three French Hens	Three French Hens	Three French Hens
Four Calling Birds	Four Calling Birds	Four Calling Birds
Five Golden Rings	Five Golden Rings	Five Gold Rings
Six Geese-A-Laying	Six Geese-A-Laying	Six Geese-A-Laying
Seven Swans-A-Swimming	Seven Swans-A-Swimming	Seven Swans-A-Swimming
Eight Maids-A-Milking	Eight Maids-A-Milking	Eight Maids-A-Milking
Nine Ladies Dancing	Nine Ladies Dancing	Nine Drummers Drumming
Ten Lords-A-Leaping	Ten Pipers Piping	Ten Pipers Piping
Eleven Pipers Piping	Eleven Lords-A-Leaping	Eleven Ladies Dancing
Twelve Drummers Drumming	Twelve Drummers Drumming	Twelve Lords-A-Leaping

	ITEM #	INTRO	RETIRED	OSRP	GBTRU	
ASHLEY POND SKATING PARTY	58405	1997	CURRENT	$70	**$70**	NO CHANGE

Dickens' Village Series® accessory. Set of 6. Ladies, gentlemen, family groups and children skate on the local frozen pond using old-fashioned long blade skates. Small warming house.

DATE: _____ $ _____
O WISH   O HAVE

'98
$70

	ITEM #	INTRO	RETIRED	OSRP	GBTRU	
FIRE BRIGADE OF LONDON TOWN, THE	58406	1997	CURRENT	$70	**$70**	NO CHANGE

Dickens' Village Series® accessory. Set of 5. Horses pull wheeled water tank pumper. Men pull hose cart and carry buckets and axes. One man sounds horn to clear the roadway.

DATE: _____ $ _____
O WISH   O HAVE

'98
$70

	ITEM #	INTRO	RETIRED	OSRP	GBTRU	
FATHER CHRISTMAS'S JOURNEY	58407	1997	CURRENT	$30	**$30**	NO CHANGE

Dickens' Village Series® accessory. Set of 2. Track Compatible. Santa pulls a colorful old-fashioned sleigh with toys, trinkets and ornaments.
Notable: First Santa representation for the Dickens' Village Series®. A variation of this was produced for North Pole City of Oklahoma as a 1998 promotional piece that has a **GBTru$ of $40**.

DATE: _____ $ _____
O WISH   O HAVE

'98
$30

	ITEM #	INTRO	RETIRED	OSRP	GBTRU	
CHRISTMAS PUDDING COSTERMONGER	58408	1997	CURRENT	$32.50	**$32.50**	NO CHANGE

Dickens' Village Series® accessory. Set of 3. Festive seasonal booth sells holiday dinner treats. Family chooses a Plum Pudding for Christmas dinner.

DATE: _____ $ _____
O WISH   O HAVE

'98
$32.50

STEPPIN' OUT ON THE TOWN

ITEM #	INTRO	RETIRED	OSRP	GBTRU	NO
58885	1997	CURRENT	$35	$35	CHANGE

Christmas In The City® accessory. Set of 5. Midyear release. Track Compatible. Doorman stands by limo that transports a couple in evening clothes ready for an evening on the town. Musicians hurry to the nightclub to take their places on the bandstand.

DATE: ____ $ ____
O WISH   O HAVE

'97	'98
$35	35

JOHNSON'S GROCERY... HOLIDAY DELIVERIES

ITEM #	INTRO	RETIRED	OSRP	GBTRU	NO
58897	1997	CURRENT	$18	$18	CHANGE

Christmas In The City® accessory. Track Compatible. Delivery man pedals a three-wheeled cart bringing holiday treats to shoppers' homes.

DATE: ____ $ ____
O WISH   O HAVE

'98
$18

SPIRIT OF THE SEASON

ITEM #	INTRO	RETIRED	OSRP	GBTRU	NO
58898	1997	CURRENT	$20	$20	CHANGE

Christmas In The City® accessory. Winged Angel statue captures the spirit of the holiday. Pigeons rest on the base.

DATE: ____ $ ____
O WISH   O HAVE

'98
$20

LET'S GO SHOPPING IN THE CITY

ITEM #	INTRO	RETIRED	OSRP	GBTRU	NO
58899	1997	CURRENT	$35	$35	CHANGE

Set of 3. Christmas In The City® accessory. Women shopping, Grandmother and grandson, and two girls with baby carriage.

DATE: ____ $ ____
O WISH   O HAVE

'98
$35

BIG SMILE FOR THE CAMERA

ITEM #	INTRO	RETIRED	OSRP	GBTRU	NO
58900	1997	CURRENT	$27.50	**$27.50**	CHANGE

Christmas In The City® accessory. Set of 2. Photographer gets ready to take picture of celebrity signing girl's autograph book.

DATE: _____ $ _____
O WISH   O HAVE

'98
$27.50

POINSETTIA DELIVERY TRUCK

ITEM #	INTRO	RETIRED	OSRP	GBTRU	NO
59000	1997	CURRENT	$32.50	**$32.50**	CHANGE

Old-fashioned wood paneled truck with roll-up canvas top delivers holiday flowers.
Notable: A variation of this truck was produced in 1998 as a promotional piece for William Glen of California. Its **GBTru$ is $50.**

DATE: _____ $ _____
O WISH   O HAVE

'98
$32.50

OUR OWN VILLAGE PARK BENCH

ITEM #	INTRO	RETIRED	OSRP	GBTRU
VARIOUS	1998	PROMO	$10	**$12**

Notable: This back of the bench was customized with the store's name on it and used as a promotional piece. It was also sold without any name printed on it.

photo not available

DATE: _____ $ _____
O WISH   O HAVE

TENDING THE COLD FRAME

ITEM #	INTRO	RETIRED	OSRP	GBTRU	↑
2208	1998	PROMO	$35	**$60**	71%

Set of 3. Henry and Hattie Bachman are seen with several of their children. The children care for young plants in a cold frame–a makeshift greenhouse made from window frames. Tiny plants can be seen. Cold frame has working hinges and metal lid.
Notable: Created for Bachman's® Village Gathering. It was re-issued as the 1998 *Tending the Cold Frame,* Item #58416.

DATE: _____ $ _____
O WISH   O HAVE

'98
$35

LORD & TAYLOR DELIVERY WAGON	ITEM # 7880	INTRO 1998	RETIRED PROMO	OSRP $32.50	GBTRU $95	↑ 192%

Notable: This wagon, produced as a promotional piece exclusively for the Lord & Taylor department stores, is a variation of *The Fezziwig Delivery Wagon*, 1996 Item #58400.

photo not available

DATE: ____ $ ____
○ WISH   ○ HAVE

'98
$32.50

PEPPERMINT SKATING PARTY

ITEM # 56363	INTRO 1998	RETIRED CURRENT	OSRP $64	GBTRU $64	NO CHANGE

North Pole Series™ accessory. Set of 6. Skating party consists of Mr. and Mrs. Claus, elves and a fallen-down reindeer. Warming hut helps take out the chill of winter. The weathervane always points to the North.

DATE: ____ $ ____
○ WISH   ○ HAVE

'98
$64

SEA CAPTAIN & HIS MATES

ITEM # 56587	INTRO 1998	RETIRED CURRENT	OSRP $32.50	GBTRU $32.50	NO CHANGE

New England Village® accessory. Set of 4. Captain and crew from the Emily Louise sailing ship. Girl holds ship in bottle and boy sails toy boat tied to a tiny rope.

DATE: ____ $ ____
○ WISH   ○ HAVE

'98
$32.50

CHRISTMAS APPLES

ITEM # 58308*	INTRO 1998	RETIRED EVENT G/S ACC.	OSRP *	GBTRU *

Set of 3. This set includes a boy, girl, and an apple seller. **Notable:** *This accessory is part of the Dickens' Village Series® *Seton Morris Spice Merchant Gift Set*, 1998 Item #58308. It is not usually individually available on the secondary market.

DATE: ____ $ ____
○ WISH   ○ HAVE

5¢ PONY RIDES

ITEM #	INTRO	RETIRED	OSRP	GBTRU
58871*	1998	Event G/S Acc.	*	*

Set of 3. A mother and child get a closer look while another child approaches the pony ride.
Notable: *This accessory is part of the Christmas In The City® *Scottie's Toy Shop*, 1998 Item #58871. It is not usually individually available on the secondary market.

DATE: _____ $ _____
○ WISH ○ HAVE

LOADING THE SLEIGH

ITEM #	INTRO	RETIRED	OSRP	GBTRU
52732	1998	Current	$125	**$125**

North Pole Series™ accessory. Set of 6. This animated handcar with track features elves bringing toys from the factory to an awaiting sleigh.

DATE: _____ $ _____
○ WISH ○ HAVE

PAINTING OUR OWN VILLAGE SIGN

ITEM #	INTRO	RETIRED	OSRP	GBTRU
55501	1998	Promo	$12.50	**$12.50**

Notable: This accessory was customized with the store's name on it and used as a promotional piece.

DATE: _____ $ _____
○ WISH ○ HAVE

STARS AND STRIPES FOREVER

ITEM #	INTRO	RETIRED	OSRP	GBTRU
55502	1998	Event Piece	$50	**$50**

Notable: Plays "Stars And Stripes Forever." Second music box in the Heritage Village Collection®, available during the 1999 July event.

photo not available

DATE: _____ $ _____
○ WISH ○ HAVE

TREKKING IN THE SNOW

ITEM #	INTRO	RETIRED	OSRP	GBTRU
56202	1998	CURRENT	$27.50	**$27.50**

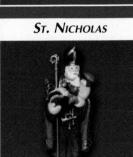

Alpine Village Series™ accessory. Set of 3. Two snowshoers and a skier make their way across the snow-covered fields.

DATE: _____ $ _____
O WISH   O HAVE

ST. NICHOLAS

ITEM #	INTRO	RETIRED	OSRP	GBTRU
56203	1998	CURRENT	$12	**$12**

Alpine Village Series™ accessory. This colorful rendition of the patron saint of children includes a metal staff and sisal tree.

DATE: _____ $ _____
O WISH   O HAVE

WELCOME TO ELF LAND GATEWAY ENTRANCE

ITEM #	INTRO	RETIRED	OSRP	GBTRU
56431	1998	CURRENT	$35	**$35**

Elf Land accessory. Elf Land. The official gateway to Elf Land has three peaks with bells on top.

DATE: _____ $ _____
O WISH   O HAVE

CHRISTMAS FUN RUN

ITEM #	INTRO	RETIRED	OSRP	GBTRU
56434	1998	CURRENT	$35	**$35**

North Pole Series™ accessory. Set of 6. Three elves are resting as two elves are racing towards the Fun Run banner.

DATE: _____ $ _____
O WISH   O HAVE

DELIVERING REAL PLASTIC SNOW

Item #	Intro	Retired	OSRP	GBTru
56435	1998	Current	$17	**$17**

North Pole Series™ accessory. A single elf pushes a hand-truck carrying two boxes of Department 56® Real Plastic Snow.

Date: ____ $ ____
○ Wish ○ Have

REINDEER TRAINING CAMP

Item #	Intro	Retired	OSRP	GBTru
56436	1998	Current	$27.50	**$27.50**

North Pole Series™ accessory. Set of 2. An instructor elf offers advice to two reindeer as another instructor praises a reindeer that just left the ground.

Date: ____ $ ____
○ Wish ○ Have

HAVE A SEAT ELVES

Item #	Intro	Retired	OSRP	GBTru
56437	1998	Current	$30	**$30**

North Pole Series™ accessory. Set of 6. Two female elves are busy talking while one elf is sleeping. Two more elves are looking over another elf's shoulder as he reads the *Glazier Gazette* newspaper.

Date: ____ $ ____
○ Wish ○ Have

DASH AWAY DELIVERY

Item #	Intro	Retired	OSRP	GBTru
56438	1998	Current	$40	**$40**

North Pole Series™ accessory. Elf in hot air balloon laden with toys prepares to lift off while two elves release the mooring line.

Date: ____ $ ____
○ Wish ○ Have

DOWNHILL ELVES

ITEM #	INTRO	RETIRED	OSRP	GBTRU
56439	1998	CURRENT	$9	**$9**

North Pole Series™ accessory. Set of 2.
Notable: These elves could be used as alternate pieces on
the 1997 *Village Animated Sledding Hill,* Item #52645.

DATE: _____ $ _____
O WISH   O HAVE

LOAD UP THE WAGON

ITEM #	INTRO	RETIRED	OSRP	GBTRU
56630	1998	CURRENT	$40	**$40**

New England Village® accessory. Set of 2. A farmer loads
up the wagon before heading to market. Actual wood is
used for the logs.

DATE: _____ $ _____
O WISH   O HAVE

UNDER THE MISTLETOE

ITEM #	INTRO	RETIRED	OSRP	GBTRU
56631	1998	CURRENT	$16.50	**$16.50**

New England Village® accessory. A couple celebrates the
season with a kiss.

DATE: _____ $ _____
O WISH   O HAVE

FLY-CASTING IN THE BROOK

ITEM #	INTRO	RETIRED	OSRP	GBTRU
56633	1998	CURRENT	$15	**$15**

New England Village® accessory. This angler's rod has a
porcelain reel and handle and a fishing line made of thin
wire.

DATE: _____ $ _____
O WISH   O HAVE

Heritage Village Collection® Accessories

VOLUNTEER FIREFIGHTERS	**ITEM #** 56635	**INTRO** 1998	**RETIRED** CURRENT	**OSRP** $37.50	**GBTRU** **$37.50**

New England Village® accessory. Set of 2. Two people work a hand pumper as three others pass water buckets.

DATE: _____ $ _____
○ WISH   ○ HAVE

FARMER'S MARKET	**ITEM #** 56637	**INTRO** 1998	**RETIRED** CURRENT	**OSRP** $55	**GBTRU** **$55**

New England Village® accessory. Set of 2. A farmer offers produce, cider, butter, and other goods for sale at this roadside stand.

DATE: _____ $ _____
○ WISH   ○ HAVE

AN ARTIST'S TOUCH	**ITEM #** 56638	**INTRO** 1998	**RETIRED** CURRENT	**OSRP** $17	**GBTRU** **$17**

New England Village® accessory. A man paints a summer scene. The "canvas" is made of porcelain with a decal, and the easel is metal.

DATE: _____ $ _____
○ WISH   ○ HAVE

HERE WE COME A-WASSAILING	**ITEM #** 58410	**INTRO** 1998	**RETIRED** CURRENT	**OSRP** $45	**GBTRU** **$45**

Dickens' Village Series® accessory. Set of 5. Eight characters dress in festive attire to celebrate the holiday season.

DATE: _____ $ _____
○ WISH   ○ HAVE

SITTING IN CAMDEN PARK

ITEM #	INTRO	RETIRED	OSRP	GBTRU
58411	1998	CURRENT	$35	**$35**

Dickens' Village Series® accessory. Set of 4. The first sitting characters for Dickens' Village, a family of seven and their dog relax as the day goes by.

DATE: _____ $ _____
O WISH   O HAVE

ELEVEN LORDS A-LEAPING—XI

ITEM #	INTRO	RETIRED	OSRP	GBTRU
58413	1998	CURRENT	$27.50	**$27.50**

Dickens' Village Series® accessory. Set of 3. *The 12 Days Of Dickens' Village.* Man on horse leaps a hedge.

DATE: _____ $ _____
O WISH   O HAVE

UNTIL WE MEET AGAIN

ITEM #	INTRO	RETIRED	OSRP	GBTRU
58414	1998	CURRENT	$27.50	**$27.50**

Dickens' Village Series® accessory. Set of 2. A gentleman offers a farewell gift to a lady as she prepares to leave on a voyage.

DATE: _____ $ _____
O WISH   O HAVE

CHILD'S PLAY

ITEM #	INTRO	RETIRED	OSRP	GBTRU
58415	1998	CURRENT	$25	**$25**

Dickens' Village Series® accessory. Set of 2. Two children bat their hoops along as another waits his turn.

DATE: _____ $ _____
O WISH   O HAVE

TENDING THE COLD FRAME

ITEM #	INTRO	RETIRED	OSRP	GBTRU
58416	1998	CURRENT	$32.50	**$32.50**

Dickens' Village Series® accessory. Set of 3.
Notable: Like the Bachman's® *Tending The Cold Frame*, Item #2208, that was available at the 1998 Bachman's® Village Gathering, this includes a cold frame with working hinges and metal lid.

DATE: _____ $ _____
○ WISH   ○ HAVE

ALE MATES

ITEM #	INTRO	RETIRED	OSRP	GBTRU
58417	1998	CURRENT	$25	**$25**

Dickens' Village Series® accessory. Set of 2. One man carries a keg of King's Ale as his companion leans on another while drinking a pint.

DATE: _____ $ _____
○ WISH   ○ HAVE

A CARRIAGE RIDE FOR THE BRIDE

ITEM #	INTRO	RETIRED	OSRP	GBTRU
58901	1998	CURRENT	$40	**$40**

Christmas In The City® accessory. Track Compatible. A bride and groom are whisked away after tying the knot.

DATE: _____ $ _____
○ WISH   ○ HAVE

TO PROTECT AND TO SERVE

ITEM #	INTRO	RETIRED	OSRP	GBTRU
58902	1998	CURRENT	$32.50	**$32.50**

Christmas In The City® accessory. Set of 3. One officer looks on as another speaks to a little girl. A mounted officer pauses so a mother and toddler can pet his horse.

DATE: _____ $ _____
○ WISH   ○ HAVE

CITY POLICE CAR

ITEM #	INTRO	RETIRED	OSRP	GBTRU
58903	1998	CURRENT	$16.50	**$16.50**

Christmas In The City® accessory.
Notable: With its battery-operated beacon, it's the first animated accessory for Christmas In The City®.

DATE: _____ $ _____
O WISH   O HAVE

1919 FORD® MODEL-T

ITEM #	INTRO	RETIRED	OSRP	GBTRU
58906	1998	CURRENT	$20	**$20**

Christmas In The City® accessory. A replica of the famous Ford® Model-T.
Notable: One of the first two licensed pieces for Christmas In The City®.

DATE: _____ $ _____
O WISH   O HAVE

READY FOR THE ROAD

ITEM #	INTRO	RETIRED	OSRP	GBTRU
58907	1998	CURRENT	$20	**$20**

Christmas In The City® accessory. Featuring a rider on a Harley-Davidson®.
Notable: One of the first two licensed pieces in Christmas In The City®.

DATE: _____ $ _____
O WISH   O HAVE

NOTES: _____
_____
_____
_____
_____
_____

Heritage Village Collection® Accessories

Item#	Name	Intro	Retired	OSRP$	GBTru$	Wish	Have	Date	Qty	Paid Each	Total
	SEASONS BAY™										
53300	Grandview Shores Hotel	1998	Current	150	150	O	O				
53301	Bay Street Shops	1998	Current	135	135	O	O				
53302	Chapel On The Hill	1998	Current	72	72	O	O				
53303	Side Porch Café	1998	Current	50	50	O	O				
53304	Inglenook Cottage #5	1998	Current	60	60	O	O				
53305	Grand Creamery, The	1998	Current	60	60	O	O				
			SB Totals:	527.00	527.00						
	SEASONS BAY™ ACCESSORIES										
53307	Relaxing In A Garden	1998	Current	25	25	O	O				
53308	A Stroll In The Park	1998	Current	25	25	O	O				
53309	I'm Wishing	1998	Current	13	13	O	O				
53311	Sunday Morning At The Chapel	1998	Current	17	17	O	O				
53313	Fishing In The Bay	1998	Current	13	13	O	O				
53314	Here Comes The Ice Cream Man	1998	Current	35	35	O	O				
53317	4th Of July Parade	1998	Current	32.50	32.50	O	O				
53319	Trick Or Treat	1998	Current	25	25	O	O				
53320	Back From The Orchard	1998	Current	27.50	27.50	O	O				
53322	Afternoon Sleigh Ride	1998	Current	27.50	27.50	O	O				
53323	Fun In The Snow	1998	Current	15	15	O	O				
53324	Skating On The Pond	1998	Current	20	20	O	O				
53326	A Day At The Waterfront	1998	Current	20	20	O	O				
53327	Garden Cart, The	1998	Current	27.50	27.50	O	O				
			SBA Totals:	323.00	323.00						

Item#	Name	Intro	Retired	OSRP$	GBTru$	Wish	Have	Date	Qty	Paid Each	Total
	SEASONS BAY™ GENERAL ACCESSORIES (ITEMIZED HERE, NOT INCLUDED IN THE LISTINGS.)										
52763	Mini Sisal Evergreens	1998	Current	13	13	○	○				
53330	Garden Fountain	1998	Current	40	40	○	○				
53331	Potted Flowers	1998	Current	12.50	12.50	○	○				
53332	Flowering Potted Tree	1998	Current	20	20	○	○				
53333	Garden Park Bench	1998	Current	12	12	○	○				
53334	Planter Box Topiaries	1998	Current	15	15	○	○				
53337	Leafy Tree	1998	Current	25	25	○	○				
53338	Garden Gazebo	1998	Current	15	15	○	○				
53343	Seasons Bay Sign	1998	Current	10	10	○	○				
53344	Flowering Vine	1998	Current	20	20	○	○				
53345	Geranium Window Box	1998	Current	12	12	○	○				
53355	Beach Front	1998	Current	15	15	○	○				
53366	Park Street Lights	1998	Current	15	15	○	○				
53370	Potted Topiaries	1998	Current	15	15	○	○				
53374	Beach Front Extensions	1998	Current	15	15	○	○				
53375	Stone Foot Path Sections	1998	Current	15	15	○	○				
53376	Lattice Obelisk	1998	Current	8.50	8.50	○	○				
53377	Ivy Vine	1998	Current	7.50	7.50	○	○				
53380	Lawn	1998	Current	N/A	N/A	○	○				
53381	Grassy Ground Cover	1998	Current	N/A	N/A	○	○				
53382	Spring/Summer Trees	1998	Current	24	24	○	○				
53383	Autumn Trees	1998	Current	24	24	○	○				
53384	Winter Trees	1998	Current	24	24	○	○				
			SBGA Totals:	357.50	357.50						

SB Totals: 527.00   527.00
SBA Totals: 323.00   323.00
SBGA Totals: 357.50   357.50

SB Grand Totals: 1,207.50   1,207.50

GRANDVIEW SHORES HOTEL

ITEM #	INTRO	RETIRED	OSRP	GBTRU
53300	1998	CURRENT	$150	**$150**

Notable: The First Edition of this building features two gold flags, a weathervane, and a First Edition decal on its bottom. The regular production building, Item #53400, has different color flags, no weathervane and no decal.

DATE: ____ $ ____
○ WISH   ○ HAVE

BAY STREET SHOPS

ITEM #	INTRO	RETIRED	OSRP	GBTRU
53301	1998	CURRENT	$135	**$135**

Set of 2.
Notable: The First Edition of this building features two gold flags, four small gold flags, and a First Edition decal on its bottom. The regular production building, Item #53401, has different color flags, no weathervane and no decal.

DATE: ____ $ ____
○ WISH   ○ HAVE

CHAPEL ON THE HILL

ITEM #	INTRO	RETIRED	OSRP	GBTRU
53302	1998	CURRENT	$72	**$72**

Notable: The First Edition of this building features a gold cross and a First Edition decal on its bottom. The regular production building, Item #53402, does not have a gold cross or a decal.

DATE: ____ $ ____
○ WISH   ○ HAVE

SIDE PORCH CAFÉ

ITEM #	INTRO	RETIRED	OSRP	GBTRU
53303	1998	CURRENT	$50	**$50**

Notable: The First Edition of this building has a First Edition decal on its bottom. The regular production building, Item #53403, does not have a decal.

DATE: ____ $ ____
○ WISH   ○ HAVE

Seasons Bay™

INGLENOOK COTTAGE #5

ITEM #	INTRO	RETIRED	OSRP	GBTRU
53304	1998	CURRENT	$60	**$60**

Notable: The First Edition of this building has a First Edition decal on its bottom. The regular production building, Item #53404, does not have a decal.

DATE: ____ $ ____
○ WISH   ○ HAVE

GRAND CREAMERY, THE

ITEM #	INTRO	RETIRED	OSRP	GBTRU
53305	1998	CURRENT	$60	**$60**

Notable: The First Edition of this building features a gold flag and a First Edition decal on its bottom. The regular production building, Item #53405, has a different color flag and no decal.

DATE: ____ $ ____
○ WISH   ○ HAVE

Meet Dennis Brose
An Interview With The Seasons Bay™ Designer

Many collectors are intrigued by Seasons Bay™, Department 56, Inc.'s newest village. I wrote about the unique aspects of the Village in the January/February '99 issue of *the Village Chronicle*.

These included the fact that there is no snow on the porcelain buildings, that the accessories are pewter and represent all four seasons, and that the buildings are lit from the bottom.

I believe, however, that there is no better way to get the "feel" of the new village than to speak to the person who created it. With that in mind, I would like to present Dennis Brose.

Peter: "What is your designing background?"
Dennis: "Though my background is business related, architecture has been a passion for as long as I remember, particularly historic and traditional architecture."

Peter: "How did your relationship with Department 56, Inc. develop?"
Dennis: "In early December 1995, I watched a profile of Department 56, Inc. on the evening news. Though I was vaguely familiar with the miniature building industry, I had no idea of the magnitude of interest in this "art form." The enthusiasm generated

Continued page 326

Seasons Bay™

An Interview With The Seasons Bay™ Designer

continued from page 325

by collectors was contagious, compelling me to create a concept and a series of designs that was unique to the industry—one that would transcend time and place and, hopefully, enjoy universal appeal by not being restricted to any one season or region. Thus the idea for Seasons Bay™ was born, and, after considerable research and a reduction of design ideas to paper, the concept was presented to Department 56, Inc."

Peter: "What do you perceive the Village to represent?"
Dennis: "Seasons Bay™ represents the embodiment of 'the age of innocence,' the idealized reality of an earlier, gentler time."

Peter: "What do you use for inspiration for the buildings and accessories of Seasons Bay™?"
Dennis: "The buildings are modeled after the shingle style architecture of late-19th century resort towns and villages situated near a soothing body of water across the United States."

Peter: "Have you ever lived in an area such as those represented by your designs?"
Dennis: "Though I have never permanently resided in an area such as Seasons Bay™, I have visited several late-19th century towns and villages over the years."

Peter: "Though there are only a few designs introduced so far, do you have a favorite?"
Dennis: "I am rather attached to all the designs in the collection. However, if I must choose a favorite from among the pieces available to date, it would be a toss up between the *Grandview Shores Hotel* and the *Bay Street Shops*. The former epitomizes my ideal of enchanting holiday accommodations while the latter best represents the asymmetrical complexity and exuberance of the shingle style."

Peter: "The International Collectible Exposition in Long Beach, California offered you your first time to meet a large base of Department 56® collectors. Were you excited?"
Dennis: "Needless to say, I was very excited and extremely grateful for the opportunity to meet Department 56® collectors to talk about the collection and to sign their pieces."

At this point I had another question or two concerning Seasons Bay™'s near and distant futures, but it didn't surprise me that, in the long-standing Department 56, Inc. tradition, questions such as these would have to go unanswered. And that's probably a good thing because one of my favorite aspects about collecting is the fact that there is always something new and exciting around the corner.

the **Village Chronicle.**

Seasons Bay™

RELAXING IN A GARDEN

ITEM #	INTRO	RETIRED	OSRP	GBTRU
53307	1998	CURRENT	$25	**$25**

Spring Accessory. Set of 3. Two Villagers tend to their flowers while two others sit and enjoy the day.

DATE: _____ $ _____
○ WISH   ○ HAVE

A STROLL IN THE PARK

ITEM #	INTRO	RETIRED	OSRP	GBTRU
53308	1998	CURRENT	$25	**$25**

Spring Accessory. Set of 5. A woman and her children take a leisurely walk through the park and meet two of its inhabitants.

DATE: _____ $ _____
○ WISH   ○ HAVE

I'M WISHING

ITEM #	INTRO	RETIRED	OSRP	GBTRU
53309	1998	CURRENT	$13	**$13**

Spring Accessory. A boy and girl make their wishes at the local well.

DATE: _____ $ _____
○ WISH   ○ HAVE

SUNDAY MORNING AT THE CHAPEL

ITEM #	INTRO	RETIRED	OSRP	GBTRU
53311	1998	CURRENT	$17	**$17**

Spring Accessory. Set of 2. A family of five heads to church in their Sunday best.

DATE: _____ $ _____
○ WISH   ○ HAVE

Seasons Bay™ Accessories

FISHING IN THE BAY

ITEM #	INTRO	RETIRED	OSRP	GBTRU
53313	1998	CURRENT	$13	**$13**

Summer Accessory. A girl and dog look on as a boy casts his line into the water in hopes of catching "the big one."

DATE: _____ $ _____
○ WISH   ○ HAVE

HERE COMES THE ICE CREAM MAN

ITEM #	INTRO	RETIRED	OSRP	GBTRU
53314	1998	CURRENT	$35	**$35**

Summer Accessory. Set of 4. Two children and their dog greet the ice cream vendor at his horse-drawn cart.

DATE: _____ $ _____
○ WISH   ○ HAVE

4TH OF JULY PARADE

ITEM #	INTRO	RETIRED	OSRP	GBTRU
53317	1998	CURRENT	$32.50	**$32.50**

Summer Accessory. Set of 5. Everyone including the family dog takes part in celebrating the nation's birthday.

DATE: _____ $ _____
○ WISH   ○ HAVE

TRICK OR TREAT

ITEM #	INTRO	RETIRED	OSRP	GBTRU
53319	1998	CURRENT	$25	**$25**

Fall Accessory. Set of 4. Dressed in their Halloween attire, the children head off for some fun and trick-or-treating.

DATE: _____ $ _____
○ WISH   ○ HAVE

BACK FROM THE ORCHARD

ITEM #	INTRO	RETIRED	OSRP	GBTRU
53320	1998	CURRENT	$27.50	**$27.50**

Fall Accessory. Children and their dog bring back their bounty from the local apple orchard.

DATE: _____ $ _____
O WISH   O HAVE

AFTERNOON SLEIGH RIDE

ITEM #	INTRO	RETIRED	OSRP	GBTRU
53322	1998	CURRENT	$27.50	**$27.50**

Winter Accessory. Two vacationers enjoy a brisk winter day in a horse-drawn sleigh.

DATE: _____ $ _____
O WISH   O HAVE

FUN IN THE SNOW

ITEM #	INTRO	RETIRED	OSRP	GBTRU
53323	1998	CURRENT	$15	**$15**

Winter Accessory. Set of 2. Children spend the day at a hillside on their sled and toboggan.

DATE: _____ $ _____
O WISH   O HAVE

SKATING ON THE POND

ITEM #	INTRO	RETIRED	OSRP	GBTRU
53324	1998	CURRENT	$20	**$20**

Winter Accessory. Set of 2. You can almost hear skates cutting into the ice as a family of five skates on the local pond.

DATE: _____ $ _____
O WISH   O HAVE

Seasons Bay™ Accessories

A Day At The Waterfront

Item #	Intro	Retired	OSRP	GBTru
53326	1998	Current	$20	**$20**

Summer Accessory. Set of 2. A mother relaxes in a chair as her children busy themselves by making sand castles.

Date: ____ $ ____
○ Wish   ○ Have

Garden Cart, The

Item #	Intro	Retired	OSRP	GBTru
53327	1998	Current	$27.50	**$27.50**

Spring Accessory. A boy sits atop a horse which is pulling a cart carrying his mother and sister.

Date: ____ $ ____
○ Wish   ○ Have

You Asked For It...You Got It

Who says companies don't listen to consumers? Let's face it, they have to. Sure they can turn a deaf ear from time-to-time, but could they survive if they didn't pay attention to the marketplace? You only have to look to Detroit in the 1980's to witness what happens when they don't.

When the U.S. automobile industry ignored the demands of its consumers, it lost market share and was rolling towards disaster. Finally, it realized that it must listen and also react. When it did, it turned itself around and, for the most part, is a viable industry once more. How do cars tie in with villages? They don't. Those companies are simply an example of sharp contrasts to Department 56, Inc.

Over the years Department 56, Inc. has responded to its consumers with various changes. When collectors demanded highly detailed designs, Department 56, Inc. responded. When they wanted more landscaping products, Department 56, Inc. answered with the introduction of additional trees, hedges, gravel, and stone fences to name a few. When collectors requested that only two or three buildings be introduced per village, per year, Department 56, Inc. responded by...OK...you knew that wasn't about to happen. But that doesn't detract from the company's fine record.

Now let's take a look at some of the items still on the "Collectors' Wish List." First, there's a non-winter village. Though Department 56, Inc. was reluctant to introduce such a village because it was a producer of **snowhouses**, the company has recently swayed from its stance. For instance, The Original Snow Village®'s *Haunted Mansion* has no snow; nor does the Dickens' Village Series® *Kensington Palace*. This building, in fact, has removable wreaths and garland so winter and non-winter scenes can be created. (The idea was commendable, but its implementation may have left a little to be desired.) Now the Literary Classics Series will feature snow-less buildings. Even so, these are only a few buildings in otherwise snow-dominated villages.

Next is scale…or lack of it. This has long been a pet peeve of many collectors. Statements of frustration such as "The people can't fit in the door" and "The people are bigger than the cars" are heard from coast-to-coast. And scale is a major concern for model railroad collectors, many of whom employ Department 56® buildings and accessories in their scenes. Yet Department 56, Inc. never addressed this matter.

Then there is the question of why lights aren't inserted in the bottom of the buildings. Collectors have been stumped when trying to determine why the lights are still inserted in the back, especially since Department 56, Inc. has acknowledged the value of all four sides of a building in a scene.

Well, guess who was listening and has responded. Yup! None other than your favorite village maker. With the recent introduction of Seasons Bay™, Department 56, Inc. has answered many long-awaited, but not really anticipated, changes. This series, which is not part of either The Original Snow Village® or The Heritage Village Collection®, is unlike any other. The highly detailed buildings are designed by an architect and have no snow on them. And yes, they are lit by bulbs that are inserted in the bottoms. (The *Grandview Shores Hotel* has three lights, meaning there will be no "dark spots" in areas like its twin towers.) And get this…the accessories are pewter so they are highly detailed, yet small enough to be close to scale, if not actually in scale. Furthermore, you can buy accessories designed to represent each of the four seasons.

Seasons Bay™ also departs from the usual in another manner. There will be two versions of each building. First Editions will sport a "First Edition" decal and will be sold through Gold Key dealers only. Regular production pieces will be sold through Showcase dealers and eventually Gold Key dealers. Consequently, there will be pieces for those who want limited editions, yet everyone will be able to purchase the like designs.

I am anxious to see how collectors respond to the new village, the one that, in many ways, they designed. I think it will be well received once collectors accept that it's not intended to be like the other villages. I also believe it will attract collectors that the other villages did not. And I am certain about one thing; the introduction of this village demonstrates that Department 56, Inc. does pay attention. When you see Seasons Bay™ for the first time, keep in mind the slogan used by an automobile manufacturer that gained tremendous market share because it listened, "You asked for it, you got it!"

the **Village Chronicle.**

Seasons Bay™ Accessories

Item#	Name	Intro	Retired	OSRP$	GBTru$	Wish	Have	Date	Qty	Paid Each	Total
	MEADOWLAND										
5050-0	Thatched Cottage	1979	1980	30	595	O	O	——	——	——	——
5051-8	Countryside Church	1979	1980	25	490	O	O	——	——	——	——
5052-6	Aspen Trees (Accessory)	1979	1980	16	170	O	O	——	——	——	——
5053-4	Sheep (Accessory)	1979	1980	12	125	O	O	——	——	——	——
	MEADOWLAND TOTAL:			**83.00**	**1,380.00**						
	BACHMAN'S®										
670-0	Hometown Boarding House	1987	1988	34	325	O	O	——	——	——	——
671-8	Hometown Church	1987	1988	40	325	O	O	——	——	——	——
672-6	Hometown Drugstore	1988	1989	40	585	O	O	——	——	——	——
	BACHMAN'S® TOTAL:			**114.00**	**1,235.00**						
	PROFILES™										
7826	Heinz House, The	1996	N/A	28	70	O	O	——	——	——	——
56000	State Farm–Main Street Memories	1997	N/A	35.50	115	O	O	——	——	——	——
05600	Heinz Grocery Store, The	1998	N/A	34	65	O	O	——	——	——	——
	PROFILES™ TOTAL:			**97.50**	**250.00**						
	HISTORICAL LANDMARK SERIES™										
58500	Tower Of London	1997	1997 Annual	165	250	O	O	——	——	——	——
58501	Old Globe Theatre, The	1997	1998 Annual	175	220	O	O	——	——	——	——
55500	Independence Hall With Sign	1998	1999 Annual	110	110	O	O	——	——	——	——
58341	Big Ben	1998	Current	95	95	O	O	——	——	——	——
	HISTORICAL LANDMARK SERIES™ TOTAL:			**545.00**	**675.00**						
NONE	NCC Collectors Club House	1998	Clubs Exclusive	56	80	O	O				
	TOTAL:			**56.00**	**80.00**						

Special Pieces GB History LIst

MEADOWLAND

This "non-winter" series was very short-lived. Made of ceramic, it is considered by many to be a companion series to The Original Snow Village®.

DATE: _____ $ _____
○ WISH ○ HAVE

THATCHED COTTAGE

ITEM #	INTRO	RETIRED	OSRP	GBTRU	↓
5050-0	1979	1980	$30	**$595**	8%

Small thatched cottage with attached tree. Chimney at rear of stucco and timber trim house.

see above

DATE: _____ $ _____
○ WISH ○ HAVE

'96	'97	'98
$725	690	645

COUNTRYSIDE CHURCH

ITEM #	INTRO	RETIRED	OSRP	GBTRU	↓
5051-8	1979	1980	$25	**$490**	4%

Countryside Church in a springtime setting. There's a large green tree against a simple white wood church with a steeple rising from the entry to the nave.
Notable: For a snow version, see Original Snow Village® 1979, *Countryside Church,* Item #5058-3.

see above

DATE: _____ $ _____
○ WISH ○ HAVE

'96	'97	'98
$685	545	510

ASPEN TREES (ACCESSORY)

ITEM #	INTRO	RETIRED	OSRP	GBTRU	↓
5052-6	1979	1980	$16	**$170**	15%

The trees that shiver and tremble in the wind. Small leaves on a hardwood tree.

see above

DATE: _____ $ _____
○ WISH ○ HAVE

'96	'97	'98
NE	$265	200

SHEEP (ACCESSORY)	**ITEM #**	**INTRO**	**RETIRED**	**OSRP**	**GBTRU**
	5053-4	1979	1980	$12	**$125**

Set of 12 includes 9 white and 3 black sheep. The photograph shows one white sheep only.

see previous page

DATE: _____ $ _____		'96	'97	'98
○ WISH ○ HAVE		NE	NE	NE

NOTES: _____

_____

_____

_____

_____

_____

_____

_____

_____

_____

_____

_____

_____

_____

_____

_____

_____

_____

_____

_____

BACHMAN'S®

This short-lived series was produced for Bachman's® Inc. of Minneapolis, MN, the original parent company of Department 56, Inc. Three buildings were manufactured and distributed, but a planned fourth building, a bookstore, never made it past the drawing board.

DATE: _____ $ _____
○ WISH   ○ HAVE

HOMETOWN BOARDING HOUSE

ITEM #	INTRO	RETIRED	OSRP	GBTRU	↓
670-0	1987	1988	$34	**$325**	6%

Three-story brick building with rented rooms above the main floor parlor and dining room.
Notable: Inspired by the Sprague House in Red Wing, MN.

DATE: _____ $ _____
○ WISH   ○ HAVE

'92	'93	'94	'95	'96	'97	'98
$275	330	330	325	300	300	345

HOMETOWN CHURCH

ITEM #	INTRO	RETIRED	OSRP	GBTRU	↓
671-8	1987	1988	$40	**$325**	11%

Building has cross-shaped floor plan with a spire rising from one side of the transept. A simple entry door at the base of the spire is in contrast to the large arched windows that fill the end walls.
Notable: Designed after a St. Paul, MN church.

DATE: _____ $ _____
○ WISH   ○ HAVE

'92	'93	'94	'95	'96	'97	'98
$300	300	300	325	305	305	365

HOMETOWN DRUGSTORE

ITEM #	INTRO	RETIRED	OSRP	GBTRU	↓
672-6	1988	1989	$40	**$585**	3%

Drugstore is corner store in a two attached buildings structure. Taller three-story building houses barber shop on main level and eyeglass shop above. Garlands decorate the awnings over display windows.
Notable: Same mold as the Christmas In The City® *Variety Store,* 1988 Item #5972-2. Inspired by a store in Stillwater, MN.

DATE: _____ $ _____
○ WISH   ○ HAVE

'92	'93	'94	'95	'96	'97	'98
$675	675	675	625	565	595	600

PROFILES™

This is a series of buildings produced by Department 56, Inc. for use as promotional pieces by other companies. Many collectors, however, have adapted them into some of the Heritage Village Collections®.

DATE: ____ $ ____
○ WISH ○ HAVE

HEINZ HOUSE, THE

ITEM #	INTRO	RETIRED	OSRP	GBTRU	↓
7826	1996	N/A	$28	**$70**	13%

Notable: This building was manufactured by Department 56, Inc. for the H.J. Heinz Company for them to use in promotions. Heinz gave it as a gift to its vendors and suppliers in late 1996 and sold it to their stockholders by a direct mail campaign in early 1997. It is packed in a white, flap-top box with red lettering.

DATE: ____ $ ____
○ WISH ○ HAVE

'97	'98
$75	80

STATE FARM–MAIN STREET MEMORIES

ITEM #	INTRO	RETIRED	OSRP	GBTRU	↑
56000	1997	N/A	$35.50	**$115**	21%

Notable: The Main Street Memories building was made available by State Farm Insurance to its agents, employees and their families. It depicts a building highlighted in Randy Souders painting that is also called Main Street Memories. A State Farm agent is located on the right side of the building, a barber shop is on the left side and a drug store in the corner shop.

DATE: ____ $ ____
○ WISH ○ HAVE

'98
$95

HEINZ GROCERY STORE, THE

ITEM #	INTRO	RETIRED	OSRP	GBTRU
05600	1998	N/A	$34	**$65**

Notable: Like *The Heinz House*, 1996 Item #7826, this building was manufactured by Department 56, Inc. for the H.J. Heinz Company for them to use in promotions. Heinz gave it as a gift to its vendors and suppliers in late 1998 and sold it to their stockholders by a direct mail campaign in early 1999. It is packed in a white, flap-top box with sepia-type photos on all four sides.

DATE: ____ $ ____
○ WISH ○ HAVE

HISTORICAL LANDMARK SERIES™

In 1997, Department 56, Inc. began a series of buildings depicting Historical Landmarks. It first appeared as though it would be a sub-series within the Dickens' Village Series®. However, the 1998 introduction of *Independence Hall* changed that.

DATE: ____ $ ____
○ WISH ○ HAVE

TOWER OF LONDON

ITEM #	INTRO	RETIRED	OSRP	GBTʀu	↓
58500	1997	1997 Annual	$165	$250	28%

Set of 5. Midyear release. Lighted main structure, non-lighted gate/tower, sign, raven master with 2 ravens, wall with 4 ravens.
Notable: This, the White Tower, is one of the many towers that comprise the actual Tower Of London. Famous for housing a royal prison as well as the Crown Jewels. Legend says six ravens must be kept at the tower to preserve the monarchy.

DATE: ____ $ ____
○ WISH ○ HAVE

	'97	'98
	$165	345

OLD GLOBE THEATRE, THE

ITEM #	INTRO	RETIRED	OSRP	GBTʀu	↑
58501	1997	1998 Annual	$175	$220	26%

Set of 4. Theatre built in the round with stage in the center. Many of Shakespeare's plays were performed here. Timber beam decorative design. Theatre sign. Two trumpeters to announce the opening.
Notable: First proofs were made in two pieces. For production, it is one piece. Some early shipments have "The City Globe" stamped on the bottom. The Globe Theatre was demolished in 1644. It was rebuilt in 1996 near the site of the original.

DATE: ____ $ ____
○ WISH ○ HAVE

	'98
	$175

INDEPENDENCE HALL WITH SIGN

ITEM #	INTRO	RETIRED	OSRP	GBTʀu
55500	1998	1999 Annual	$110	$110

Notable: A replica of Philadelphia's Independence Hall, this was the first building in the Historical Landmark Series® which was not part of Dickens' Village Series®. Available during the 1999 July event.

DATE: ____ $ ____
○ WISH ○ HAVE

Big Ben

Item #	Intro	Retired	OSRP	GBTru
58341	1998	Current	$95	**$95**

Set of 2. Big Ben, one of the world's most well known landmarks, is not the structure itself, but the largest bell within the tower.

Notable: Features a working clock on one of its four faces. The other three faces read "5 of 6."

Date: _____ $ _____
○ Wish   ○ Have

Notes: _____

_____

_____

_____

_____

_____

_____

_____

_____

_____

_____

_____

_____

_____

_____

_____

_____

_____

_____

_____

_____

NCC COLLECTORS CLUB HOUSE

ITEM #	INTRO	RETIRED	OSRP	GBTRU
NONE	1998	CLUBS EXCLUSIVE	$56	**$80**

Notable: An exclusive for members of National Council of 56 Clubs related collectors clubs, this building was available directly from Department 56, Inc. It includes a sign and a man and woman walking to the club. The man is carrying a Snow Village bag and refreshments, and the woman is carrying a Heritage Village bag. Collectors who purchased *Club Houses* could have decals of their clubs' logos affixed to the sign.

DATE: _____ $ _____
O WISH   O HAVE

NOTES: _____

_____

_____

_____

_____

_____

_____

_____

_____

_____

_____

_____

_____

_____

_____

_____

_____

_____

_____

_____

_____

Special Pieces—Club Piece

Trees

1987–1995
#6597-8
SPRUCE TREE WITH WOODEN BASE, MEDIUM
Size: 9".
LSRP: $5/ea

1986–1992
#6537-4
PORCELAIN TREES
Set of 2.
Two different size snow-covered evergreens.
GBTru$ is $33.
LSRP: $14/set

1987–1995
#6598-6
SPRUCE TREE WITH WOODEN BASE, LARGE
Size: 12".
LSRP: $7/ea

1987–1990
#6594-3
SPRUCE FOREST
Set of 22.
LSRP: $90/set

photo not available

1988–1991
#5111-0
CHRISTMAS WREATHS
8 pieces per package.
Sizes: 1" & 3/4".
LSRP: $5/pkg

1987–1995
#6595-1
SPRUCE TREE WITH WOODEN BASE, SMALL
Size: 6".
LSRP: $3.50/ea

1988–1991
#5112-8
SV GARLAND TRIM
3 pieces per package.
Each piece is 24" long.
LSRP: $4.50/pkg

photo not available	1988–1990 #5115-2 **FROSTED TOPIARY VILLAGE GARDEN** Set of 8. 4 cones & 4 ovals. LSRP: $16/set	1989–1998 #5175-6 **VILLAGE FROSTED NORWAY PINES** Set of 3. Sizes: 7", 9" & 11". LSRP: $12.95/set

1988–1990
#5115-2
FROSTED TOPIARY VILLAGE GARDEN
Set of 8.
4 cones & 4 ovals.
LSRP: $16/set

1989–1998
#5175-6
VILLAGE FROSTED NORWAY PINES
Set of 3.
Sizes: 7", 9" & 11".
LSRP: $12.95/set

1988–1992
#5185-3
TOPIARY GARDEN SISAL
36 pieces assorted.
Sizes: 2 1/2", 4", 6", 8" & 12".
LSRP: $50/set

1989–1990
#5184-5
WINTER OAK TREE WITH 2 RED BIRDS
LSRP: $16/ea

1988–1989
#5193-4
FROSTED CONE TREE WITH WOOD BASE, LARGE
LSRP: $10/ea

1989–1989
#5186-1
SISAL TOPIARY, LARGE
Size: 12".
LSRP: N/A

1989–1989
#587-0
SISAL TOPIARY, MEDIUM
Size: 8".
LSRP: N/A

1989–1989
#5188-8
SISAL TOPIARY, SMALL
Size: 6".
LSRP: N/A

Trees

1989–1989
#5189-6

SISAL TOPIARY, MINI

photo not
available

Size: 4".

LSRP: N/A

1989–Current
#5202-7

**VILLAGE FROSTED
TOPIARY, LARGE**

Set of 8.
Sizes: 4 cones &
4 oblong, 4" each.

SRP: $12.50/set

1989–1994
#5192-6

**VILLAGE POTTED
TOPIARY PAIR**

Sisal trees in white
resin planters.
2 pieces per package.
Size: 4 ³/₄".

LSRP: $15/pkg

1989–Current
#5203-5

**VILLAGE FROSTED
TOPIARY, SMALL**

Set of 8.
Sizes:
4 @ 2" round,
4 @ 3" high.

SRP: $7.50/set

1989–Current
#5200-0

**VILLAGE FROSTED
TOPIARY, LARGE**

2 pieces per package.
Size: 11 ¹/₂".

SRP: $12.50/pkg

1989–1990
#6579-0

MINI SPRUCE FOREST

photo not
available

Set of 26.
Sizes: 5", 4", 3".

LSRP: $50/set

1989–Current
#5201-9

**VILLAGE FROSTED
TOPIARY, MEDIUM**

Set of 4.
Sizes:
2 @ 7 ¹/₂" &
2 @ 6".

SRP: $10/set

1990–1994
#5181-0

**VILLAGE WINTER
OAK, SMALL**

Size: 4 1/4".
Name changed from
Winter Oak, Small to
*Bare Branch Winter
Oak, Small* in 1993.

LSRP: $4.50/ea

Trees

1990–1994
#5182-9

VILLAGE WINTER OAK, LARGE

Size: 7 3/4".
Name changed from *Winter Oak, Large* to *Bare Branch Winter Oak, Large* in 1993.

LSRP: $8/ea

1991–1998
#5419-4

SISAL WREATHS

6 pieces per package.
Size: 1" diameter.

LSRP: $4/pkg

photo not available

1990–1990
#5183-7

SISAL TREE SET

Set of 7.
4 cones & 3 ovals.

LSRP: $16/set

1991–1998
#5527-1

VILLAGE POLE PINE FOREST

Set of 5.
4 trees in a snow base.
Size: 10" x 5" x 12".

LSRP: $48/set

1990–1996
#6582-0

FROSTED EVERGREEN TREES

Set of 3.
Sizes:
8 1/2", 6 1/2" & 4 1/2".
Papier-mâché.

LSRP: $16/set

1991–1998
#5528-0

VILLAGE POLE PINE TREE, SMALL

Size: 8".

LSRP: $10/ea

1991–1997
#5205-1

EVERGREEN TREES

Set of 3.
Sizes: 3 1/4", 4 1/4" & 6 1/2".
Cold cast porcelain.

LSRP: $12.95/set

1991–1998
#5529-8

VILLAGE POLE PINE TREE, LARGE

Size: 10 1/2".

LSRP: $12.50/ea

Trees

1992–1997
#5218-3
***VILLAGE PORCELAIN
PINE, LARGE***
Size is 8 ¹/₂".
LSRP: $12.50/ea

1994–1996
#5231-0
***VILLAGE FROSTED
SPRUCE TREE***
Size: 15".
LSRP: $12.50/ea

1992–1997
#5219-1
***VILLAGE PORCELAIN
PINE TREE, SMALL***
Size is 7".
LSRP: $10/ea

1994–1996
#5232-9
***VILLAGE FROSTED
SPRUCE TREE***
Size: 22".
LSRP: $27.50/ea

1993–1996
#5216-7
***VILLAGE WINTER
BIRCH TREE***
Size: 11 ¹/₂".
LSRP: $12.50/ea

1994–Current
#5243-4
***VILLAGE BARE
BRANCH TREE, WITH
25 LIGHTS***

This item is Battery
Operated or can be
used with Adapter,
Item #5225-6.
Size: 9".

SRP: $13.50/ea

1993–1995
#5221-3
***VILLAGE PINE CONE
TREES***
Set of 2.
Sizes: 8 ³/₄" &
7 ¹/₄".
Resin.
LSRP: $15/set

1994–1998
#5246-9
***VILLAGE PENCIL
PINES***
Set of 3.
Sizes: 12", 8" & 5".
LSRP: $15/set

Trees

1994–1997
#5251-5
PORCELAIN PINE TREE
Set of 2.
Sizes: 4 ³/₄" & 3 ³/₄".
LSRP: $15/set

1995–1996
#5248-5
SPRUCE TREE FOREST
Set of 4.
Size: 16" x 14".
LSRP: $25/set

1994–1997
#5254-0
VILLAGE AUTUMN MAPLE TREE
Size: 11".
LSRP: $15/ea

1995–1996
#5249-3
VILLAGE FROSTED ZIG–ZAG TREE, WHITE
Set of 3.
Sizes: 9", 7" & 4 ¹/₂".
LSRP: $15/set

1995–1996
#5241-8
VILLAGE FROSTED BARE BRANCH TREE, SMALL
Size: 9 ¹/₂".
LSRP: $6.50/ea

1995–1996
#5250-7
VILLAGE FROSTED ZIG–ZAG TREE, GREEN
Set of 3.
Sizes: 9", 7" & 4 ¹/₂".
LSRP: $15/set

1995–1996
#5242-6
VILLAGE FROSTED BARE BRANCH TREE, LARGE
Size: 13".
LSRP: $12.50/ea

1995–1996
#5255-8
SNOWY WHITE PINE TREE, SMALL
Size: 18".
LSRP: $15/ea

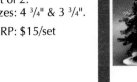

Trees

1995–1996
#5256-6
SNOWY WHITE PINE TREE, LARGE
Size: 24".
LSRP: $20/ea

1995–1997
#52603
LIGHTED SNOWCAPPED REVOLVING TREE
Lighted. Battery Operated or can be used with Adapter, Item #5225-6.
Size: 8".
Resin.
LSRP: $35/ea

1995–Current
#52590
VILLAGE LANDSCAPE
Set of 14.
SRP: $16.50/set

1995–1997
#52604
LIGHTED SNOWCAPPED TREES
Set of 2.
Lighted.
Sizes: 10" & 8".
Resin.
LSRP: $45/set

1995–Current
#52596
VILLAGE FLEXIBLE SISAL HEDGE
3 pieces per package. Each piece is 12" long.
SRP: $7.50/pkg

1995–1998
#52605
VILLAGE FROSTED FIR TREES
Set of 4.
Sizes:
15", 12", 9" & 6 $1/4$".
LSRP: $15/set

1995–Current
#52600
VILLAGE HYBRID LANDSCAPE
Set of 22.
SRP: $35/set

1995–1998
#52606
VILLAGE CEDAR PINE FOREST
Set of 3.
Sizes: 12", 10" & 8".
LSRP: $15/set

Trees

1995–1998
#52607

VILLAGE PONDEROSA PINES

Set of 3.
Sizes: 12", 10" & 9".
LSRP: $13/set

1995–Current
#52613

VILLAGE SNOWY EVERGREEN TREES, MEDIUM

Set of 6.
Sizes:
7 1/4", 5 1/2",
5 1/4", 5" & 4 1/4".
Resin.
SRP: $25/set

1995–1998
#52608

VILLAGE ARCTIC PINES

Set of 3.
Sizes: 10", 8" & 6".
LSRP: $12/set

1995–Current
#52614

VILLAGE SNOWY EVERGREEN TREES, LARGE

Set of 5.
Sizes:
9 1/4", 9", 7 1/4" & 7".
Resin.
SRP: $32.50/set

1995–Current
#52610

VILLAGE FALLEN LEAVES

Size: 3 oz. bag.
Fabric.
SRP: $5/bag

1995–Current
#52615

VILLAGE SNOWY SCOTCH PINES

Set of 3.
Sizes: 7", 5 1/4" & 5".
Resin.
SRP: $15/set

1995–Current
#52612

VILLAGE SNOWY EVERGREEN TREES, SMALL

Set of 6.
Sizes:
3 1/2", 3", 2 1/4" & 2".
Resin.
SRP: $8.50/set

1995–1998
#52616

VILLAGE AUTUMN TREES

Set of 3.
Sizes:
7 3/4", 6" & 4 3/4".
Resin.
LSRP: $13.50/set

Trees

1995–1998
#52617
VILLAGE WAGON WHEEL PINE GROVE

Size:
6 ³/₄" x 6 ¹/₄" x 6 ¹/₂".
Resin.
LSRP: $22.50/ea

1996–Current
#52623
VILLAGE BARE BRANCH TREES

Set of 6.
SRP: $22.50/set

1995–Current
#52618
VILLAGE PINE POINT POND

Size: 9 ¹/₄" x 8" x
5 ³/₄".
Resin.
SRP: $37.50/ea

1996–Current
#52630
VILLAGE HOLLY TREE

Size: 7".
SRP: $10/ea

1995–1998
#52619
VILLAGE DOUBLE PINE TREES

Size:
5 ¹/₄" x 5 ¹/₂" x 6".
Resin.
LSRP: $13.50/ea

1996–Current
#52631
VILLAGE BIRCH TREE CLUSTER

With 2 mailboxes.
SRP: $20/ea

1996–Current
#52622
VILLAGE JACK PINES

Set of 3.
SRP: $18/set

1996–Current
#52632
VILLAGE TOWERING PINES

Set of 2.
With cardinals.
Sizes: 7" & 9".
SRP: $13.50/set

1996–Current
#52636

VILLAGE WINTER BIRCH

Set of 6.
Sizes:
12", 9 ½" & 7 ½".
SRP: $22.50/set

1997–Current
#52655

VILLAGE AUTUMN BIRCH/MAPLE TREE

Set of 4.
Sizes: 12" & 8".
SRP: $27.50/set

1996–Current
#52637

VILLAGE FROSTED SPRUCE

Set of 2.
Sizes: 15 ½" & 12".
SRP: $25/set

1997–Current
#52660

VILLAGE WINTER-GREEN PINES

Set of 3.
Sizes: 3", 4 ¼" & 5 ¼".
SRP: $7.50/set

1996–1998
#52638

VILLAGE FROSTED HEMLOCK TREES

Set of 2.
Sizes: 15 ½" & 12".
LSRP: $32.50/set

1997–Current
#52661

VILLAGE WINTER-GREEN PINES

Set of 2.
Sizes: 7" & 8 ½".
SRP: $15/set

1996–Current
#52639

VILLAGE TOWN TREE

With 50 LED Lights.
Size: 14".
SRP: $35/ea

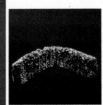

1997–Current
#52662

VILLAGE FLEXIBLE SISAL HEDGE

Set of 3.
Size: 12".
SRP: $10/set

Trees

1997–Current
#52665

VILLAGE LOG PILE

Wood crib holds cut logs.
Size: 4".

SRP: $3/ea

1998–Current
#52703

VILLAGE FLEXIBLE AUTUMN HEDGES

Set of 2.
Size: 12" long.

SRP: $10/set

1997–Current
#52683

VILLAGE LIGHTED SNOWY TREE

45 LED lights/adapter.
Size: 8 ¹/₂".

SRP: $27.50/ea

1998–Current
#52714

DECORATED SISAL TREES

2 assorted.

SRP: $12.50/ea

1997–1998
#52690

VILLAGE LIGHTED CHRISTMAS TREE

With 50 LED lights/adapter.

LSRP: $48/ea

1998–Current
#52748

CRAGGY OAK TREE

SRP: $12.50/ea

1997–Current
#59001

VILLAGE PORCELAIN PINE TREE

Set of 4.

SRP: $17.50/set

1998–Current
#52769

SWINGING UNDER THE OLD OAK TREE

SRP: $30/ea

Trees

1998–Current
#52770
HALLOWEEN SPOOKY TREE

SRP: $15/ea

Trims

---

photo not available

1998–Current
#52771
PINE TREES WITH PINE CONES
Set of 3.
SRP: $15/set

1987–1993
#5109-8
VILLAGE PARK BENCH
Size: 2 ½".
LSRP: $3.20/ea

---

photo not available

1998–Current
#52772
WINTER PINE TREES WITH PINE CONES
Set of 3.
SRP: $15/set

1988–1998
#5110-1
VILLAGE TOWN CLOCK
2 assorted–green or black.
Size: 3 ½" tall.
LSRP: $3/ea

---

photo not available

1998–Current
#53367
FLOCKED PINE TREES
Set of 3.
SRP: $15/set

1988–Current
#5139-0
UP ON A ROOF TOP
2 pieces.
Size: 4" long.
Pewter.
SRP: $6.50/ea

Trees/Trims

1989–1998
#5176-4

VILLAGE STOP SIGN

2 pieces per package.
Size: 3" tall.

LSRP: $5/pkg

1989–1997
#5513-1

TOWN SQUARE GAZEBO

Resin.

LSRP: $24/ea

1989–1998
#5178-0

VILLAGE PARKING METER

4 pieces per package.
Size: 2" tall.

LSRP: $6/pkg

1989–1992
#5516-6

BOULEVARD

Set of 14. 4 sidewalk
pieces, 4 removable
5" trees, 2 benches,
4 hitching posts.
GBTru$ is $45/set.

LSRP: $25/set

1989–1994
#5180-2

VILLAGE BIRDS

6 pieces per package.

LSRP: $3.50/pkg

1990–1998
#5209-4

CHRISTMAS TRASH CANS

Set of 2.
Two galvanized refuse
cans filled with holiday
wrappings and
garbage. Tops come
off.

LSRP: $7/set

1989–Current
#5511-5

'CHRISTMAS EAVE' TRIM

Non-electric bulb
garland.
Size: 24" long.

SRP: $3.50/ea

1990–Current
#5211-6

VILLAGE ACRYLIC ICICLES

4 pieces per package.
Each piece is 18"
long.

SRP: $4.50/pkg

1991–Current
#5208-6

***VILLAGE MYLAR
SKATING POND***

2 sheets per package.
Each sheet is
25 1/4" x 18".

SRP: $6/pkg

1991–1998
#5512-3

UTILITY ACCESSORIES

Set of 8.
2 stop signs,
4 parking meters,
2 traffic lights.
Sizes: 1 3/4", 2" & 3".

LSRP: $12.50/set

1991–Current
#5210-8

VILLAGE BRICK ROAD

2 strips per package.
Each strip is
4 3/4" x 36".
Vinyl.

SRP: $10/pkg

1991–Current
#5984-6

***VILLAGE COBBLE-
STONE ROAD***

2 strips per package.
Each strip is
4 3/4" x 36".

SRP: $10/pkg

1991–1997
#5417-8

***"IT'S A GRAND OLD
FLAG"***

2 pieces per package.
Size: 2 1/4".
Metal.

LSRP: $4/pkg

1992–1992
#948-2

***HERITAGE VILLAGE
COLLECTION®
PROMOTIONAL LOGO
BANNER***

Giveaway at 1992
events.

LSRP: N/A

1991–1994
#5418-6

VILLAGE GREETINGS

Set of 3.

LSRP: $5/set

1992–Current
#5217-5

TACKY WAX

Size: 1" diameter x
1" deep tub.

SRP: $2/tub

Trims

1992–1994
#5524-7
"VILLAGE SOUNDS" TAPE WITH SPEAKERS

23 minute tape.
LSRP: $25/ea

1993–Current
#5233-7
VILLAGE SLED & SKIS

Set of 2.
Sizes: 2" & 2 1/4".
SRP: $6/set

1992–1994
#5525-5
"VILLAGE SOUNDS" TAPE

23 minutes, continuous play.
LSRP: $8/ea

1993–Current
#5456-9
WINDMILL

Size: 11 1/2" high.
Metal with earthen base.
SRP: $20/ea

1992–1995
#5526-3
HERITAGE BANNERS

Set of 4, 2 each of 2.
Size: 1 1/4".
LSRP: $6/set

1994–Current
#98841
"THE BUILDING OF A VILLAGE TRADITION" VIDEO, WITH INSTRUCTION BOOKLET

35 Minutes.
SRP: $19.95/ea

1993–Current
#5230-2
VILLAGE WROUGHT IRON PARK BENCH

Size: 2 1/4".
Metal.
SRP: $5/ea

1995–1998
#52594
VILLAGE LET IT SNOW SNOWMAN SIGN

Size: 6".
Resin.
LSRP: $12.50/ea

Trims

1995–Current
#52595

***VILLAGE PINK
FLAMINGOS***

4 pieces per package.
Size: 1 ³/₄".

SRP: $7.50/pkg

1996–Current
#52591

***VILLAGE SQUARE
CLOCK TOWER***

Battery-operated
watch.

SRP: $32.50/ea

1995–1997
#52599

***VILLAGE ELECTION
YARD SIGNS***

Set of 6, assorted.
Size: 2 ¹/₄".

LSRP: $10/set

1996–Current
#52620

***VILLAGE MAGIC
SMOKE™***

Pine Scent.
6 oz. bottle.

SRP: $2.50/ea

1995–Current
#52601

***VILLAGE BRICK
TOWN SQUARE***

Size: 23 ¹/₂" square.
Vinyl.

SRP: $15/ea

1996–Current
#52629

***VILLAGE STONE
WALL***

2 assorted.
Size: 5 ¹/₂" x 1 ¹/₂".

SRP: $2.50/ea

1995–Current
#52602

***VILLAGE COBBLE-
STONE TOWN
SQUARE***

Size: 23 ¹/₂" square.
Vinyl.

SRP: $15/ea

1996–Current
#52633

***VILLAGE MILL CREEK
(STRAIGHT SECTION)***

Straight section of
creek bed with
evergreens.
Size: 9 ¹/₄" x 4 ¹/₂".

SRP: $12.50/ea

Trims

1996–Current
#52634

VILLAGE MILL CREEK (CURVED SECTION)

Curved section of creek bed with evergreens.
Size: 8 1/2" x 4 1/2".

SRP: $12.50/ea

1997–Current
#52651

VILLAGE MILL CREEK POND

SRP: $55/ea

1996–Current
#52635

VILLAGE MILL CREEK BRIDGE

Stone bridge over section of creek.
Size: 10 3/4" x 5 3/4".

SRP: $35/ea

1997–Current
#52652

VILLAGE GAZEBO

SRP: $22.50/ea

1997–Current
#52646

VILLAGE STONE FOOTBRIDGE

Size: 7" x 3 1/2".

SRP: $16/ea

1997–Current
#52653

VILLAGE MILL CREEK WOODEN BRIDGE

Size: 10 3/4" x 5 1/4" x 4 3/4".

SRP: $32.50/ea

1997–Current
#52647

VILLAGE STONE TRESTLE BRIDGE

Size: 9" x 4 3/4".

SRP: $37.50/ea

1997–Current
#52654

VILLAGE MILL CREEK PARK BENCH

Size: 6" x 4 1/2".

SRP: $14/ea

1997–Current
#52656
TELEPHONE POLES

Set of 6.
Individual "wires"
complete with
perched birds can
connect poles.
SRP: $15/set

1997–Current
#52667
***PEPPERMINT ROAD,
CURVED SECTION***

SRP: $5/ea

1997–Current
#52658
TELEVISION ANTENNA
Set of 4.
SRP: $5/set

1997–Current
#52668
***TWO LANE PAVED
ROAD***
Set of 2.
SRP: $15/set

1997–Current
#52659
WEATHER VANE
Set of 5 assorted.
SRP: $6.50/set

1997–Current
#52669
CANDY CANE BENCH

SRP: $5/ea

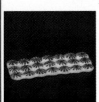

1997–Current
#52666
***PEPPERMINT ROAD,
STRAIGHT SECTION***

SRP: $5/ea

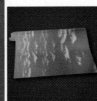

1997–Current
#52685
***VILLAGE BLUE SKIES
BACKDROP***
Size: 39" x 59".
SRP: $7.50/ea

Trims

1997–Current
#52686

***VILLAGE STARRY
NIGHT SKY BACK-
DROP***

Size: 39" x 59".
SRP: $7.50/ea

1998–Current
#52705

***VILLAGE CAMDEN
PARK FOUNTAIN***

Set of 3. Compatible
w/Camden Park Square
pieces.
Working fountain
complete with a water
pump.

SRP: $84/set

1997–Current
#52687

***VILLAGE CAMDEN
PARK SQUARE***

Set of 22.
SRP: $75/set

1998–Current
#52712

***HOLIDAY TINSEL
TRIMS***

photo not
available

Set of 11.
SRP: $8/set

1997–Current
#52691

***VILLAGE CAMDEN
PARK COBBLESTONE
ROAD***

Set of 2.
SRP: $10/set

1998–Current
#52713

TINSEL TRIMS

photo not
available

Set of 8.
SRP: $8/set

1998–Current
#52704

***VILLAGE HALLOWEEN
SET***

Set of 22. Set includes 1
scarecrow, 3 wheat
shocks, 1 ghost, 2 black
cats, 12 pumpkins, 2
trees & a bag of Village
Fallen Leaves.

SRP: $50/set

1998–Current
#52719

SLATE STONE PATH

photo not
available

SRP: $3/ea

1998–Current
#52720
WOODLAND ANIMALS AT MILL CREEK

SRP: $32.50

1998–Current
#52740
PUTTING GREEN

SRP: $22.50/ea

photo not available

1998–Current
#52725
STONE STAIRWAY

SRP: $16.50/ea

1998–Current
#52742
MOOSE IN THE MARSH

SRP: $25/ea

photo not available

1998–Current
#52729
CLEAR ICE

SRP: $6.50/ea

1998–Current
#52743
BEARS IN THE BIRCH

SRP: $25

photo not available

1998–Current
#52739
GREEN
24" by 36".
SRP: $12.50/ea

1998–Current
#52744
FOXES IN THE FOREST

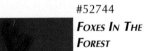

SRP: $22.50

Trims

1998–Current
#52747
THOROUGHBREDS
Set of 5.
SRP: $45/set

1998–Current
#52754
REAL GRAY GRAVEL

photo not available

SRP: $5

1998–Current
#52751
GRAY COBBLESTONE SECTION
Set of 2.
SRP: $7.50/set

photo not available

1998–Current
#52755
GRAY COBBLESTONE CAPSTONES
Set of 2.
SRP: $6/set

photo not available

1998–Current
#52752
GRAY COBBLESTONE ARCHWAY

photo not available

SRP: $10/ea

1998–Current
#52756
GRAVEL ROAD

photo not available

SRP: $10/ea

1998–Current
#52753
GRAY COBBLESTONE TUNNEL

photo not available

SRP: $6.50/ea

1998–Current
#52765
WOLVES IN THE WOODS

SRP: $25

Trims

1998–Current
#52766
WOODEN PIER
Set of 2.
SRP: $32.50/set

1998–Current
#53347
GRASSY GROUND COVER

photo not available

SRP: $7.50/ea

photo not available

1998–Current
#52767
SLATE STONE PATH

SRP: $3/ea

Snow

photo not available

1998–Current
#52775
SNOW VILLAGE UTILITY ACCESSORIES
Set of 9.
SRP: $15/set

1977–Current
#4998-1
REAL PLASTIC SNOW
7 oz. bag.
SRP: $3/bag

photo not available

1998–Current
#52776
HERITAGE VILLAGE UTILITY ACCESSORIES
Set of 11.
SRP: $15/set

1977–Current
#4999-9
REAL PLASTIC SNOW
2 lb. box.
SRP: $10/box

1991–Current
#4995-6

***VILLAGE "BLANKET
OF NEW FALLEN
SNOW"***

Size: 2' x 5' 1".
SRP: $7.50/ea

1995–1997
#52592

***VILLAGE LET IT SNOW
MACHINE, WITH 1 LB.
BAG VILLAGE FRESH
FALLEN SNOW***

Size:
38 1/2" x 9" x 5 1/2".
Battery Operated.
LSRP: $85/ea

---

photo not
available

1991–1992
#4996-4

***"LET IT SNOW"
CRYSTALS, PLASTIC
SNOW***

Size: 8 oz. box.
LSRP: $6.50/box

photo not
available

1998–Current
#53362

GLISTENING SNOW

SRP: $10

1995–Current
#49979

***VILLAGE FRESH
FALLEN SNOW***

7 oz. bag.
Compatible with *Let
It Snow Machine.*
SRP: $4/bag

Fences

1995–Current
#49980

***VILLAGE FRESH
FALLEN SNOW***

2 lb. box.
Compatible with *Let
It Snow Machine.*
SRP: $12/box

1987–Current
#5100-4

***VILLAGE WHITE
PICKET FENCE***

One of the first metal
accessories.
Size: 6" x 1 3/4".
Cast Iron.
SRP: $3/ea

1987–1997
#5101-2
**VILLAGE WHITE
PICKET FENCE**

Set of 4.
Each piece is
6" x 1 ³/₄".
Cast Iron.

LSRP: $12/set

1989–1989
#5509-3
**LAMP POST
EXTENSION**

photo not
available

Set of 12.
Metal.

LSRP: N/A

1989–1991
#5506-9
LAMP POST FENCE

Set of 10.
2 lamps,
4 posts,
4 fence pieces.

LSRP: $13/set

1989–1998
#5998-6
**WROUGHT IRON
FENCE**

White & black or
white & green.
Each piece is 4" long.

LSRP: $2.50/ea

1989–1989
#5507-7
LAMP POST FENCE

photo not
available

Set of 10.
Metal.

LSRP: N/A

1990–1998
#5212-4
**TREE-LINED COURT-
YARD FENCE**

1 ¹/₂" high x 4" long.
Metal with resin.

LSRP: $4/ea

1989–1991
#5508-5
**LAMP POST FENCE
EXTENSION**

Set of 12.
6 posts &
6 fence pieces.

LSRP: $10/set

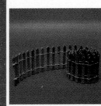

1991–1998
#5204-3
**VILLAGE SNOW
FENCE, FLEXIBLE
WOOD & WIRE**

2" high x 36" long.

LSRP: $7/ea

Fences

1991–1997
#5207-8

Frosty Tree-Lined Picket Fence

3 posts & 3 attached trees.
Size: 5 3/4" x 2 1/2".
Metal with resin.

LSRP: $6.50/ea

1991–1998
#5999-4

Wrought Iron Fence

4 pieces per package.
White & black.
Size: 4" long.

LSRP: $10/pkg

1991–1998
#5514-0

Village Wrought Iron Gate And Fence

Set of 9.
Gate & 4 fence pieces with 4 posts.
Size: 9 1/4" x 3".
Metal.

LSRP: $15/set

1992–1998
#5220-5

Courtyard Fence With Steps

1 1/4" high x 4 1/4" long.
Metal with resin.

LSRP: $4/ea

1991–1998
#5515-8

Village Wrought Iron Fence Extensions

Set of 9.
4 fence pieces & 5 posts.
Size: 9 1/4" x 3".
Metal.

LSRP: $12.50/set

1992–1997
#5864-5

Lionhead Bridge

LSRP: $22/ea

1991–1998
#5541-7

City Subway Entrance

Size:
4 1/2" x 2 3/4" x 4 1/2".
Metal.

LSRP: $15/ea

1993–1998
#5234-5

Chain Link Fence With Gate

Set of 3.
Size: 2" high.

LSRP: $12/set

Fences

1993–1998
#5235-3

CHAIN LINK FENCE EXTENSIONS

Set of 4.
Each piece is 4 ¹/₂"
long.
LSRP: $15/set

1995–Current
#52598

VILLAGE TWIG SNOW FENCE, WOOD

2 ³/₄" x 4' roll.
SRP: $6/ea

1994–Current
#5252-3

VICTORIAN WROUGHT IRON FENCE WITH GATE

Set of 5.
Size: 5 ¹/₂" x 3".
Metal.
SRP: $15/set

1996–1998
#52624

VILLAGE WHITE PICKET FENCE WITH GATE

Set of 5.
Size: 3" & 3 ³/₄".
LSRP: $10/set

1994–Current
#5253-1

VICTORIAN WROUGHT IRON FENCE EXTENSION

Size: 3".
Metal.
SRP: $2.50/ea

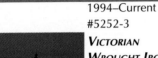

1996–1998
#52625

VILLAGE WHITE PICKET FENCE EXTENSIONS

Set of 6.
Size: 3 ³/₄".
LSRP: $10/set

1995–1997
#52597

VILLAGE SPLIT RAIL FENCE, WITH MAILBOX

Set of 4.
Hand-hewn wood.
LSRP: $12.50/set

1997–Current
#52648

STONE HOLLY CORNER POSTS AND ARCHWAY

Set of 3.
Sizes: 4 ¹/₄",
3 ¹/₂" x 4".
SRP: $20/set

Fences

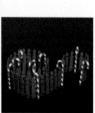

1997–Current
#52649
***VILLAGE STONE
HOLLY TREE CORNER
POSTS***
Set of 2.
Size: 4 1/4".
SRP: $8.50/set

1997–Current
#52689
***VILLAGE CAMDEN
PARK SQUARE STONE
WALL***

SRP: $2.50/ea

1997–Current
#52650
***VILLAGE STONE
CURVED
WALL/BENCH***
Set of 4.
SRP: $15/set

1998–Current
#52702
***VILLAGE HALLOWEEN
FENCE***

Set of 2.
Flexible wooden
fence with orange
pumpkins and a
black cat.
SRP: $12.50/set

1997–Current
#52657
SNOW FENCE
White.
SRP: $7/ea

1998–Current
#52717
FIELDSTONE WALL
3 assorted.
SRP: $3.50/ea

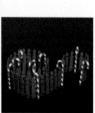

1997–Current
#52664
CANDY CANE FENCE
Size: 24".
SRP: $8.50/ea

1998–Current
#52718
***FIELDSTONE ENTRY
GATE***

SRP: $10/ea

Fences

1998–Current
#52722
**HOLLY SPLIT RAIL
FENCE**

photo not
available

Set of 4.
SRP: $18/set

1998–Current
#52768
**FIELDSTONE WALL
WITH APPLE TREE**

SRP: $25/ea

1998–Current
#52723
**HOLLY SPLIT RAIL
FENCE WITH SEATED
CHILDREN**

SRP: $13.50/ea

Mountains

1998–Current
#52724
**STONE WALL WITH
SISAL HEDGE**

photo not
available

SRP: $5/ea

1992–Current
#5226-4
**VILLAGE MOUNTAIN
WITH FROSTED SISAL
TREES, SMALL**

Set of 5.
With 4 trees.
Size: 12" x 10 $\frac{1}{2}$" x
8".
Foam and sisal.
SRP: $32.50/set

1998–Current
#52746
CORRAL FENCE
Set of 6.
SRP: $8/set

1992–Current
#5227-2
**VILLAGE MOUNTAIN
WITH FROSTED SISAL
TREES, MEDIUM**

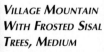

Set of 8. With 7 trees
and 1 niche to display
Village piece.
Size:
22" x 12" x 10 $\frac{1}{2}$".
SRP: $65/set

1992–Current
#5228-0

***VILLAGE MOUNTAINS
WITH FROSTED SISAL
TREES, LARGE***

Set of 14. With 13 trees.
Can accommodate 3
lighted pieces.
Size: 35" x 13" x 15 ¹/₂".
Foam and sisal.

SRP: $150/set

Lights

1994–Current
#5257-4

***VILLAGE MOUNTAIN
BACKDROP***

Set of 2.
Without trees.
Sizes:
27" x 11" & 22" x
9 ¹/₂".
Foam.

SRP: $65/set

1987–1989
#3632-3

***MULTI COLOR 10
LIGHT SET***

photo not
available

Green Cord.

LSRP: N/A

1994–Current
#52582

***VILLAGE MOUNTAIN
TUNNEL***

Size:
19 1/2" x 9 ¹/₂" x
5 ¹/₂".

SRP: $37.50/ea

1987–1989
#3633-1

***MULTI COLORED 10
LIGHT SET***

Clear Cord.

LSRP: N/A

1996–Current
#52643

***VILLAGE MOUNTAIN
CENTERPIECE***

Size: 24" x 15" x
7 ¹/₂".

SRP: $45/ea

1987–1989
#3635-8

AMBER 10 LIGHT SET

photo not
available

Green Cord.

LSRP: N/A

1987–Current
#3636-6

STREET LAMPS

6 pieces per package. Battery Operated (2 "AA" Cells) or can be used with Adapter, Item #5502-6. Cord 60" long, lamps 2 1/4" tall.

SRP: $10/pkg

1989–Current
#5501-8

RAILROAD CROSSING SIGN

2 signs per package. Battery Operated or can be used with Adapter, Item #5502-6.
Size: 4 1/4" tall.

SRP: $12.50/pkg

1988–1988
#5993-5

STREETLAMP WRAPPED IN GARLAND

2 pieces per package. Size: 4".

LSRP: $10/pkg

1989–1991
#5503-4

OLD WORLD STREETLAMP

4 pieces per package. 2 "C" Cells.
Size: 4".

LSRP: $22/pkg

1988–1988
#5994-3

STREETLAMP WITH GARLAND

4 pieces per package. Size: 4".

LSRP: N/A

1989–Current
#5504-2

TURN OF THE CENTURY LAMPPOST

4 pieces per package. Battery Operated (2 "C" Cells) or can be used with Adapter, Item #5502-6.
Size: 4" tall.

SRP: $16/pkg

1989–Current
#5500-0

TRAFFIC LIGHT

2 lights per package. Battery Operated (2 "C" Cells) or can be used with Adapter, Item #5502-6.
Size: 4 1/4" tall.

SRP: $11/pkg

1989–1991
#5505-0

TURN OF THE CENTURY LAMPPOST

6 pieces per package. 2 "C" Cells.
Size: 4".

LSRP: $22/pkg

Lights

1989–Current
#5996-0

**VILLAGE DOUBLE
STREET LAMPS**

4 pieces per package.
Battery Operated (2
"C" Cells) or can be
used with Adapter,
Item #5502-6.
Size: 3 ¹/₂" tall.

SRP: $13/pkg

1996–Current
#52611

VILLAGE SPOTLIGHT

Set of 2.
Battery Operated or
can be used with
Adapter, Item
#5225-6.
Size: 1 ³/₄".

SRP: $7/set

1990–1994
#5206-0

**CANDLES BY THE
DOORSTEP**

4 pieces per package.
2 "AA" Cells.
Size: 2 ¹/₄".

LSRP: $6.95/pkg

1996–Current
#52621

**NORTH POLE CANDY
CANE LAMPPOSTS**

4 pieces per package.
Size: 3".

SRP: $12.50/pkg

1991–Current
#5215-9

**VILLAGE MINI
LIGHTS**

14 bulbs.
Battery Operated or
can be used with
Adapter,
Item #5502-6.
Size: 27" long cord.

SRP: $12.50/ea

1996–1998
#52626

**VILLAGE MINI
LIGHTS**

20-light strand.

LSRP: $10/set

1992–1994
#5416-0

**YARD LIGHTS (2
SANTAS, 2
SNOWMEN)**

Set of 4.
Size: 1 ³/₄".

LSRP: $12.95/set

1996–Current
#52627

**VILLAGE BOULEVARD
LAMPPOSTS**

4 pieces per package.
Size: 3 ³/₄".

SRP: $15/pkg

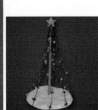

1996–1997
#52628
***VILLAGE COUNTRY
ROAD LAMPPOSTS***
2 pieces per package.
LSRP: $12/pkg

1997–Current
#52680
***ROAD CONSTRUC-
TION SIGN***
Set of 2.
Blink on/off to warn
of road work.
SRP: $12/set

1997–Current
#52663
***VILLAGE COUNTRY
ROAD LAMPPOSTS***
Set of 4.
Size: 5".
SRP: $15/set

1997–Current
#52681
***VILLAGE WALKWAY
LIGHTS***
Set of 2.
3-light sections.
Size: 6".
SRP: $12/set

1997–Current
#52678
***VILLAGE 45 LED
LIGHT STRAND***
With adapter.
SRP: $22.50/ea

1997–Current
#52682
***VILLAGE FROSTY
LIGHT SPRAYS***
Set of 2.
SRP: $12/set

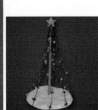

1997–Current
#52679
***VILLAGE LIGHTED
CHRISTMAS POLE***
With 48 LED Lights.
With adapter.
Size: 9".
SRP: $32.50/ea

1997–Current
#52684
***VILLAGE STRING OF
STARRY LIGHTS***
With 20 LED lights.
SRP: $12.50/ea

Lights

1998–Current
#52700

VILLAGE STRING OF 12 PUMPKIN LIGHTS

LED lights.
Battery Operated or
Brite Lites™ adapter
compatible.

SRP: $13/ea

1998–Event Piece
#52727

VILLAGE FIREWORKS

photo not
available

SRP: $25/ea

1998–Current
#52701

VILLAGE JACK-O'-LANTERNS

LED lights.
Battery Operated or
AC/DC adapter
compatible.

SRP: $10/pair

1998–Current
#52728

STRING OF 25 MINI LED LIGHTS

photo not
available

SRP: $10

1998–Current
#52706

CARNIVAL CAROUSEL LED LIGHT SET

With adapter.
Special light set to
coordinate with *The
Carnival Carousel.*

SRP: $20/set

1998–Current
#52738

HALLOWEEN LUMINARIES

SRP: $15

1998–Current
#52715

CHRISTMAS LUMINARIES

SRP: $15

1998–Current
#52760

RAILROAD LAMPS

photo not
available

Set of 2.
SRP: $15/set

Lights

Brite Lites™

All Brite Lites™ are
Battery Operated
or they can be used
with Adapter,
Item #5225-6.

1993–Current
#5225-6

***VILLAGE BRITE
LITES™ ADAPTER***

For use with 2 "Brite
Lites™" only.
SRP: $10/ea

1993–1997
#5222-1

***VILLAGE BRITE
LITES™ 'I LOVE MY
VILLAGE', ANIMATED***

Size: 6 ¹/₂".
LSRP: $15/ea

1993–Current
#5236-1

***VILLAGE BRITE
LITES™ FENCE,
ANIMATED***

Set of 4.
Size: 11".
SRP: $25/set

1993–Current
#5223-0

***VILLAGE BRITE
LITES™ 'MERRY
CHRISTMAS',
ANIMATED***

Size: 7 ¹/₂".
SRP: $15/ea

1993–Current
#5237-0

***VILLAGE BRITE
LITES™ SNOWMAN,
ANIMATED***

Size: 3 ³/₄".
SRP: $20/ea

1993–Current
#5224-8

***VILLAGE BRITE
LITES™ REINDEER,
ANIMATED***

Size: 3 ¹/₄".
SRP: $13.50/ea

1993–Current
#5238-8

***VILLAGE BRITE
LITES™ TREE,
ANIMATED***

Size: 3 ¹/₂".
SRP: $13.50/ea

1993–Current
#5239-6
***VILLAGE BRITE
LITES™ SANTA,
ANIMATED***
Size: 3 ¹/₂".
SRP: $20/ea

1994–1998
#5482-8
***COCA–COLA® BRAND
NEON SIGN***
Size: 4 ¹/₂" x 2".
LSRP: $16.50/ea

1993–1997
#9846-9
***VILLAGE BRITE
LITES™ 'DEPARTMENT
56®', ANIMATED***
Size: 5".
LSRP: $10/ea

1997–Current
#52670
***VILLAGE BRITE
LITES™ CANDY
CANES***
Set of 2.
Size: 3".
SRP: $18/set

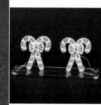

1994–1997
#5244-2
***VILLAGE BRITE
LITES™ WAVING
FLAG, ANIMATED***
Size: 5".
LSRP: $12.50/ea

1997–Current
#52671
***VILLAGE BRITE
LITES™ ANGEL***
Size: 3 ¹/₄".
SRP: $15/ea

1994–1997
#5245-0
***VILLAGE BRITE
LITES™ SET OF 20
RED LIGHTS,
FLASHING***

LSRP: $9/ea

1997–Current
#52672
***VILLAGE BRITE
LITES™ SNOW
DRAGON***
Size: 9 ¹/₂" x 2".
SRP: $20/ea

1997–Current
#52673
VILLAGE BRITE LITES™ SANTA IN CHIMNEY
Size: 3 ¹/₂".
SRP: $15/ea

1988–1990
#9900-2
REPLACEMENT LIGHT BULB
6 Watts, 12 Volts.
LSRP: N/A

photo not available

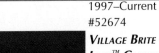

1997–Current
#52674
VILLAGE BRITE LITES™ CANDLES
Set of 4.
Size: 3".
SRP: $17/set

1988–Current
#9902-8
SINGLE CORD SET, WITH SWITCHED CORD AND BULB

SRP: $3.50/set

1997–Current
#52675
VILLAGE BRITE LITES™ HOLLY ARCHWAY

SRP: $25/ea

1988–Current
#9927-9
VILLAGE 6 SOCKET LITE SET WITH BULBS, WHITE SWITCHED CORD
Size is 12'.
SRP: $12.50/set

Electrical

1989–Current
#5502-6
AC/DC ADAPTER, FOR BATTERY OPERATED ACCESSORIES
Not for use with Brite Lites™.
SRP: $10/ea

1990–1991
#9926-0

BATTERY OPERATED LIGHT

6 Watts, 12 Volts.
LSRP: $2.50/ea

1996–Current
#99245

VILLAGE REPLACEMENT ROUND LIGHT BULBS

Set of 3.
6 Watts, 12 Volts.
SRP: $2/set

1991–1994
#5213-2

VILLAGE "LIGHTS OUT" REMOTE CONTROL

Turns lights on/off in up to 60 houses at once. Electric eye with remote.
LSRP: $25/ea

1996–Current
#99247

VILLAGE LED LIGHT BULB

Battery Operated.
SRP: $6.50/ea

1991–Current
#9924-4

VILLAGE REPLACEMENT LIGHT BULBS

3 pieces per package.
6 Watts, 12 Volts.
SRP: $2/pkg

1996–Current
#99278

VILLAGE 20 SOCKET LIGHT SET WITH BULBS

SRP: $25/set

1991–Current
#9933-3

VILLAGE MULTI-OUTLET PLUG STRIP, 6 OUTLETS

UL Approved.
Size: 12" x 2" x 1 1/2".
SRP: $10/ea

1997–Current
#99246

VILLAGE SPOTLIGHT REPLACEMENT BULBS

Set of 6.
SRP: $2.50/set

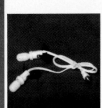

1997–Current
#99280

VILLAGE DOUBLE LIGHT SOCKET ADAPTER

SRP: $4/ea

1988–1996
#5980-3

VILLAGE EXPRESS TRAIN

Set of 22.
Manufactured by Bachmann Trains.
GBTru$ is $125.

LSRP: $95/set

photo not available

1998–Current
#52779

STRING OF SPOTLIGHTS

SRP: $15

1994–Current
#5229-9

VILLAGE ANIMATED SKATING POND

Set of 15.
UL Approved.
Size: 17 1/2" x 14".

SRP: $60/ea

Animated

1994–1998
#5240-0

VILLAGE STREETCAR

Set of 10.
With transformer.
Car lights up.

LSRP: $65/ea

1987–1988
#5997-8

VILLAGE EXPRESS TRAIN—BLACK

Set of 22.
Manufactured by Tyco.
GBTru$ is $275.

LSRP: $90/set

1994–1996
#5247-7

VILLAGE ANIMATED ALL AROUND THE PARK

Set of 18.
GBTru$ is $120.

LSRP: $95/ea

1996–Current
#52593

VILLAGE UP, UP & AWAY, ANIMATED SLEIGH

UL Approved.
Size: 17" tall.

SRP: $40/ea

1996–Current
#52644

VILLAGE WATERFALL W/ELECTRIC PUMP

Water cascades down hilly terrain to form small lake before entering creek.

SRP: $65/ea

1996–Current
#52640

VILLAGE REVOLVING TURNTABLE

SRP: $50/ea

1997–Current
#52645

VILLAGE ANIMATED SLEDDING HILL

SRP: $65/ea

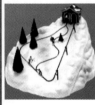

1996–1998
#52641

VILLAGE ANIMATED SKI MOUNTAIN

With 3 skiers.
Size: 20" x 17" x 14".

LSRP: $85/ea

1998–Current
#52710

VILLAGE EXPRESS ELECTRIC TRAIN SET

Set of 24. Manufactured by Bachmann Trains. Includes plaques for each Village.

SRP: $270/set

1996–Current
#52642

VILLAGE ANIMATED ACCESSORY TRACK

Accepts all Track Compatible pieces by fitting included adapter to base.
Size: 38" x 24".

SRP: $65/ea

1998–Current
#52711

UP, UP & AWAY WITCH

SRP: $50/ea

Animated

photo not
available

1998–Current
#52731
**BIPLANE UP IN THE
SKY**

SRP: $50/ea

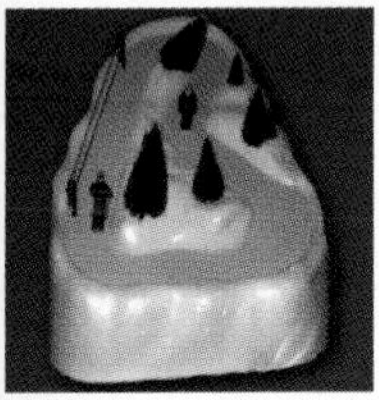

1998–Current
#52733
SKI SLOPE

SRP: $75/ea

NOTES: _____
_____
_____
_____
_____
_____
_____
_____
_____
_____
_____
_____
_____
_____

_____
_____
_____
_____
_____
_____
_____
_____
_____
_____
_____
_____
_____

Animated

1982–1983

#5099-7

SNOW VILLAGE WOODEN ORNAMENTS

These six wooden ornaments are replicas of six Original Snow Village® buildings from 1982. They include *Carriage House, Centennial House, Countryside Church, Gabled House, Pioneer Church* and *Swiss Chalet.* They have mono-filament lines attached to the tops and/or clips attached to the bottoms.

GBTru$ is $495.

 **GABLED HOUSE**

 **CENTENNIAL HOUSE**

 **SWISS CHALET**

 **COUNTRYSIDE CHURCH**

 **PIONEER CHURCH**

 **CARRIAGE HOUSE**

1997–1997 Annual
#8961

RONALD MCDONALD HOUSE® ORNAMENT (THE HOUSE THAT ♥ BUILT™)

A miniature, flat version of the 2-story home piece, Item #8960. A portion of the proceeds from the sale of this ornament were donated to the Ronald McDonald House®s across the country.

LSRP: $15

1998–Current
#98635

photo not available

LIGHTHOUSE
ORNAMENT

Original Snow Village® Classic Ornament Series. Lighted w/adapter.

SRP: $20

1997–1998
#98630

NANTUCKET
ORNAMENT

Original Snow Village® Classic Ornament Series. (Non-lighted.)

LSRP: $15

1998–Current
#98637

photo not available

PINEWOOD LOG
CABIN ORNAMENT

Original Snow Village® Classic Ornament Series. Lighted w/adapter.

SRP: $20

1997–1998
#98631

STEEPLED CHURCH
ORNAMENT

Original Snow Village® Classic Ornament Series. (Non-lighted.)

LSRP: $15

1998–Current
#98642

NANTUCKET
ORNAMENT

Original Snow Village® Classic Ornament Series. Lighted w/adapter.

SRP: $20

1997–1998
#98632

J. YOUNG'S
GRANARY ORNAMENT

Original Snow Village® Classic Ornament Series. (Non-lighted.)

LSRP: $15

1998–Current
#98643

STEEPLED CHURCH
ORNAMENT

photo not available

Original Snow Village® Classic Ornament Series. Lighted w/adapter.

SRP: $20

1998–Current
#98644
J. YOUNG'S GRANARY ORNAMENT

Original Snow Village® Classic Ornament Series. Lighted w/adapter.

SRP: $20

1996–1996
Annual
#98729
GRAPES INN ORNAMENT, THE

Miniature version of Signature Collection lit piece. Special Keepsake box.

LSRP: $25

The Heritage Village Collection® Ornaments

1996–1996
Annual
#98730
CROWN & CRICKET INN ORNAMENT

Miniature version of Signature Collection lit piece. Special Keepsake box.

LSRP: $25

1994–1994
Annual
#9872-8
DEDLOCK ARMS ORNAMENT

Miniature version of Signature Collection lit piece. Special Keepsake box.

LSRP: $25

1996–1996
Annual
#98731
PIED BULL INN ORNAMENT, THE

Miniature version of Signature Collection lit piece. Special Keepsake box.

LSRP: $25

1995–1995
Annual
#9870-1
SIR JOHN FALSTAFF INN ORNAMENT

Miniature version of Signature Collection lit piece. Special Keepsake box.

LSRP: $25

1997–1997
Annual
#98732
GAD'S HILL PLACE ORNAMENT

Miniature version of Signature Collection lit piece. Special Keepsake box.

LSRP: $25

1997–1998
#98733

DICKENS' VILLAGE MILL ORNAMENT

The Heritage Village® Classic Ornament Series. (Non-lighted.)

LSRP: $15

1997–1998
#98739

CRAGGY COVE LIGHTHOUSE ORNAMENT

The Heritage Village® Classic Ornament Series. (Non-lighted.)

LSRP: $15

1997–1998
#98734

SANTA'S WORKSHOP ORNAMENT

The Heritage Village® Classic Ornament Series. (Non-lighted.)

LSRP: $16.50

1997–1998
#98740

DOROTHY'S DRESS SHOP ORNAMENT

The Heritage Village® Classic Ornament Series. (Non-lighted.)

LSRP: $15

1997–1998
#98737

DICKENS' VILLAGE CHURCH ORNAMENT

The Heritage Village® Classic Ornament Series. (Non-lighted.)

LSRP: $15

1997–1998
#98741

CITY HALL ORNAMENT

The Heritage Village® Classic Ornament Series. (Non-lighted.)

LSRP: $15

1997–1998
#98738

OLD CURIOSITY SHOP ORNAMENT, THE

The Heritage Village® Classic Ornament Series. (Non-lighted.)

LSRP: $15

1997–1998
#98742

SANTA'S LOOKOUT TOWER ORNAMENT

The Heritage Village® Classic Ornament Series. (Non-lighted.)

LSRP: $15

1998–Current
#98745

CHRISTMAS CAROL COTTAGES ORNAMENTS

The Heritage Village®
Classic Ornament
Series.
Set of 3.
Lighted w/adapter.

SRP: $50

1998–Current
#98759

CATHEDRAL CHURCH OF ST. MARK ORNAMENT

The Heritage Village®
Classic Ornament
Series.
Lighted w/adapter.

SRP: $20

photo not
available

1998–Current
#98756

CAPTAIN'S COTTAGE ORNAMENT

The Heritage Village®
Classic Ornament
Series.
Lighted w/adapter.

SRP: $20

1998–Current
#98762

REINDEER BARN ORNAMENT

The Heritage Village®
Classic Ornament
Series.
Lighted w/adapter.

SRP: $20

photo not
available

1998–Current
#98757

STEEPLE CHURCH ORNAMENT

The Heritage Village®
Classic Ornament
Series.
Lighted w/adapter.

SRP: $20

1998–Current
#98763

ELF BUNKHOUSE ORNAMENT

The Heritage Village®
Classic Ornament
Series.
Lighted w/adapter.

SRP: $20

1998–Current
#98758

RED BRICK FIRE STATION ORNAMENT

The Heritage Village®
Classic Ornament
Series.
Lighted w/adapter.

SRP: $22.50

1998–Current
#98766

DICKENS' VILLAGE MILL ORNAMENT

The Heritage Village®
Classic Ornament
Series.
Lighted w/adapter.

SRP: $22.50

1998–Current
#98767

DICKENS' VILLAGE CHURCH ORNAMENT

The Heritage Village®
Classic Ornament
Series.
Lighted w/adapter.

SRP: $20

---

photo not available

1998–Current
#98768

OLD CURIOSITY SHOP ORNAMENT, THE

The Heritage Village®
Classic Ornament
Series.
Lighted w/adapter.

SRP: $20

1998–Current
#98769

CRAGGY COVE LIGHTHOUSE ORNAMENT

The Heritage Village®
Classic Ornament
Series.
Lighted w/adapter.

SRP: $20

1998–Current
#98770

DOROTHY'S DRESS SHOP ORNAMENT

The Heritage Village®
Classic Ornament
Series.
Lighted w/adapter.

SRP: $20

---

photo not available

1998–Current
#98771

CITY HALL ORNAMENT

The Heritage Village®
Classic Ornament
Series.
Lighted w/adapter.

SRP: $20

---

photo not available

1998–Current
#98772

SANTA'S WORKSHOP ORNAMENT

The Heritage Village®
Classic Ornament
Series.
Lighted w/adapter.

SRP: $22.50

1998–Current
#98773

SANTA'S LOOKOUT TOWER ORNAMENT

The Heritage Village®
Classic Ornament
Series.
Lighted w/adapter.

SRP: $20

NOTES: _____

_____

_____

_____

_____

_____

Name Index

Name Index

NAME INDEX

NAME INDEX

ITEM NUMBER INDEX

ITEM NUMBER INDEX

ITEM NUMBER INDEX

ITEM NUMBER INDEX

As we were on press ...

You can look forward to seeing these pieces arrive at Department 56®
retail stores this fall:

The Original Snow Village®

54977	2000 Holly Lane, Set/11	$65.00
54978	Cinema 56	$85.00

The Original Snow Village® Accessories

54982	Preparing For Halloween, Set/2	$40.00
54983	The Looney Loons® Animated Film Festival, Set/4	$40.00

Dickens' Village Series®

58352	Chancery Corner, Set/8	$65.00
58353	Dudley Docker	$70.00

New England Village®

56606	*Little Women* The March Residence, Set/4 plus Book	$90.00

North Pole Series™

56407	Santa's Visiting Center, Set/6	$65.00
56408	Marie's Doll Museum	$55.00

Christmas In The City®

58947	Parkview Hospital	$65.00
58948	Wintergarten Cafe	$60.00

The Heritage Village Collection®

55510	The Times Tower, Set/3	$185.00

The Heritage Village Collection® Accessories

56442	Tee Time Elves, Set/2 (NP)	$27.50
56443	Happy New Year! (NP)	$17.50
56639	It's Almost Thanksgiving (NE)	$60.00
58387	XII, The 12 Days Of Dickens' Village, Twelve Drummers Drumming (DV)	$65.00
58420	A Good Day's Catch, Set/2 (DV)	$27.50
58909	Bringing Home The Baby, Set/2 (CIC)	$27.50
58910	The City Ambulance (CIC)	$15.00